Insurance Company Operations

Volume I

Insurance Company Operations

Volume I

BERNARD L. WEBB, CPCU, FCAS
Professor of Actuarial Science and Insurance
Georgia State University

J. J. LAUNIE, Ph.D., CPCU
Professor of Finance and Insurance
California State University, Northridge

WILLIS PARK ROKES, J.D., Ph.D., CPCU, CLU
Peter Kiewit Distinguished Professor
of Law and Insurance
University of Nebraska at Omaha

NORMAN A. BAGLINI, Ph.D., CPCU, CLU
Senior Vice President and Dean
American Institute for Property and Liability Underwriters

Third Edition • 1984

AMERICAN INSTITUTE FOR
PROPERTY AND LIABILITY UNDERWRITERS
Providence and Sugartown Roads, Malvern, Pennsylvania 19355

Foreword

The American Institute for Property and Liability Underwriters and the Insurance Institute of America are companion, nonprofit, educational organizations supported by the property and liability insurance industry. Their purpose is to provide quality continuing education programs for insurance personnel.

The Insurance Institute of America offers programs leading to the Certificate in General Insurance, the Associate in Claims (AIC) designation, the Associate in Management (AIM) designation, the Associate in Risk Management (ARM) designation, the Associate in Underwriting designation, the Associate in Loss Control Management (ALCM) designation, the Associate in Premium Auditing (APA) designation, the Accredited Adviser in Insurance (AAI) designation, and the Associate in Insurance Accounting and Finance (AIAF) designation. The Insurance Institute of America also offers a one-semester course, INTRO—An Introduction to Property and Liability Insurance. The American Institute develops, maintains, and administers the educational program leading to the Chartered Property Casualty Underwriter (CPCU) professional designation.

Throughout the history of the CPCU program, an annual updating of parts of the course of study took place. But as changes in the insurance industry came about at an increasingly rapid pace, and as the world in which insurance operates grew increasingly complex, it became clear that a thorough, fundamental revision of the CPCU curriculum was necessary. This text is the third edition of one of those which were written for, and published by, the American Institute for use in the revised 10-semester CPCU curriculum which was introduced in 1978.

Throughout the development of the CPCU text series, it has been—and will continue to be—necessary to draw on the knowledge and skills of Institute staff members. These individuals receive no royalties on texts sold; their writing responsibilities are seen as an integral part of their professional duties. We have proceeded in this way to avoid any possibility of conflicts of interests. All Institute textbooks have been—and will continue to be—subjected to an extensive review process. Reviewers are drawn from both industry and academic ranks.

We welcome criticisms of our publications. Such comments should be directed to the Curriculum Department of the Institutes.

Edwin S. Overman, Ph.D., CPCU
President

Preface

This text is divided into two volumes. Volume I begins with an overview of insurance company operations. It is intended to introduce each of the major insurance functions which are dealt with in detail in later chapters. Chapter 1 discusses the interrelationship and interdependency of insurance company operations. Chapters 2 and 3 deal with marketing, including a discussion of recent developments in the marketing of property and liability insurance. Chapters 4, 5, and 6 analyze the underwriting function. Chapter 4 analyzes basic principles of underwriting, the organization of underwriting activities, and underwriting decision making. These principles are applied to selected property and liability lines in Chapters 5 and 6. Chapters 7 and 8 provide an in-depth study of the major types of reinsurance, including an analysis of reinsurance programs and reinsurance transactions.

Volume II begins with two chapters on rate making. Basic principles of rate making are explained in Chapter 9, and these principles are applied to the major property and liability lines of insurance in Chapter 10. The loss control activities of insurance organizations are examined in Chapter 11, including examples of such activities in selected lines of insurance. The next three chapters deal with claims handling and stress the interdependence that exists between the claimsperson and personnel involved in other insurance company functions. Chapter 12 explains the basic principles of claims adjusting. Chapters 13 and 14 continue with the examination of claims adjusting; however, each chapter addresses itself to specific types of property and liability claims handling. Finally, Chapter 15 discusses other insurance company functions—completing the analysis of insurance company operations.

No review or discussion questions appear in this text. These are included in a companion study aid—the CPCU 5 Course Guide. The Course Guide contains educational objectives, outlines of the study material, key terms and concepts, review questions, and discussion questions.

This book would not have been possible without the assistance of a great many people. Sincere thanks are extended to J. Wesley Ooms, CPCU, CLU, AIM, AIU, Assistant Vice President, Product Planning and Development, State Farm Fire and Casualty Company, who read and commented on the entire manuscript. The authors wish to thank all of the capable individuals who reviewed portions of the text in their specialty areas, especially James E. Brennan, CPCU, CLU, ARM, AIM, Assistant Director, Center for Insurance Education and Research, University of Connecticut; James S. Burkart, CPCU, ARM, Assistant Vice President, Collier Cobb & Associates of Alabama, Inc.; Walter G. Butterworth, CPCU, Vice President, INA Reinsurance Company; Charles W. Cook, CPCU, AIM, ARM, Vice President, Data Processing Services, Michigan Mutual Insurance Company; Patrick Doyle, CPCU, CLU, Vice President, Office of General Chairman, Nationwide Insurance Companies; Francis P. Flood, Ph.D., CPCU, CLU, President, Viva Management Corporation; George M. Gottheimer, Jr., CPCU, CLU, Vice President, North Star Syndicate, Inc.; Paul J. Kelley, CPCU, Vice President, Johnson & Higgins of Virginia, Inc.; Dean A. Ockerbloom, CPCU, Director—Product Management Division, Travelers Insurance Company; Frank J. Pellegrino, CPCU, Vice President—Director, Motors Re Management Corporation; Lewis R. Plast, CPCU, Vice President, State Farm Fire and Casualty Company; R. B. Reynolds, Jr., RHU, FLMI, Assistant Vice President—Compliance, The ERC Life Companies; Paul I. Thomas, Consultant to the National Committee on Property Insurance, Boston; and Advisory Board Member of Insurance Technical Training Institute, Dallas; and Albert J. Walsh, CPCU, FCAS, Vice President—Manager, Interinsurance Exchange of the Auto Club of Southern California.

Finally, the authors wish to offer their thanks to all of the Institute staff members who have been involved in this project over the last few years. They have made this book possible by assuming the tasks of editing, proofreading, and production.

The authors accept full responsibility for all errors and omissions. It would be greatly appreciated if readers would send us their criticisms and suggestions so that subsequent editions may be improved.

Bernard L. Webb
J. J. Launie
Willis Park Rokes
Norman A. Baglini

Contributing Author

The American Institute for Property and Liability Underwriters and the authors acknowledge, with deep appreciation, the work of the following contributing author who helped to make this text possible:

Ronald M. Hubbs
Retired Chairman and Former President
The St. Paul Companies, Inc.

Table of Contents

Chapter 5 — Underwriting Property Insurance 213

Fire Insurance Underwriting ~ *Introduction; Construction; Occupancy; Protection; Exposure; the Human Factor — Moral and Morale Hazards*

Underwriting Other Perils ~ *Windstorm; Hurricanes; Tornadoes; Hail; Explosion; Sprinkler Leakage and Water Damage; Vandalism or Malicious Mischief; Earthquake*

Underwriting Time Element Coverages ~ *Types of Time Element Coverages; Underwriting the Gross Earnings Form; Disaster Contingency Plans*

Underwriting Crime Insurance ~ *Personal Lines; Commercial Lines*

Underwriting Ocean and Inland Marine Insurance ~ *The Marine Concept; Ocean Marine; Inland Marine*

Chapter 6 — Underwriting Liability and Multiple Lines Insurance 269

Underwriting Automobile Insurance ~ *The Regulatory Environment; The Legal Evironment; Private Passenger Automobile Underwriting Factors; Private Passenger Automobile Loss Control; Commercial Automobile Underwriting Factors; Commercial Automobile Underwriting Characteristics Summarized; Commercial Autombile Loss Control; ICC Regulations on Commercial Automobiles*

Workers' Compensation Underwriting ~ *The Evaluation of Workers' Compensation Submissions; Occupational Safety and Health Act*

Underwriting General Liability Lines ~ *Comprehensive Personal Liability; General Liability; Professional Liability; Underwriting Umbrella and Excess Liability Policies*

Underwriting Fidelity and Surety Bonds ~ *Fidelity Bonds; Surety Bonds*

Package and Account Underwriting ~ *Interaction of Multi-Line Hazards; Pyramiding Limits of Liability; Other Underwriting Considerations*

CHAPTER 1

Overview of Insurance Operations

INTRODUCTION

Insurance evolution spans centuries. It is now in a dynamic phase influenced by unprecedented rates of change in the economic, social, technological, and regulatory environments. Insurance operations are influenced by these accelerating pressures, and insurance companies (also known as insurers) are finding it necessary to be more flexible, more productive, and better organized. Performance, measured by both financial and societal criteria, is a prominent factor. These considerations will emerge from time to time in this overview.

From a distant perspective, insurers have many similarities in structure and function. Production, underwriting, and claims handling are always present. The financial and administrative support services are there as necessary adjuncts. A closer and more critical view, however, makes it apparent that there are many specialized ways to assemble and use these components. Traditional operations become enlarged, diminished, or even disregarded. Change brings into view and dramatizes new functions. These, too, must be recognized in an overview of insurance operations. The following pages will introduce the reader to the nature and scope of insurance operations and their relationships.

For purposes of study, the major insurance company operations have been assembled into six groups:

- product design and development
- production and distribution
- product management
- services

- administration
- finance and investment

Some activities could be included in more than one of these groups. In fact, a later section of this chapter is devoted to the interrelationship and interdependency among insurance company activities. These six groups are not intended to be an organizational structure but are presented here to provide a framework for study.

PRODUCT DESIGN AND DEVELOPMENT

Historical

The evolution of insurance to deal with fortuitous loss began in antiquity. In the ancient civilizations of the Chinese, Babylonians, Greeks, Romans, and others, practical schemes for risk distribution or guarantee against loss were developed. It is reasonable to assume that the agreements underwent scrutiny and, from time to time, some change.

Colonists from England brought the fire insurance policy to America. It became formalized in 1873 when Massachusetts adopted the first standard fire policy. Since then, the standard fire policy, often with different forms to accommodate opinions of legislators of the various states, spread to all of the states.

These were evolutionary steps in the development of a fire insurance policy, but much more was going on around this venerable contract. The automobile had been invented, jewelry and fine arts were becoming available to the affluent, goods were being transported within the country as well as without, owners of property were discovering that they were incurring liabilities to the public, and employers found they had obligations to compensate injured employees. These changes that were taking place in this century influenced the evolution of new insurance contracts. The ancient marine and fire policies were surrounded by a myriad of new exposures to loss, and even though old policies were altered by endorsements that took them into areas not foreseen, the old policies also evolved. As new exposures and hazards appeared, new policies were developed to insure them.

Insurance policy innovations developed rapidly after the great depression of the 1930s. Automobile insurance began to grow. This period witnessed the introduction of the extended coverage endorsement, which was considered a daring innovation in its time. It was also then that the first efforts were made to combine property and liability insurance coverages and to introduce the new comprehensive property insurance forms. It cannot be said that any one of these changes was solely responsible for the steadily accelerating interest in product development. Competitive forces certainly were partly responsible, along with technological change and consumer needs.

Pertinent here would be some reflection on the overworked phrase, *public demand,* to which credit for a new policy is so frequently assigned. John N. Cosgrove put this phrase in perspective:

> "Public demand" is a mistaken concept that has been confused with public acceptance. There is plenty of the latter. When an enterprising company comes up with what appears to be a novel type of policy—particularly when price is a factor—the public responds with alacrity. Many buy it, and others approach their customary source of protection to see if the new policy is available. The companies which lack the product are soon forced to develop an attractive and matching alternative. This is dictated by public acceptance of the originator's idea and not by public demand.
>
> It is important to distinguish between the two. Those who refer to public demand are saying, in effect, that people in the mass originate coverage ideas. They do not. Some lonely and creative insurance man germinates the idea, and the next thing he knows, it is in the hands of a committee of his associates and superiors where it is scrutinized, improved, priced and brought to market.[1]

Product design and development is a primary responsibility of management regardless of where origination and execution take place. The need for a new policy or a modification in an existing one can be voiced by a producer, an insured, a prospective insured, a company employee, or even by the government (e.g., OSHA, flood insurance, no-fault). An underwriter (a most likely source) can see a possible demand for this new product. The genesis can come from loss control personnel, actuaries, claims people, or field representatives.

Regardless of the source, the first acid test is convincing the underwriters. If the concept is approved there, it must be reviewed by the claims department or the legal department to clarify the legal and practical consequence as well as to unmask hidden dangers. The review must assess the probabilities of paying losses under circumstances not contemplated in the policy. In addition, actuaries must provide calculations on price, and marketing personnel must consider the potential sales of the new coverage.

The need for new insurance products cannot be doubted. Rising consumer demands, changes in the law, and the restless growth in technology will see to that. It is predicted that people will soon be spending more for services than for the goods they consume. Many are expecting that science will change our weather, mine the seas, and solve the secrets of cell biology. In a word, there will be a wealth of new concepts that will bring with them product opportunities beyond measure. These will include the unique as well as the commonplace.

Competition against large, established insurers requires innovation in product design and development. This is an incentive for the entrepreneur and the small and new insurance companies to bring to the market new or modified products for the consumer.

Marketing methods also stimulate the discovery of new insurance policies. Mass merchandising and payroll deduction plans cause the invention or adaptation of contracts with wide appeal. Not infrequently, this is the direction of association and franchise business, which builds its market on population segments as diverse as retired persons, teachers, hardware dealers, and fast-food vendors.

The discussion up to this point has dealt primarily with internal considerations affecting product design and development. Many outside forces also come to bear.

The influence of consumerism, regulation, and environmental changes as progenitors will be reviewed below. All three of these forces are causing product changes and developments in unprecedented modes and volume.

Consumer Needs

Readability To many lay people, insurance contracts are almost incomprehensible. A constant warning to policyholders to read their policies has been in the main ignored. In response to these unpleasant truths and recurring agitation to simplify insurance contracts, most insurance companies now use "easy to read" policies.

Reasons for resistance to change are fairly well known. Legal counsel, underwriters, claims people, and others warn that many terms and clauses have been interpreted by the courts. Tampering with the agreed-upon language is dangerous, they argue. Some oppose changes to language because they fear this could convey meanings not intended by those who designed the policy. The insurance business does have its own language which many are loath to vary. Some contend that simpler policies will also not be read. Hence, the expense and effort in redrafting is really lost.

Several insurance companies have, in fact, redesigned their policies to make them easier to read. Applications and invoices have also been simplified.

The typical simplified language policy is written in informal English. There are no long paragraphs listing conditions and exceptions. There are few words unfamiliar to the average reader; no "whereins" are found in the new policy and there is no fine print. Any term that is defined in the policy appears in boldface type. The typographical design has clearly defined headings and the text is set in larger type—larger than most newspapers and magazines.

The more consumers know before they buy insurance, the more insurers save on the cost of adjustments, complaints, and explanatory correspondence.

Packaging Bringing together insurance policies of many kinds into one package has been the dream of producers and underwriters for years. Experimentation dates from the early history of inland marine insurance. The strongest stimulant came when separate property and liability insurance companies began to merge. Also pushing in the package direction was removal of artificial barriers created by rating bureaus. The advent of Public Law 15 lessened the power of bureaus to interfere with insurance contract changes. Regulators relaxed ideas about conformity.

Packaging has caused some of the more radical changes in the insurance business. It has meant merging various contracts to meet insureds' needs—a process that often avoids gaps and overlaps in coverage. Packaging has experienced a tremendous growth since the days when editorial changes were not permitted by law, regulation, or bureau rules.

Early experiments involved scissors and paste to put several contracts together under one binder. Actually, it was no real improvement over separate policies, except that insureds probably found it more convenient and it seemed to be a package.

Now, there are some novel ways in which policies are packaged. There are contracts that are completely tailored to fit a specific situation. Many of the conventional insurance clauses are bypassed. These freely written policies—that is, free as to language used and coverage granted—depend on the willingness of the underwriters to experiment with the perils covered and to say more simply and clearly what is covered. Many of the contracts of this type can be considered very broad.

Many believe that packaging helps an insured to better understand an insurance program. Dissenters say it forces the buyer to use one insurer when several insurers, because of competitive coverages, could give better protection. Adherents say that it gives an insured greater leverage with the insurer and a better chance for a more favorable rate since the amount of business can be greater.

Consumer desire to have a common expiration date favors packaging, but it could interfere with staggering premium dates, if that is desired, unless the insured is willing to use a premium finance plan. Underwriters state that it is much easier to account underwrite (determining the acceptability and pricing of all of an insured's coverages on an overall basis) when all the contracts are in one package. Skeptics warn against putting all the eggs in one basket.

Two more criticisms of packaging should be considered: (1) it essentially skims off the cream, accelerating the process of creating shared markets (insurance facilities to provide insurance for high risk insureds unable to obtain insurance through the conventional market) with attendant problems, and (2) within an insurance company it can cause morale problems, especially when packaging takes over the better-than-average monoline account and places it in another area beyond the reach of the monoline underwriter. This leads to producers' criticisms that within one insurance company there are two or three separate companies with different underwriting attitudes.

Standard or Independent Policy Clauses

For most of the major lines of business, a large number of insurance companies use a standard insurance contract form. Standard forms have identical or similar wording that has evolved through custom or law. Standard forms are prepared, amended and distributed by rate-making organizations or bureaus that are responsible for developing policy forms as well as rates. In this text, the term *"bureau"* will be used to refer to any organization that publishes rates and policy forms such as the Insurance Services Office (ISO) and other national or regional rating bureaus or boards. Many insurers use bureau forms exclusively. However, an increasing number of insurers are now using "independently filed" forms that may deviate only slightly from standard forms or may be significantly different.

A policy form is *independently filed* when it is submitted for approval to the state insurance department by a single insurer (or group under common ownership) rather than by a bureau on behalf of many insurers.

Advantages of Standard Forms The advantages, to an insurer, of using standard forms are:

1. *Comparable Statistics.* Claims experience of different insurers is easily compared when they use standard forms. Insurance rate making becomes more complicated if premium and loss experience reported by insurers is based on different coverages. Insurers that use independently filed forms which deviate from standard forms must evaluate the effect of differences in coverages so that they can adjust their rates to reflect those differences.

2. *Court Tested.* Standard forms use words, phrases and provisions whose meaning has been established through court decisions. Since insureds usually have no opportunity to modify

their insurance contracts, any ambiguities are generally interpreted against the insurer. Using standard forms with court-tested language minimizes this problem.

3. *Concurrency.* Insurance policies are "concurrent" if they contain identical clauses. Losses involving two or more insurers are less complicated if insurers use standard forms. Large amounts of insurance on (1) buildings (for property insurance) or (2) activities (for liability insurance) are often shared by several insurers or through reinsurance. Standardized forms help to facilitate this risk-sharing practice.

4. *Simplicity.* Widespread use of standard forms is beneficial to insureds and producers who do not have to compare differences in policy language among different insurers. Also, the training of insurance personnel is simplified by learning a standard form and then studying deviations from the standard. Producers representing more than one insurer and underwriters competing for business can quickly learn another insurer's coverage if they are familiar with the standard form and can recognize nonstandard clauses.

5. *Economy.* Without standard forms, it would be necessary for each insurance company to have its own policy design experts, and to develop its own policies, resulting in duplication of effort and unnecessary costs. Through bureaus, standardization permits a concentration of experts in policy design, and the cost of developing standard policy forms is shared by all member companies.

Advantages of Nonstandard Forms   The major advantages of nonstandard (independently filed) policy forms are:

1. *Flexibility.* Nonstandard independently filed forms usually provide greater flexibility and allow for experimentation. New coverages may be developed more quickly because bureaus, due to their size and nature, require more time and study to develop new coverages.

2. *Competition.* Short run competitive advantages may be gained by the use of independent forms. Independently filed nonstandard forms allow for innovation such as eliminating an exclusion or broadening coverage. These points of difference may be important sales advantages. Interestingly, some standard forms began as independently filed forms that became standardized over time.

The disadvantages of standard forms are simply the opposite of the advantages of independent ones—less flexibility and lack of competition. Likewise, the disadvantages of independent forms are seen in the advantages of standard forms: lack of comparable statistics, language not court tested, possibility of nonconcurrency, less simple to administer and to use in training, and finally, an increase in expenses.

The use of standard or independent forms depends upon the marketing and underwriting philosophy of the insurance company. Many insurers use both types of forms. For example, an insurance company could use standard forms for personal lines (personal auto and homeowners), and independent forms for commercial packages.

Regulatory Restraints

Product design is of course restricted to what insurance regulators will permit. The rates for a new policy must agree with prior filings or may require special filings. In any event, the rates must be approved by the regulatory authority in many jurisdictions.

In most states, policy forms must also be approved. Occasionally, states will disapprove a form on the grounds there is no public demand for it! Some states have disapproved a new policy simply because it crossed traditional property and liability lines or because it was not possible to segregate the experience into the historical classes. There are also regulatory constraints that will not permit certain types of package policies.

Many states require a policy with multi-peril conditions to incorporate the standard fire policy directly or by reference. Some will permit improvements that broaden the language of the standard fire policy in favor of the insured. However, regulation and statute will rarely permit a reduction of coverage contained in the statutory contract. Mixtures of filed and nonfiled rates are permitted in some states but are prohibited in others. A few states grant some latitude in computing premiums on a retrospective basis or in payment of dividends to policyholders.

The method of premium payment is a cause for concern in some areas. Type size of insurance contracts is a concern to some regulators, but not to others. Licensing variations that require or dispense with countersignatures add additional speculation in the treatment of certain policies.

Regulatory constraint is always present in subtle ways. If an insurer is uneasy about rate adequacy and its ability to get increases when needed, few new policies will find their way to market, and upgrading of current policies will be infrequent.

Environmental Changes
Requiring New Forms of Coverages

Attitudes to environmental changes, in their broadest implications—physical, social, legal, economic—are generating new forms of insurance coverage. Many of these changes are now embedded in national and state laws and regulations. It is questionable if all are insurable or within the capacity of insurers; nevertheless, the insurance business is responding to new legislation through coverages and services. Notable examples are the Occupational Safety and Health Act (OSHA), Air and Water Pollution Acts, the Consumer Product Safety Act, FAIR plans, joint underwriting associations, and crime and flood insurance programs.

New emphasis is also being placed on directors' and officers' liability and on errors and omissions in all professional groups because of legal environmental changes. These new developments cause the insurance industry to redirect its thinking.

There almost certainly will be new industries and products arising from the search for alternate sources of energy. The space age is also introducing new potentials for loss. Something that has been around for a long time, but is now once again catching the public eye, is weather modification. It carries with it a substantial peril, and it has interested some insurers from time to time.

PRODUCTION AND DISTRIBUTION

Marketing

All businesses must operate with some type of marketing strategy, expressed or not.

In insurance company operations, the responsibility for marketing is vested in a major division. The charge from senior management is to develop, motivate, and maintain an effective sales and marketing force that produces the desired quantity and quality of business established by company objectives. To do this a field sales force must be recruited and trained to supply services to producers. Management must also establish realistic production objectives, marketing policies and strategies, implement advertising and promotion campaigns, and select and develop producers.

The marketing division or department should discover producer and consumer needs as well as maintain an awareness of all changes and trends in the functions of the producer to assure the company's competitive position. Good communications must be maintained with producers and the supporting field force. Finally, the marketing department must make systematic performance audits of field offices to make certain these vital operations are functioning as they should.

An analysis of marketing activities of a field office may well embrace the subjects outlined below. The analysis will include a review of written programs previously prepared by the local manager for operations in that area. In every case, improvements, suggestions for improvements, and effectiveness will be noted. Important items are:

1. Review of field personnel—evaluate performance of each field representative and interview field supervisors and specialists (the latter is not a performance evaluation).
2. Producer analysis and premium objective setting—review producers and premium objectives.
3. New producer prospecting and appointments—inspect appointment files and appointment objectives and examine records of producers appointed and closed.
4. Producer development—review progress of selected producers.
5. Account balances—inspect past due notices as to repeaters and suspensions.
6. Travel and call planning—inspect written travel schedules to see if they follow general adherence to planning.
7. Specific sales promotion activity—what has been initiated by the marketing manager during the period of examination? Review new product strategy, sales meetings.
8. Supervision and development of field supervisors—check on accompanied travel by marketing and general managers, marketing manager travel without field supervisors, frequency that marketing manager reviews with each field supervisor his or her performance and results, number of field supervisor meetings and what has been accomplished at those meetings with respect to education, communications, and sales training activities. Also check number of field supervisors engaged in job-related educational courses and examine results of producer service questionnaires, and what is done to correct inefficiency. Finally, review field staffing and field assignments, supervision, and development of field supervisors.
9. Interview with General Manager—inquire on conditions existing in other divisions that impede marketing effort. Get manager's evaluation of the performance of the marketing manager and relationship with the home office marketing division.

The audit reveals actual and potential problem areas or areas in which performance is especially good. Using management by exception, the marketing department can focus on problems and share with other field offices the ideas or programs that have been especially successful.

Advertising

Insurers are frequently beset with doubts about how to spend their advertising dollars. Some seek public recognition and identity on a broad scale. Others think of producers as their public. Still others seek a specialized audience. The format of an insurer's distribution system influences where the money is to be spent.

The direct writers, exclusive agency companies, and mail order insurers (discussed in Chapter 2) appear to be successful in national advertising. Advertising by independent agency companies often is aimed at agents because of the conviction that this is their market. Heavy use is made of trade publications for this purpose, and some insurers advertise in national magazines, newspapers, and other periodicals aimed at special audiences.

Much of the advertising budget is used for sales promotion materials useful to producers. This includes sales brochures, yellow page listings in telephone books, technical production guides, audio cassette product presentations, and share-the-cost items (e.g., fire extinguishers, atlases, calendars, and so on).

The advertising function will often be found in the marketing division of a company. In some insurance companies it is part of a marketing services department, which is a subdivision of marketing. As a part of the marketing services department, advertising is allied with marketing research, planning, and new products. The director of advertising and sales promotion typically performs the following functions:

1. Determines and prepares the advertising budget needed to carry out the advertising strategy and submits it for approval.
2. Approves the content of all advertising, direct mail, and promotion material directed to consumers and producers, and is responsible for the company's public posture as influenced by these activities.
3. Directs the advertising agency in its development of advertising campaigns.
4. Sees that the company uses the advertising agency in an efficient manner so as to minimize costs.
5. Directs the corporate identity program, including monitoring the use of the company's trademark and symbol.

Research

Insurers use research to coordinate the companywide marketing strategies, marketing planning, and premium goal procedures. Research is also used for marketing studies, including new products and services, consumer and producer attitudes, market and area potentials, sales forecasting, and advertising effectiveness. Research is applied to sales and economic analyses for gathering and evaluating competitive information. In some instances, it is used to design and maintain the agency data base. Increasingly, research is used to gather data for computer planning models.

Marketing research does not mark, by any means, the limit of company research in many fields. An established company department exclusively labeled research is unusual; however, several insurers do have research and development activities that are fairly well formalized. Others are certain to have ad hoc research task forces that set out to solve specific problems. In any event, research does go on in every function of a company, centralized, formalized, directed, or not.

Product research is extensive. An example is the change by professional liability insurers to the claims-made policy in lieu of the occurrence form. The difficult, penetrating research focused in part on defining the problem, measuring the extent of professional liability, analyzing statistical data, searching the law, examining public relations trends, pricing the product, marketing the new product, and organizing the task to accomplish the change.

Most serious research undertakings have high-level implications. Almost certainly they are approved by senior executives. Important decisions are likely to be influenced by them. For all these reasons, it is vital that key people know the goal and purposes of the project. Coordination and communication to others must be carefully planned.

The interrelationship among functional departments makes it necessary, too, that these units that have shared responsibilities be fully briefed on what is to take place. The success of the research project may depend on it. In any event, management knows that any large research venture that infers change as a possible consequence is a real threat to employee cooperation and morale if not satisfactorily explained in the very beginning.

PRODUCT MANAGEMENT

The functions grouped under the heading Product Management are those that focus on managing the internal operations that deal with selection and pricing. This section will discuss rate making, underwriting, and reinsurance.

Rate Making

Rate making and rating are directed toward one major objective—the determination of the proper premium to be charged to each insured and line of business. The premium involves developing a rate (rate making) and applying that rate or rating plan to exposure units (rating). These activities may be collectively referred to as *pricing*.

Pricing of insurance contracts has the same objective as the pricing of any other product offered for sale. It is to cover the provider's cost (including contingencies and catastrophes), and a margin for profit needed for financial strength, growth, and dividends to the policyholders or stockholders.

In this pricing process there is a unique difference for the insurance business. The "cost of goods sold" will not be known until the policy expires—and often several years beyond that time. Insurance is purchased to protect against a fortuitous loss. It is this very element of uncertainty that adds a novel and often formidable dimension to insurance pricing. *Past* loss data are used to develop *present* rates that must be adequate to pay *future* losses.

To be useful, a rate or rating plan must pass several tests. It must satisfy the underwriter that it will cover ultimate costs. It is desirable that it have built-in incentives for loss control. The producer must believe that the product is competitively priced, and the regulator must be satisfied that the rates meet the established regulatory standards. Finally, and most important, the public must be willing and able to pay the price asked.

There are several ways in which rates can be produced. One is through rating organizations established for that purpose. Premiums, losses, and expense statistics are furnished to the rating bureau, which promulgates rates for its members and subscribers or supplies them with advisory rates. Another way is through insurance company actuarial departments working with their own loss and expense figures. In this respect, insurance companies are becoming more and more independent. Finally, rates may be mandated by law or regulation in some states (generally for private passenger auto).

The insurer's capability, and perhaps need, to be independent in rating is enhanced and supported by several factors. One is, of course, the availability of skilled actuaries. The tremendous power of the computer is an element. Another factor is the trend for rating bureaus to be exclusively statistical units—providing only loss data and leaving it to the insurers to develop a final rate. Prompt rating responses to inflationary forces must be on the list. Special policy forms will frequently require independent rates. Competition is also a factor.

It is obvious that a rating scheme cannot produce certainty in result. Experience, judgment, highly refined schedules, and careful scrutiny of hazards all can lead to tentative conclusions, but none can be predictive with precise accuracy. This is the dilemma. An insurance policy with a fixed premium today must insure against tomorrow's uncertainties with unknown costs.

Underwriting

The purpose of underwriting can best be determined by a consideration of the manner in which the insurance business serves the general public. Since private (non-government) insurance is based on the transfer of risk, the basic purpose of insurance is to provide protection to businesses, individuals, and other institutions against a wide variety of losses on mutually acceptable terms. The role of underwriting is to screen the various insurance proposals for acceptability and to determine the rates, terms, and conditions for the coverage. This is an important role, because if an insurance company did not properly screen all proposals for insurance, it would become the victim of *adverse selection.*

Adverse selection occurs when the applicants for insurance are largely those most likely to suffer a loss. It is more prevalent in some lines of insurance, such as flood, than in others. Where flood insurance is offered, only those with serious flood exposures are likely to apply for coverage. The person whose property is on high ground is much less likely to purchase the coverage than the person whose property is on low land next to a river. Because of adverse selection, an insurance company must "select or be selected against." If the insurance company does not practice selection competently, applicants will adversely select against the company.

The fundamental purpose of underwriting, then, is to protect the insurance company against the consequences of adverse selection. An insurance company can fulfill its commitments to its insureds, stockholders, employees, and the community at large only if it is financially sound. The senior underwriting officer in charge, reporting to the president, would consider the primary responsibility of the assignment centered around the following tasks:

- formulation and implementation of underwriting policy to meet profit and premium volume objectives
- selection, development, and motivation of key subordinates to assure performance and management continuity

- formulation of plans to meet company and division objectives
- direct development of new products that meet market acceptance and profit objectives
- development of a reinsurance program
- review of results and the initiation of changes to correct inefficiencies or improve results within the division
- development and maintenance of an organizational structure for the underwriting division to meet its current and long-range objectives
- maintaining of close coordination with other divisions, especially marketing, claims, and accounting

Types of business and how they will be underwritten vary with insurers. The same generalization can be made about underwriters. Attitudes depend not only upon policy, but backgrounds, training, experience, intuition, judgment and, naturally, the *classes of business* (a sub-group in a line of business such as the youthful driver class in the personal auto line of business) under consideration. Insurance companies usually will establish formal or informal policies and underwriting guidelines. Underwriters also do this on their own initiative, but in time, experience and knowledge will have more influence on decisions.

The underwriter is influenced by the policy forms and contracts, the rates they bear, the expense ratios, and, of course, the nature of the exposure. Underwriting must also take into account the reinsurance treaties in effect. The process inquires not only into hazards, but includes loss control measures and rating programs as well.

The producer is also involved in the underwriting function. The agent, broker, or company marketing specialist is in a good position to know relevant information about an insured. It is assumed that a reliable producer would not submit an application if the moral or physical hazards were clearly undesirable. The power to bind a company in almost unlimited amounts is a serious responsibility. The underwriting obligation is obvious and awesome.

Reinsurance

Underwriters must be constantly alert in the selection of insureds to obtain and maintain a safe and profitable distribution of business. One very important tool available to underwriters in this connection is reinsurance. Reinsurance may be defined as a contractual arrangement under which one insurer, known as the ceding company, transfers to another insurer, called the reinsurer, some or all of the losses incurred by the ceding company under insurance contracts it has issued or will issue in the future. The ceding company is sometimes referred to by other terms, such as the primary insurer, cedent, direct writer, direct insurer, or the reinsured.

Regardless of the size of the insurance company, the use of reinsurance in some measure is universal. The reinsurance mechanism is not a bottomless well into which the insurer tosses undesirable business. A valued axiom is that an insurer over time eventually pays in premiums all that it ever recovers from its reinsurer. Why then should there be reinsurance?

The transaction between the primary insurer and reinsurer is not a frivolous exchange of money. The primary insurer can be saved from ruinous catastrophe, smooth its loss experience from one year to another, avoid emotional alarms from investors because of shock losses, and reduce the necessity to liquidate assets disadvantageously.

Reinsurance is a critical problem for top management, not in an administrative sense but in its dramatic effect on capacity and profit or loss. Major commitments are sure to have front office attention.

Organization of the reinsurance function within a company may be charged to an underwriting officer, or a department may be created for that particular purpose. Assuming the latter format, the department chief will, for example, be charged with these responsibilities:

1. Formulate and implement reinsurance policies which promotes achievement of objectives.
2. Obtain reinsurance terms which protect the insurer's surplus and lend stability to underwriting results.
3. Investigate new ways to reinsure and assemble relevant information upon which to base alternative courses of action.
4. Negotiate with reinsurance markets which are determined to be financially sound; new treaties and substantial changes are subject to approval by the division head and the president.
5. Assume incoming reinsurance within guidelines approved by the division head and the president.
6. Assume administrative responsibility for the underwriting associations in which the company has membership.

SERVICES

The services provided by property and liability insurers are many and varied. The major service activities discussed in this chapter are claims adjusting, legal, loss control, risk management services, policyholders' service, policywriting, premium audits, electronic data processing, and producer, consumer, and employee education.

Claims Adjusting

Claims adjusting must take its place with marketing and underwriting as one of the three essential and basic functions of an insurance company. The ultimate worth of an insurance contract is determined in the event of loss.

One of the most constructive evolutions in the adjustment of losses has been organizing to deal with a catastrophe. Insurance companies send teams to the stricken area to provide immediate loss adjustment. These people work under trying conditions and for long hours. Frequently, they may use herculean efforts to keep building materials costs in line, provide temporary relief, and get quality work done where repairs are required. Insurance associations move their staffs into the area to provide information for the public on where and how to have their losses adjusted. Some insurers use sound trucks and set up temporary headquarters where the public can submit claims. All of this has been successful in allaying anxieties by providing prompt service. As a dividend, the procedure has done much for the public image of insurance companies.

At the home office level, the senior officer in charge of claims controls a network of claim facilities directly and indirectly on a policy or operational level. This network is operated by delegating the claims function and setting limits of authority.

The responsibilities for the chief of the claims division include the following:

- developing and communicating the practices and procedures for the investigation, evaluation, direction, disposition, and audit of the claim payments to insureds
- making certain that the disbursements are proper and in accord with the insurance contract provisions
- seeing that the policyholder receives the service, protection, and benefits purchased
- making certain that there is adequate resistance to faulty, unreasonable, or questionable claims
- overseeing active and effective pursuit of salvage, subrogation, and reinsurance recovery
- supervising the establishment and maintenance of procedures for the prompt and efficient processing of claims and claims data

The claims chief also has a major responsibility for monitoring the litigation that arises out of the very few claims that go to court, including the everyday management of lawsuits in the hands of defense attorneys. This is to make sure that cases are not overworked and that unnecessary expenses are not incurred. Since outside lawyers usually represent a number of clients, it is only prudent to make sure that a company's cases are receiving proper attention. The monitoring function embraces not only accuracy and honesty but also a continuous audit of open and closed files to determine operating effectiveness.

There are some regulatory aspects to claims handling that should be noted. Because of an antitrust consent decree, insurance companies cannot direct auto repairs to a particular garage. This decree diminishes the ability of insurers to control repair costs. There are some statutes that deal with alleged unfair claims practices. A growing number of states require loss adjustments to be completed within a specified time, or penalties are exacted. There are regulators who advocate that claimspersons should be licensed in order to establish their competency.

Legal

Legal staffs are needed not only to cope with claims but also to cope with other corporate problems. Today, it is not uncommon to have a general counsel as an officer of the insurance company even though outside counsel will frequently be used. This is an indication of the increasingly litigious nature of our society.

The legal department will frequently be involved with insurance regulators as well as with the legality of certain aspects of the property and liability insurance operation. They will also be active in enunciating the company's position in legislative matters.

While actuaries and underwriters decide on rates and rating plans, a mechanism is needed to file rates. Often, lawyers supervise this process and supervise the state-by-state licensing procedures for the company. Duties of the legal department may also involve relations with trade associations and other business organizations.

Corporate counsel usually report to the chief executive or a senior officer because many high-level policy decisions will be based on legal advice. The legal department includes lawyers and paralegal assistants. The chief counsel will usually assume the responsibility for relations with outside counsel and will direct litigation in which the insurer is involved. If there are other insurance subsidiaries (such as life or title insurance companies), the corporate counsel may assign a company lawyer as their chief legal counsel. There may also be a staff assistant to deal with tax problems.

The chief counsel must be especially careful to provide guidance to officers and directors in meeting their responsibilities as defined in law and recent court cases as well as fulfilling requirements imposed by regulatory authorities such as the Securities and Exchange Commission and state insurance departments. The maze of federal and state statutes and regulations requires constant vigilance and expert legal advice.

Loss Control

The conservation of lives and property is a primary objective of every insurance organization. Loss control efforts of property and liability insurers contribute to social and economic welfare and to the image of the insurance industry.

The cost of loss control services is more than offset by the benefits derived from them. The loss control representative is a connecting link with the insuring public, providing one of the few means that insurers have, not only to articulate sound policies for loss control, but also to assist in their implementation. The communicating value of loss control personnel is a demonstrable asset.

Loss control services can also add a new dimension to a company's marketing efforts. Here, after all, is something constructive that insurance companies have to offer in addition to the indemnity provided by their policies.

The advent of the Occupational Safety and Health Act, the Consumer Product Safety Act, and other legislative actions have broadened the expected services provided by loss control specialists.

Loss control is an example of how far flung the internal and external relationships can be in an insurance company. Operationally, personnel from the department have frequent contact in daily operations with underwriting, field offices, employee relations, general services, marketing, claims, producers, and insureds. Because of special expertise and research abilities, loss control personnel have frequent contact with industries; trade associations; department of labor and safety councils; organizations dedicated to standards, research safety, nuclear energy, building security, and disaster planning; and associations of commerce and industry.

Risk Management Services

In the recent past, more and more corporate insureds have adopted large deductibles, or retention (self-insurance) programs. Others have established captive insurance companies. To meet the need for increased insurer services, many insurance companies have developed risk management services departments to provide inspection, claims adjusting, actuarial, and risk analysis services to insureds on a fee basis. It appears that more property and liability insurers will be offering these insurance-related services to take the place of or to supplement a corporate insurance program.

Premium Audit

Some policies are written with an estimated or deposit premium subject to a final premium based on a variable factor such as payroll or sales. Upon expiration, it is the premium audit department's responsibility to audit the insured's books and obtain the actual figures to determine the final premium. The actual earned premium can then be computed and an additional premium collected, or a return premium paid, depending on the amount of the estimated deposit premium. The audit may be a physical audit of the larger insureds by a company premium auditor or a self-audit prepared by the insured.

The premium audit process involves the monies of both the insured and the insurer and is one of the few direct contacts the insured has with company personnel. Consequently, the timeliness and accuracy of the audit and the impression created by the auditor are important because both can influence the customer's image of the insurance company.

Some companies have combination loss control-auditing personnel. Because of their knowledge of the customer's operations, they can better classify the premium bases; they also avoid duplication in travel to the same insured and provide a company person in a territory that could not support both a loss control representative and an auditor.

The premium audit function of an insurance company is a significant part of cash flow. Cash flow can be accelerated by completing and billing audits promptly and accurately, by determining additional exposures covered and the additional premium due because of them, and by prompt notification of inadequate deposit premiums or excessive additional premiums. Obviously, a high percentage of additional premiums indicates an earlier loss of cash flow from deposit and earned premiums. The billing and clerical functions in a premium audit department appear to be moving toward computerization. The speed and accuracy of computer operations will also help to increase cash flow benefits.

Electronic Data Processing

The computer is one product from the technological age known to all. It processes data in a fraction of a second and can handle billions of figures with ease. Although it is responsible for a love-hate relationship with many, insurers of any size would be operationally stymied without its capability twenty-four hours a day.

The computer has now become an essential element of the small as well as the large insurance company. For the manager of tomorrow, there is no escape from the computer. Business can recount some successes from the application of EDP, especially in accounting, policy issuance and the like; but all of these are only in the frontier of data processing knowledge. Its enormous capabilities are only dimly perceived. With us now are simulation routines, operations research, underwriting advice, systems for information retrieval, teleprocessing, telecommunication, management information, and computer-assisted training and education. This is only the beginning. These devices are used more and more to assist in decision making. There are few businesses that will profit from this technical and flexible virtuosity as much as insurance.

The processing of raw data by computer must be a well-organized effort. The EDP unit has not only a variety of computers and supporting peripheral equipment, but it is often staffed by specialists in programming, systems design, telecommunications and even those skilled in operations research and other exotic arts. Because of the immense importance of the computer center, as well as the skills involved and the dependence of almost the entire organization on its product, it is usually organized as a completely separate function headed by a senior officer often reporting to the president, depending upon the company's organizational concepts.

The chief of EDP is responsible for several essential operations. Examples are systems design, programming, use of computers (large and small) and their extensive peripheral gear—which includes optical scanners, high-speed printers, tape drives, remote terminals, storage devices, and data entry paraphernalia, all of which make up the various links that join this equipment into a functioning network. The data processing responsibility is an imaginative and exacting one.

What does management expect from computers? First, it expects the computer to process a large amount of data, assimilate it, have it in a readily accessible data bank, print it out in a variety of forms, and do all of this in a timely fashion. The amount of data used internally and externally is staggering. This trend shows no sign of abatement. EDP is the only effective way to deal with this outsized problem.

Second, it expects accuracy. Program system design and data source failures are correctable, and the computer's discipline inevitably exposes most errors. There is no sweeping them under the rug. This enforces the discipline of determining what is an acceptable error ratio.

Producer, Consumer, and Employee Education

Many insurance companies offer their producers a number of

opportunities to attend educational seminars and formalized classes and to take correspondence courses. Usually, these courses are prepared and monitored by the home office staff and may be held in different localities. They are useful, too, in communicating the company point of view.

Employees are given many opportunities to enlarge their insurance education. Some companies make a substantial effort to provide opportunities for enrollment in national continuing education programs and in degree programs at the undergraduate and graduate school levels. Several companies maintain an educational staff that prepares and teaches correspondence courses and advises employees about educational opportunities. Other companies provide computer-assisted educational programs through terminals in company offices.

Staff personnel organize and conduct classes that range from orientation for the new employee to courses in management techniques and administration. They include accounting, EDP, law, and personnel, plus training in special skills (e.g., communications, supervision, general management, time management).

The educational role of the company is large, varied, and certain to grow. At a given time, a large percentage of an insurance company's employees are involved in training or education. Many insurers offer their employees incentives by paying part or all of their tuition and examination fees.

Educational policy and objectives are requisites for an effective educational training program within a company. An announced goal of such a program may be to assure an adequate supply of knowledgeable employees to carry out the company's objectives.

Success or failure of the employee educational programs should be monitored by management, not only to be prudent about cost-benefit, but to make certain that this supremely important goal is attained. Periodic reports from the company's education and training executives should inform top management and measure progress.

Consumer education is widely dispersed. Some is attempted through advertising. Some is through leaflets and other material inserted in policy mailings or premium billings. Insurers and producers also participate in industry symposia or in professional groups or schools that lecture to students and interested citizens on certain phases of insurance. Those engaged in loss control are constantly educating employers and employees in conservation of life and property. Consumer education is also found in the efforts of trade associations to inform the public on a variety of issues such as highway and product safety, protection against fraud and crime, and safety in the home and at school.

ADMINISTRATIVE

The magnitude and diversity of insurance company operations require careful administration of activities that enable the company to achieve its objectives. The major administrative functions discussed here include planning and development, personnel administration, accounting, coding, field office administration, and public and community relations.

Planning and Development

Planning is essential. It causes a company to think about where it wants to go and how it can best get there. The planning process includes both goal setting (establishing what the company wants to be in the future) and detailed action steps designed to move the company toward its goal. Top management is most concerned with goal setting, while other levels are much more involved in determining the proper action steps. A good plan will include the following: What does the company want to be? How is it going to accomplish this? What is the timing of each significant action? Who should take the action?

The mission of planning is to carry out the purpose and priorities of the company. Concern of top management should be directed toward what to do and not how to do it. A planner must react not only to factors inside the organization but also to what is happening outside.

Participation in the planning process is necessary at all levels. This participation creates commitment on the part of individuals. Commitment motivates the organization to focus on the desired goals and objectives. The task is not only to see that the plans are good, are specific, have deadlines, and can be measured, but that an accounting is rendered. Without an accounting, plans are a wasted effort.

Personnel Administration

In this generation, perhaps no business responsibility has elevated its status so dramatically and meaningfully as personnel administration. There is now full realization among insurance executives that employee morale and productivity are among their greatest concerns. Coping with human concerns requires skillful judgment. Personnel administration has grown from a subsidiary staff exercise to a high-level function involved in many operational phases of a company. Its mission is the development of people and the management of the company's human resources.

The organization of the employee relations department at the highest level may have certain subordinate sections and functions such as salary administration, employment, upward communication, minority relations, employee benefits and services, education and training, management development, human resource planning, and employee data control.

To be effective, an insurer must use the same management techniques as other well-managed businesses. There must be clear assignments of responsibilities at all levels; standards and measurement of performance at all levels; compensation related to performance and job content; a system of accountability; and communication of a belief in the worth of the individual and in that person's need to know that he or she is performing vital, useful work. People are management's most crucial responsibility, most valuable resource, and the essence of business success.

Personnel Planning Alert insurance companies do not leave to chance encounter the knowledge of what future personnel requirements may be. As a part of the planning process, estimates of future needs are calculated and targets set. Companies also must know what the composition of the staff should be, when a new activity will be started, or when a new office will be opened. Personnel administration counsels operating departments on personnel planning and control. Often the ratio of premium dollars to salary dollars is an important index to the health of the enterprise.

Employee Communications Companies should make certain that there is a flow of communications downward, laterally, and upward. This is accomplished in many ways. Formal announcements, letters, bulletins, memoranda, radio, television, conference telephone calls, and meetings are among the many methods used. Employee polls, however, document that learning the news directly from the chief of the unit is by far the best way. Special training in communications is often given to supervisors to reinforce this influence.

Upward communication is more difficult to manage. Many companies maintain what is called an open-door policy. Under this plan, an employee with a grievance or problem can approach anyone in management to seek a solution. Another device is attitude surveys. As a corollary to all of this, it is essential that supervisors receive the training necessary to handle employees' problems with sensitivity and understanding.

Salary Administration Salary administration commences with the job description and evaluation. It requires careful construction of salary ranges that fit the responsibilities of the position. The ranges must be competitive and administered equitably.

The trend in salary administration is toward consideration of the total compensation for employees, cash and noncash, including employee fringe benefits. Internal equity is attained by sophisticated job structuring and review. Salary surveys are used to maintain a competitive position externally.

Modern practice is to disseminate widely information on salary levels that can be expected in various career patterns. Reasons for granting or withholding increases must be frankly communicated. This is probably one of the most urgent responsibilities for a personnel administrative unit.

Human Relations In many organizations, there is an officer who coordinates and manages the urban affairs and social responsibility of a company to ensure maximum benefit from company resources. In the event there are several subsidiaries with independent personnel functions, the officer develops and maintains an effective corporate employee relations policy and coordinates this policy throughout the entire organization. He or she may also prepare the company's contributions budget and supervise its administration.

Accounting

There are several operational formats that are suitable for the accounting function. In a few organizations, accounting may be grouped with other financial activities. In the case of a large organization, the accounting work probably will be separated, and the department head will report to the treasurer or controller.

Because of the enormous number of transactions and dollar volume now being transacted in the insurance business, accounting has grown in magnitude. Procedures have been complicated by regulatory requirements, valuation of assets, accounting changes, and the necessary use of electronic data processing. Where there are several insurance companies under one management, the interchange of funds, reinsurance transactions, and common use of facilities add additional problems.

The accounting unit at times is the processor and compiler of information provided by others (e.g., loss reserves) and in other instances the originator of the data (e.g., accounts receivable). The distribution of organizational duties will usually determine whether data are originated by the accounting department or others.

Coding

The coding concept is simple. It is a process of reducing information to alphabetic and numeric characters that can be used by the computer to represent that data. Grave consequences may result from coding mistakes. The physical act of coding may be simple, but coding plans and schemes are complicated.

The ramification in coding errors may be seen in four examples. The writer of a code ticket mistakenly enters the number 8 for 7; result, a million dollar salvage recovery was entered as a loss reserve, throwing the annual underwriting statement out of balance by $2 million. A coding plan was rewritten, but code Block A should have been in code Block B; result, 600 insureds who paid their premiums received delinquency notices. For the month of April, the number 5 was used instead of 4 for the period of time on automobile policies, and the following year the computer failed to renew April policies. The coder transposed the code numbers used to instruct the computer to make automatic adjustments in insured values to reflect inflation; the result, a $60,000 increase on dwelling contents on all renewals until the error was detected.

Simplification of the process is not easy because of the inordinate demands for data in many forms and by many users. However, computer editing of data is going a long way towards remedying the problem.

Field Office Administration

A field office may range from one person to an office that has all the major activities represented: production, underwriting, claims, loss control, and even accounting. In the latter case, the local manager's problems will be similar to those at the home office level. The manager's ability to solve these problems will depend not only on experience and competence but also on vested authority.

The relation of the field office with the producer is of the utmost importance. In many respects, this office *is* the company. Producer reaction to it will often decide the future of the company. Effectiveness of the field office can well be determined by the extent of its decision-making authority.

Under a centralized operation, supervision of personnel in a field office might be charged to each executive responsible for a similar function at the home or regional office level. That is, field representatives responsible for production would report to a manager for production at the home office, claims personnel to a claims manager, and so on. The same might also be true of underwriting and loss control personnel. At the field office level, all these functions might be housed together, with one of the employees acting as chief administrator for the group. Each administrator, however, would be independent of the others.

A more unified scheme, but one requiring authentic decentralization, is to have an overall manager of the field office accountable to the home office or regional level for all activities and functions in that field office. The specialized services—underwriting, claims, field representatives, loss control—would have a reporting relationship on technical, procedural, and advisory matters with an executive at the home office or regional level. If an overall manager is established at each field office, that person's responsibility would be to only one executive at the higher level. That executive would be responsible for the success of the enterprise at that location.

Public and Community Relations

The importance of a good public image to a company cannot be overemphasized. This has always been true, but companies now spend more time and money in attempting to project that image as they see it. One observer said, "The art of public relations is doing what's good and right and getting credit for it." In any event, the deeds must have substance, and they must be communicated. Companies are learning that earnest and effective communication about problem areas to concerned constituents pays dividends. The responsibility for good communications rests with all individuals and all groups, and management must be the prime mover in attaining continuous and anticipatory communications.

In recent years, insurers have also been conscious of the need to make their involvement with community relations better known. Most insurers are heavy contributors of money and personnel in support of civic, cultural, and charitable enterprises. These objectives and activities often are interpreted by a public or community relations department, which frequently has responsibilities for shareholder relations and for monitoring the internal communication programs.

The mission for public and community relations is to interpret the corporation, its businesses, its activities, and its accomplishments to the various internal and external publics to assure that the company is accurately and well known; to monitor, appraise, and interpret for management the social trends and public attitudes that affect the company and to recommend courses of action; to develop and coordinate programs in support of the company's civic and public affairs objectives; to provide communication services to the various internal departments; to maintain communications to shareholders; and to audit, evaluate, and advise on employee communications programs.

One of the duties of a public relations officer is to deal with the media. This embraces trade, general, financial, and specialized news media, including newspapers, magazines, radio, and television. One significant objective is to maintain credibility with the media as a reliable source of information about the company. The same requirement applies to prompt, adequate, and accurate information of value to be disseminated to the financial community and shareholders. In some instances, public relations is responsible for the design, writing, and production of the annual report, as well as the interim reports and other publications directed towards the shareholders.

Public relations, as an operation, must also be concerned with a broad range of other company communications, including those directed towards employees, management, producers, government officials, and the general public. This might also include institutional advertising, as distinguished from marketing advertising.

A substantial responsibility for the public relations function is to operate an early warning system on external social developments and trends that could affect the company. This embraces public attitudes towards the company and the insurance industry.

Another important public relations function is to maintain an annual audit of the internal communications program of the company to measure how well it is meeting corporate objectives. The purpose of this audit is to (1) measure the effectiveness of the company's internal communications program and (2) determine if the program meets corporate standards. The audit is not concerned with the methods or techniques of internal communications. There is no one way in which to communicate effectively. What is communicated is more important than how it is communicated.

FINANCE AND INVESTMENT

Insurance company accounting and finance is so important that a major portion of CPCU 8 is devoted to it. However, a brief overview of investment strategy, portfolio management, cash flow management, and relations with financial institutions is presented here to illustrate their effect on insurance company operations.

Investment Strategy

Strategy for investing money is dependent upon a company's recognition of its needs. If its motivation is to minimize the vulnerability of its net worth from market action, the strategy would be directed towards government, corporate, or municipal bonds to protect a leveraged position in capital to premiums or loss reserves. The company might also be expanding or have heavy commitments in high hazard underwriting areas.

There is a need to consider the interrelationships between underwriting and investment operations in order to assure that compatible goals are being pursued. Special attention must be given to the nature of the risks to which the company is exposed. Insurance accounting rules provide some insulation of policyholders' surplus (net worth) from the risk of fluctuating asset values by permitting insurers to value government, municipal, and corporate bonds in good standing at amortized cost rather than at current market value. To the extent that the investment portfolio can be valued on this stabilized basis, one aspect of investment risk is reduced.

If the company's investment objective is to earn a high aftertax yield on its assets, the investment strategy should emphasize securities that are currently providing high returns in the form of interest and dividends. Insurance companies that are experiencing significant underwriting losses probably cannot take full advantage of tax-exempt income from municipal bonds. These insurers may choose to invest extensively in high-grade corporate bonds. On the other hand, insurers experiencing taxable underwriting profits may invest more heavily than otherwise in tax-exempt public debt issues.

Another insurance company may believe that it can build policyholders' surplus faster by investing for portfolio appreciation through increases in the market value of common stocks. In this case, the insurer's investment portfolio will be more heavily weighted with equity securities. This strategy does create greater risk of fluctuations in policyholders' surplus because stocks are shown in the balance sheet at their market values. Moreover, an equity-oriented portfolio may also yield a lower current return than bonds, but the insurer may be motivated by total return (i.e., current income plus market value appreciation) rather than current return only.

Investment strategy and the appropriate debt/equity mix of the portfolio are influenced by a number of factors, such as current return versus total return; the composition of the portfolio; the accuracy and stability of estimated liability values; the company's current net worth, its growth plans, and its dividend policy; the condition of the money and capital markets and the forecast for the future; and the effects that future inflation is expected to have on the economy in general and the insurer in particular. Many of these issues are dealt with in CPCU 8 and elsewhere in the CPCU curriculum.

Portfolio Management

The management of a portfolio is, in fact, implementation of the investment strategy or policy. Attention is then directed to the entire investment program. Component parts must be structured in detail.

Asset mix as to stocks and bonds must be settled. The specific issues to be owned must be determined, as well as the segmentation with regard to industry, service, and financial groupings. Time to buy and time to sell must be foreseen. Economic forecasts must be reviewed and updated.

The management of the portfolio is generally lodged with an investment division operating within the policies established by the board of directors and implemented by senior management. An investment officer or financial vice president will be in charge of the activity. The responsibilities of this person are to develop investment policy, direct research, and supervise investment officers and analysts. The chief financial officer will brief directors and top management of the company's investment position. That officer must also be conversant with finance and economics; be able to judge stock, bond, and money market trends; and have insights on tax consequences and regulatory requirements in the securities industry. The responsibility for accomplishing all of this is divided within the investment staff according to its respective specialties and abilities.

Establishing and maintaining the portfolio is an art. Generally, a company will maintain a list of common stocks recommended by the staff and approved by the directors. Preceding the listing will be research either originating within the concern or acquired from outside analysts and investment firms. The list is constantly reviewed and updated. With equities, limits will usually be placed on any one holding or category.

Property and liability insurers are large investors in municipal bonds. A high percentage of the portfolio will be in these debt instruments. As mentioned, they give the financial statements some stability because they are valued on an amortized basis. The fact that these bonds are almost always in demand does not make trading in them a simple exercise. Rated and unrated bonds require careful selection and consideration, field trips, independent judgments, and a sensitivity to current and future interest rates. Success in buying and selling bonds requires good timing, care, and good judgment.

The performance of portfolio managers is monitored as is any other function in the operations of an insurer. Usual yardsticks are Dow-Jones or Standard and Poor's averages as well as goals established by the investment division and top management.

Cash Flow Management

Only in recent years have insurance companies become acutely aware of the importance of cash flow management. It used to be habitual, especially for annual statement purposes, to have large sums of cash on deposit in various banks all over the country. The first move toward cash flow management was in consolidating unnecessary bank accounts. In the 1960s and 1970s, it became obvious that many insurers had been operating under a passive cash flow management policy. But changing times and higher short-term interest rates brought sophistication about money; cash flow must be managed with all that the words imply.

Cash flow management depends on three essentials: (1) policy must be established and implemented; (2) cash must be managed and monitored (reports required and accountabilities established); and (3) cash must be used where maximum benefits can be realized, which usually means through investments. A few of the techniques available are described in the following examples.

The use of lock boxes is a time- and money-saving practice. In this method, customers or others at distant points send payments to a lock box under the custody of a bank. The sums can then be quickly recorded on the company books. With agency collections, the practice reduces mail and collection time by three to five days. Another use of the lock box is for investment transactions. It speeds cash flow and eliminates in-house processing of large items. All funds in both types of box deposits are wired to the company on the following day and are then available for investment.

Another vantage point for watching cash flow is monitoring credit terms in conjunction with accounts receivable. Changes needed will be obvious. Transfer of funds by wire is becoming standard practice in cash management. When securities are delivered for sale, it is an especially useful method. Direct billing is used by many companies for personal lines. This procedure speeds up the flow of cash to the home office.

The daily cash flow through an insurance company generally is large enough so that it is not necessary to sell securities to meet losses. This fact makes it possible to keep money constantly invested. For the same reason, companies find it desirable to keep bank deposits at the lowest possible amount.

Many companies keep elaborate records on the cash flow and forecast its course. In this way, they know at all times how much money will be available for uses other than losses and expenses. The cash flow chart sets forth the amount in redemptions, bonds, and stocks bought and sold, dividends to be received and paid, and money that is available week by week from operations of the business. Some companies control cash flow daily with at least a weekly reading on future cash expectancies.

Relations with Financial Institutions

Because of the large sums of money that are invested, officers responsible for investment policy and its implementation have constant two-way communication with the financial community. This group will include analysts from large institutional investors, traders in stocks and bonds, commercial and investment bankers, economists, and financial journalists. Reams of material are also flowing to and from companies and financial institutions. While banking relations are important, insurance companies are not bank borrowers. They are depositors and frequently use bank services.

The relationship between investment houses and insurers is that of buyer and seller. An investment officer of an insurer buys a selected stock or bond at the best market price at the time of purchase. This is a fiduciary and management responsibility. Investment brokers perform several services for companies by providing economic and investment information. Not many companies maintain elaborate research facilities. They usually depend on outside sources.

Investment bankers are used by insurers to underwrite offerings of new capital stock or debentures when the company wishes to increase its capital strength. Some companies that are owned by holding companies have an affiliation with stock exchanges, mutual funds, investment bankers, consumer loan companies, leasing, savings and loan organizations, and other financial service companies.

INTERDEPENDENCY AMONG INSURANCE ACTIVITIES

The management structure of an insurance company consists of several major departments and many smaller divisions within such departments. Each department and division must have some degree of autonomy if it is to function effectively and efficiently in reaching the company's goals and objectives and to serve its purpose in the development of skilled and practiced management personnel. However, the autonomy cannot be complete. The departments and divisions are interdependent to a very large degree. The effective coordination of the activities of the departments and divisions is the principal function of the top management team of an insurer. The paragraphs that follow discuss the interactions among a few representative departments to illustrate the interdependency that exists among virtually all company operations.

Marketing and Underwriting

Marketing and underwriting are cooperative activities that depend heavily on each other regardless of market conditions. While marketing has a responsibility to underwriting to make it aware of the needs of the consumer, it is underwriting that is the manufacturer of the product. In that capacity, underwriting must develop products that fulfill the needs of the consumer; are acceptable to the sales force; and are priced at a profit and within a reasonably competitive range. If these conditions are not met, the product is not a salable item.

Marketing is further responsible for development of a sales force capable of reaching those consumers who are prospects for the products and developed in sufficient numbers to allow the selective process of underwriting to function. In addition, marketing must see that proper communication takes place between the company and its producers to make them aware of the products available, the underwriting attitudes of the company, and the conditions of sale. It cannot do this without careful coordination with underwriting.

While the underwriter ultimately decides what the rates will be for a given contract, it is necessary to know if that rate will hamper or aid sales. Obviously, marketing and underwriting have a shared responsibility for this decision.

If a policy or any coverage, new or old, is to be sold with confidence, it is necessary for producers, and especially field representatives, to understand the nature and conditions of the contract. This requirement places a duty on the underwriter to describe clearly what the product does and does not do and why.

To provide an incentive to sell a policy, it is necessary that a commission be established. Cost of selling is certainly a part of the price. Underwriting is heavily involved in the commission decision but must work closely with the marketing department in this part of pricing.

Service is what the producer and consumer expect. Without the close cooperation between marketing and underwriting, service will suffer. The field representative makes a commitment which can be carried out only if underwriting agrees and is capable of meeting it. Failure of the two departments to understand or support each other in the service area is often the cause of serious damage to the producer-consumer relationship.

Underwriting philosophy is certain to be influenced by marketing considerations. An ultraconservative underwriting philosophy might guarantee the insurer a riskless world, but the public is not likely to buy if the price is unaffordable or if the contract provisions are too restrictive. On the other hand, selling only at the lowest price and on the broadest terms is not a very successful goal for the insurer. Underwriting and marketing must be in harmony on this point.

The principal objectives of underwriting and marketing may appear divergent: underwriting for profit and marketing for sales. However, the total thrust and success of their joint effort stem from a common company philosophy and strategy understood and supported by both. Production and profitability are not mutually exclusive.

Claims and Underwriting

The relationship between claims and underwriting requires tact. Second-guessing or interference must not be a part of it. Working as a team can accomplish much. Working independently, many beneficial opportunities can be lost. The underwriter must underwrite, and the claims representative must adjust, but recognizing their interdependence will make life easier for both. It is the duty of a claims department to advise the underwriters about various items of cost, dangerous conditions, unfavorable laws, areas with high incidence of claims, and so on. It is likewise incumbent on underwriting to brief claims personnel on stress situations developing among the producer, company, and insured.

To evaluate a submission, the underwriter must rely on a number of facts concerning the insured. These are gleaned from many sources, but a number come from the claim records. The claim history may be short but expensive, or long but not too costly. Or perhaps a number of small occurrences might indicate a proneness to accident or just bad luck. Not only will claims files contain information on the desirability of an account, but they may indicate what might be needed to make it acceptable.

Claim files give an underwriter insight into what can go wrong. They introduce the reader to the world of damages, the cost of different types of accidents, and reserving practices. This information helps the underwriter to price the product more realistically. It also brings an appreciation of the size and number of possible losses that can be generated.

An underwriter could fail to consider the expense in handling claims. Attention tends to center on the loss itself, overlooking the expenses incurred in the investigation and negotiation process, plus the cost of litigation. In some lines, such as directors' and officers' liability, the cost of defense is the main cost.

An area of concern, especially with the manuscript policies, is the meaning and clarity of the language used by underwriters in a policy. It happens, too, that an underwriter introduces a policy with one concept in mind and the claims department has another interpretation. This means that claims personnel need thorough explanation of the genesis of new products. If the policy is new to the market, it is almost certain to carry in it words and phrases untested in court or in the adjustment of claims. It is necessary then that the claims department know well what was in the minds of the underwriters when the product was designed so that the claims department will perform its task properly.

When dealing with litigation or problems that may be litigated, the wording of the policy or endorsement is all important. The courts will assert that the common meaning is what is intended. Ambiguities are certain to be held against the insurer. Sometimes an underwriter can testify as to the intent, but the written word is usually final. Claims people, drawing on education, training, and experience, can help the underwriter with policy language.

A postmortem on a serious loss is often necessary. An evaluation of the insured can be made by conference between claims and underwriting, often bringing in loss control and marketing personnel. The claims representative is the only one who deals with all the parties at interest: the insured, the producer, the attorneys, the courts, and the underwriter.

The adjuster is in a good position to make judgments while investigating a claim. This is often valuable input for the underwriter. It is also an opportune moment to evaluate the credibility of the data supplied by or to the producer.

Marketing and Claims

Marketing and claims people represent the insurer to the public. However, the approaches are different. Both render service to producers, but the claims people do so through the producers' customers, the insureds. Claimspersons also give opinions on coverage and keep producers informed on developments that can influence the sellers' relationships with clients. Lines of communication must be open between claims and marketing so that each is aware of the other's position with respect to the producer. This is significant with coverage problems or where service or lack of it is evident.

A claim tests the performance of the product. If the settlement is unsatisfactory to the buyer, the reasons should be obvious. In such a case, the product is failing to perform its function and fill its intended need. Failure of a product can arise from slow service, poor customer relations, inaccurate explanations or understanding, poor evaluations, and unfair settlements. Marketing, claims, and underwriting must look for improvements in their combined operations.

Marketing should collaborate with claims, a natural checkpoint for producers anxious to know what the delivery end of the company has to say about the product. Claims people often see shortcomings in coverage and a solution. Insurance is flexible. Frequently, it can be tailored to meet unusual situations. Facts developed from claims experiences should improve the insurance products.

Underwriting and Rate Making

The interdependency of underwriting and rate making is self-evident. Actuarial support is necessary to arrive at rates of most products, although the final decision makers are the underwriters. It is the underwriters who have ultimate accountability for policy drafting, selection of insureds, and pricing; but they can fail if the antecedent preparation by the actuarial staff is ignored or inaccurate.

Underwriting and rate making must respond together to changes in coverage and deductibles imposed by experience, competition, or outside forces such as law and inflation. Rate-making techniques are an underwriter's tool to identify and pursue profitable areas, and the rate-making department is dependent on the underwriter for input to modify statistical weights to accommodate the practical world. Frequently, a weakness between underwriting and rate making is the absence of cost figures on processing and maintaining the policy. Also, data gathering can be so ponderously slow at times that techniques are needed for short cuts in rating that will be more timely and consistently accurate.

Loss Control and Claims

Input from the claims department broadens the loss control specialist's understanding of what to look for and what to guard against. Numerous items from claims files provide good examples for use with insureds in selling them on needed safety improvements and changes. A more recent concept for loss control is in the pre-claim activity directed towards mitigating losses. This approach is used frequently in products liability, but it also applies to other types of claims, especially in the category of what to do after the accident or occurrence. Too often, necessary evidence is lost or irretrievable after the loss. With claims and loss control cooperation, a system can be established to prepare and maintain records and routines that will be invaluable should a loss occur. The insured can protect and preserve evidence and identify witnesses. Such a system documents programs on quality control of the product, identifies experts who can testify as to the methods a manufacturer employed, identifies suppliers of components, provides data on production formulas and processes, plus other types of information that, if not preserved prior to loss, would be almost impossible to obtain later. This is a joint enterprise that merges the talents of the loss control staff with the imagination and claims experiences of the claimspersons to improve preparation for the legal cases that will inevitably occur. Not to be overlooked is the joint input of both departments which will give the underwriter knowledge in deciding whether or not the insured's loss potential is desirable.

Loss control people are usually well informed in engineering, mechanical, and technological areas which may not be well known to claims personnel. Working together is necessary not only in preventing and reducing losses but also in solving technical problems that accompany claims. In workers' compensation, it is the practice to inspect an insured location very closely for safety in the beginning. Claims and loss control collaboration develops routines and practices that will be prescriptions for action when an accident occurs. Immediate medical attention, prompt reporting to the insurance company, and avoidance of delay in paying just compensation to the injured are basic requirements.

Loss control and claims personnel, in performing their usual roles, encounter many areas that overlap, and the information thus developed can be exchanged to the advantage of both. Claims personnel can often reveal situations, conditions, and trends that are useful to the loss control representative in correcting unsatisfactory conditions with proper loss control techniques. The loss control department can provide codes, standards, technical opinion, laboratory analyses, and other assistance to the claims department in the investigation and settlement of losses. Product recall procedures can be worked out by a loss control specialist to assist claims personnel and insureds in controlling specific product losses.

Thorough original engineering surveys, with presentation and discussion of findings and recommendations to management, followed by periodic resurveys and safety services, are necessary ingredients in the program to help control losses. Accurate loss information is necessary to emphasize to the insured and other interested parties the trends and costs of accidents, their effect on rates and premiums, and the need for an effective safety program.

Loss Control and Underwriting

Underwriters have learned that adequate rates are not enough to guarantee insurability for many commercial and industrial insureds. To this must be added loss control service to improve the quality of the loss exposures. For an underwriter to select good business and price it properly, there is a strong dependency on a sound loss control department to advise underwriting on desirability from a physical, moral, and operational standpoint. The loss control representatives verify the accuracy of underwriting information; provide data needed to set lines of exposure correctly; advise if there are changes in the status of existing business; report on legislative changes that could affect a class or a line in the realm of safety; estimate costs to provide service for an insured; assist in training underwriters in the classroom and in the field; and keep underwriters up to date on new exposures, new protection, and emerging needs.

Marketing and Life Insurance

There are property and liability insurers that own life companies or are affiliated with life companies through a parent company. In some instances, the marketing of life insurance is directed as an adjunct effort of the property and liability insurer. Results in the field can be a responsibility of the local manager. In some cases, the life marketing staff is headed and operated by personnel with property and liability backgrounds.

In addition to the described staffing, the source of business may be mostly producers who are in the general insurance business. These producers are not only involved in the sale of ordinary life insurance, but in group insurance as well. In the latter case, the producer has excellent access to qualified prospects.

For this kind of enterprise to succeed, it is necessary for each group to understand the production, commission, and underwriting differences in the two types of insurance. Life and property-liability producers can prosper independently, but joining the two establishes a formidable competitive weapon for those who can balance the two systems as a cooperative venture.

AN ILLUSTRATION OF INTERDEPENDENCY AMONG DEPARTMENTS

The case study that follows should help to clarify the nature of the interactions among departments in the solution of problems facing an insurer. This situation is an actual example from the experience of a major insurer, though it has been simplified for presentation here.

The president of the XYZ Insurance Company has just reviewed a printout from the electronic data processing department which indicates that the loss experience on professional liability insurance (a substantial block of business) has deteriorated badly in the state of Nevcal. He calls a conference of his underwriting, actuarial, claims, law, and marketing officers and his chief assistant to resolve the problem.

After statement of the problem by the president, the claims officer points out the influence on verdicts of expert testimony, relaxation of rules of evidence, and weaknesses in the statute of limitations in the state of Nevcal. He is not at all optimistic about reversing these trends.

The actuary has charts showing the long-tail influence on reserves caused by claims developing years after the alleged incident occurs. The law officer points out that requests for rate increases (if that is the solution) require prior approval in the state of Nevcal and might even require a public hearing, thus delaying the effect of the increase even if it is granted.

The president then observes that the experience must be improved or the company will have to withdraw from the market. The marketing officer points out the long-term benefits to the company in providing a market to all of its producers and the state medical association. It is a substantial block of business, and the insureds' needs are great.

The senior underwriting officer expresses the opinion that the company cannot overcome inadequate premiums charged as well as inadequacy and untimeliness of reserve changes because of the *occurrence* policy form. He recommends staying in the market by changing to *a claims-made* form, with a modest rate increase and moving in that direction immediately.

The actuary responds by asserting that she can no longer rate the occurrence forms with any reasonable profit expectations; but with more pricing information, she has confidence that the claims-made form could be at least an interim solution.

After considerable discussion, the conference concludes that it might be more responsible to stay in the market, but to do so the company must stabilize the pricing and the loss ratio. The president approves remaining in the professional liability field, provided occurrence policies can be converted to claims-made policies. He sets a six-month deadline and appoints a task force to accomplish the mission and devise a strategy. If the appropriate forms and rates are not acceptable to insureds and regulators in that time, the company will discontinue professional liability business in Nevcal. He assigns the assistant to the president as chairman of the task force.

The reason for the task force is to combine talents and responsibilities on an unusual problem, assure coordination, and, most important, make certain that communications are exceptionally good. A plan of action under supervision of the coordinating officer is drafted.

1. *Underwriting*, with assistance from actuarial, law, claims, and perhaps outside counsel, must draft the claims-made form; within the department this will require consultation with professional liability underwriters.

2. *The chief actuary* will construct rates for a claims-made policy, after reviewing experience with statistics (completeness and quality of figures), claims (discussion on time lags for developing claims), and underwriting (forms to be used).

3. *The law officer* will plan procedures for filing new rates and forms, have conversations with regulatory officials at the appropriate time, and assess regulatory climate.

4. *Public relations* is assigned the responsibility for developing with underwriting, marketing, and others how this change will be communicated to several audiences including the producers, medical association, media, employees, financial community, regulators, and legislators. The public relations officer will develop all of the material (including explanations of the professional liability problem and the claims-made policy) to assure uniformity in telling the story and in dissemination, using oral, written, and audio visual techniques. Responsible operational and staff units will further disseminate information through their established channels.

5. *Marketing* will communicate appropriate responses and action to marketing personnel at both field and home office levels as policy develops, positions are established, and problems arise. Marketing will also coordinate recommendations with underwriting, communications, actuarial, and claims.

6. *Loss control* will be informed (by the assistant to the president) of the moves being made in case inspection and safety programs might be involved in any way.

7. *The treasurer's department* is to be consulted on booking premiums and segregation of statistics by EDP and on figures required in annual statements.

8. *The field office* responsible for Nevcal must be consulted by the senior officer in charge of regional operations on action to be taken. Each staff and operational department (claims, underwriting, marketing, and loss control) must do likewise.

9. *The field office general manager* will plan on how best to stay in touch with interested producers, the medical association, and local media. He must arrange coordination within his own office and home office.

10. *The president's assistant* establishes a timetable and deadlines for all of these activities. He or she will be responsible for testimony and conferences with legislators, the governor, and other state officials if required; will initiate required research, arrange for periodic meetings with all concerned officers, and make periodic reports of progress to the president; and will establish feed-back routines to assure early warning of ap-

Exhibit 1-1
Departmental Interrelatedness

Department	Responsibility	Coordinates with
Executive	Coordination, timetables, high level conferences, reports to CEO, feed-back procedures	All departments
Marketing	Communication with producers, medical association, field office	Underwriting, actuarial, claims, public relations
Actuarial	Preparation of rates	Statistics, claims, underwriting
Underwriting	Drafting of forms, agreeing on rates	Actuarial, marketing, EDP, treasurer, field office, public relations, outside sources, law, claims
Claims	Interpreting forms	Underwriting, marketing, law
Law	Regulation/filings	Underwriting, public relations, marketing, claims
Public relations	News media	Underwriting, marketing, regional operations
Loss control	Inspection models	Underwriting, field offices
Field offices	Policyholders, producers, medical association, local media, regulators	All home office counterparts, plus public relations, law

proaching problems involving policyholders, producers, regulators, and the media.

A summary of interrelated activities is shown in Exhibit 1-1.

The major point made in this example is the interdependence of the various components that make up an insurance company. No one department or division can operate effectively or efficiently without the cooperation and assistance of all the other departments and divisions.

The principal job of top management is to facilitate interdepartmental communication and cooperation so that the company's plans can be carried out and its goals and objectives reached. This function includes the establishment of a workable organizational format, effective channels of communication, and the clear and specific delineations of duties, responsibilities, and privileges of departments, divisions, and individuals within the organization.

Chapter Note

1. John N. Cosgrove, "Still True," *The National Underwriter*, Property & Casualty Insurance Edition, 12 March 1976, p. 16.

CHAPTER 2

Marketing

INTRODUCTION

The term *marketing* has been defined as "the performance of business activities that direct the flow of goods and services from producer to consumer."[1] This definition stresses the distributive aspects of marketing and the notion that marketing is a broader concept than sales.

In the property and liability insurance business, marketing activities include the sales function and many other services expected by the consumer. Unlike most tangible products, the selling of insurance often involves the seller in all aspects of servicing the account. (In this text, the term *account* refers to the set of insurance policies held by an insured.) In the insurance industry, the term marketing may also refer to the "placing" of business with various insurers. This form of marketing applies to existing business as well as new business and is beyond the scope of this text.

This chapter is the first of two chapters dealing with the marketing function. It focuses on the sales function, sales management, producer motivation and supervision, and marketing systems. Chapter 3 deals with developments in marketing.

The Sales Function

The importance of the sales function to property and liability insurers is perhaps indicated most clearly by the fact that the salesperson, agent, or broker usually is referred to as the *producer*. The term producer is usually reserved in other businesses for the people who create, or manufacture, the product, rather than those who sell it.

While producers are the front-line sales force, conducting most of the direct sales contact with insurance consumers, they are not the only people in the insurance industry who are concerned with sales. Most insurance companies engage in advertising and market research activities to facilitate and support the sales efforts of producers. Also, sales management staffs or marketing departments are maintained to assist and supervise producers.

Statistics concerning the extent of these sales support activities are not available in fine detail. However, some general indication of their cost can be obtained from available statistics. Exhibit 2-1 shows the percentages of direct premiums spent in 1982 on (1) commissions and brokerage expenses and (2) other acquisition costs for stock property and liability insurers.

The remuneration paid to producers consists largely of commissions and brokerage expenses. Other acquisition costs include advertising, sales management costs, and other similar expenses related to sales.

Need for Technical Expertise

Successful insurance producers must develop other skills in addition to sales skills. Many insurance consumers depend heavily upon producers to guide them in the selection of the proper combination of insurance products to cover their loss exposures. Insurers rely upon producers to provide necessary information to enable them to select the persons and firms that meet their underwriting standards.

Insurance Principles and Coverages Insurance contracts are complex legal documents not readily understood by the general public. This complexity has led to a movement by insurers and consumer advocates for "readable" policies, which, in some states, are mandated by law. Producers must be thoroughly familiar with insurance principles and practices to understand insurance contracts and explain them to their clients, especially at the time of sale. Consumers, expecting a high degree of professional service from producers, may bring legal action against the producer for errors and omissions. In 1968 the number of insurance agents' errors and omissions claims was 5 per 100 agents. That figure increased to 10.2 per 100 agents in 1975, and 14 per 100 agents in 1984.[2]

Also, the producer frequently is the first person contacted when a loss occurs. Consequently, producers must be sufficiently familiar with the insuring agreements, exclusions, and conditions of policies to advise

Exhibit 2-1
Direct† Commissions, Brokerage and Other Acquisition Expenses—
Stock Insurers—1982*

Line	Commissions and Brokerage	Other Acquisition Costs
Fire	20.1%	5.1%
Allied	17.4	5.6
Homeowners	17.3	4.8
Comm. Multiple Peril	17.5	6.2
Ocean Marine	15.4	3.9
Inland Marine	15.9	6.2
Medical Malpractice	7.5	2.7
Workers' Compensation	6.8	3.2
Liability other than Auto	12.9	5.6
Private Passenger Auto. Liab.	12.1	5.7
Private Passenger Auto. Ph. Dam.	13.6	5.5
Comm. Auto. Liability	15.0	5.1
Comm. Auto. Ph. Dam.	16.6	5.3
Fidelity	16.1	9.1
Surety	23.5	11.7
Glass	19.0	10.4
Burglary and Theft	20.1	7.9
Boiler and Machinery	18.4	10.9

†Direct expenses are those paid by the insurer, without reflecting any reinsurance transactions.

*Adapted from *Best's Aggregates and Averages-1983* (Oldwick, NJ: A.M. Best Company, 1983).

the insured of his or her rights under the contract. The skill of the producer in handling the first contact in a claim situation frequently determines whether the insured will be satisfied or dissatisfied with the insurance program and the performance of the insurer and producer involved.

Consumer Needs In addition to the possession of knowledge of insurance principles and coverages, producers must develop skills in the analysis of consumer needs and the tailoring of insurance programs to meet those needs. While much insurance is still sold on a single policy basis, the trend is toward the development by the producer of a complete and integrated insurance program designed to meet the needs of the client. For business firms, many sophisticated producers offer complete programs to cope with all fortuitous loss exposures, whether insurable or not. The noninsurable loss exposures may be handled through a program combining loss control, risk transfer, and retention (including self-insurance). The insurable loss exposures may also utilize these noninsurance techniques as well as a comprehensive insurance program.

The first step in meeting consumer needs is the analysis of the loss exposures to which the consumer is subject. The insurance survey is one way of discovering loss exposures.

In the course of an insurance survey, the producer must become thoroughly familiar with the activities, whether personal or business, of the client. The familiarization process may take several routes. Perhaps the oldest and least complex method of finding a client's loss exposures is the questionnaire method. In this method, the producer and the client, working together, complete a questionnaire designed to reveal the loss exposures to which the client is subject. The producer then designs an insurance program to protect against these exposures.

Many insurance companies and other organizations have published survey questionnaires for personal exposures, business exposures, or both. However, the questionnaire, regardless of length, is seldom sufficient for a thorough insurance survey except for personal exposures and the very smallest business firms. For larger business firms, governmental bodies, and institutions, the questionnaire must be supplemented, at least, by a personal inspection of the client's premises. An examination of the client's financial statement and the preparation of a flow chart of the firm's operations also assist the producer in determining the client's insurance needs. In addition, information gathered from employees, such as internal auditors, foremen, etc., and information from other firms in the industry may greatly improve the risk analysis activities of producers.

Many producers have progressed beyond the insurance survey to the practice of risk management. The process of risk management uses some of the tools of the insurance survey. However, the insurance survey is designed to find insurable loss exposures and to protect against them with insurance. Risk management is concerned with both insurable and uninsurable loss exposures, and uses both insurance and noninsurance devices to cope with them. Noninsurance devices used in risk management include retention, either funded or unfunded, loss avoidance, and loss control.

A detailed treatment of insurance surveys and risk management is beyond the scope of this chapter but is covered in detail in CPCU 1, 2, 3, and 4. The producer who serves substantial business firms needs to be familiar with these techniques.

Profit from Insurance Operations
Not Directly Related to Sales

The insurance business differs from many other businesses in that insurer profits are not directly related to sales. In most businesses that deal in tangible products, the cost of producing and marketing the product either remains constant or decreases as the sales volume increases. The same is true in most service industries. The identity and characteristics of the buyer do not, in most cases, affect the cost of the product to the seller. Consequently, an increase in sales usually means greater profit (or a smaller loss), and most such businesses will sell their products to any person who can pay for them.

Property and liability insurance operations do not appear to be subject to economies of scale, at least with regard to the relationship between premium volume and loss payments. That is, the insurers' loss payments per unit of coverage do not decrease significantly with an increase in the number of units sold. In fact, if the increase in sales is obtained by relaxing underwriting standards, the insurer's largest expense—loss payments—may increase sharply. Thus, an insurer may find itself in the incongruous position of seeking additional sales while refusing to provide insurance to many applicants because they fail to meet its underwriting standards. Also, the producer is placed in the position of having to screen potential customers to avoid soliciting business that will be rejected by the insurer.

Insurance Sales Compared to Sales of Other Products

Insurance, like most other intangible products, presents some sales difficulties which must be overcome by the producer. It is seldom possible, for example, to sell insurance through the use of sales appeals involving prestige, since the purchase of an insurance policy is not as conspicuous as the purchase of an expensive automobile or a large home.

Insurance must be sold primarily on the basis of the human need for security and the ability of the insurance product to provide financial security from fortuitous losses.

In some lines of insurance, the absence of some of the more emotional sales approaches is offset by legal compulsion to insure. For example, purchase of automobile liability insurance is required by law in many states and is strongly encouraged by financial responsibility laws in other states. Purchase of physical damage insurance usually is required by lending institutions that finance the purchase of automobiles. Banks and other mortgagees usually require at least fire and extended coverage insurance on houses and other buildings they finance. Other examples could be cited. In such cases, the producer does not need to persuade the prospective purchaser of the need for insurance. It is necessary only to convince the prospective purchaser that the producer is better able than competing producers to meet the customer's needs for service or that the producer's company can provide the required coverage(s) on more desirable terms and conditions with better claims service or possibly a lower price than its competitors.

The lines of insurance that some persons are legally compelled to purchase represent only a small percentage of the available kinds of property and liability insurance. However, they account for a much larger percentage of the total premium volume of the insurance industry because they include such major lines as automobile, workers' compensation, fire, and homeowners insurance. But even in the case of compulsory insurance, the skills of the producer come into play in connection with classification, rating, claims handling, and recommendations of alternative rating plans and loss control measures.

The professional skills of the producer are more clearly demonstrated by the ability to determine and meet the needs of clients for the noncompulsory lines of insurance. For those lines, the producer must discover the client's needs and make those needs clear to the client. This is an educational process for both the producer and the client.

Sales as an Educational Process

The producer must educate and gain the trust of the client if he or she is to succeed in meeting the insurance needs of clients. The producer must be able to impart to the client sufficient knowledge of the client's loss exposures, and of the insurance coverages and other mechanisms available to meet them, to facilitate the development of a risk management program adequate for the client's needs.

Need for Increased Counseling of Consumers The increasing complexity of technology and the increasing complexity of our legal system have created many new loss exposures and have increased the potential amount of loss from many existing loss exposures. The insurance industry has responded by creating new coverages and amending existing coverages to meet the newly created exposures. In addition, new policies and new rating plans have been developed to meet increasing competition within the insurance industry.

The development of atomic energy and the increased use of radioactive isotopes for testing purposes have created exposures to loss from radioactive contamination in industrial plants. Previously, such exposure was limited to hospitals and the few plants that handled or processed radium. The adoption of the Employee Retirement Income Security Act of 1974, sometimes referred to as ERISA or the Pension Reform Act of 1974, created new liability exposures for persons involved in the management of employee benefit plans. Increasingly liberal court decisions have expanded the liabilities of providers of professional services and the manufacturers and sellers of products, among others. Legislatures in almost half of the states have enacted no-fault automobile laws of one form or another. These new or changing loss exposures require that producers keep their clients informed.

The insurance industry's response to these changes has been a number of new policies, new endorsements, and new rating plans. In most cases, these responses have resulted in broadened coverage. In addition to the nuclear facility policies for operators of nuclear reactors, the industry has developed two endorsements to add radioactive contamination coverage to fire and multiple peril policies. Several insurers have developed special fiduciary liability policies to cover the new liability exposures related to employee benefit plans. Unlike the radioactive contamination endorsements, the fiduciary liability policies are not standardized; there are substantial variations in the coverage provided.

The National Flood Insurance Program provides still another example of the role of producers in educating and counseling consumers. Under the terms of the program, all agents licensed in the individual states are automatically licensed to write flood insurance. Most mortgagees require flood insurance as a condition to obtaining a loan on property located in flood-prone areas. Beginning in 1983, many insurance companies added flood coverage to their homeowners policies, with the coverage subsidized by the federal government.

In an attempt to cope with the expanded liability of physicians, surgeons, and some other professionals, many insurers have adopted policies that cover claims made during the policy period rather than events which occur during the policy period. If a policy is written on an occurrence basis, coverage is provided on those claims arising out of events that *occur* during the policy period even if claims are not brought against the insured for years after the coverage has expired. If a policy is written on a claims made basis, coverage is provided only on those *claims made* against the insured during the policy period. The adoption of policies that cover claims made has major implications for purchasers of professional liability insurance and to producers who have a responsibility to inform and educate their clients.

The producers have at least two important reasons for informing their clients of changes in exposures and coverages. First, producers have both a moral and a legal obligation to provide their clients with adequate information concerning the clients' loss exposures and methods of protecting against them. Second, changes in exposures and coverages create new sales opportunities for producers and the insurers they represent.

The changes in legal theories which have expanded the liabilities of others have also expanded the professional liabilities of producers. Errors for which producers have been held liable include (1) failure to renew a policy, (2) failure to warn of a new restriction in a renewal policy, (3) failure to issue binders, (4) failure to find a market for a coverage when one exists, (5) failure to point out the need for a coverage (e.g., fire legal liability), (6) failure to inform the insured of the coinsurance clause contained in a fire insurance policy, and (7) failure to inform the insured of a warranty in a policy.

The producer's function of providing greater information to his or her clients is carried out in many ways. Oral communication during sales presentations and upon delivery of policies is an important educational method. The same is true of advice and guidance in claims handling. Written reports of insurance surveys are important informational tools and may also be useful in proving that the producer has properly executed his or her duty to inform the client. Also, some producers furnish their clients with newsletters, pamphlets, and similar materials which discuss the latest developments in loss exposures and insurance coverages.

These educational efforts of producers, along with similar programs of insurers, assist insurance consumers in avoiding errors in planning their insurance programs. Consequently, they avoid much dissatisfaction on the part of the insured and many errors and omissions claims against producers.

Effects of Increasing Price Consciousness The price structure of property and liability insurance has changed drastically during the past two decades. Until the middle fifties, there was substantial price uniformity within the industry. Most large insurers belonged to rating bureaus and charged bureau rates. Though many mutuals and reciprocals and a few stock insurers paid dividends to policyholders, only a few insurers deviated downward from bureau rates.

During the intervening years, the bureaus have lost much of their power to influence or set rates. The resulting diversity of rates has been accompanied by increasing price consciousness on the part of consumers.

One national survey showed that almost half of the respondents who had purchased automobile insurance had tried to compare prices among companies before purchasing coverage. Of those who compared price, slightly over half bought coverage from the company that quoted the lowest cost. Of those respondents under age twenty-nine, slightly more than half had compared prices, while only a third of those over age fifty had compared prices. The greater prevalence of price shopping among younger buyers may foreshadow even greater price consciousness in the future. Almost one out of six (14 percent) of the respondents expressed a willingness to change insurers for a price difference of less than 10 percent. An additional 23 percent of the respondents would change for a price reduction of less than 20 percent.[3]

In another survey, price was mentioned by 28 percent of the respondents as the reason for selecting their agent or insurer. Price was second only to the reputation of the company or agent, which was mentioned by 54 percent.[4]

Price consciousness among business buyers of insurance seems to be even greater. In one survey, 67 percent of the respondents thought it desirable to shop around for insurance. Half of the respondents perceived a real difference in price among insurers.[5] In an earlier survey, 62 percent of the nation's 500 largest business firms indicated that they had changed from one insurer to another to obtain a lower price.[6]

Price shopping, especially in commercial lines, is not a simple matter. Coverage may differ substantially, and various combinations of coverage and rating plans may make price comparisons misleading. In addition, differentials in the quality of service may account for some price differences.

Price consciousness of insurance consumers has had significant effects on the marketing of property and liability insurance. Producers who represent more than one insurer have found it desirable and sometimes necessary to shop for the best price for their clients in order to avoid losing accounts to competitors. The aggressive shopping by producers and consumers may lead to price cutting by insurers to obtain business, which contributes to underwriting losses. A continuation of lower prices and underwriting losses may, in turn, result in more rigid underwriting standards and consequent unavailability of insurance to many consumers who would have been insurable at more adequate rate levels.

MARKETING SYSTEMS

There are four distinguishable systems for marketing property and liability insurance in the United States. They are (1) the independent agency system, sometimes referred to as the American agency system; (2) the exclusive agency system, sometimes called the captive agency system; (3) the direct writing system; and (4) the direct mail system. The first three systems use producers (employees or independent contractors) to solicit business from consumers. The last named system does not use producers but depends upon mail or telephone solicitation or advertising in periodicals and other mass media to produce business.

The Independent Agency System

The independent agency system consists of a very large number of independent business firms, either agencies or brokerage firms or both. An independent agent is a representative of one or more insurance companies and usually has been given authority to bind these insurers to contracts of insurance. A broker is a representative of the applicant for insurance rather than of the insurer and therefore does not have authority to bind insurers to contracts of insurance. The broker's function is to find insurers that are willing to provide coverages their clients wish to purchase. Sub-agents who place business with different agencies are also sometimes called brokers.

With the exception of the legal distinction just mentioned, and possibly some clerical functions, the operations of agents and brokers are quite similar. In fact, the same person may act as both agent and broker, though not in the same transaction. A person may act as an agent when placing insurance with those companies for which he or she is licensed as an agent; however, the same person may act as a broker in the placement of business with other companies for which he or she is not licensed as an agent. A survey conducted by the Independent Insurance Agents of America showed that 60 percent of the responding agents also held broker's licenses.[7]

Both independent agents and brokers are independent business people. They are *independent contractors* and not employees of insurers. They may represent several insurers, and business is allocated among the companies they represent on a policy-by-policy basis. The independent agency or brokerage firm solicits business on its own behalf; the producer alone has the authority to decide which of the companies he or she represents will be offered the coverage that has been solicited.

Ownership of Expirations One of the principal distinguishing features of the independent agency system is the producer's ownership of expirations. A typical agency contract spells out the ownership of expirations as follows:

> In the event of termination of this agreement, the agent having promptly accounted for and paid over premiums for which he may be liable, the agent's records, use and control of expirations shall remain

the exclusive property of the agent and shall be left in his undisputed possession. Otherwise the records, use and control of expirations shall be vested in the company.

The agency ownership of expirations also has been upheld in the courts. The lead case in this regard is the so-called "Yonkers Case" (The National Fire Insurance Company of Hartford vs. Benjamin E. Sullard, 97 App.Div. 233, 89 N.Y.S. 934), decided by the New York Appellate Division in 1904. Sullard had purchased an insurance agency from Albert K. Shipman of Yonkers, N.Y. Among the assets purchased was the expiration register of business written by Shipman in the National Fire Insurance Company. When National Fire refused to appoint Sullard as its agent, he proceeded to renew the business in other companies.

National Fire filed suit asking that Sullard be enjoined from using any information from the expiration register to solicit renewal of the business. However, the court held that the expiration information was owned by Shipman and purchased by Sullard, and was not the property of National Fire. The court's decision was based on judicial notice of the well-established custom of agency ownership of expirations, and not on any provision of Shipman's agency contract or of any statutory provision.

The records of the expiration dates of the policies of clients are a major asset of the agency or brokerage firm. These records are an important tool in the retention of business the agency has produced and would be of great help to a competitor who wished to take away the business. It should be noted that the insurer also has records of expiration dates and other information concerning the agent's or broker's business.

In the absence of producer ownership of expirations, the insurer, upon termination of the agency contract, might solicit the producer's clients or furnish policy information to another of its producers. The contract provision quoted above specifically prohibits such actions by the insurer.

The independent agency and brokerage firms have guarded their ownership of expirations jealously. The tangible assets of an agency or brokerage firm consist primarily of office furniture and equipment. The good will of the firm, of which the expirations are a major part, accounts for a large portion of the value of the agency. Both assets have a substantial market value and a ready market if the producer wants to go out of business or merge his business with another firm.

Independent Agency Firms   The independent agency system frequently is referred to as though it were composed of a large number of essentially similar firms. However, that is not the case. Producer firms within the independent agency system vary from small firms with only one producer and less than $100,000 in annual premiums to giant firms with thousands of employees in the United States and abroad and annual premiums measured in the hundreds of millions of dollars. They include firms that serve the world's largest corporations and those that write only personal lines. Some producers write virtually all lines of insurance for any kind of personal or business client, while others specialize in coverages for banks, surety bonds for contractors, or other relatively narrow classes of clients or coverages. Some represent only stock insurers; others represent only mutuals or reciprocal exchanges; and still others may represent all three. The only things they all have in common are (1) their independent contractor status, (2) the right to represent more than one insurer, and (3) the ownership of their expirations.

Size of Firms. One measure of the size of an agency or brokerage firm is its annual premium volume. There are no statistics available for all producer firms, but the Independent Insurance Agents of America has published the results of surveys of a sample of its members. The responding agencies were distributed by size as shown in Exhibit 2-2.

The proportion of agencies with premium volumes of $500,000 or more has grown from 32 percent in 1973 to 69 percent in 1982. This trend to larger agencies results from a combination of real sales growth, inflation, and agency mergers.

While most producer firms are small businesses, one group of firms, frequently referred to as national brokerage houses, are conspicuous for their size. National brokerage firms enjoy a substantial advantage over local agency and brokerage firms in the competition for large commercial accounts. Their national and international branch office system makes it easier for them to service national and international accounts, and their large premium volumes enable them to support their own loss control engineers and other specialized personnel.

The local agency and brokerage firms have responded to this competitive situation by banding together into organizations to assist each other in this servicing of national accounts. One such organization has member firms in sixty-one cities in the United States and abroad. Services provided by one member firm to another member firm are billed on an hourly basis, with the amount of the hourly fee depending upon the qualification of the person providing the service. All of the member firms employ loss control and claims personnel.[8]

Producer Compensation. Though some producers may require their clients to pay fees for some services, the principal source of compensation is commissions received from insurers. Exhibit 2-3 shows

Exhibit 2-2

Distribution of Agencies by Annual Premium Volume—The Independent Insurance Agents of America, Inc., 1973*, 1975**, 1978***, 1981**** and 1982****

Premium Volume	Percentage of Agencies				
	1973	1975	1978	1981	1982 (Est.)
Less than $199,999	30%	23%	18.3%	11%	7%
200,000—299,999	18	17	12.0	8	8
300,000—399,999	12	13	9.3	7	8
400,000—499.999	8	9	9.2	8	8
500,000—749,999	13	13	14.9	16	16
750,000—999,999	6	8	10.3	14	14
Over 1,000,000	13	15	23.9	34	39

* Adapted with permission from Stuart V. d'Adolf, "Profile of the Independent Agent," *Independent Agent*, January 1975, p. 18.

** Adapted with permission from Stuart V. d'Adolf, "Who Is the Independent Agent?" *Independent Agent*, January 1977, p. 14 and January 1979. The totals do not equal 100% because some of the respondents did not indicate their premium volume.

*** Adapted with permission from Stuart V. d'Adolf, "Who Is the Independent Agent?" *Independent Agent*, January, 1979. The total for 1978 does not equal 100% because some respondents did not report their premium volumes.

**** Adapted with permission from "Profile of the Independent Agent," *Independent Agent*, January 1983, p. 36. Note: The percentages may not add to 100% due to the failure of some respondents to provide premium data.

the commissions, as a percentage of premiums, received by agents responding to the Rough Notes Agency Cost Survey.

Exhibit 2-4 shows, by line, the percentage of net written premiums paid in commissions and brokerage in 1982 by selected large insurers operating through the independent agency system. The figures shown are the average for each line; there may have been a substantial variation within the line by classification, territory, and producer.

It should not be assumed that the commission is all profit to the producer. The agency or brokerage firm, as an independent business firm, incurs substantial operating expenses which must be paid from commission income. For example, the average agency with $550,000 of annual premiums in the Rough Notes Survey received commission income of $88,305 in 1981. However, the cost of clerical salaries, office supplies, rent, telephones, and other office expenses totaled $44,397. Selling expenses, such as salaries and commissions to subagents and brokers, advertising, automobile, and entertainment expenses con-

Exhibit 2-3
Agency Commissions as a Percentage of Premiums—Rough Notes
Agency Cost Survey, 1973, 1975, 1977 and 1981*

Agency Annual Premium Volume	Average Commissions As a Percentage of Premiums			
	1973	1975	1977	1981
$ 15,000— 60,000	20.53%	—[1]	—[2]	—[2]
60,000— 100,000	19.81	16.89%	—[2]	—[2]
100,000— 200,000	18.32	18.43	—[2]	—[2]
200,000— 400,000[3]	19.54	18.33	17.4%	17.0%
400,000— 600,000[4]	18.46	18.42	17.1	17.0
600,000—1,000,000[5]	18.83	18.15	16.8	17.0
Over 1,000,000 (1973) and 1,000,000—2,000,000 (1975, 1977 and 1981)	18.20	17.28	16.7	17.0
Over 2,000,000 (1975)[6]	—	16.49	16.4	16.0
Over 4,000,000 (1977)	—	—	14.3	16.0

1. The $15,000—$60,000 and the $60,000—$100,000 categories were combined in the 1975 study.
2. This category was eliminated in the 1977 study.
3. This category included agencies, with volumes of $100,000 to $400,000 in the 1977 and 1981 studies.
4. $400,000—700,000 for 1977 and 1981.
5. $700,000—1,000,000 for 1977 and 1981.
6. $2,000,000—4,000,000 for 1977 and 1981.

*Adapted with permission from Carl O. Pearson, *What It Costs to Run an Agency*, Rough Notes Company, 1975, 1977 and Tom McCoy, *What It Costs*, Rough Notes Company, 1979, 1983.

sumed an additional $13,166. Salaries and drawing accounts of agency owners and net profits totaled $43,532.[9]

A producer may receive two kinds of commissions: (1) a straight or sliding-scale percentage commission, and (2) a contingent or profit-sharing commission. The flat percentage commission, which varies by line of insurance and even by classification within a line, is paid at the inception of the policy, or when the premium is paid, if that is later. If the producer bills and collects the premium, the commission is deducted and the net amount forwarded to the insurer. If the insurer bills and collects the premium, commissions are forwarded to the producer

Exhibit 2-4
Selected Agency Company Average Commission Rates[†] for Selected Lines—1982*

Company Group	Fire	Homeowners	Commercial Multiple Peril	Ocean Marine	Private Passenger Automobile Liability	Private Passenger Automobile Physical Damage	Workers' Compensation
Aetna Life & Casualty	19.8%	19.6%	16.8%	15.9%	14.6%	14.7%	6.7%
CNA	12.2	20.3	14.2	N.A.	15.0	15.4	5.5
Crum & Forster	19.3	21.2	20.8	13.1	16.4	16.5	8.9
Fireman's Fund	19.4	21.3	19.2	15.4	16.5	17.0	6.8
Royal-Globe	18.7	21.3	19.2	16.4	15.2	15.3	10.0
Safeco	20.2	21.1	18.0	N.A.	15.4	15.5	9.1
Atlantic Mutual	21.1	18.2	16.4	10.4	15.7	13.5	8.6
Central Mutual	21.9	20.1	20.4	N.A.	15.0	15.3	7.9
Employers Mutual Casualty	30.6	20.9	21.5	21.6	15.2	15.9	6.4
Lumbermen's Mutual Casualty	24.9	20.1	16.1	16.7	14.6	15.1	2.9
Utica Mutual	21.2	22.6	19.8	22.0	16.7	15.7	9.2
Worcester Mutual	22.2	23.1	22.5	N.A.	N.A.	N.A.	N.A.

N.A. - Not Available

[†] Percentage of net premiums written.

* Adapted from *Best's Aggregates and Averages: Property-Casualty, 1983* (Oldwick, NJ: A.M. Best Company, 1983).

Exhibit 2-5
Profit Sharing Commission
Based on Loss Ratio

Loss Ratio	Profit-Sharing Commission as Percentage of Earned Premiums
0.00	14.00%
0.05	12.05
0.10	10.35
0.15	8.65
0.20	7.15
0.25	5.65
0.30	4.50
0.35	3.30
0.40	2.25
0.45	1.30
0.50	0.60
0.55	0.00

periodically, frequently monthly, after the premiums are collected. It is customary in the independent agency system to pay the same percentage commission on new business and renewal business.

The contingent commission is usually paid annually but is occasionally paid semi-annually or quarterly. It is not a fixed percentage of premiums but varies with the volume, rate of growth, and loss ratio of the business the producer has placed with the insurer. If the volume is too low or if the loss ratio is too high, the producer may not receive any contingent commission. The use of a contingent commission is therefore an effective method for encouraging the producer to write an adequate volume of business which is desirable from an underwriting standpoint.

There is considerable variation in the contingent commission contracts used by various insurers. However, the plan illustrated by Exhibits 2-5 and 2-6 is reasonably representative. It was taken from an agency contract in use by a major independent agency company.

In this contract, the agency's profit sharing (or contingent) commission depends on three factors: (1) the company's loss ratio on the agency's business, (2) the agency's premium volume with the company, and (3) the rate of growth of the agency's premium volume with the company. The portion of the profit-sharing commission dependent solely on the loss ratio is shown in Exhibit 2-5. Thus, an

Exhibit 2-6
Percentage Increase in Profit-Sharing Commission Based on
Premium Volume and Growth Rate*

Earned Premiums	Percentage Growth in Premium Volume					
	10%	15%	20%	30%	40%	60%
$ 50,000	3.50%	7.00%	10.50%	17.50%	24.50%	38.50%
75,000	4.69	8.50	12.31	19.94	27.56	42.81
100,000	5.87	10.00	14.12	22.38	30.62	47.12
150,000	8.25	13.00	17.75	27.25	36.75	55.75
200,000	10.62	16.00	21.37	28.37	42.87	64.38
250,000	13.00	19.00	25.00	37.00	49.00	73.00
400,000	20.12	28.00	35.87	51.62	67.37	98.87
500,000	24.87	34.00	43.12	61.37	79.62	100.00

agency with a loss ratio of 25 percent would receive a profit-sharing commission of 5.65 percent of earned premiums based solely on the loss ratio.

However, if the agency had both (1) a premium volume with the company of $50,000 or more and (2) a growth in its premium volume of 10 percent or more, then its profit-sharing commission from Exhibit 2-5 would be increased by the appropriate percentage from Exhibit 2-6. Thus, an agency with (1) a loss ratio of 25 percent, (2) a premium volume of $250,000, and (3) a growth rate of 20 percent, would receive a profit-sharing commission of 7.06 percent (5.65% × 1.25).

The profit-sharing plan includes definitions of earned premiums, incurred losses, expenses, and profit. It also places a limitation of $100,000 on the amount for any single loss to be used in calculating the agency's loss ratio.

With the high loss ratios of the late 1970s and early 1980s, the profit-sharing commissions paid to agents decreased sharply, frequently to the point of complete disappearance. To avoid hardship to agents, a few insurance companies began sharing a part of their investment income with agents whose loss experience and production records met specified goals. The amount of investment income shared with an agent is usually a function of the unearned premium and loss reserves generated by the agent's business.

The practice of sharing investment income with agents is not widespread. A comprehensive report on profit-sharing commissions compiled by the IIAA mentioned the possibility of sharing investment income but stopped short of recommending the practice.[10]

Some observers have criticized the practice of compensating

producers through commissions. They believe that commissions place the producer in a conflict of interests. Producers have a moral, and perhaps legal, obligation to provide professional insurance advice to their clients. This obligation may require the producer to place a client's insurance with the insurer that offers the lowest cost if all other factors are equal. Yet the act of placing the client's coverage at a lower cost will very likely reduce the producer's compensation. Thus, the producer's compensation may be reduced if he expends extra effort on behalf of the client.

The commission basis of compensation has also been criticized on the ground that the producer's remuneration is not related to the effort expended to earn it. A policy may have a high premium, and thus a high commission, even though it requires very little effort on the part of the producer. On the other hand, another policy may require substantial effort but have a low premium and a low commission. A graded commission scale in workers' compensation insurance was developed, in part, to correct this situation.

To rectify these stated defects in the commission system, it has been proposed that insurers quote premiums net of commissions. The producer and the insured could then negotiate a fee commensurate with the effort expended by the producer on the insured's behalf.

In fact, some brokers now charge fees for their services either in lieu of or in addition to commissions. Such practices are permitted in some jurisdictions but prohibited by law in others. Also, it is not uncommon for a producer to agree with the insurer to accept a lower percentage commission on a specific policy (usually a large commercial account), provided the insurer will reduce the premium on the policy by an equivalent or greater amount. In the absence of filings, allowing for such expense reductions, such commission reductions may constitute rebating, discrimination, or both. These reductions generally are not extended to all of the producer's clients but are likely to be reserved for those competitive situations where price is a major factor in the selection of producer and insurer.

Functions Performed by Producers. Agents and brokers within the independent agency system perform many other functions in addition to the sales function. One survey found that 73 percent of responding agents had authority to adjust small first-party claims, usually up to $250 or $500, and to issue drafts in payment of such claims. Similar authority for third-party claims was held by 29 percent of respondents, and 62 percent of the agencies had authority to assign claims to independent adjusters.[11] All independent agents are active in claim processing at least to the extent of accepting the first notice of claims and forwarding it to the insurer concerned. Also, some producers may be asked to perform a test marketing function on behalf of the insurers.

Some large producers also provide loss control services, employing fire control engineers, accident prevention engineers, industrial hygienists, claims analysts, and actuaries. Some insurers are willing to grant higher commission rates when the producer provides such services. However, a producer must control a rather large premium volume in order to justify the outlay for loss control personnel and equipment.

Traditionally, independent agents prepared policies and billed or collected premiums. They still do in many areas. However, these clerical functions have been performed by insurers to an ever-increasing extent in recent years. The advent of large-scale electronic data processing equipment made it possible for insurers to perform these functions at a cost lower than that which could be achieved by agencies through manual processing. In some cases, the insurer prepares the policy and bill and forwards them to the agent for delivery and collection. Other insurers mail the policy and bill directly to the policyholder, and the premium is paid to the insurer rather than to the agency. The latter procedure is usually referred to as direct billing. Some insurers will either provide direct billing service or permit agency billing, at the option of the agency, but the commission rate to the agent is usually a few percentage points lower on direct-billed business than on agency-billed business.

The change from agency billing to direct billing has been achieved only with much controversy, and the change is still far from complete. The principal objections voiced by producers were (1) direct billing poses a threat to the producers' ownership of expirations; (2) direct billing results in reducing the producers' opportunities for direct contact with their customers; and (3) direct billing results in lower commissions, which may not be offset fully by lower agency expenses.

The first objection was met by strengthening the agency contract provisions dealing with ownership of expirations. The second objection was countered with the argument that bill collection is an unpleasant contact at best, and that transferring that contact to the insurer would improve the relationship between producer and client. Insurers also argued that the economies of direct billing were necessary in order for the independent agency system to offer prices competitive with those of the direct writer, direct mail, and exclusive agency systems. In addition, it has been claimed that direct billing will permit the producers to increase sales because it will relieve them of the time-consuming collection function.

With regard to the third objection, one study estimated that direct billing would reduce agency commissions by $6.45 per $100 of automobile insurance premium but would reduce agency expenses only

$2 or $3 per $100 of premium even if the agency wrote 80 percent or more of its automobile insurance on a direct billed plan.[12] The proponents counter this objection with the argument that the lower, more competitive premium for direct billed policies, along with the additional sales time released by direct billing, will enable the producer to increase his volume sufficiently to more than offset the lower rate of commission.

The Exclusive Agency System

The exclusive agency system is somewhat younger than the independent agency system. The former dates only from the first quarter of this century, while the latter can trace its beginning to the 1790s.

Description The producers in the exclusive agency system also are independent contractors. They differ from independent agents in that exclusive agents are required by their contracts to represent only one insurer, or perhaps several insurance corporations under common ownership or management. The independent agent, on the other hand, may, and usually does, represent several unrelated insurers. One exclusive agency contract spells out the agent-insurer relationship as follows:

> You are an independent contractor for all purposes. As such you have full control of your activities, with the right to exercise independent judgment as to time, place and manner of soliciting insurance, servicing policyholders, and otherwise carrying out the provisions of this agreement.

Ownership of Expirations Exclusive agency contracts vary somewhat with regard to ownership of expirations. Some insurers do not grant their agents any ownership interest in expirations. Others may grant limited ownership. For example, some insurers grant ownership of expirations while the contract is in force, but the agent is required to sell the expirations to the insurer when the contract is terminated.

One insurer specifies the ownership of expirations as follows:

> Information regarding names, addresses, and ages of policyholders of the companies; the description and location of insured property; and expiration or renewal dates of (the company's) policies acquired or coming into your possession during the effective period of this agreement, or any prior agreement, are trade secrets wholly owned by (the company). All forms and other materials, whether furnished by (the company) or purchased by you, upon which this information is recorded shall be the sole and exclusive property of (the company).

> We will leave in your account all policies assigned to your account so long as the policyholder resides within a 25-mile radius of your principal place of business and within a state in which you are duly licensed, except that we may, after prior written notice to you, transfer any policy to the account of another (company) agent when the policyholder makes a bona fide request in writing.

The foregoing contract provisions make it clear that the agent has some ownership interest in expirations during the term of the contract; however, such interest ceases when the agency contract is terminated. These provisions contrast rather sharply with the comparable provisions of independent agency contracts, which vest the ownership of expirations in the agent upon termination of the contract. Many exclusive agency companies offer retirement benefits in lieu of ownership of expirations.

Compensation of Producers Exclusive agents usually are compensated on a commission basis, though some insurers may provide a drawing account or guarantee during a training period. Exclusive agency companies frequently pay a lower commission percentage on renewal business than on new business. For example, the commission rates might be 15 percent on new business and 7 percent on renewal business. The reduced renewal commission is not practical for the independent agency system because the agent could get the new business rate by the simple expedient of shifting the policy to another insurer. The exclusive agent, who represents only one insurer, cannot use that expedient. The higher first year commission tends to encourage the exclusive agent to emphasize the production of new business, and may be one reason for the rapid growth of exclusive agency companies. The lower renewal commission helps to support the greater sales management and advertising efforts of the exclusive agency companies.

Functions Performed by Producers There is some variation in the functions performed by producers in the exclusive agency system. Some insurers restrict their agents exclusively to the sales function. All other services are performed by the company. Other insurers permit their agents to settle small first-party losses, and in some cases, producers perform loss control and premium auditing functions. Policy issuance and premium collection are performed by the insurer in virtually all cases.

Direct Writer System

The direct writer system might be considered the oldest insurance marketing system in the United States. The first insurance companies in this country did not employ agents; persons who wished to purchase insurance applied directly at the home office of the insurer. However, the present direct writer system operates somewhat differently from this original method.

Description The direct writer system, as it now operates, bears a striking resemblance to the exclusive agency system. The only essential difference is the nature of the relationship between the producer and the insurer. The direct writer producer is an employee of the insurer, not an independent contractor.

Ownership of Expirations In the direct writer system, the ownership of expirations usually is vested solely in the insurer. The producer usually does not have any ownership rights in expirations even during the effective period of the employment.

Compensation of Producers There is wide variation in the compensation plans in the direct writer system. Some producers receive only a salary; others receive a salary plus a bonus or commissions; still others receive only commissions. When commissions are paid, the commission rate for new business is usually higher than for renewal business.

Functions Performed by Producers The direct writer producers frequently are restricted to performing the sales function, with all other functions performed by other employees of the insurer. Some insurers permit producers to settle small first-party claims. Policy issuance and premium collection are performed by the insurer in almost all cases.

Mail Order System

The mail order marketing system, sometimes called direct mail system or the direct response system, differs from the other three systems in that no producers are involved. The insurer's sales message is communicated to the prospective purchaser either through the mail or through the mass media, such as newspapers, magazines, radio, or television. The prospective purchaser is expected to contact the office of the insurer directly by mail, or sometimes by telephone.

The principal advantages to the insurer of mail order selling are (1) lower selling expenses than the personal producer systems and (2) more precise market segmentation. The principal disadvantages are the possibly slower growth rate resulting from the lack of personal solicitation and the inability to provide some personal services. Mail order marketing has been restricted almost entirely to the personal lines of insurance. The complexity of commercial lines makes the services of a producer almost indispensable.

The principal advantage to the consumer is lower insurance cost, and the principal disadvantage is the lack of personal service. Consumers must make their own choices of coverages and limits without the benefit of advice from a skilled producer.

The lower cost of mail order insurance results partly from the lower insurer expenses resulting from the elimination of producer commissions and partly from careful selection of persons and property to be insured. The former lowers the expense ratio and the latter lowers the loss ratio. Insurers that solicit applications only by mail can select the persons to whom they wish to appeal by their occupation, income group, or other characteristics. Mailing lists segregated by such characteristics are available from many sources. Several mail order insurers specialize in insuring teachers, engineers, accountants, or other occupational groups that are likely to have fewer claims than the average for the population as a whole. By mailing their sales materials only to these selected groups, the mail order insurers avoid writing the less desirable groups. Also, since they do not have producers to intercede on behalf of applicants, the mail order insurers are better able to reject undesirable applicants.

Mixed Systems

Up to this point, the various marketing systems have been treated as though they were mutually exclusive—as though a given insurer could use only one system. However, there seems to be a trend in recent years toward mixed systems. One mail order company does have some exclusive agents, and a large direct writer has found it expedient to appoint independent agents in some rural areas and small towns. One large independent agency insurer conducted, through an affiliate, an unsuccessful experiment in mail order marketing and is promoting a modified independent agency system which bears a striking resemblance to the exclusive agency system. Another insurer, originally a direct writer, has extensive independent agency operations and has experimented with mail order marketing. It seems likely that this experimentation with mixed marketing systems will continue in the future. (Mixed marketing systems are discussed in detail in the next chapter.)

Perpetuating the Production Force

If the insurance industry is to survive and continue to grow, it must develop new producers for the existing marketing systems as well as new sources of production.

Developing New Producers The development of new producers seems to be a relatively simple, though expensive, problem for the direct writer and exclusive agency companies. Because of the nature of their operations, they have adequately staffed personnel and sales management departments to recruit, train, and supervise new producers. Because the companies own the expirations, they usually can assign to a new producer a sufficient number of accounts for support during the first few years of employment. Also, they usually have arrangements for providing a salary, drawing account, or advance against commissions during the training period.

However, the problem is much more difficult for the independent agency companies. Because the independent agent represents several insurers, usually no one insurer is willing to provide financing for a new agent. Also, since the independent agency companies do not own the expirations, they cannot assign accounts to a new agent to help him or her get started. Therefore, the prospective new agent must have sufficient financing to support the agency through the start-up period until a reliable commission flow can be developed.

For this reason, relatively few new independent agencies are started, in comparison with the number of new exclusive agents or direct writer producers who enter the field.

Most persons who want to enter the independent agency business do so by purchasing an existing agency or a share of such an agency. Frequently, a person will become associated with an existing agency as an employee solicitor for the agency, with the understanding that he or she will be able to acquire a share (or possibly all) of the ownership of the agency at some future time.

However, even this avenue of entry into the independent agency system may not always be easy. Most independent agencies are very small businesses. They do not have adequate financial resources to support a new producer for the relatively long period required for him or her to become established. Also, the principals of the agency may not have the time or background to select a properly qualified producer or to train the producer after selection.

The Independent Insurance Agents of America is attacking the problem on three fronts. The association, with the assistance of consultants, is attempting to develop scientific methods of selecting sales personnel. IIAA is also providing training material to help the new salesperson acquire the necessary insurance knowledge and selling skills to function adequately. Finally, a financing plan has been developed whereby the agency can borrow the money from a bank to finance the new producer during the initial period of employment. The bank makes monthly loans of from $800 to $1,400 to the agency, not to the new producer. These loans are paid back to the bank in installments, and the payments should be covered by the commissions earned by the efforts of the new producer.

The National Association of Professional Insurance Agents (PIA) has developed a program to help agents finance expansion and acquisitions. Professional Resource Organization (PRO), a for-profit subsidiary of PIA, was formed to provide services for subscribing agencies. PRO, in conjunction with a group of insurance companies, provides surety bonds to guarantee repayment of bank loans or to guarantee payment under installment purchase agreements for the acquisition of other agencies. The bonds should enable the agencies to qualify for lower interest rates for their bank loans and should encourage sellers of agencies to agree to installment payment of the purchase price.[13]

A newly formed agency holding company, ADAPT, takes a different approach to agency perpetuation. ADAPT, which is owned by the Hartford Insurance Group and a number of independent insurance agencies, acquires majority stock interest in agencies and provides financial and management assistance as needed. It leaves the existing management in place and permits the agencies to operate autonomously. ADAPT wants the management of each agency to hold a substantial amount of the agency's stock so they will continue to have a financial interest in the operation of the agency.[14]

A few independent agency insurers are experimenting with methods of recruiting producers. The usual approaches are (1) joint financing and training of a new producer by an existing agency, and (2) company financing of a new agency. A given company may follow either or both approaches. Under one company's program, the new agent operates from an insurance center maintained by the company. Interest-free loans are available from the company along with free office space, telephones, and secretarial help. When the new producer completes the program, he or she owns the business produced and may either take it to an existing agency or establish a new agency. After leaving the program, the new producer is free to represent other insurers also. Another insurer's program is aimed at helping existing agencies recruit, finance, and train new producers. The insurer will finance up to 75 percent of the salary paid by the agency to the new producer.

In 1983, the CNA companies launched a new program to support the agency system by providing assistance in agency management and marketing. The program also provides assurance that the CNA companies will provide a stable market for the business produced by participating agencies and will not reduce commissions unilaterally. To qualify, an agency must agree to give CNA companies at least 40 percent of the agency's premium volume.[15]

Several insurance companies are trying to preserve the independent agency system by buying agency and brokerage firms. While this technique may preserve the marketing system of the companies involved, it seems like an unlikely method for preserving the independent agency system as it now exists.[16]

New Sources of Production Insurers and producers are looking for new sources of production in two ways. First, they are looking for new ways for producers to sell their traditional product—insurance. Second, they are trying to sell new services, which previously were furnished only in conjunction with insurance, including loss control, loss adjustment services, and administrative services for captive insurers.

New Methods of Selling. Producers, especially independent agents, are making much more extensive use of telephone selling and direct mail campaigns to produce personal lines business. Several agencies have established insurance counters in department stores, supermarkets, and other high traffic retail locations. Agencies, through mergers, acquisitions of other agencies, or internal expansion, have established networks of branch offices, blanketing metropolitan areas. This geographic spread enables such producers to make more efficient use of advertising through the mass media, such as radio, television, newspapers, and billboards.

New Services. Several insurers have adopted the practice of selling, on a fee basis, some of the services they previously furnished only in connection with insurance. For example, an insurer might provide loss control or loss adjustment services, on a fee basis, to self-insured commercial and industrial firms. In fact, some insurers, or their subsidiaries, go even further and advise employers in the establishment of self-insurance programs, with the insurer or subsidiary then providing loss adjustment and loss control services, surety bonds, and excess insurance coverage if needed. Advice and assistance in the rehabilitation of accident victims also may be furnished.

The sale of such services may be of benefit to the insurer in two ways. First, and most obvious, it provides a source of income from the self-insurers, income which would otherwise be lost entirely to the insurance companies. Second, it enables the insurance companies to support more elaborate and sophisticated loss adjustment and loss control facilities, which can then be used to provide services to purchasers of insurance. The growing trend toward self-insurance among major commercial and industrial firms probably will add greater emphasis to the sale of services in the future.

Producer Trade Associations

Independent agents and brokers, like other independent business firms, have found it expedient to form trade associations to protect and promote their interests. The largest such associations are the Independent Insurance Agents of America (formerly the National Association of Insurance Agents), the National Association of Professional Insurance Agents, and the National Association of Insurance Brokers. The first two of these associations have affiliated associations at the state level and, in many cases, at the city or county level. Many producers maintain memberships in two or all three of the national associations.

The oldest and largest of the three associations is the Independent Insurance Agents of America which has over 35,000 member agencies with over 220,000 agents and their employees. For many years, various rules of the Independent Insurance Agents of America and its state and local affiliates precluded agents of mutual insurers from membership therein. Mutual agents formed their own association, the National Association of Mutual Insurance Agents in 1931. Through the next forty years, agents began to represent both stock and mutual companies. In 1975, the mutual agents association changed its name to the National Association of Professional Insurance Agents (PIA) and allowed both types of agents in its association. The Independent Insurance Agents of America also accepted mutual agents. PIA has more than 39,000 independent agents in its membership.

The National Association of Insurance Brokers was formed in 1934. Its membership consists of independent agents and brokers who are engaged primarily in meeting the insurance needs of commercial and industrial firms.

Another producer trade association is the National Association of Casualty and Surety Agents which was formed in 1913 and numbers about 300 members.

A specialty producer organization is the National Association of Surety Bond Producers. Formed in 1943, it has approximately 350 member agencies or brokers which constitute the majority of large surety producers.

These associations, and other similar associations, perform essentially the same functions for their members. These functions might be classified as (1) research, (2) education, (3) lobbying, (4) litigation, and (5) advertising, all in the protection and promotion of the interests of the members.

Research   The producer associations conduct research operations by two methods. First, the associations have committees, both standing committees and special committees, that research many problems and issues. Among the issues studied by such committees in recent years are (1) mass merchandising, (2) direct billing, (3) provisions of agency contracts, (4) establishment of an electronic data processing network for producers, (5) ways of meeting the competition from other marketing systems, (6) standardization of applications, and many others.

Second, outside consulting organizations may be retained when a research project requires skills not available within the membership or when more time is required than committee members can be expected to devote to the project. Another motive for retaining outside research organizations may be the value of the organizations' reputation and prestige in influencing association members, insurers, and legislators. For example, in the late 1960s, the Independent Insurance Agents of America retained the Stanford Research Institute to evaluate the then existing market position of the independent agency system, the reasons for the declining market share of the system, and possible strategies to improve the market share of independent agents.[17] A prestigious management consulting firm was retained to research the effects upon the independent agency system resulting from the development of direct billing and mass merchandising.[18] The Committee on Independent Business Institutions, of which the Independent Insurance Agents of America is a member, retained an independent research firm to prepare a report on the threat to small business firms arising from the diversification programs of bank holding companies.[19] A prestigious Washington law firm was retained to study the insurance activities of savings and loan associations.[20]

In general, the research conducted by the trade associations is intended to (1) provide guidance for the effective management of producer firms; (2) assist producers in negotiations with insurers concerning agency contracts, commissions, and similar matters; (3) assist in and encourage the development of better insurance policies and improved industry practices; (4) guide the associations in their efforts to protect the interests of their members through lobbying and litigation activities, and other similar purposes.

Education   The trade associations conduct their educational activities in a number of ways. First, they publish newsletters and magazines to keep members abreast of the latest developments in the industry and to provide information on sales techniques and agency management problems and techniques. Second, they conduct meetings, seminars, and short courses for the benefit of producers and their employees. Also, the research projects conducted by the associations have substantial educational value for members, and reports on such projects are widely distributed among the membership.

Lobbying and Litigation The trade associations engage in extensive lobbying activities with legislative and administrative agencies at the federal, state, and local levels. Lobbying at the federal level is conducted primarily by the national associations, while state and local lobbying usually is the responsibility of the state and local affiliates of the national associations. The associations also frequently engage in litigation designed to protect and further the interests of their members. The campaign against bank holding companies is perhaps the best illustration of these activities, since it included both lobbying and litigation at the federal and state levels.

Advertising Independent agency firms, being small and local in nature, cannot afford individually to sponsor major radio and television programs or to advertise in national publications. However, their national trade associations can use the national media for institutional advertising to create a desirable image for independent agents and brokers as a group. The "Big I" campaign sponsored by the Independent Insurance Agents of America is an example of such advertising. The national media were used to create a favorable image of independent producers as a group and to familiarize the public with the "Big I" symbol. Participating member agencies then used local advertising media to identify their own firms with the "Big I" trademark and to tie in with the national advertising. Associations may also offer other advertising assistance or advertising materials to their members at cost or as a part of normal membership services.

There are no significant producer trade associations in either the exclusive agency system or the direct writer system. Such associations would, of course, be inappropriate for direct writers, since they are employees of the insurers and not independent business firms. Producers of some direct writers have formed or joined labor unions, which, in addition to representing them in negotiations with their employers, perform for them some of the functions which trade associations perform for independent producers.

Surplus Lines Brokers

Most insurance agents and brokers are licensed by the states to represent only *admitted* insurers, those insurers licensed to do business in the state that granted the agent's or broker's license. However, it sometimes happens that a prospective purchaser cannot obtain insurance from an admitted insurer, usually because the loss exposure is too severe or because the amount of insurance required is too great. All of the states now have laws that provide for a special class of brokers, called surplus lines brokers, specially licensed to place business with *nonadmitted* insurers. Surplus lines brokers frequently do not sell insurance directly to consumers, but they deal with other insurance brokers and agents. However, some firms are licensed to place business with both admitted and nonadmitted insurers.

Regulation Nonadmitted insurers are not and cannot be regulated directly by the states in which they are not licensed. Therefore, the principal thrust of regulation is through the surplus lines broker. State laws require the surplus lines brokers to collect premium taxes and forward them to the state. Insurance in alien (chartered outside the U.S.) nonadmitted insurers is also subject to a 4 percent federal excise tax, payable by the insured. However, some alien insurers have worked out agreements to come under the United States income tax laws and to be exempt from the excise tax. The surplus lines broker may also be required to file with the state an affidavit stating that the coverage to be placed in a nonadmitted insurer has been rejected by admitted insurers. The number of admitted insurers by whom the coverage must have been rejected varies by state. For example, New York requires rejection by five admitted insurers.

Some surplus lines laws require the surplus lines broker to ascertain the financial condition of the nonadmitted insurers in which he obtains coverages. For example, Regulation 41 of the New York Insurance Department requires the broker to inquire into the financial status of the insurer and obtain and retain in the broker's office a copy of the insurer's latest annual statement; the broker is prohibited from placing coverage with the insurer unless the insurer's surplus to policyholders exceeds either (1) the minimum required of an admitted carrier in New York or (2) the minimum required of an admitted carrier in its home state if it is domiciled outside New York but within the United States. In addition, if the insurer is domiciled outside the United States, it must maintain a trust fund of at least $300,000 in a New York bank for the protection of policyholders and claimants in the United States. If the surplus lines broker cannot obtain an alien insurer's financial statement, he or she is required to notify the prospective insured of that fact. As of the middle of 1983 there were over 160 alien insurers that had established trust funds in the United States. The largest of these, with a trust fund of $4.3 billion, was maintained by the underwriters at Lloyd's of London.[21]

Surplus lines brokers are not left entirely to their own devices to establish the financial condition of nonadmitted insurers. About half of the states publish lists of approved nonadmitted insurers. In addition, the Nonadmitted Insurers Information Office of the National Association of Insurance Commissioners tracks the activities of nonadmitted insurers in the United States and furnishes information on nonadmitted insurers to state authorities and other interested persons.

New York and some other states require surplus lines brokers to see that policies issued by nonadmitted insurers include an agreement that the insurer will accept service of process in the state. Without such an agreement it might be necessary for an insured or claimant to file suit in the insurer's country of domicile in the event of a dispute. Such a procedure obviously would be impractical unless the dispute involved a great deal of money.

Size of Market Precise figures on surplus lines premiums are not available. However, some information on the size of the market does exist.

Richard E. Willey estimated that 1982 surplus lines premiums in the United States were approximately three billion dollars, or approximately 3.0 percent of total property and liability insurance premiums.[22] Some surplus lines premiums handled by U.S. brokers may involve premiums through insurers domiciled in Bermuda, the Cayman Islands, or Lloyd's of London.

Reasons for the Market One could reasonably ask why an insurance company, especially one domiciled in the United States, would choose to operate on a nonadmitted basis. There are several reasons. Lloyd's of London, which is not an insurance company, cannot qualify for admission to most states because most state laws do not permit individuals to act as insurers, except possibly through reciprocal exchanges. Consequently, the nonadmitted market is the only avenue available for the underwriters at Lloyd's to operate in most states.

Insurers that can qualify for admission may choose not to do so in order to avoid the somewhat rigid rate regulatory laws of the states. Also, some of the nonadmitted insurers may not do enough business in any one state to justify the expense and trouble of obtaining a license.

Finally, the surplus lines market deals extensively in policies tailored to cover unusual exposures. An admitted insurer might be required to file such policies for approval in each case.

SALES MANAGEMENT

Whether an independent agency, exclusive agency, or direct writer, every insurer needs sales management to assure the success of its marketing program.

Sales management involves the direction of the sales force to secure the kinds and amounts of business desired by the insurer. Persons responsible for sales management must determine:

1. the segments of the available market that can be reached most effectively by the company's producers;
2. the nature of the product that will be most appealing to the selected market segments and most profitable to the insurer; and
3. how best to select, train, and motivate producers to sell to the selected market segments.

Market Segmentation

Only the very largest insurers can afford the luxury of trying to appeal simultaneously to all segments of the national market. It is doubtful that even they can do so effectively. Most insurers, especially smaller companies, must concentrate their sales efforts on selected geographic, demographic, or industrial segments of the market, or concentrate on a limited range of coverages in order to use their limited resources effectively.

Geographic Segmentation There are several reasons an insurer may limit its marketing activity to a state or region. The first, and perhaps the most important reason, is cost. An effective sales management program involves many people. There must be producers situated at key places throughout the sales territory unless the insurer sells only by mail. The maintenance of a producer force requires the expense for supervisory and service personnel, including sales managers or special agents, loss control engineers, adjusters, and premium auditors. Consequently, the expense of servicing a given volume of business is lower if the business is concentrated in a small geographic area.

Second, the loss exposures may vary substantially among geographic areas. An insurer may elect to concentrate its business in the less hazardous areas. For example, the earthquake hazard is more serious on the Pacific Coast than in most of the remainder of the United States. The windstorm exposure is more serious in the hurricane belt of the Gulf Coast and the tornado belt of the Midwest. California has been experiencing about one medical professional liability judgment per month in excess of $1 million, while some less urbanized states have never had such a judgment in excess of $100,000. While the medical professional liability differences reflect demographic or social, rather than geographic differences, it is sometimes easier to reflect demographic differences through geographic segmentation.

Third, geographic segmentation may reflect regulatory patterns. An insurer may want to avoid a state in which regulatory authorities have held rates at unrealistically low levels or have imposed other unfavorable regulatory constraints. Conversely, insurers may seek to enter states with favorable regulatory patterns.

Finally, a geographic area may be sought or avoided because of patterns of growth or competition. For example, a strong local insurer may dominate an area's market to such an extent that it is difficult to enter, or localized price competition may make an area unattractive from the standpoint of profitability.

Demographic and Industry Segmentation Many insurers concentrate their marketing efforts on selected demographic groups. The groups may be delineated by such characteristics as age, income, occupation, and others. For example, one large insurer specializes in insuring officers and warrant officers of the United States armed forces. Several insurers offer coverage exclusively or primarily to teachers. Many fraternal organizations were formed to offer insurance protection to religious, racial, ethnic, or occupational groups.

There are at least two advantages to demographic specialization. First, a company that specializes in insuring a demographic group becomes more familiar with the needs, likes, and dislikes of the group and can specialize its advertising and sales appeals to reach group members more effectively. Also, the natural cohesion of racial, ethnic, and religious groups may make sales easier for those insurers who succeed in identifying with the group. Familiarity with group characteristics and communication with group leaders may also facilitate underwriting selection.

Second, some demographic groups have been shown to have fewer claims in some lines of insurance than the population as a whole. Specialization in insuring these groups may enable the insurer to offer them lower rates and thus compete for their business more effectively than insurers that do not specialize.

Specialization by industry group offers substantially the same advantages as specialization by demographic group. It is for this reason that many insurers include in their names references to such industries as hardware, canners, transportation, and others.

Product Segmentation The market also may be segmented by insurance product. That is, an insurer may specialize in one or a limited number of insurance products, rather than attempting to offer all lines. For example, a few insurers specialize in surety bonds, others may offer only personal lines of coverage, and at least one insurer specializes in coverage for contact lenses.

The advantages of product specialization are:

1. better loss control, claims handling, and underwriting as a result of the greater familiarity possible through specialization;
2. simplification of personnel and training functions; and
3. reduced expenses due to the more limited inventory of forms, manuals, and other materials required.

Of course, specialization, whether geographic, demographic, or product, places a limit on an insurer's growth. It is for this reason that many insurers that begin as specialists later expand their operations to encompass broader horizons. In designing products and preparing sales plans, insurers must consider not only the characteristics of the market segments but also the demands of producers in account selling.

Account selling is the idea that one producer or underwriter should endeavor to write all of the insurance for a particular insured rather than only part of the account. Thus, personal auto business is a lead to homeowners business, which may lead to personal life insurance, commercial property and liability insurance, and business life insurance.

Product Differentiation

A company that plans to maintain or increase its market share must find some way to differentiate its products from those of its competitors. The term product, as used here, includes not only the actual insurance contract but also the services associated with the contract. An insurer may differentiate its products from the competition by (1) changing the coverage provided by the contract, (2) charging a different price, (3) providing a different level of service, or (4) a combination of the three.

Contract Differentiation Many of the policies and endorsements that are now considered standard insurance products have their origins in the efforts of insurers to differentiate their products from those of their competition. For example, the homeowners policy was developed for that purpose in the 1950s. It has now become a standard product, and some insurers are attempting to differentiate their homeowners policies by offering new or expanded coverages. For example, some insurers now offer replacement cost coverage on contents under their homeowners policy, thus avoiding the perennial problem of setting a value for used furniture and clothing to reflect depreciation.

It is through contract differentiation that the insurance industry has progressed, in approximately one hundred years, from offering policies which covered only against fire and lightning to the rather common availability of "all-risks" coverages. Some insurers are now offering a combination policy covering property, liability, life, and health insurance. While contract differentiation can be desirable, it can also be disadvantageous. Excessive contract differentiation can complicate the settlement of claims when a loss is covered by two or more insurers with varying contract provisions. Also, there are additional complications in analyzing loss data from policies that are not identical.

Legislation has been enacted in many states to place some control on excessive contract differentiation. For example, many states have statutes that specify the wording, and even the type size, of the standard fire insurance policy. Some states require certain minimum provisions in life and health insurance policies, and some states require that automobile insurance policies cover all persons who operate the insured vehicle with the owner's consent. Other minimum provision statutes could be cited.

The standard policy laws and minimum provision laws, along with the requirement that policy forms be approved by regulatory authorities, restrict contract differentiation and product improvement to some degree, but substantial room for change remains.

Price Differentiation In the marketing of tangible products, price differentiation may result from charging either more or less than the competition. Some products with prestige value are purchased, at least in part, because they cost more and therefore offer the opportunity for ostentatious consumption. Upward price differentiation has little application in insurance marketing.

An insurer that wishes to charge a lower price than its competitors must find some way to reduce its costs, its profits, or both, below those of its competitors. Not only must it comply with the statutory requirement that its rates be adequate, but it must also comply with the economic necessity of having enough income to cover its outgo if it plans to remain in business over the long term.

An insurance rate usually consists of allowances for (1) losses, (2) expenses, and (3) profit. An insurer might justify a reduction in rate on a reduction of any one or more of the foregoing three elements of the rate. The allowance for losses might be reduced through more careful underwriting selection or less generous claim settlement practices. The allowance for expenses may be reduced through strict expense control measures in the areas of underwriting, inspection, and overhead. Acquisition expenses may be reduced by lowering commissions to producers but that could discourage producers' sales efforts. The record of various industry segments in reducing expenses is discussed in later sections of this chapter. Price differentiation may also result from refinement of rating classes. For example, one rating class might be divided into two classes, with a lower rate for the least hazardous members of the old class and higher rates for the more hazardous members. Experience, retrospective, and schedule rating plans also may be used as means of price differentiation. These concepts are discussed more fully in Chapters 8, 9, and 10.

Service Differentiation Many insurers use service differentiation in their marketing programs. For example, several large workers' compensation insurers advertise their loss control services and their capabilities to assist employers in complying with the Occupational Safety and Health Act. The insurer's capabilities in the rehabilitation of injured workers have also been used for sales appeals. Of course, these services may also be promoted in the guise of price differentiation, since both, if successful, tend to reduce insurance costs.

Service differentiation is less common in personal lines property and liability insurance, except in the area of prompt and fair claim settlement. Several large personal lines insurers advertise the convenience of their drive-in claims centers, and one insurer advertises that it will guarantee automobile repair work for which it pays, provided the repairs are made by one of its recommended repair shops. Many less specific slogans and trademarks are used by insurers to at least create the impression that their services are superior to those of their competitors.

Producer Motivation

Even the best product will not sell well unless potential customers are told about it. Insurers use a wide variety of inducements to motivate their producers to sell. Some of the inducements are monetary or material, but others are psychological.

Money, of course, is a principal inducement offered to producers, since most producers depend upon income from insurance as their principal source of livelihood. Although some producers are active in other business, such as real estate, the number of part-time producers is diminishing.

While some producers may receive a salary from their principals, many receive commissions or bonuses in addition to, if not in lieu of, salary. The commissions or bonuses can be powerful motivators to persuade the producer to sell the kinds and amounts of coverage that the insurer wants to write. By lowering the commission or bonus on undesirable business and raising it on desirable business, the insurer can, to a large degree, channel the efforts of the producer in the desired direction. However, insurers do not frequently raise or lower commissions because of the confusion that may result, the increased administrative and accounting costs, the regulatory requirements, and producer resistance.

Sales contests may also be used to motivate producers to sell more business in general, to sell specific kinds of coverage, or to sell to specific classes of consumers. The prizes in such contests may be money, merchandise, or perhaps a trip to some very desirable resort for a combination business-pleasure meeting.

Nonmaterial or psychic incentives may also be used to motivate producers, as they are used to motivate others. Such incentives consist of conspicuous recognition of their performance by their supervisors or by the company or a professional group, possibly through the granting of a specific title or membership in a club or organization.

Many insurers (especially life insurers) insert advertisements in trade journals recognizing their top producers, or publish articles in their in-house journals to inform other producers and employees of the outstanding accomplishments of selected producers. Insurers also have organizations, sometimes called the President's Club, the Millionaires' Club, or something similar, to which leading producers are given membership. Many producers are highly competitive by nature and place great value on such recognition of their achievements.

Of course, the final incentive, though a negative one, is the threat of termination of the producer's relationship with the insurer. Producers may be terminated because they do not produce enough business, because their business is consistently unprofitable, or because the business they produce is not the kind the insurer wants. Termination of agency contracts is subject to restrictions in some states.

Producer Supervision

An insurer must provide some means of supervising its producers in order (1) to motivate them to sell the kinds and amounts of business it wants, (2) to assist them in handling unusual or difficult insurance situations, (3) to continually reappraise their performance so that corrective action may be taken promptly when needed, and (4) to recruit additional or replacement producers when necessary. Small insurers operating in restricted geographic areas may be able to provide this supervision through home office officials. However, larger insurers with more widespread operations usually find it desirable to provide supervision in or near the locality in which each producer operates. There are, in general, two systems in use in the United States for providing producer supervision. They are (1) the branch office or regional system and (2) the managing general agency system.

The Branch Office System   Under the branch office system, as the name implies, the insurer maintains offices in strategically located cities and towns in its operating territory. A small branch office, sometimes called a service office, may consist of only a sales manager, special agent, or field representative (the title varies by company) whose principal duty is maintaining contact with and supervision of producers. Larger branch offices may also include company officers, management personnel, underwriters, claim people, loss control engineers, premium auditors, and other service personnel.

Some insurers may have two or more levels of branch offices. For example, a large branch office, sometimes called a regional office, may supervise smaller branches scattered throughout one or more states. Regional offices of some insurers are largely autonomous and perform most of the insurance functions, though not the investment functions, usually associated with home office operations. Others function primarily as a communications facility, gathering information from producers, forwarding it to the home office, and returning home office decisions to the producer.

As one might expect, there is a great deal of expense involved in maintaining a widespread system of branch offices. An insurer can afford to maintain such offices only in those territories in which it has, or expects to obtain, a substantial volume of business.

The Managing General Agency System   A managing general agency is an independent business firm that performs for one or more separate insurers some or all of the functions usually performed by company branch offices. A managing general agent may perform such services for a single insurer, though it is more common for them to represent several insurers. The general agency usually does not sell directly to insurance consumers but appoints and supervises producers throughout the territory. Its territory may consist of an entire state or several states. A few managing general agencies cover very large territories, though frequently for specialty lines of insurance.

The advantage to an insurer of operating through a managing general agent is the low fixed cost. The general agency is compensated by an overriding commission on the business sold by the producers it appoints. Consequently, the insurer does not have the large fixed cost of maintaining a branch office. The general agency, by writing relatively small amounts of business for each of several insurers, earns enough commissions to cover its expenses and earn a profit.

The managing general agency system was a major marketing system for property and liability insurers in the nineteenth century when most insurers were small and much of the nation was sparsely populated. As the population and insurers grew larger, many insurers accumulated sufficient premium volume to operate through branch offices in many areas. In some cases, the insurers merely terminated their relationships with managing general agencies and established their own branch offices staffed with their own personnel. In other cases, insurers purchased the general agencies and converted them to branch offices.

As a result of additional insurers moving to the branch office system, the total number of managing general agencies had been significantly reduced by the 1960s, and many of the remaining general agencies had their underwriting authority restricted as insurers increased their producer supervision activities at the home office level. As the result, most managing general agencies were forced into the excess and surplus lines and into specialty markets such as mobile homes, snowmobiles, nonstandard automobile, and other lines not normally sought by the majority of insurers.

However, during the 1974-75 underwriting crunch when a number of insurers significantly reduced their writings, the excess and surplus lines and specialty markets grew, and managing general agencies were the primary beneficiaries. With few exceptions, the trend continues to be a managing general agency system devoted primarily to excess and surplus lines and specialty markets with some also offering standard facilities from smaller companies unable to promote their product through the branch office system.

COMPARISON OF RESULTS UNDER VARIOUS MARKETING SYSTEMS

The sections that follow present some statistical comparisons of the operating results of the various marketing systems. Some caution must be exercised in the interpretation of these statistics for several reasons.

First, the statistics will be shown by company or by company group. As indicated elsewhere, some companies and company groups use more than one of the marketing systems. It is not possible to separate their statistics by marketing system.

Second, two companies writing the same nominal line of insurance may, in fact, be assuming quite different loss exposures and incurring quite different expenses. For example, it is customary to use a graded scale of commissions in workers' compensation insurance, with the commission scale on policies with small premiums being much higher than for policies with large premiums. Thus, an insurer that specializes in insuring large industrial firms would show a lower commission expense on a given premium volume than would an insurer specializing in, for example, automobile dealers.

Third, commission and brokerage expense does not indicate the entire cost of producing business. The other acquisition costs also must be considered, particularly since changes in operating methods may change large blocks of expense from commissions and brokerage to other acquisition expense. For example, when an insurer changes from agency policy issuance and billing to direct billing, it usually reduces the producer's commission by as much as five percentage points. However, the insurer must include in other acquisition expenses the newly assumed cost of issuing and billing policies. Thus, the commission and brokerage expense would decrease more than total acquisition expense.

The division between commissions and other acquisition expense may also cause misleading conclusions when comparing independent agency companies with direct writers. Salaries of direct writer producers are included in other acquisition expense, rather than in commission and brokerage expense.

Most of the comparisons that follow will compare the independent agency system on the one hand with the combination of exclusive agency, direct writer, and mail order systems on the other hand.

Market Shares

The market share of the independent agency companies has been declining for many years. At the turn of the century, the independent agency system controlled virtually all of the property and liability insurance in the United States, and only a few relatively small insurers used other marketing systems. By 1982, the independent agency system's share of the market for all property and liability lines had dropped to 61.4 percent. Exhibit 2-7 shows the changes in market share from 1970 through 1982.

As shown in Exhibit 2-7, the all-lines market share of the independent agency system has declined steadily over the thirteen-year period, as it has since World War II. However, the decline has not been even over all lines. The independent agency system's share of the personal lines has decreased more sharply than its share of the commercial lines. The growth of the exclusive agency and direct writer systems and the entry of the giant life insurers into property and liability insurance are largely responsible for this decline. The downward trend slowed in the early 1970s as indicated by the decrease from 1972 to 1974 of 0.3 percent, as compared to the decrease from 1970 to 1972 (0.9 percent), but the rate of decrease accelerated again after 1974.

Exhibit 2-8 shows the market shares for automobile liability

Exhibit 2-7
Market Shares by Marketing System—All Property-Liability Lines Combined*

System	Market Share As Percentage of Industry Premiums						
	1970	1972	1974	1976	1978	1980	1982
Independent Agency	69.0%	68.1%	67.8%	66.1%	64.1%	63.0%	61.4%
Other	31.0	31.9	32.2	33.9	35.9	37.0	38.6

*Adapted from *Best's Executive Data Service* for various years.

Exhibit 2-8
Market Shares by Marketing System—Automobile Liability Insurance*

System	Market Share As Percentage of Industry Premiums						
	1970	1972	1974	1976	1978	1980	1982
Independent Agency	56.1%	54.6%	54.2%[1]	52.7%	50.4%	48.7%	47.6%
Other	43.9	45.4	45.8[1]	47.3	49.6	51.3	52.4
1. Calculated from data shown in *Best's Executive Data Service*.							

*Adapted from *Best's Exectuive Data Service* for various years.

insurance, private passenger and commercial combined, for the years 1970 through 1982. While the independent agency system's share of all automobile liability insurance is still near half, it has dropped almost 10 percentage points in the thirteen-year period. If private passenger automobile insurance is taken alone, the independent agency system now controls much less than half of the market. Private passenger insurance business was not reported separately on the annual statement blank prior to 1972, but Exhibit 2-9 shows the market shares for 1972 through 1982. [23]

As shown in Exhibit 2-10, the homeowners market is following in the footsteps of the private passenger automobile insurance market, with the independent agency system having lost more than 20 percentage points of market share in the thirteen-year period.

As shown by Exhibit 2-11, the independent agency system has held its market share in ocean marine insurance since 1970.

The downward trend in the independent agency companies' share

Exhibit 2-9
Market Share by Marketing System—Private Passenger
Automobile Liability Insurance*

| System | Market Share As Percentage of Industry Premiums | | | | | |
	1972	1974	1976	1978	1980	1982
Independent Agency	48.5%	48.3%	45.6%	41.8%	39.3%	38.6%
Other	51.5	51.7	54.4	58.2	60.6	61.4

*Adapted from *Best's Executive Data Service* for various years.

Exhibit 2-10
Market Shares by Marketing System—Homeowners Insurance*

| System | Market Share As Percentage of Industry Premiums | | | | | | |
	1970	1972	1974	1976	1978	1980	1982
Independent Agency	74.6%	71.9%	68.3%	63.6%	59.5%	55.7%	54.3%
Other	25.4	28.1	31.7	36.4	40.5	44.3	45.7

*Adapted from *Best's Executive Data Service* for various years.

of the workers' compensation market was reversed in the years 1978-1982, with their market share rising 5.1 percentage points during the period. The general liability market share of the independent agency companies remained rather constant at approximately 84 percent from 1970 to 1982.

As shown in Exhibit 2-12, the independent agents' share of commercial multiple peril coverages has declined steadily since 1972. However, they seem to have stabilized their share of the markets for inland marine and surety business. In spite of the loss of market share, the independent agency companies still dominate the commercial multiple-peril market, with fourteen of the fifteen largest writers using the independent agency system. State Farm was the third largest writer of commercial multiple-peril insurance in 1982, although it had not been in the top 15 as recently as 1975.

The marketing plans of most of the exclusive agency, direct writer, and mail order insurers have placed heavy emphasis on the personal lines. This emphasis has resulted in their dominance of the private

Exhibit 2-11
Market Shares by Marketing System—Ocean Marine, Workers' Compensation, General Liability*

System	Market Share As Percentage of Industry Premiums						
	1970	1972	1974	1976	1978	1980	1982
Ocean Marine							
Independent Agency	90.6%	93.2%	96.1%	92.5%	89.7%	91.0%	89.8%
Other	9.4	6.8	3.9	7.5	10.3	9.0	10.2
Workers' Compensation							
Independent Agency	73.1%	74.6%	75.6%	75.2%	73.6%	75.7%	78.7%
Other	26.9	25.4	24.4	24.8	26.4	24.3	21.3
General Liability							
Independent Agency	83.7%	84.3%	84.8%	85.4%	83.6%	84.4%	83.5%
Other	16.3	15.7	15.2	14.6	16.4	15.6	16.5

*Adapted from *Best's Executive Data Service* for various years.

passenger automobile insurance market and their rapidly growing position in the homeowners market.

The exclusive agency, direct writer, and mail order insurers placed such high emphasis on personal lines for several reasons. First, automobile insurance, to which they first turned their attention, is the major property and liability insurance line, accounting for about 42 percent of the industry's total premium volume. Private passenger auto insurance alone accounts for about 35 percent of the industry's volume.

Second, because of its relative simplicity when compared with commercial lines, private passenger automobile insurance can be sold and serviced with relative ease. In fact, it has been sold successfully by mail without a personal producer. The combination of a large market and relative simplicity permitted exclusive agency and direct writer insurers to build large forces with a minimum of training delays and expenses.

Third, these insurers were able to mechanize the policywriting, billing, and other internal service functions, thus reducing expenses and prices.

Having secured many automobile policyholders, it was natural for these insurers to offer homeowners insurance to the same customers. In addition, homeowners coverage possessed many of the same

Exhibit 2-12
Market Shares by Marketing System—Commercial Multiple-Peril,
Inland Marine, Surety*

	Market Share As Percentage of Industry Premiums						
System	1970	1972	1974	1976	1978	1980	1982
Commercial Multiple-Peril							
Independent Agency	94.1%	94.7%	93.7%	92.9%	90.9%	87.9%	87.6%
Other	5.9	5.3	6.3	7.1	9.1	12.1	12.4
Inland Marine							
Independent Agency	86.0%	85.5%	84.4%	83.6%	83.3%	83.8%	82.0%
Other	14.0	14.5	15.6	16.4	16.7	16.2	18.0
Surety							
Independent Agency	99.3%	99.2%	97.7%	95.8%	97.4%	95.8%	96.9%
Other	0.7	0.8	2.3	4.2	2.6	4.2	3.1

*Adapted from Best's *Executive Data Service* for various years.

characteristics that made automobile insurance an attractive product
for them.

The major exclusive agency and direct writer insurers may be
approaching a point at which they cannot expect to continue their rapid
growth in the personal lines market, especially in the private passenger
automobile insurance market. The slowing of growth is due, among
other things, to the increasingly competitive prices offered by independent agency insurers, and possibly complete penetration of that group
of consumers for whom price is an overriding consideration in the
selection of an insurer.

However, growth in premium volume may continue at a healthy
rate because of the increase in premiums on existing business and
additional premiums from collateral business. In property insurance,
premium volume is a function of the amount of insurance and has been
steadily increasing due to inflation. In liability insurance, rate increases
brought about by rising claims costs and higher limits of liability have
the same effect.

It is almost inevitable that exclusive agency and direct writing
companies will expand into the commercial lines markets, and some of
them have been moving aggressively in that direction. It is doubtful

that mail order insurers can market commercial lines successfully because of the greater complexity of the coverages and the greater skill needed to assess the needs of commercial lines buyers.

Growth Rates

As indicated by the changes in market shares, the growth rate of the independent agency insurers, as a group, has been slower than that for companies using the other marketing system. Of course, the group growth rates are averages; as such, they mask a wide variation of growth rates within the groups.

Exhibit 2-13 gives a rather dramatic indication of the more rapid growth rate for the exclusive agency and direct writer companies. It compares the net premiums written for (1) the industry as a whole, (2) State Farm Mutual Automobile Insurance Company, and (3) Allstate Insurance Company, all for the thirty-eight years 1945 through 1982. It should be noted that the industry figures include premiums for State Farm and Allstate. Also, the State Farm and Allstate figures are only for the two corporations named and not for all of the State Farm and Allstate companies.

The companies comprising the property and liability insurance industry wrote $32.19 of premiums in 1982 for every dollar written in 1945. At the same time, Allstate Insurance Company wrote $636.44 in 1982, and State Farm Mutual Automobile Insurance Company wrote $184.70 in 1982 for every dollar written in 1945. Both Allstate and State Farm, especially the latter, would have had even higher ratios if all of their affiliated companies had been included.

To state the relative growth rates in another way, the industry grew at an average rate of 9.6 percent compounded annually during the period from 1945 through 1982. The comparable rates for Allstate Insurance Company and State Farm Mutual Automobile Insurance Company were 18.5 percent and 14.7 percent, respectively.

As shown in Exhibit 2-13, Allstate's annual growth rate has exceeded the growth rate of the industry every year except three since World War II, though the gap has narrowed in the last few years (except for 1979). State Farm's growth rate has exceeded the industry's every year but five since World War II. If all State Farm companies had been included in Exhibit 2-13, they would have developed a combined annual growth rate higher than the industry rate during three of those five years. However, as in the case of Allstate, their growth rate in the last few years would have been closer to the industry average than it was in the earlier years.

The growth rates of the largest exclusive agency and direct writer insurers have declined over the last few years and are now approaching

Exhibit 2-13
Net Premiums Written, Growth Indexes, and Growth Rates—Property and Liability Insurance Industry,*
Allstate Insurance Company,† and State Farm Mutual Automobile Insurance Company,† 1945-1982

Year	Net Premiums Written[1]			Growth Indexes			Annual Growth Rates		
	Industry	Allstate	State Farm	Industry	Allstate	State Farm	Industry	Allstate	State Farm
1945	3,230	9	37	1.000	1.000	1.000			
1946	4,052	15	55	1.254	1.677	1.486	25.4%	66.7%	48.8%
1947	5,113	20	70	1.583	2.222	1.892	26.2	33.3	27.3
1948	5,877	32	76	1.820	3.556	2.054	14.9	60.0	8.6
1949	6,356	41	81	1.968	4.556	2.189	8.2	28.1	6.6
1950	6,866	58	98	2.130	6.444	2.649	8.0	41.5	21.0
1951	7,775	75	119	2.407	8.333	3.216	13.2	29.3	21.4
1952	8,770	103	141	2.715	11.444	3.811	12.8	37.3	18.5
1953	9,673	156	191	2.995	17.333	5.162	10.3	51.5	35.5
1954	9,908	190	214	3.067	21.111	5.784	2.4	21.8	12.0
1955	10,539	230	242	3.263	25.555	6.541	6.4	21.1	13.1
1956	11,130	259	287	3.446	28.778	7.757	5.7	12.6	18.6
1957	12,096	287	341	3.745	31.889	9.216	8.7	10.8	18.8
1958	12,828	372	397	3.972	41.333	10.730	6.1	29.6	16.4
1959	14,084	432	447	4.360	48.000	11.784	9.8	16.1	12.6
1960	14,973	495	478	4.640	55.000	12.919	6.3	14.6	6.9
1961	15,474	525	514	4.791	58.333	13.891	3.3	6.1	7.5
1962	16,034	569	581	4.964	63.222	15.703	3.6	8.4	13.0

Year									
1963	17,175	622	662	5.317	69.111	17.892	7.1	9.3	13.9
1964	18,317	667	753	5.671	74.111	20.351	6.6	7.2	13.7
1965	20,063	759	840	6.211	84.333	22.703	9.5	13.8	11.6
1966	22,090	889	973	6.839	98.778	26.297	10.1	17.1	15.8
1967	23,829	1,036	1,088	7.377	115.111	29.405	7.9	16.5	11.8
1968	26,026	1,205	1,268	8.058	133.889	34.270	9.2	16.3	16.5
1969	29,225	1,393	1,478	9.048	154.778	39.946	12.3	15.6	16.6
1970	32,867	1,639	1,685	10.176	182.111	45.541	12.5	17.7	14.0
1971	35,715	1,966	1,888	11.057	218.444	51.027	8.7	20.0	12.0
1972	39,318	2,167	2,046	12.172	240.778	55.297	10.1	10.2	8.4
1973	42,075	2,343	2,184	13.026	260.333	59.027	7.0	8.1	6.7
1974	45,152	2,522	2,295	13.980	280.222	62.027	6.4	7.6	5.1
1975	49,967	2,804	2,582	15.470	311.555	69.784	10.7	11.2	12.5
1976	60,813	3,383	3,272	18.83	375.89	88.43	21.7	20.6	26.7
1977	72,397	4,078	4,027	22.41	453.11	108.84	19.0	20.5	23.1
1978	81,690	4,046	4,675	25.29	449.56	126.35	12.8	−0.8	16.1
1979	90,123	4,708	5,320	27.90	523.11	143.78	10.3	16.4	13.8
1980	95,569	5,156	5,843	29.59	572.89	157.92	6.0	9.5	9.8
1981	99,276	5,226	6,201	30.74	580.67	167.59	3.9	1.4	6.1
1982	103,968	5,728	6,834	32.19	636.44	184.70	4.7	9.6	10.2

1. In millions of dollars.

*Adapted from *Insurance Facts* for various years.
†Adapted from *Best's Insurance Reports, Property-Casualty,* for various years.

the industry average growth rate. Also, the gains in market share by these companies in the automobile insurance market have been slower than in the past. The aggressive entry of direct writer companies affiliated with large mutual life insurers may increase the market share of the nonindependent agency insurers as a group but probably will help to slow the growth rates of leaders, at least in the personal lines markets.

The increasing market shares of the exclusive agency and direct writer companies have not gone unnoticed by the independent agents and the companies they represent. Numerous studies have been made by various trade associations and individual insurers in an effort to find a way to stabilize the market share of the independent agency system. More recently, the four major trade associations in the independent agency system (American Insurance Association, Independent Insurance Agents of America, National Association of Casualty and Surety Agents, and the National Association of Professional Insurance Agents) joined forces to suggest ways to meet the challenge from the other marketing systems. Their principal proposals are:

> Insurance companies need to develop consistent and predictable marketing strategies based on identification of target markets and determination of the mix of products, prices, distribution channels, and other methods needed to reach those markets. They could use better market research to determine their target markets. They could select agents that are compatible with this marketing strategy, working closely with these agents to develop the strategy and then to help them carry it out.

> Innovative products could aid the competitiveness of the American Agency System. Ongoing price competitiveness could be sought through improved ratemaking, reduction and reallocation of overhead costs, improved claims procedures, and programs designed to attract business with lower loss cost potential. With such price competitiveness, advertising could be strengthened by concentrating on target markets and increasing the visibility of the American Agency System.

> In the area of representation, companies could weigh what increased efficiencies would result from future appointment of a smaller number of carefully selected, qualified agencies. Agents, in turn, could consider reducing the number of companies they represent.

> Performance standards can be established in a variety of areas for both agents and companies. Companies can also assist agents in building the agency sales force and in management and perpetuation of the agency. They can commit to a more formal program of agency rehabilitation instead of terminating an agency in difficulty. They could also upgrade the caliber and authority of their field personnel who work with agents.

> Agents' advisory councils can be made more effective channels of communication and coordination with companies. Agents' associa-

tions can help upgrade the professional qualifications of agents as well as provide training and education services.

A number of steps could be considered to reduce or eliminate duplication of functions, including:

- Giving complete underwriting authority to selected agents.
- Resolving the question of responsibility for verification of data.
- Having companies produce policies and endorsements mechanically, as well as upgrade values for renewal, bill the insured, and handle informational messages.
- Increasing the use of modern information processing systems in agents' offices.
- Continuing and expanding the ACORD project and the Insurance Institute for Research.
- Developing the most efficient process for claim handling, considering the ability and location of each agent.
- Reevaluating the issue of direct contact by companies with insureds.

Current compensation methods could be reviewed to determine whether they provide sufficient incentives to agents for producing new business, assuming varied functions, and meeting competitive pricing and providing an adequate overall return for the agent.

There are several ways to achieve better coordination and cooperation between companies and agents to improve the legislative and regulatory climate in which they operate.

In summary, there may be a number of opportunities to increase the competitiveness of the American Agency System in personal lines and reduce the mistrust and misunderstanding in the relationship while maintaining adequate levels of profitability for companies and agents. Current practices and past traditions need to be examined objectively and innovations made if the American Agency System is to remain a significant factor in the insurance market during the rest of this century.[24]

Profitability

The sections that follow will show the expense ratios and the loss ratios for the leading insurers to compare the profitability of the companies under the various marketing systems. In all cases, the loss ratio used will be the ratio of incurred losses and loss adjustment expenses to earned premiums.

Statistics for 1982 will be used in the tables that follow because that is the latest year for which data are available at the time of writing.

Automobile Bodily Injury Liability Exhibit 2-14 shows the loss ratio, expense ratio, and underwriting profit ratio for ten large writers of private passenger automobile liability insurance. This line appears to have been more profitable (or at least less unprofitable), with

Exhibit 2-14
Underwriting Profitability—Private Passenger Automobile Liability, 1982*

Company	Marketing System[1]	Loss Ratio[2]	Expense Ratio[3]	Underwriting Profit or Loss[4]
State Farm	0	84.2%	17.0%	− 1.7%
Allstate	0	87.1	22.3	−10.0
Farmers Group	0	87.6	24.6	−12.9
Nationwide	0	90.1	25.7	−16.2
Aetna Life & Casualty	A	88.4	28.7	−17.2
Travelers	A	92.2	31.1	−24.7
Government Employees	0	83.8	13.6	1.8
Liberty Mutual	0	100.8	18.7	−20.4
United Services	0	86.9	10.8	1.8
Continental	A	84.2	33.3	−18.5

1. A indicates independent agency system; 0 indicates other than independent agency system.
2. Ratio of incurred losses and loss adjustment expenses to earned premiums.
3. Ratio of commissions, brokerage, taxes, and fees to written premiums plus ratio of loss adjustment, other acquisition, and general administrative expenses to earned premiums.
4. After policyholder dividends.

*Adapted from *Best's Aggregates and Averages: 1983* (Oldwick, NJ: A.M. Best Company, 1983).

some exceptions, for the other marketing systems than for the independent agency system in 1982.

While the profitability of the coverage may change from year to year, the relative positions of the marketing systems remain substantially as shown in Exhibit 2-14. That is, the other systems have been, in general, more profitable in good years and less unprofitable in bad years than the independent agency companies.

Homeowners The underwriting results for homeowners coverage are shown in Exhibit 2-15. Homeowners seems to be less profitable for the independent agency system than for the other marketing systems, although the insurers using the other systems are expanding their market shares more rapidly. Homeowners loss ratios were higher for the exclusive agency and direct writer companies than for some of the independent agency companies in 1982. However, their lower expense ratios permitted State Farm and Allstate to show some profits.

Commercial Multiple Peril State Farm was the only exclusive agency, direct writer, or mail order insurer among the ten largest writers of commercial multiple-peril coverages. To permit comparison among the systems, Allstate is also included in Exhibit 2-16 although its premium volume would place it well below the other members of the group.

Workers' Compensation Underwriting results for the large writers of workers' compensation are shown in Exhibit 2-17. The two direct writers had the lowest and the third lowest expense ratios among the ten largest writers of this line in 1982.

Fire Insurance Exhibit 2-18 shows the underwriting results of ten large writers of fire insurance along with State Farm. The latter insurer is included for comparison purposes because nine of the ten largest writers are independent agency companies. Allstate is the ninth largest writer of fire insurance, and State Farm is seventeenth.

Critique The foregoing sections have demonstrated that the companies operating through the exclusive agency, direct writer, and mail order marketing systems have displaced the independent agency system as the leading writers of private passenger automobile insurance. They are making a strong, and seemingly successful, bid to become the leading writers of homeowners insurance.

The success of those companies in the personal lines markets seems to depend on two factors: (1) their lower expense ratios and lower prices and (2) their ability to focus their selling efforts more effectively upon the markets they wish to reach.

Some of the exclusive agency and direct writer insurers that have dominated the personal lines markets in recent years are now trying to

Exhibit 2-15
Underwriting Profitability—Homeowners Insurance, 1982*

Company	Marketing System[1]	Loss Ratio[2]	Expense Ratio[3]	Underwriting Profit or Loss[4]
State Farm	0	72.5%	24.9%	1.2%
Allstate	0	70.0	22.9	6.1
Aetna Life & Casualty	A	66.9	33.1	0.1
Farmers Group	0	80.0	29.4	—11.6
Continental	A	79.9	33.9	—15.2
Nationwide	0	76.0	31.9	— 9.2
CIGNA	A	64.4	37.4	— 2.5
Travelers	A	64.1	34.8	— 1.8
Safeco	A	67.2	34.0	— 1.2
Fireman's Fund	A	66.7	35.7	— 5.1

1. A indicates independent agency system; 0 indicates other than independent agency system.
2. Ratio of incurred losses and loss adjustment expenses to earned premiums.
3. Ratio of commissions, brokerage, taxes, and fees to written premiums plus ratio of loss adjustment, other acquisition, and general administrative expenses to earned premiums.
4. After policyholder dividends.

*Adapted from *Best's Aggregated and Averages: 1983* (Oldwick, NJ: A.M. Best Company, 1983).

Exhibit 2-16
Underwriting Profitability—Commercial Multiple-Peril Policies, 1982*

Company	Marketing System[1]	Loss Ratio[2]	Expense Ratio[3]	Underwriting Profit or Loss[4]
CIGNA	A	84.2%	41.5%	—18.5%
Travelers	A	66.9	27.7	— 0.5
Fireman's Fund	A	69.5	44.9	—15.6
Aetna Life & Casualty	A	68.2	35.6	— 1.6
Hartford	A	62.8	43.0	— 4.5
Continental	A	75.8	36.9	—13.8
State Farm	O	75.4	31.1	— 8.3
Home	A	83.0	41.7	—22.5
Royal-Globe	A	86.8	39.9	—26.8
AIG	A	128.3	28.2	—55.9
Allstate	O	78.7	52.2	—31.0

1. A indicates independent agency system; O indicates other than independent agency system.
2. Ratio of incurred losses and loss adjustment expenses to earned premiums.
3. Ratio of commissions, brokerage, taxes, and fees to written premiums plus ratio of loss adjustment, other acquisition, and general administrative expenses to earned premiums.
4. After policyholder dividends.

*Adapted from *Best's Aggregates and Averages; 1983* (Oldwick, NJ: A.M. Best Company, 1983).

Exhibit 2-17
Underwriting Profitability—Workers' Compensation, 1982*

Company	Marketing System[1]	Loss Ratio[2]	Expense Ratio[3]	Underwriting Profit or Loss[4]
Liberty Mutual	O	80.8%	12.8%	6.3%
Aetna Life & Casualty	A	82.8	21.3	— 2.9
Travelers	A	80.4	16.7	2.1
CIGNA	A	71.4	18.7	11.6
Hartford	A	75.0	23.1	1.8
Fireman's Fund	A	68.8	24.6	5.6
Wausau Group	O	73.5	17.3	9.3
Home	A	78.2	19.3	3.3
USF & G	A	83.2	22.1	— 4.7
Crum & Forster	A	68.2	21.8	10.7

1. A indicates independent agency system; O indicates other than independent agency system.
2. Ratio of incurred losses and loss adjustment expense to earned premiums.
3. Ratio of commissions, brokerage, taxes, and fees to written premiums plus ratio of loss adjustment, other acquisition, and general administrative expenses to earned premiums.
4. After policyholder dividends.

* Adapted from *Best's Aggregates and Averages; 1983* (Oldwick, NJ: A.M. Best Company, 1983).

Exhibit 2-18
Underwriting Profitability—Fire Insurance, 1982*

Company	Marketing System[1]	Loss Ratio[2]	Expense Ratio[3]	Underwriting Profit or Loss[4]
St. Paul	A	48.3%	41.2%	11.4%
AIG	A	84.0	39.6	—30.5
Aetna Life & Casualty	A	54.5	49.2	— 0.7
Continental	A	68.7	42.0	— 8.3
Hartford	A	42.9	48.3	11.3
USF & G	A	52.0	41.0	6.7
Crum & Forster	A	65.6	38.1	— 1.9
Allstate	A	62.6	33.4	4.0
CIGNA	A	54.6	47.3	2.2
Home	A	49.6	38.9	16.7
State Farm	O	54.0	31.3	16.4

1. A indicates independent agency system; O indicates other than independent agency system.
2. Ratio of incurred losses and loss adjustment expenses to earned premiums.
3. Ratio of commissions, brokerage, taxes, and fees to written premiums plus ratio of loss adjustment, other acquisition, and general administrative expenses to earned premiums.
4. After policyholder dividends.

*Adapted from *Best's Aggregates and Averages: 1983* (Oldwick, NJ: A.M. Best Company, 1983).

become major factors in the commercial lines. Although they made substantial progress in the 1970s and early 1980s, it is still too early to judge their success. They have not yet demonstrated that they can maintain lower expense ratios in the commercial lines than the independent agency system companies. Their lower expense ratios in the personal lines come primarily from two sources. They pioneered mechanization and mass production in policy issuance and billing. They also reduced compensation paid to producers. Because of their exclusive representation contracts, the exclusive agency and direct writer insurers were also able to pay lower commissions on renewals than on new business. This provided an incentive for their producers to spend more time producing new business.

The exclusive agency and direct writer companies have not yet demonstrated that they can mechanize and mass produce commercial policies or at least that they can do so ahead of the independent agency companies. Neither have they shown that they can reduce producer compensation.

Regulatory restrictions on underwriting prerogatives have not yet been fully applied to commercial lines. It is possible that strict underwriting practices might be applied to produce a lower rate for competitive purposes.

However, as this is written, it is too early to judge the success of the major exclusive agency and direct writer companies in penetrating the commercial lines markets. Indications are that they are enjoying some success, but the final extent of that success remains to be seen.

Chapter Notes

1. Committee on Definitions of the American Marketing Association, *Marketing Definitions* (Chicago: American Marketing Association, 1960), p. 15.
2. National Association of Professional Insurance Agents, Washington, DC.
3. *National Opinion Study: A Profile of Consumer Attitudes Toward Auto and Homeowner's Insurance* (Stevens Point, WI: Sentry Insurance, 1974), pp. 53, 54.
4. *The Auto Insurance Consumer: Patterns and Profiles* (Long Grove, IL: Kemper Insurance Cos., 1975), p. 6.
5. *National Opinion Study: Businessmen's Attitudes Toward Commercial Insurance* (Stevens Point, WI: Sentry Insurance, 1975), p. 39.
6. *How Major Industrial Corporations View Property/Liability Insurance* (New York: Fortune Market Research, 1973), p. 17.
7. Stuart V. d'Adolf, "Profile of the Independent Agent," *Independent Agent* (January 1975), p. 20.
8. Elizabeth M. Wechsler, "Assurex Shuns National Brokerage Image While Fostering Nationwide Newtwork," *Business Insurance*, 28 July 1975, p. 24.
9. *What It Costs*, Ed. Tom McCoy, Indianapolis, IN: Rough Notes, 1983, pp. 8, 9.
10. "An Agent's Guide to Profit Sharing Agreements and Additional Compensation Alternatives," *Independent Agent*, December 1983, p. 53.
11. Stuart V. d'Adolf, p. 21.
12. *The Booz, Allen & Hamilton Report: Research Studies on Direct Billing and Mass Merchandising* (New York: National Association of Insurance Agents, 1971), pp. 16-18.
13. Sam Friedman, "PIA Subsidiary Offers Surety Bonds to Help Agents Get Bank Loans," *National Underwriter*, Property & Casualty Insurance Edition, 28 October 1983, p. 3.
14. Linda Kocolowski, "New Angle on Agency Continuity Problems," *National Underwriter*, Property & Casualty Insurance Edition, 10 June 1983, p. 6.
15. Steven Brostoff, "CNA Hitches Up to Agency Survival," *National Underwriter*, Property & Casualty Insurance Edition, 12 August 1983, p. 36.
16. For a more detailed discussion of this phenomenon and the IIAA's view of it, see Frederick B. Carl, "The Changing Industry," *Independent Agent*, April 1983, p. 37.
17. Stanford Research Institute, *The Stanford Report* (New York: National Association of Insurance Agents, 1967).
18. *The Booz, Allen & Hamilton Report.*
19. Stanley W. Black III, Glenn Brian Canner, and Robert G. King, *The Banking System: A Preface to Public Interest Analysis* (Washington, DC: The Public Interest Economic Center, 1975).
20. Wilkinson, Cragun & Barker, *Study of Insurance Agency Activities of*

Savings and Loan Associations (New York: National Association of Insurance Agents, 1972).

21. "Mid-Year Report on Trust Funds Maintained in the U.S. by Non-Admitted Foreign Carriers," *Weekly Underwriter*, Annual Excess-Surplus Edition, 1983, p. 63.

22. Richard E. Willey, "Surplus Lines—An Optimistic Viewpoint; Market Seen Moving Toward Specialty Products," *National Underwriter*, Property & Casualty Insurance Edition, 11 November 1983, p. 3.

23. The annual statement, also known as the convention form of annual statement, or convention blank, is a comprehensive statement on financial position and results of insurance operations. Insurance statutes in all states require that every insurance company authorized to transact business in the state prepare an annual statement verified under oath by an officer of the company.

24. *Improving the American Agency System* (New York: American Insurance Association, 1979), pp. 5-6.

CHAPTER 3

Developments in Marketing

INTRODUCTION

Marketing methods, in insurance as in other fields, are constantly under review as companies seek new distribution methods and marketing techniques that may reduce costs or enhance the companies' competitive positions. Methods of marketing insurance change more rapidly than marketing methods in most other kinds of business, especially in those businesses which market tangible products. There are several reasons for such rapid changes.

First, insurance marketing is not hampered by the need for extensive physical facilities for the transportation or storage of products. The insurance "product" usually refers to the policy itself, but includes the services which the policy provides. The mail system is the principal transportation system, and only office space is required. An automobile manufacturer illustrates the opposite extreme. It needs extensive physical equipment, such as railroad cars or motor trucks, to transport its products, and its marketing representatives need large storage areas and extensive service facilities. These expensive physical facilities act as a substantial deterrent to major marketing changes.

Second, the insurance industry, unlike most other industries, is characterized by the existence of a large number of suppliers (sellers). There are almost three thousand property and liability insurers in the United States, of which about nine hundred operate in all or almost all states. By way of contrast, there are only four significant producers of private passenger automobiles in the United States. Banking and the construction industry are also characterized by large numbers of sellers, but virtually all are small, local businesses. The existence of a large number of insurers, each seeking its share of the market, fosters experimentation and innovation in insurance marketing.

Finally, the insurance industry is characterized by relative ease of entry. Because of the limited need for physical facilities, an insurance company can be started with less investment than would be required for most manufacturers or retailers with comparable sales. Also, a new insurer need not prove a public need for its services as some other financial corporations are required to do. Each new insurer must find a way to market its products.

The combination of these factors has created a marketing system that is subject to change. One recent change is the growth of mixed marketing systems.

MIXED MARKETING SYSTEMS

Marketing systems have been categorized as (1) independent agency, (2) exclusive agency, (3) direct writer, and (4) direct mail or mail order. A *mixed marketing system* is defined as the simultaneous use of any two or more of the foregoing marketing systems by a single insurer or by a group of insurers under common ownership or management.

Evolution of the Concept

It is not possible to determine the time or place of the first use of a mixed marketing system. Some of the large direct writers of commercial lines have marketed, at least to some degree, through independent brokers for many years. This practice was and is especially prevalent among the direct writers who specialize in workers' compensation insurance, such as Wausau Insurance Companies.

In the mid-1960s, Sentry Insurance, a direct writer, acquired control of Dairyland Insurance Company and its affiliates. Dairyland was and is an independent agency company. The Sentry Group also began to use the independent agency system when it started Sentry Indemnity Company and acquired the Middlesex Insurance Company and its affiliates, which are also independent agency companies.

The entry of the commercial lines direct writers into the independent agency system seems to have attracted relatively little attention. The accounts obtained by the workers' compensation insurers through brokers were very large accounts, mostly large industrial firms. Since those accounts were already controlled by the large brokerage firms, the placement of them with the direct writers apparently did not alarm the independent agent associations.

However, the entry of Allstate Insurance Company into the independent agency system in 1974 stirred considerable resistance among both independent agents and Allstate's own sales force. Allstate's direct writer marketing system had not been able to reach many rural areas and small towns which include an estimated 20 percent of the property and liability insurance market.

In order to reach these areas, the company began appointing independent agents in March 1974. One survey showed that the new Allstate independent agencies were located in towns of five thousand to ten thousand population in trading areas with populations of ten thousand to twenty-five thousand. Most of the agents appointed in the United States are members of the Independent Insurance Agents of America.[1] Allstate also has appointed independent agents in Canada.[2] The independent agents who represent Allstate may also represent other insurers. The Allstate independent agency contract includes the usual provision to grant ownership of expirations to the agent.

More recently, Allstate formed the Northbrook Property and Casualty Insurance Company, a wholly owned subsidiary, to market through the independent agency system. Northbrook agents are not restricted to small towns as the original Allstate independent agencies were.

The movement has not been entirely directed toward the independent agency system. Several independent agency companies have been attempting to become, in part, exclusive agency companies. That is, they have been trying to persuade their agents to limit representation to one insurer or one group of insurers under common ownership or management. The Insurance Company of North America, which claims to have started the independent agency system in 1807, has attracted the most attention in this regard.

INA's exclusive agency arrangement, called One-Compar, grants to the agency the ownership of expirations but requires the agency to represent only INA. In exchange for exclusive representation, INA offers its exclusive agencies (1) assistance in establishing marketing plans, (2) cooperative advertising programs, (3) help in recruiting and training sales personnel, and possibly (4) financial backing.[3] The One-Compar agencies will not have exclusive territories. They will compete with other INA agents as well as with producers for other insurers.

The Continental Insurance Companies also have experimented with single-company representation.[4] One survey of agents attending an association meeting showed that two-thirds of them would be willing to give all of their personal lines business to one insurer if that insurer would agree to provide a stable market and competitive rates.[5]

INA also experimented briefly with mail order selling of automobile insurance. The program provided for a 15 percent reduction in rates and for a 1 percent commission, apparently for countersigning the policies. The direct mail campaign was launched in Indiana in 1972 and later expanded to other states. It immediately stirred a storm of protest among producer organizations.[6]

Early in 1984, the Hartford Insurance Group launched a direct mail campaign to sell personal lines property and liability insurance to members of the American Association of Retired Persons (AARP). The plan has been condemned by the IIAA, which alleges that the program puts the independent agents "in the untenable position of not having equivalent coverage and prices through Hartford."[7]

In spite of the IIAA's condemnation of the Hartford-AARP program, there are signs that the independent agents are beginning to accept company experimentation with mixed marketing systems. An officer of an agent association was quoted as saying:

> I don't know of any insurance company that isn't in some way using direct writing as well as independent agents in their marketing. ... We all have to realize that both companies and agents are cutting back in the interests of their bottom-line profit. You need room to do this and still design innovative marketing programs.[8]

Implications for Consumer, Insurer, and Producer

The implications of mixed marketing systems for the consumer are not completely clear. It seems likely that experimentation with the various marketing methods will result in lower insurance costs for some consumers. However, the lower rates may be obtained through a reduction of service. Many consumers may consider the service of their agents to be worth the difference.

Movement from one form of producer to another, e.g., from independent agent to exclusive agent, may have little effect upon the consumer. Changes in cost are likely to be small, and changes in service will depend primarily upon the capabilities of individual producers and not upon the form of their relationships with their insurer-principals.

The effect upon producers is not much clearer. Movement from independent agent to exclusive agent (or direct writer producer) is likely to result in lower commission rates, but this may be offset, in part or in whole, by increased insurer support in advertising and services. Of course, the exclusive agent or direct writer producer does not have the opportunity, as an independent agent does, to build a large business by employing subproducers or to become part of an even larger firm through merger.

Any major expansion of mail order selling would, of course, reduce the market available to all personal producers. However, it seems unlikely that mail order marketing will ever become the major method of selling even personal lines. It is likely to be even less significant in commercial lines.

Mixed marketing systems give insurers a method for reaching virtually all segments of the market. This provides them with not only the opportunity for greater premium volume but also with the possibility of more stable underwriting results because of the greater diversity of business. These advantages for insurers may be offset to some extent, at least initially, by the dissatisfaction generated by such changes within their existing marketing forces.

CHANGING COMPENSATION ARRANGEMENTS

This section will deal with changing concepts in the compensation of producers in the independent agency system. A comparable treatment for producers in other systems is not practical because of the wide variety of compensation plans and the complexity of such plans used in the other systems. Independent agents and brokers, on the other hand, traditionally have been compensated exclusively on a commission basis.

It has been customary to compensate independent agents by a percentage commission, with the same percentage applying to new and renewal business. In addition, many producers receive a contingent (or profit-sharing) commission if the loss ratio on their business is lower than the objective loss ratio established by the insurer. In contrast with the level commission arrangements of independent agents, most exclusive agency and direct writer insurers pay a lower commission on renewal business than on new business. Also, even their new business commission is frequently lower than the commissions paid to independent agents.

The lower commission scale of most exclusive agent and direct writer insurers has been a major factor in their lower rates for personal lines and therefore a major factor in their competitive success against the independent agency system. The lower renewal commission, in addition to recognizing the lower service requirement of renewal business, has motivated their producers to spend more time soliciting new business.

Independent agency insurers are moving to meet the competition in two ways. First, commission rates are being reduced by some insurers even in the face of strong resistance by producers. Second, independent agency companies and producers are exploring the possibility of adopting a system with lower commissions on renewal.[9]

On the other hand, it has been suggested that the independent agency companies should pay *higher* commissions on renewals than on new business. The purpose of this suggested change is to discourage producers from switching business among companies on renewal, a practice that increases company expenses.[10] Other suggested changes include: (1) graded commission scales, in which the percentage commission decreases as the premium size increases (as in workers' compensation), and (2) higher commission rates for those producers who provide loss adjustment or loss control services or other services usually provided by insurance companies.[11]

Producer remuneration changes for commercial lines are being discussed and considered, and practiced to a limited degree, for another reason. Many risk managers for large commercial and industrial firms believe that remuneration by percentage commissions is inappropriate for two reasons. First, the percentage commission results in producer remuneration which varies with the premium size and not necessarily with the amount of effort required. Second, a producer who recommends measures for reducing the insured's premium automatically reduces the producer's compensation, thus introducing a conflict of interests. It has been suggested, therefore, that producers should be compensated, at least for large commercial lines, by fee, with the fee to be negotiated between the producer and the client on the basis of the time and effort required to handle the client's account. The fee would be paid by the client and not by the insurer.

Some producers already receive some compensation on a fee basis, particularly if they place coverage with an insurer that will not pay them a commission. Also, some producers enter into contracts with clients under which the clients pay them a specified annual fee for managing their insurance programs. The producers then credit any commissions received against the agreed fees, and the clients pay only the balance.

Producers who plan to seek fees from clients should determine the legality of that practice under state law. Surveys of insurance commissioners have indicated that fees are illegal in many states, at least under some circumstances.[12]

COMPUTER NETWORKS

The insurance industry is one of the largest users of computers. They have been used for (1) accounting, (2) statistical analysis and rate making, (3) issuance of policies and endorsements, (4) market research, (5) budgeting and planning, and many other purposes. However, the potential of computers for insurance marketing has hardly been realized.

Present Status

For the purpose of this section, a computer network may be defined as a computer, or quite possibly several computers linked together, which may be accessed by users either on a *real-time* or on a *time-sharing* basis from terminals located away from the computers. Real-time or time-sharing simply means that the user can instruct the computer to do a certain job, and the computer will execute the necessary procedures and give the user the required answer while the user is still on the line. To most persons, a familiar application of a real-time computer network is the airline reservation system. An airline employee at almost any ticket office or airport ticket counter can immediately determine the availability of space on any of the major airlines and confirm a reservation at that time. Many ticket offices are equipped with terminals which even enable the computer to prepare the ticket.

The computer networks now in operation in the insurance industry are not as sophisticated as the airline reservation system. However, several minor networks are in operation. Some of them are sponsored by producer associations, some by insurance companies, and some by private business firms that sell their services to producers.

Producer Associations The network of the Georgia Association of Independent Insurance Agents (GAIIA) can be used to illustrate the association-sponsored networks and the independent system, though there are variations among systems.

Functions performed by the GAIIA computer include (1) preparation of invoices, (2) comparison of automobile rates among insurers represented by the agency using the service, (3) pro-rata and short-rate calculations, (4) premium finance calculations, and (5) accounting.

A computer terminal is located in the office of each subscribing agency and is connected to the central computer system by telephone lines. Necessary information is entered into the computer through the terminal. The operation of the terminal is relatively simple and does not require extensive training.

Because the tasks can be initiated from the terminal, the accounting function is accomplished much quicker than through the older computerized accounting systems. Under the older systems, it was necessary for the producer to mail the accounting records to the computer firm; the records were then converted to computer readable form, such as punched cards; and finally, the necessary invoices and reports were printed out by the computer and mailed back to the producer. The entire process, including mail time, might require a week or more.

In addition to the time factor, the old system also required the agency to duplicate many of its records so that operations could continue while agency records were in the hands of the computer firm. This duplication of records is avoided under the GAIIA network, since necessary data are transmitted almost instantly from the terminal in the agency office.

Of course, the comparison of automobile insurance rates for various companies for a specific applicant was not possible under the older systems because of the delays in mail transmission. Under the GAIIA network, the necessary information can be entered from the terminal in the agency office; the computer prepares a quotation based on the rates for each company in the agency and transmits the quotations back to the terminal in the agency office, all in a matter of a very few minutes.

The computer can also prepare invoices for monthly billings. Such invoices are typed on the terminal in the agency office. The system can also check the producer's accounts receivable records and alert the producer to past due accounts.

Insurer Networks Several insurance companies have established computer networks with terminals in the offices of their larger agencies. The networks differ somewhat in their capabilities. However, some general observations can be made regarding them. In general, the producer can order automobile, homeowners, and dwelling fire policies by typing the necessary information into the computer through the terminal. The computer then rates the policy, prepares the declarations page, and prepares an invoice. The declarations page and invoice may be typed on the terminal in the agency office, or they may be prepared at the company computer center and mailed to the producer or the insured, depending upon the network involved.

The complete policy record also is stored in computer memory and may be retrieved by the producer from the terminal in the agency office. Policy changes also may be initiated from the terminal.

Some insurers are known to be experimenting with the preparation of quotations for commercial multi-peril policies through their computer networks.

As producer firms have grown larger and computer costs have decreased, a substantial number of agency and brokerage offices have purchased computer systems. It is estimated that approximately 5 percent of the independent agency and brokerage offices had some kind of computer system in the fall of 1980, and the number of offices with such equipment was increasing rapidly.[13] A survey conducted in 1983 showed that 19 percent of responding agencies owned computers.[14] It became apparent that much time and paper could be saved if producers' computers could interface (communicate) with insurance company computer systems.

Several insurance companies have developed the necessary systems to permit their computers to interface with the computers in the offices of their agents. In addition to preparing quotations, policies, and invoices, the systems also may be used to prepare sales proposals and to prepare statistical reports for agency management purposes. They also provide a means of rapid communication between producers and companies to facilitate loss adjustment, underwriting, adjustment of billing and accounting problems, and other company-producer relationships.

IIR/ACORD   As the desirability of company-producer computer communication became apparent, many insurance industry executives became concerned about the possibilities that computer networks developed by individual insurance companies might not be compatible with each other. The existence of many noncompatible networks would work a considerable hardship on agency and brokerage offices because each office would need the equipment and expertise to communicate with the systems of all of the companies with which the office deals. The Insurance Institute for Research (IIR) was formed in an attempt to avoid the problems of noncompatible computer networks.

In 1983, IIR was merged with another nonprofit, industry-supported corporation called ACORD (Agency-Company Operations Research and Development). The merger was a natural one since IIR's primary purpose is to guide the development of voluntary standards for computer systems to facilitate communication between producer and company computers, and ACORD's primary purpose is to develop standard forms and procedures to facilitate communications between independent agents and the companies they represent.

IIR/ACORD expects the development of an agency-company computer network to reduce:

1. the time required to communicate forms and messages between producers and companies;
2. errors in forms and messages communicated;
3. telephone communications between producers and companies;
4. storage of forms in agency offices; and
5. the overall time required to complete a transaction.

If these benefits are realized, the network should reduce agency and company expenses and aid the agency-company marketing effort by facilitating transactions and providing the producer with more time for selling.

In 1983, IIR entered into a contract with IBM Information

Network to provide computer network services for its members. The new network is known as IVANS, for Insurance Value-Added Network Services. At the end of 1983, twenty insurance companies and three hundred agencies were connected to the network.

IVANS offers three kinds of memberships. Class A members are insurance companies. They exercise management control of IVANS, receive its services, and are billed directly for the services. Class B memberships are for rating bureaus, credit reporting organizations, and similar entities. They receive IVANS services and are billed directly for the services, but do not exercise any management control over the network. Class C members are agents and brokers. They receive IVANS services but are not billed directly for the services received.[15]

Projections for the Future

The present networks are rather elementary although IVANS has great potential for future development. Far more sophisticated networks can be anticipated in the future.

A network designed by Transystems International (but never actually implemented) can be used to illustrate the possible nature of a future network. It was contemplated that the Transystems network would be available to producers and insurers. In addition, it was hoped that it could be connected to state motor vehicle record offices, reporting bureaus, and rating bureaus.

The computer would be programmed to handle applications and perform rate calculations for virtually all lines of insurance. However, the handling of a private passenger automobile application can be used to illustrate the probable operation of the system.

The producer would enter the information for the application into the computer from the terminal or minicomputer in the agency or brokerage office. The application could then be directed to any insurer or insurers selected by the producer, provided the insurer or insurers were subscribers to the system. An application could even be directed to a specific underwriter within the company.

If an underwriter was interested in writing the applicant, the underwriter could request a motor vehicle report and an inspection report from a credit bureau through the network, and they would be supplied, if available, in a matter of seconds. If the underwriter decided in the affirmative, the producer would be notified through the network. The Transystems network did not have the capability of preparing policies and invoices, but future networks will have that capability. The network also could maintain agency and company policy records and claim records in computer memory for ready access by the producer.

Implications for Consumer, Insurer, and Producer

Computer networks, when they are perfected, will have substantial advantages to all parties involved in insurance marketing, either as buyer or seller. One of the biggest advantages is speed. If enough insurers participate in the network, it will be possible for a producer to shop widely for a market with only a few minutes' delay. This will not only save time for the producer but will also shorten the applicant's wait for coverage. However, this will require that all participating insurers agree to accept the same types of information in a uniform format.

The computer network also should reduce the duplication of records between insurers and producers, since both will have access to the computerized records. This reduction in paperwork should reduce expenses and premiums. Hopefully, the computer network also will reduce errors in the preparation of policies, invoices, and endorsements. However, this advantage may not be realized in the early stages of the network.

There are, of course, substantial barriers to the development of such a network. The start-up costs are high and include the hardware, software, and time required to implement the system. Participating producers and insurers will need to standardize many forms and applications. Computer programs must be developed to enable the network computer to communicate directly with the proprietary computer systems of insurers, producers, rating bureaus, credit bureaus, and other participants. This is a major hurdle because of the wide variety of computer hardware used by the various entities.

The few insurers that have developed their own networks may resist the idea of a general network. They may consider the sales advantages of their proprietary networks too valuable to give up.

Finally, insurers, producers, and other participants must be convinced of the security of their computerized records and assured that such records cannot be accessed by unauthorized persons. The above implications are only a few of the factors to be dealt with in implementing a computer network.

AGENCY FRANCHISE PLANS

There are several reasons for the declining market shares of independent agents and brokers, and at least as many cures for the decline have been suggested. One that has received much attention since the late 1970s is the development of an agency-brokerage franchising organization. The franchising systems are intended to provide services that will permit the independent agents and brokers to compete with the large national brokerage houses, direct writers, and exclusive agency systems. Most of the franchising organizations are concerned primarily with commercial lines, but some emphasize personal lines.

The franchising organizations grant to a selected group of agencies and brokerage firms the right to transact business under a common trade name. This use of a common trade name may be the greatest single advantage of a franchising system if it is properly exploited. As the franchising systems reach maturity, the use of a common trade name will permit effective national advertising to develop national recognition of the trade name.

Many Americans move from one area of the country to another in any given year. If they have purchased their insurance from a national brokerage firm or from a large direct writer or exclusive agency company, they probably can continue to do business with the same firm at their new location. If they are insured by an independent agent or broker, they usually must terminate their relationship with that agent or broker and find a new one at their new location. The use of a nationally recognized trade name should be very helpful to independent agents and brokers in obtaining such business, especially if it is accompanied by a system of referrals among franchise holders in various parts of the country.

The common trade name and joint advertising of franchising organizations can also be useful in selling commercial lines by creating an image of professional skill and performance equal to the skill and performance of the national brokerage houses. Many local agency and brokerage firms already possess the necessary skill to handle complex commercial accounts, but it is difficult for them to project the image of professional skill that is often attributed to the national brokerage firms. This failure in image projection is due in part to their smaller advertising budgets. Joint advertising by franchise holders could help to alleviate this problem.

Some of the franchising firms also provide research and advisory services to assist independent producers in handling the complex problems associated with large commercial accounts. One firm maintains a toll-free telephone line, staffed around the clock, to provide answers for its franchise holders.

Other services offered by one or more of the franchising firms include:

1. agency management assistance and advice;
2. education and training support;
3. assistance in selection and recruiting of producers;

4. national countersignature service;
5. development of mass merchandising programs;
6. computer services;
7. credit card financing of premiums;
8. financial management;
9. national communications network;
10. research and product development; and
11. national advertising and public relations.

One franchising firm (ISU Companies) offers what it calls a "capital value guarantee" program under which a franchise holder can require ISU Companies to purchase the franchise holder's business at an agreed price at any time. However, the agreed price is less than the franchise holder probably could get on the open market. The principal advantage of the guarantee, according to ISU Companies, is to provide a floor for the value of an agency so the principal of the agency can use it as collateral to borrow money from a bank for expansion.

The Cost of a Franchise

There is no standard fee for a franchise. In most cases, the cost of a franchise consists of a flat dollar initial investment plus an agreed percentage of commissions or premiums.

The initial investment amounts appear to vary from $3,000 to $10,000. Thereafter, the cost varies from 2 percent to 6 percent of commissions, depending on the franchising firm selected and the premium volume of the franchised agency or brokerage firm.

Franchising Versus Agent Associations

Some agency trade associations seem to take a rather dim view of franchising because the services provided by franchising firms overlap those provided by the associations. The president of the Independent Insurance Agents of America (IIAA) prepared the comparison shown in Exhibit 3-1, though the form shown here differs slightly from the form in which it was originally published. It is possible, of course, that all franchising firms may not agree with all of the IIAA's analysis, but it does indicate the possible overlap between association services and those provided by franchising firms.

The Future

As this is written (January, 1984), it is too early to assess the future of agency franchising. At least nine firms have announced their

Exhibit 3-1

Comparison of Services of and Obligations to IIAA and Franchising Organizations*

Service	IIAA	Franchisers
Local, state, national affiliation	Yes	No
Representation on board of directors	Yes	No
Federal, state legislative action	Yes	No
National trade magazine	Yes	No
State, local, national communications	Yes	No
State and national conventions (optional)	Yes	No
Applied research	Yes	No
Youth programs (IYC, project In/Vest)	Yes	No
National advertising	Yes	Perhaps
National public relations	Yes	No
Educational programs and seminars	Yes	No
National identification through Big "I" advertising	Yes	Franchise Identified
Representation on Insurance Institute for Research and ACORD	Yes	No
Company contacts of top level	Yes	No
Liaison with industry organizations	Yes	No
Political action committee	Yes	No
Direct voting on leadership	Yes	No
6,000 agents working for you	Yes	No
Obligations		
Term obligation for duration of contract	No	Yes
Contractual obligations	No	Yes
Agency financial disclosure	No	Yes

* Adapted from Robert Reynolds, "President's Page: The Finest in Franchise." *Independent Agent*, December 1980, p. 5.

entry into the field, but the largest has less than a thousand franchisees. The others appear to have even fewer franchisees, and at least two franchising organizations have discontinued operations.

If all of the franchising firms reach their goals, about one-third of the nation's independent agencies and brokerage firms would hold franchises by 1985. However, it is very unlikely that all will succeed to that extent. Most of the franchising firms are interested only in agencies that emphasize commercial accounts. Only one is primarily interested in personal lines agencies. One seeks agencies with balanced books of commercial and personal lines.

Many agents have expressed interest in the franchising concept but have also expressed concern about the high fees required by the franchising firms. This concern may slow the growth of franchising unless the franchising firms either reduce their fees or convince the prospective franchisees that their services are worth the current fees.

THE INSURANCE EXCHANGES

The beginning of the 1980s saw the founding of three organizations that have the potential to bring substantial changes in the American insurance market. They are three insurance exchanges, bearing a resemblance to Lloyd's of London and intended to compete with that organization for the billions of dollars in premiums that it derives from the United States. They are also intended to compete with Lloyd's for business from other countries.

The states of New York, Illinois, and Florida have adopted legislation authorizing the formation of such exchanges, and all three are now in operation (January, 1984).

Like Lloyd's, the three American exchanges will be trading floors, where brokers can contact underwriters to obtain insurance for their clients. Also like Lloyd's, the underwriters will operate through syndicates on the trading floor. Unlike Lloyd's, the underwriters on the American exchanges will not all be natural persons risking their entire fortunes on the business they underwrite. The underwriters on the American exchanges may be corporations, and they are permitted to limit their liability.

At the end of 1983, over forty syndicates were in operation at the New York Insurance Exchange. The Illinois Insurance Exchange had approved eight syndicates. The Insurance Exchange of the Americas, in Florida, had nine syndicates in operation.

New York Insurance Exchange

The New York Insurance Exchange is authorized to write three classes of business:

1. reinsurance of any kind originating anywhere;
2. direct insurance originating outside of the United States; and
3. direct business originating in New York, but only if such business is eligible to be written in the New York Free Trade Zone and has been rejected by insurers operating in the free trade zone.

Note that underwriters at the New York Insurance Exchange cannot write direct business from other states of the United States and can write direct business from New York only if that business is eligible for the free trade zone and has been rejected by insurers operating in the free trade zone. These restrictions place severe limitations on the growth potential of the Exchange, and it is likely that the legislature will remove or amend the limitations in the near future.

New York Free Trade Zone

The New York Free Trade Zone is not a geographic zone, as other free trade zones are. It is merely a section of the New York Insurance Code (Section 168-d) which permits the granting of special licenses to any insurer authorized to transact an insurance business in the state of New York. The special licenses permit the insurers to write two classes of business without being subject to the rate and form regulations applicable to other insurers. Two classes of business are eligible for the free trade zone: (1) accounts that produce at least $100,000 of annual premiums for any one line of insurance or at least $200,000 of annual premiums for all lines of insurance to be written and (2) unusual risks specified in Regulation No. 86 of the New York Insurance Department. There are 305 categories of unusual risks listed in the regulation.

Florida and Illinois Exchanges

The exchanges in Florida and Illinois are not subject to limitations as severe as those imposed on the New York Insurance Exchange. Underwriters at the Illinois Insurance Exchange can write any insurance for which the annual premium is $50,000 or more. Coverages with smaller premiums may be written if the broker certifies that a diligent but unsuccessful attempt has been made to place it with insurers licensed in Illinois. There is no restriction on writing direct business from other states. Underwriters at the Insurance Exchange of the Americas (the Florida Exchange) can write:

1. reinsurance of all kinds of insurance;
2. direct insurance of all kinds originating entirely outside of the United States; and
3. surplus lines insurance eligible for export under the Florida insurance code and written through a licensed surplus lines broker.

This provision is only slightly less restrictive than the comparable New York Law.

Operating Methods

All of the exchanges will operate in a similar manner, though there will be some differences in detail. Any person or firm seeking to buy coverage from the exchange must do so through a broker approved by the exchange to do business on the exchange floor. The New York exchange recognizes two classes of brokers. Broker members are voting members of the exchange and may place business at the exchange either for their own accounts or for the accounts of others. Associate brokers are not voting members of the exchange and can place business at the exchange only for their own accounts. In either case, the broker goes onto the exchange floor and negotiates with the underwriting managers of the various syndicates in an effort to find one or more syndicates willing to provide the needed coverage on acceptable terms.

The exchange corporations provide a trading floor, accounting and data processing services, regulation of underwriting syndicates and brokers, and other services necessary for the efficient functioning of the markets. The exchange corporations are not insurers: all insurance is provided by the various syndicates at the exchanges.

MASS MERCHANDISING AND GROUP MARKETING

The term *mass merchandising* encompasses a wide variety of marketing methods, but they are all characterized by efforts to sell insurance, either personal lines or commercial lines, to individual purchasers whose only relationship is membership in a common organization. While mass merchandising is the generally accepted term for this marketing method, quasi-group marketing would seem to be more descriptive because of the strong resemblance to group marketing techniques used in connection with life and health insurance. The name collective merchandising also has been used to describe this method of selling.

The Nature of Mass Merchandising

There are no generally accepted definitions for mass merchandising or quasi-group marketing. However, the definitions shown below categorize the existing *personal lines* plans according to their major variants.

Basic Concepts Because of inherent differences in personal lines and commercial lines, slightly different definitions are used. Personal lines programs are categorized according to (1) the method of premium collection, (2) the restrictions, if any, on the underwriting prerogatives of the insurer, and (3) the effect of the plan on the cost of insurance to participants.

Franchise merchandising is a plan for insuring a number of employees of an employer under a single plan of insurance with premiums payable by payroll deduction without any reduction in premiums but with the insurer retaining the right of individual underwriting selection.

Mass merchandising is a plan for insuring a number of otherwise independent purchasers of insurance under a single program of insurance at premiums lower than those charged for similar loss exposures for persons who are not members of the program, but with the insurer retaining the right of individual underwriting selection.

Group marketing is a plan for insuring a number of otherwise independent purchasers of insurance under a single program of insurance with guaranteed issue, without individual underwriting selection or individual proof of insurability, and at premiums lower than those charged for similar loss exposures for persons not participating in such programs.

Franchise merchandising programs, which were once quite common, have now become rare. They have been replaced by mass merchandising programs and, in a few instances, by group marketing programs. In general, such programs have been provided most often for employees of a single employer or for members of a labor union. However, some plans have been written for members of social organizations or for customers of a specified business firm, such as a credit card issuer, a public utility, or a credit union.

The foregoing definitions do not apply to commercial lines marketing. Franchise marketing, as defined, would be meaningless for commercial lines programs; and at the time of this writing, the authors are not aware of any commercial lines programs that have been written on a guaranteed issue basis. Consequently, all known programs in the commercial lines area would fall into the mass merchandising category as defined in this chapter. Unfortunately, within the industry, a mass merchandising program is variously referred to as "commercial group," "association/franchise," or "commercial mass marketing."

Commercial lines programs can be categorized as *trade association plans* and *safety group plans*. Under a trade association plan, any member firm of the trade association would be eligible to participate provided it meets the insurer's underwriting requirements. Safety group plans usually are not restricted to the members of a trade association but are available to any firm in the selected industry, provided the firm meets the insurer's underwriting requirements and agrees to undertake a loss control program specified by the insurer. For example, a trade association plan written for a state restaurant association would be available only to members of that associaton and only to those members which meet the underwriting standards of the insurer. On the other hand, a safety group plan for restaurants would be available to any restaurant in the state which (1) meets the insurer's underwriting standards and (2) agrees to adopt the loss control program specified by the insurer. Membership in the trade association would not be a requirement for participation in the safety group program. However, adoption of a loss control program may also be required as a condition of participation in a trade association program.

Comparison to True Group Insurance Mass merchandising or quasi-group marketing of property and liability insurance, as practiced up to the present time, differs somewhat from true group insurance as exemplified by group life and health insurance.

Under quasi-group property and liability insurance plans, the insurer usually reserves the right to refuse coverage or to charge a higher rate for an insured whose loss exposures are more severe than anticipated for its rating class. In group life and health insurance, this right to refuse coverage is generally not reserved by insurers, except for very small groups. There are several reasons for this difference.

First, it is customary for the employer to pay at least a part of the premium for group life and health insurance, thus encouraging employees to participate in the plan and reducing adverse selection. It is not now customary for employers to pay property and liability insurance premiums, though some employers do so.

Second, most group life and health insurance plans require the participation of at least 75 percent of eligible persons. Quasi-group property and liability plans generally do not include such a requirement, and most of them do not reach that proportion of participation.

Third, group life and health insurance plans usually restrict the amount of coverage for a participant either to a stated amount or to an amount determined by a rigid formula, frequently related to the participant's income. Quasi-group property and liability plans do not place such restrictions on the amount of insurance a participant can purchase, and it is doubtful that such restrictions are practical. If the coverage under a group life or health plan is inadequate for the needs of a participant, additional coverage can be obtained from other sources without adverse effect on the group coverage, assuming that the participant can show insurability. However, clauses of some automobile and homeowners policies may result in reduced coverage if two policies are carried with different insurers. For example, if the participant owns two cars and insures both of them with the same insurer, there will be automatic coverage if the participant acquires an additional car. If the cars are insured with different insurers, there is no automatic coverage. The resulting gap may be covered by endorsement, however.

Fourth, the requirement of group life and health plans that the employee be on the job when coverage becomes effective imposes at least a minimum health requirement. However, the fact that an employee is able to be on the job gives very little assurance of underwriting acceptability from the standpoint of automobile or homeowners insurance.

Finally, group life and health insurers look for groups with a steady influx of younger workers because such workers generally have lower loss exposures under life and health insurance. On the other hand, younger people tend to have higher loss exposures for automobile insurance. The property and liability insurer, however, may minimize this by seeking groups with a "stable" mature work force.

These differences in coverages and loss exposures dictate a somewhat different approach to the group and mass merchandising of personal lines property and liability insurance from that used in group life and health insurance. Experience to date, coupled with the current income tax status and some lack of interest by labor unions, suggests that some major problems exist in the mass merchandising of personal lines property and liability insurance. However, these problems may be overcome, and group automobile and homeowners insurance may become available wherever employers are willing to reduce adverse selection by paying at least a part of the premium for such coverages.

Regulatory Aspects Historically, the regulatory climate has been unfavorable toward group and mass marketing of either personal lines or commercial lines of property and liability insurance, though it has become more favorable since 1971.

Initially, regulatory authorities prohibited mass merchandising on the ground that it was unfairly discriminatory against those persons or firms who were not eligible to participate in such plans. According to the regulators, the plans were unfairly discriminatory because a participant could obtain insurance at a cost lower than that available to a nonparticipant with a similar loss exposure. It was the generally accepted theory among regulators at that time that rating classifications could not be based on *expense* differences but only on differences in *loss* exposure.

Beginning in 1956, several state insurance commissioners issued so-called fictitious grouping regulations designed to prohibit mass merchandising of property and liability insurance. An investigation in 1969 and 1970 by the Subcommittee on Antitrust and Monopoly of the United States Senate called attention to the regulatory prohibitions against mass merchandising of property and liability insurance.[16] Thereafter, the regulatory climate became more favorable, though most of the fictitious grouping statutes and regulations remained on the books.

In June of 1969, while the Senate investigation was still in progress, the National Association of Insurance Commissioners (NAIC) released a report that encouraged experimentation with mass merchandising and group merchandising of automobile insurance.[17] In 1971, the NAIC released a staff report that was even more favorable to mass merchandising.[18]

The regulatory situation has continued to improve until at least some form of mass merchandising now seems to be legal in every state.

Description of Present Mass Merchandising Plans

Mass merchandising plans vary rather widely, so those that are described in the following paragraphs should be considered illustrative rather than typical.

Personal Lines   While homeowners policies, personal umbrella policies, and other personal lines have been offered through mass merchandising programs, the principal activity has dealt with automobile insurance. In most cases, the policies used have been standard family automobile policies or the same special package automobile policies offered through the usual marketing channels.

In a few cases, policies have been amended to coordinate coverage with group medical insurance policies provided by the employer. Such amendments usually consist of making automobile medical payments coverage excess over the group medical insurance benefits. In most cases, the employer does not pay any of the premium but does collect it through payroll deduction and forward it to the insurer. A few cases have been written in which the employer pays a part of the premium. In such cases, the employer's premium payments are deductible by the employer for income tax purposes, but they constitute taxable income to the employee. This is in contrast with premiums for group health and life insurance, which generally are not taxable income to the employee.

Premiums under mass merchandised automobile insurance plans are generally somewhat less than premiums charged by the same company for individually marketed policies. The reductions usually are in the range of 5 percent to 15 percent, though greater reductions have been reported in some cases. The premium reduction results from reduction in commissions to producers, premium collection expenses, and possibly other minor expenses. Producer commissions may range from as low as 2 percent, if the insurance company does all the service work and soliciting of individual group members, to a high of about 8 percent if the agent solicits and services the members. Some insurers have claimed that mass merchandising, because of the large number of insureds in one place, enables them to reduce claims through loss control programs. However, no evidence of such reductions has been made public.

Solicitation of group members is a major factor in building participation in mass merchandising plans, and high participation is necessary in order to avoid adverse selection. Solicitation may be handled in several ways. Insurance company or producer personnel may solicit employees on the premises of the employer or by telephone. In some cases, solicitation has been handled by direct mail. Personal solicitation is probably most effective but is also most expensive. Employees generally cannot be enrolled in the plan by the employer as they are for group health and accident insurance, because most state laws prohibit the sale of property and liability insurance by any person not licensed as an insurance agent or broker. Brief descriptions of some existing plans will illustrate a few of the variations.

At least one insurer mass merchandises automobile insurance through credit unions. Solicitation is handled primarily through direct mail, though some experimentation has been conducted with personal solicitation in large credit unions. Premiums are collected by the credit unions through deduction from the member's credit union account.

Another insurer mass merchandises automobile insurance to the employees of its parent organization that is not an insurer. The parent organization pays one dollar per week per employee toward the automobile insurance premium and collects the balance by payroll deduction. Solicitation is handled by company employees. The insurer reserves the right to refuse coverage to individual employees, but the right is exercised very infrequently.

One of the most successful large personal lines mass merchandising programs is that of a major airline. The airline does not pay any of the premiums, but it does collect them by payroll deduction and forward them to the insurer. The plan has been promoted vigorously through its employee magazine, payroll stuffers, and other media.

The broker for the account maintains a staff to solicit employees, both in person and by telephone. The brokerage office is connected to the airline's national telephone system and may call any employee nationally on that system. About two-thirds of eligible employees have at least one policy under the program. In addition to automobile insurance, they can purchase homeowners, umbrellas, boat coverage, and even aircraft coverage under the plan.

Commercial Lines   Commercial lines mass marketing programs are much more varied than personal lines programs. Some commercial lines programs are restricted to a single line of insurance, such as workers' compensation. Others encompass most or all of the lines required by participating firms.

The *safety group dividend plan* was among the earliest forms of commercial lines mass merchandising. Under this plan, the members of the group may receive a dividend from the insurer at the end of the policy term. The amount of the dividend will depend upon the loss experience of the *group*, and there may be no dividend at all if the loss experience of the group is unsatisfactory.

The New York Insurance Department issued a circular letter on October 22, 1959, setting forth the requirements for safety group dividend plans in that state. The requirements are

1. the dividend must remain within the discretion of the insurer's board of directors and cannot be guaranteed;
2. the method of calculating the dividend must be filed with and approved by the superintendent of insurance;
3. the group must be open to all eligible firms and not restricted to members of a trade association;
4. a safety program must be spelled out as a part of the safety group dividend plan;
5. eligibility must be limited to those classes of firms for which the loss experience can be affected significantly by the safety program;
6. records must be maintained regarding activities related to the safety program; and
7. appropriately detailed financial and experience records must be maintained for each group.

A reasonably typical safety group dividend plan provides workers' compensation and general liability insurance for restaurants. The extensive experience of the insurer with restaurant exposures has enabled its loss control department to develop effective safety programs.

When an eligible restaurant expresses an interest in the program, a loss control engineer is sent to make an inspection of the premises. If the restaurant meets the insurer's underwriting standards, or the owner is willing to make the recommended changes to meet its standards, it is admitted to the program. Thereafter, it is inspected at least twice each year and more often if necessary. There is also a constant flow of safety material from the insurer to members of the group. Individual claims are analyzed by the insurer's loss control department to determine their safety implications.

The group elects a management committee composed of representatives of member firms. The committee has the authority to recommend termination of any restaurant that fails to comply with safety recommendations of the insurer.

All policies issued under the program have a common expiration date to facilitate dividend determination. The experience is reviewed six months after the end of the policy term, and the dividend, if any, is declared by the board of directors of the insurance company. The amount of the dividend varies with (1) the amount of premium under the program and (2) the loss experience of the group. Over a period of several years, the dividends under the program have averaged about 20 percent of earned premiums.

Analysis of Existing Plans

Existing mass merchandising plans can be examined from at least five viewpoints: (1) the consumer, (2) the sponsor, (3) the producer, (4) the insurer, and (5) labor unions. The consumer may be either an individual (for personal lines) or a business firm (for commercial lines). Labor unions are concerned primarily with personal line plans.

The Consumer's Viewpoint The principal interest of the consumer in mass merchandising plans, whether personal or commercial, is in the potential reduction of insurance costs. As noted earlier, mass merchandised automobile insurance can result in reductions of up to 15 percent, or possibly more in some cases. Dividends of 20 percent to 25 percent for commercial mass merchandising programs are reported frequently. However, some commercial lines plans have failed to produce substantial savings as a result of poor loss experience.

Personal lines mass merchandising or group plans may provide for the employer to pay a part of the premium, thus resulting in even greater savings for the employee. However, under present federal tax laws, amounts paid by the employer for the property and liability insurance premiums are considered taxable income to the employee.

One consumer survey showed that 39 percent of automobile policyholders would prefer a group program to individual coverage if the group program provided a 10 percent reduction in premium. The percentage preferring group coverage increased as the annual premium size increased, reaching 45 percent for persons with annual premiums of $400 or more. Also, 43 percent of those with annual incomes of $15,000 or more preferred the group plan, as did 46 percent of those aged thirty to forty-nine, inclusive.[19] The proportion who would prefer group homeowners coverage (with the same 10 percent premium reduction) was only slightly lower, at 35 percent.[20]

Interestingly, those persons in the same survey who had unsatisfactory experiences with automobile insurance claims were more favorable toward group insurance, with 75 percent positive replies.[21] This points up another possible advantage to the consumer. The increased bargaining power of the group, as compared to that of an individual, may help the participants obtain more favorable treatment in claims and underwriting as well as pricing. While insurers retain the right to refuse coverage to an individual under most mass merchandising plans, pressure from the employer, or other sponsor, can be expected to minimize the number of instances in which the right is exercised.

A third advantage to the consumer is the payment of premiums by payroll deduction. This method of premium payment amounts to a monthly, or possibly more frequent, payment plan, usually without a finance charge.

It is also possible that the insurer and producer under a commercial lines mass merchandising plan might be in a better position to provide specialized risk management advice because of their greater exposure to the specific class of business insured under the program. For example, an insurer and producer who are engaged in marketing a mass merchandising plan for, say, motels could be expected to become more familiar with the loss exposures and loss control measures of the motel business than other insurers or producers who only insure an occasional motel. This kind of specialization is less significant for personal lines, however.

Finally, it is possible that the consumer, especially the commercial lines consumer, may be able to obtain coverage under a mass merchandising program which would not be available on an individual basis.

Of course, there are also disadvantages to mass merchandising. The plan may be terminated by either the employer (or other sponsor) or the insurer, leaving the consumer without coverage. If the termination occurs during a period of tight insurance markets and if the insurer does not offer to convert the policy to an individual basis, the consumer may have difficulty finding replacement coverage.

The consumer may lose some flexibility in insurance planning. Depending upon the program specifications, there may not be as many options under the plan as there would be on an individual basis.

Under personal lines programs, there is the possibility that the employer may obtain personal information about the employee as a result of the plan. For example, the underwriting process might disclose that the employee has an alcohol problem or some other problem which the employee would prefer that the employer not know about. However, this would rarely happen unless the employee rigorously pursues a cancellation or nonrenewal.

The Sponsor's Viewpoint The sponsor of a mass merchandising plan (the employer, labor union, trade association, and so forth) also gains some advantages from the plan at the cost of some disadvantages.

The principal advantage to an employer is the increased loyalty and improved morale of the work force. While these factors are difficult to measure, it is widely held that employee benefit plans, including mass merchandised property and liability insurance, result in lower employee turnover and probably result in greater productivity.

One survey of risk managers showed that 83 percent of the risk managers employed by companies that provided mass merchandised automobile insurance thought the program was either a very good idea or a good idea.[22] Reasons given for favoring the concept included: (1) employer offers an employee benefit for little or no employer cost; (2) employee saves money; (3) payment made easier through payroll deduction; and (4) improves employer-employee relations. In total, eighty-six respondents, or 9 percent, provided automobile insurance for employees.

Mass merchandised automobile insurance was considered a very good idea or a good idea by only 31 percent of risk managers of companies not currently providing such plans.[23] Reasons given for unfavorable replies included (1) possible assumption of part of cost by employer; (2) creation of administrative problems and costs; (3) involvement of employer in claim or policy disputes; and (4) strain on employee-employer relations.

Another survey showed that 11 percent of respondents among the top five hundred industrial corporations already provide mass merchandised automobile insurance, and an additional 10 percent were actively considering it. Of the same group, 3 percent provided homeowners coverage and 6 percent were actively considering it.[24] Of respondents from the second five hundred industrial corporations, 4 percent were providing automobile insurance and 6 percent were actively considering it. One percent were providing homeowners insurance and 3 percent were actively considering it.[25]

A survey of smaller firms, mostly in the range of from one hundred to five hundred employees, showed that 9 percent provided automobile insurance and 1 percent were actively considering it. One percent of respondents provided homeowners insurance and less than 0.5 percent were actively considering it.[26]

It would appear from these surveys that the majority of employers do not favor providing mass merchandised property and liability insurance for their employees. However, a substantial minority does tend to favor such plans, and a significant minority is now furnishing such programs. A much smaller minority now pays at least part of the premium for employees.

It is interesting to note that the first survey showed that 46 percent of those respondents not then providing automobile insurance for employees expected to provide such coverage in the future.[27]

There have not been any published surveys to reveal the attitudes of trade associations toward commercial lines mass merchandising plans. However, the principal advantage of such plans to trade associations is their ability to attract new members and help retain existing ones. Also, in a few cases, the association may receive some compensation from the insurer for services provided in connection with the program. The major disadvantage is the possible dissatisfaction of members because of disputes about claims, premiums, or other facets of the program. Dissatisfaction is almost certain to result if the anticipated savings fail to materialize because of bad loss experience.

The Producer's Viewpoint   There seem to be several producer viewpoints, depending upon the kind of business transacted by the producer. The Independent Insurance Agents of America and its state affiliates have opposed the development of mass merchandising with varying degrees of aggressiveness since at least 1925, when Chrysler Motor Company launched the first significant effort to mass merchandise automobile insurance. The National Association of Professional Insurance Agents and its state affiliates, though joining the fight somewhat later, have opposed mass merchandising at least as vigorously.

The fictitious grouping regulations and statutes mentioned earlier were adopted and enforced primarily because of lobbying by producer organizations. The opposition of producer organizations was based on three fears. First, they feared that the spread of mass merchandising would enable the direct writer companies, exclusive agency companies, and large national brokerage firms to compete more effectively for the personal lines and small to medium commercial lines that constitute the major business of the local agents. Second, the commission rates for mass merchandised insurance usually are substantially lower than for individual policies. The producers felt that they could not survive on such low commissions. Finally, there were concerns that the expansion of mass merchandising would undermine their ownership of expirations.

The first of these fears probably was more justified than the others. The national brokerage firms historically have not been interested in writing personal lines or small to medium commercial lines. Their traditional market has been the large commercial and industrial accounts. However, some national brokers were and are interested in mass merchandising both personal lines and smaller commercial lines.

The reasons for the interest of national brokerage firms in mass merchandising were partly defensive and partly offensive. They were beginning to reach the limits of expansion in their traditional markets and needed to find new markets if they were to continue to grow at a rapid pace. Since they were already providing property and liability insurance and employee benefit plans for many of the nation's largest corporations, it seemed natural to expand into selling personal lines insurance by payroll deduction to the employees of those corporations. They had already established working relationships with the corporations and had established the facilities for administering group life and health insurance, facilities which could be modified for mass merchandising. Defensively, they deemed it desirable to be the first to offer automobile and homeowners insurance to their existing accounts. Another producer who provided such coverages might use them as a competitive lever to write other coverages for the account.

The national branch office systems of the large brokerage houses also made them strong competitors for mass merchandised commercial lines. These branch office systems were expanded greatly in the 1960s and early 1970s by mergers with and acquisitions of many local agencies. Thus, the large brokerage firms are able to solicit and service mass merchandised commercial lines business over a wide geographic area. Most agency firms are local in nature and cannot provide solicitation or service over a wide area.

The direct writers and exclusive agency companies proved to be less of a threat than originally believed. Because of opposition of their own producers, or because such programs do not fit into their marketing network, most of them have not become extensively involved in mass merchandising. They could become a substantial force if they chose to do so, however, because of their large, widespread, and closely directed sales organizations.

The commission rates on mass merchandising have been inching upward during the past few years, while commission rates for individual policies have been inching downward. The differences between them are not as great as they were. In addition, the lower percentage commission on mass merchandised business may produce more commission dollars for a producer because of the greater premium volume produced.

Ownership of expirations is a matter of contract between producer and insurer. Contract changes and clarifications seem to have reduced the concern of producers on this score.

Many producers across the country have seized upon mass merchandising as a way to expand their business. They have not been able to compete successfully with the national brokers for the personal lines accounts of the largest corporations, but they have been able to compete successfully for the smaller accounts and for local and state government employees. By joining national networks of independent agencies, the local producers have been able to compete quite effectively for mass merchandised commercial lines.

Though they may differ in detail, all mass merchandising programs operate in essentially the same way. Each consists of two components: a central organization and a network of affiliated producers. Either an affiliated producer or the central organization finds a trade association or franchising organization that is interested in providing an insurance program for its members or franchise holders. The central organization, in cooperation with an insurance company, prepares the necessary policy forms, rating plans, and promotional materials. The insurance company makes any necessary filings of policy forms, rating plans, or dividend plans with the states in which the program will be offered. The central organization manages the advertising and promotional campaign in cooperation with the sponsoring organization (trade association or franchising organization), advises its affiliated producers of prospects in their territories, and follows up to see that the prospects are contacted. Underwriting, policy issuance, and similar functions may be performed by either the central organization or the insurer.

Most of the mass merchandising organizations provide only closed plans in which only member or affiliated agencies may solicit and write coverages under the plan. However, some insurance companies operate commercial lines mass merchandising plans for which any licensed agent or broker can solicit business. One list of open group plans for workers' compensation included over two hundred groups.[28] Most of them were state or regional groups on the West Coast, but about a quarter of them were national in scope.

The Insurer's Viewpoint Mass merchandising offers several advantages to insurers, especially for independent agency companies. The major advantage is the reduction in operating expenses, primarily commissions, which will enable the independent agency companies to compete effectively with the direct writer and exclusive agency companies.

Also, mass merchandising may offer insurers a means to reverse a loss of personal lines market share or provide an opportunity to increase it.

Mass merchandising enables an insurer to sell large amounts of business in an organized manner and thus speed up growth with some degree of control. By first "underwriting the group," (personal or commercial), the insurer can increase the probability that the individual policyholders will be acceptable.

Also, by obtaining a spread of business in a selected field of commercial enterprises, the insurer is able to become more familiar with the exposures of its policyholders. This familiarity is especially helpful in loss control activities but also will be helpful in policy design, underwriting, claims handling, and the providing of risk management advice.

However, there are also disadvantages from the insurer's standpoint. The reduction in commissions under mass merchandising plans has alienated some producers, though it appears that this problem has become less serious in recent years.

While mass merchandising enables an insurer to acquire large blocks of business in a relatively short time, it may result in losing large blocks of business in an even shorter time. If the sponsor becomes dissatisfied with existing service, or is offered a better program or a better price, it may shift the entire program to another insurer. This may result in some instability in the insurer's premium volume and growth.

The insurer's underwriting, and consequently its profit, may suffer. While most mass merchandising plans permit the insurer to cancel or refuse coverage to an individual member, pressure from the sponsor may limit the insurer's ability to do so. Also, there is a tendency for those who are below average to apply for insurance under the plan first because they are unable to obtain coverage on desirable terms elsewhere. This adverse selection, coupled with limitations on the insurer's underwriting prerogatives and lower rates, may result in underwriting losses, especially in the early development of a program.

Finally, a substantial amount of expense is involved in the development and promotion of a mass merchandising plan. Much of this expense is borne by the insurer, though the producer or mass merchandising organization may bear part of it, and there is always a danger that the program may be discontinued or moved to another insurer before the expenses can be recovered.

The Labor Union's Viewpoint   During the early years of mass merchandising, labor unions expressed considerable interest in providing automobile and homeowners programs for their members. Such plans would be logical additions to the life and health insurance and pension plans they presently provide.

Some automobile insurance plans were established by unions at the local level, and some employer-sponsored plans were established pursuant to union negotiatons. However, labor unions have been a relatively minor factor in mass merchandising of property and liability insurance up to the present time.

One reason for the lack of interest on the part of unions is the unfavorable tax treatment of mass merchandised property and liability insurance in relation to other employee benefit plans.

Employer contributions to group life and health insurance and pensions are not considered taxable income to employees under present federal income tax laws, though pension benefits are taxable after retirement. However, employer contributions for premiums for property and liability insurance are taxable income to employees. Consequently, the unions can provide greater after-tax benefits for the same employer contribution by negotiating increases in group life and health insurance and pensions than they can by establishing automobile and homeowners insurance plans.

Future Trends

Mass merchandising suffered a setback in the mid-1970s. Personal lines programs were affected most seriously, but commercial lines programs were also affected.

Poor underwriting results on all classes of business, mass merchandised and individual, coupled with adverse stock market developments, reduced insurers' surpluses and forced them to reduce premium volume or slow growth. Mass merchandising was still in an experimental and developmental stage and therefore relatively less profitable in many cases. Consequently, it was a good place to cut.

Several insurers have withdrawn entirely from mass merchandising, and others have terminated many individual plans. However, other insurers have remained active in mass merchandising.

Several insurers have developed group automobile insurance plans without reservation of the right to refuse or cancel coverage for an individual participant. Such plans are now being offered on a limited basis to those employers who are willing to pay part or all of the premium for their employees. It seems likely that such plans will become popular in the future.

Commercial lines mass merchandising continues to expand, though at a slower pace than in the early seventies. Again, the pace is likely to increase when insurer profits and surpluses improve. Some observers have estimated that as much as 25 to 30 percent of commercial lines policyholders will eventually be served by mass merchandising programs. However, such figures are projected far into the future.

CAPTIVE INSURERS AND RETENTION PLANS

The formation of captive insurers has been one of the most interesting and most publicized insurance phenomena of the last decade. The increase in self-insurance, though less spectacular, also has been substantial. Self-insurance is really a form of retention, but the term has been widely used as a synonym for retention. In this text, the term retention will be used. The risk management and regulatory aspects of captives and retention have been discussed at length in other assignments of the CPCU program. The paragraphs that follow are limited to the implications for insurance marketing.

Effect on the Insurance Industry

Captive insurers affect the insurance industry in four major ways:

1. by writing some or all of the insurance needed by their parent companies;
2. by competing with the industry for other commercial or personal lines business;
3. by reinsurance transactions; and
4. by providing a market for services.

Risk retention programs affect the insurance industry in the first and fourth ways mentioned.

No completely accurate figures are available to indicate the amount of U.S. premium written by captive insurers, but a report by the Bermuda government indicated that captive insurance companies headquartered there wrote premiums of $5.2 billion in 1982.[29] (Of course, all Bermuda-based captives are not owned by U.S. interests.) Most of the captives are owned by a single corporation or a group of corporations under common management, but some of them are owned by groups of corporations that are otherwise unrelated.

Some of the captives provide coverages (such as strike insurance) which are not available through normal insurance marketing channels. Those captives have little or no effect on insurance marketing unless they purchase reinsurance or services from the industry.

The other *pure* captives (which provide insurance only for their owners) are in competition with the insurance industry for the kinds of coverage they write. They may, of course, offset part of the loss of direct premiums by buying reinsurance or services from the industry.

The insurance industry is affected most by *profit center* captive insurers—those that provide insurance to their owners and sell coverages to other policyholders. For example, one captive offers reinsurance to other insurers here and abroad. It sells insurance coverages to other commercial and industrial firms besides its parent. Another parent company has established a captive that is expected to insure both its parent and other nonrelated firms as well as provide reinsurance for other insurers. Many other examples could be cited.

These profit center captives may affect the insurance industry in all four of the ways mentioned above. Of course, it is quite possible that the coverages written by the captive for its parent companies would be retained by the parent if the captive did not exist.

Risk retention also has grown rather rapidly in recent years. A survey of members of the Risk and Insurance Management Society, Inc. (RIMS) showed an expanded use of deductibles and self-insurance. The extent of retention among respondents follows.[30]

	Percent of Respondents	
	Property	*Liability*
Self-insurance	*68%*	*45%*
Deductibles	*84%*	*54%*

The Product Liability Risk Retention Act of 1981, usually referred to as the Risk Retention Act, makes it easier for organizations with products liability exposures to use alternative methods to finance their losses.

First, the Act provides for the formation of *risk retention groups*. A risk retention group is a captive insurer formed by several organizations to cover the products liability losses of those organizations. A risk retention group need meet the chartering requirements of only one jurisdiction and the capitalization requirements of only one state. This eliminates the need for a qualifying captive to meet the duplicative or conflicting requirements of a variety of states, and thus helps provide an expedient alternative to commercial insurance.

Second, the Act provides for *purchasing groups*—groups of people or businesses that have as one of their purposes the purchase, on a group basis, of product liability or completed operations insurance, either separately or together with comprehensive general liability insurance. Groups may be able to negotiate more favorable insurance terms than individual insureds.

Many pure captives are likely to enter aggressively into the insurance market in direct competition with traditional insurers. Revenue Rulings 77-316 and 78-277 held that captive insurers that insure only their parents are not insurance companies for tax purposes and that premiums paid to such captives by their parents are not deductible expenses to the parents for income tax purposes. Internal Revenue Ruling 78-338 held that a captive insurer jointly owned by thirty-one unrelated corporations (with no one of the parents accounting for more than 5 percent of the captive's premiums) was an insurance company, and premiums paid to it were deductible expenses. These rulings have encouraged captives to solicit business from firms other than their parent or affiliated firms. Several captives have already entered the marketplace for nonparent business, and some of them have been quite successful in writing such business.

The loss of premium to captives and retention plans will be offset to some degree by the sale of services to them. Several insurers are aggressively marketing their loss control, loss adjustment and management services to self-insurers and captive companies. Contracts under which an insurer provides services only, without insurance protection, are sometimes referred to as administrative services only (for ASO) contracts.

Providing reinsurance and fronting services to captives also may enable traditional insurers to recoup some of the income lost to captives. Under a reinsurance contract, the captive would write the business and then transfer all or a part of it to another insurance company. Reinsurance methods are discussed at length in Chapters 7 and 8 of this book. Some Bermuda captives have formed a reinsurance exchange to reinsure each other, thus competing with the traditional insurers for the reinsurance income.[31]

Fronting might be considered as the inverse of traditional reinsurance arrangements. Under traditional reinsurance arrangements, the business is controlled by the insurer that originally writes it, and that company determines how much, if any, of it will be reinsured and with what company or companies it will be reinsured. Under a fronting arrangement, the captive insurer or its parent company controls the business and arranges for a licensed insurer to write the business directly and to service it, but the licensed insurer (the fronting company) is required to transfer an agreed part (possibly all) of the business to the captive insurer. The fronting company receives a fronting fee to cover its expenses and a profit. The fronting fee should also be sufficient to cover the increased obligation of the fronting company under FAIR plans, automobile insurance plans, and similar residual market plans if the fronted business increases its obligations under such plans.

To illustrate a fronting operation, assume that Giant Industrial Corporation has formed a captive insurance company, Giant Indemnity and Reinsurance Company, Ltd., headquartered in Bermuda. Giant Industrial wants to place its workers' compensation coverage with Giant Indemnity, but it cannot do so because state law requires workers' compensation coverage to be written by an insurer licensed in the state. Giant Indemnity cannot qualify or does not want to qualify for a license.

Giant Industrial enters into a contract with Quaking Casualty Company, a licensed insurer, under which Quaking agrees to write Giant Industrial's workers' compensation coverage and to reinsure all of it with Giant Indemnity. Quaking is to receive a fee of 18 percent of premiums for its fronting services. Quaking also provides loss adjustment and loss control services as required.

The increasing competition from captives and retention plans also is likely to result in greater use of paid loss retrospective rating plans by traditional insurers. These plans, which are discussed in greater detail in Chapter 10 of this book, provide most of the cash flow advantage of captive insurers and retention plans while retaining most of the advantages of traditional insurance arrangements.

Selling reinsurance and services to captives and self-insurers will help offset the loss of income to them. However, it seems almost inevitable that the growth of the traditional insurers will be slowed by the continued development of these risk treatment techniques.

CAPTIVE AGENCIES

The use of captive insurance agencies by commercial and industrial firms has received less attention than the use of captive insurers. A substantial number of such agencies are known to exist. A captive insurance agency is an agency formed primarily to handle the insurance needs of its parent company. However, many of them also sell insurance to others.

Reasons for Use

One of the major reasons for the use of a captive agency is expense reduction. The profits earned by the agency on the commissions from the business of the parent can be used to reduce the cost of the insurance program. If the agency also sells to firms other than the parent, the profits from this business would be received by the parent.

A number of trade associations also have established captive agencies to provide insurance advice and coverage for member firms. Franchising firms, which sell franchises to restaurants, motels, and other businesses, have formed captive agencies to sell insurance to franchise holders. In the case of trade associations and franchising firms, the profits from the agency may go to the association or franchising firm rather than to the association member or franchise holder.

The establishment of a captive agency is, of course, much easier and much less expensive than the establishment of a captive insurer. Yet, it accomplishes part of the purpose of a captive insurer. In effect, it reduces the net cost of insurance by recapturing the producer's commission, one of the major expenses of insurers. A captive agency cannot, however, serve all of the purposes of a captive insurer. It cannot, for example, be used to write coverages that commercial insurers are unwilling to provide.

Several disadvantages of captive agencies have been suggested. First, because of the limited amount of business handled, the captive agency may not become as expert as other producers in finding the most advantageous insurance market. Second, the captive agency may not be able to afford loss control personnel and other specialized personnel that a larger brokerage firm can furnish to its clients.[32]

Regulation

There are two principal regulatory restrictions that may affect captive agencies. The first is antirebate legislation, which prohibits a producer from giving anything of value, outside of the insurance contract, to a prospect to induce the prospect to enter into the contract. Although the antirebate laws would prevent a captive agency from returning commissions directly to the parent company, they apparently would not prevent the agency from paying its profits to its owner. The laws might be a somewhat greater barrier to the captive agency of a trade association if the agency wanted to return commissions to association members.

The second regulation that may affect a captive agency is the restriction on controlled business. For example, Section 56-804b(b) of the Georgia Insurance Code says that an agent or broker must not

> ...use or intend to use the license for the purpose of obtaining a rebate or commission upon controlled business...and must not, in any calendar year, effect controlled business that will aggregate as much as 25 per cent of the volume of business effected by him during the year, as measured by the comparative amounts of premium.

The Georgia provision is reasonably typical, except that some states may permit controlled business equal to 50 percent, or some other percentage, rather than the 25 percent permitted in Georgia. The Georgia law does not define controlled business.

The NAIC Uniform Agents and Brokers Model Licensing Act defines controlled business as:

> (a) insurance written on the interests of the licensee or those of his immediate family or of his employer; or
> (b) insurance covering himself or members of his immediate family or a corporation, association or partnership, or the officers, directors, substantial stockholders, partners, employees of such a corporation, association or partnership, of which he or a member of his immediate family is an officer, director, substantial stockholder, partner, associate or employee, provided, however, that nothing in this section shall apply to insurance written in connection with credit transactions.[33]

Business written for association members by a captive agency controlled by a trade association would not appear to be controlled business within the meaning of the quoted provision. In any case, captive agencies seem to survive in spite of the legal restrictions upon them.

MULTINATIONAL OPERATIONS

Prior to World War II and for the first decade or so thereafter, only a very few American insurers operated overseas. Most of those that did operate beyond North America did so through syndicates, such as the American Foreign Insurance Association.

Beginning in the late 1950s, and accelerating through the 1960s and into the 1970s, American insurers and producers have become increasingly active in overseas markets. There are at least three reasons for this increased activity. First, American commercial and industrial firms expanded rapidly into overseas markets and sought coverage from American insurers for their multinational operations. Second, many insurers expanded into foreign lands to obtain a greater geographic spread of risks. Finally, some insurers and producers saw foreign markets as expansion room—a place to grow with less competition than in the United States.

Corporate Clients

International trade is older than history. However, until the last half century, foreign trade consisted largely of an exporter in one country shipping goods to an importer in another country. Within this century, and primarily within the last two decades, there has been a strong trend toward a new kind of international trade. Instead of moving goods across national borders, it has become common to move capital and production facilities.

Many companies own manufacturing plants in countries other than their country of domicile. The international oil companies operate almost anywhere they can find oil or customers to buy it. Even large retailers and utilities have expanded across national boundaries.

International firms may be grouped into two categories: *limited international* and *multinational* corporations. A limited international firm is a predominately domestic firm with a limited degree of involvement in international operations (manufacturing, mining, assembly, servicing, etc.). A multinational firm is one that is heavily involved in international operations and views the entire world as its market and as its source of personnel and factors of production. These categories represent stages of evolution in international business and affect, to some extent, the insurance markets utilized. One study found that the risk management and insurance buying practices varied significantly between the two categories of international firms.[34]

There are international firms domiciled in all of the major industrial nations outside of the Communist bloc. However, there are more such companies domiciled in the United States than in any other nation, though European nations and Japan are gaining rapidly. It is estimated that the combined output of international firms exceeds the gross national product of any nation except the United States.

As American firms expanded their production and distribution facilities into foreign lands, they sought to take their American insurance coverages and markets with them. There were several reasons for preferring American insurance. First, the risk managers of the new international firms were familiar with American insurers and accustomed to dealing with them. They preferred to continue dealing with them, rather than dealing with unfamiliar insurers in a foreign language.

Second, policy terms and conditions in foreign markets may be substantially different from American policy terms and conditions. These differences complicated the job of risk management because of the necessity for becoming familiar with insurance policies and customs in a number of countries. Also, it was not possible, in many cases, to obtain the extent and type of protection to which American companies had become accustomed.

Dealing in foreign currencies also presented problems. For example, if the proceeds of a fire policy were payable by a foreign insurer, they generally would be payable in the currency of the home country of the insurer. If the insured wanted to use the funds to buy replacement equipment in the United States, or simply to repatriate the money to the United States, it would be subject to risks of (1) fluctuation of the foreign currency relative to the dollar and (2) laws of the foreign country prohibiting repatriation of funds. If, on the other hand, the property had been insured in dollars by an American insurer, the exposure to currency losses could be avoided.

Finally, the use of American insurers and policies throughout the world permits the company to implement a uniform risk management program in all of its operations. Also, the entire insurance program could be negotiated in the United States, further simplifying the risk manager's job.

Insurance provided by an alien or foreign insurer not admitted to do business in a country is called "nonadmitted" insurance in that country. Prohibitions against nonadmitted insurance exist in almost two-thirds of all countries.

In response to the needs of the international firms and their employees, and to protect the coverages already written for the United States operations of these firms, many American insurers and producers found it desirable to become "multinational" themselves.

Alternatives in the Foreign Markets

There are several methods by which an American insurer can expand into foreign markets. Perhaps the easiest is to join a group of insurers that operates abroad through a common foreign management organization.

Another is to purchase an interest (sometimes a controlling interest) in insurers domiciled in foreign countries. Joint ventures between American insurers and foreign insurers are also used as a device for American insurers to enter foreign markets. Joint ventures may take several forms. Some are agreements among existing insurers stipulating that each will provide services to the other's clients in its territory. In other cases, an American insurer and a local insurer join together to form a new jointly owned insurer. The acquisition or formation of a local company helps to avoid the prejudice against foreign insurers which is common in some countries. A joint venture with a domestic insurer also helps in that respect.

It is also possible for an American insurer to operate in some foreign markets through a managing general agency, which provides production, claims, and other services for the insurer. This method of operation would be less expensive in the early stages than a company branch office, but the insurer would have less control of its operations. Finally, reinsurance may offer a method for operation in some foreign markets where direct operation is prohibited by local law.

American producers use somewhat the same tactics as American insurers in entering foreign markets. The large brokerage houses have opened branches in some cases, purchased existing brokerage offices in others, and arranged for local brokerage offices to act on their behalf in still others.

Agency and brokerage firms that are not large enough to maintain their own foreign operations have joined together into associations to provide such facilities.

Other Reasons for Multinational Operations

Service to American commercial and industrial firms was not the only reason for expansion into foreign markets. Some insurers with little exposure in the large industrial and commercial market found foreign markets attractive for other reasons.

Geographic Spread of Risks In order to operate successfully an insurer must be able to predict its loss experience with some accuracy. The geographic spread of exposures helps provide predictability. Weather conditions, for example, usually are not unfavorable in all parts of the world in the same year. A year which produces a large number of tornadoes in the United States may be a good year in Australia or Africa, or vice versa. Inflation in the United States, with its concomitant pressure on loss ratios, may be offset by stable results in Europe or Japan. Some of these advantages can be, and are, obtained by writing reinsurance for local companies in other countries, but direct foreign operations may provide an even greater spread of exposures.

Expanded Markets Some American insurers entered foreign markets simply as a means to more rapid growth. Changes in the past two decades created opportunities for American insurers to insure not only American international firms but also local businesses and personal exposures. Several predominantly personal lines insurers are now engaged in the foreign markets, either directly or through subsidiaries or joint ventures. The nature of their operations and the countries in which they operate are determined largely by the local regulations of the host countries.

Foreign Government Regulation The regulatory climate in foreign countries may range from practically no regulation to the outright prohibition of foreign insurers. A few countries, such as India and Libya, have nationalized the insurance industry, thus prohibiting the operation of all private insurers, whether foreign or local.

A number of other countries prohibit the operation of alien insurers (an insurer domiciled in another country) within their borders. Some of these countries will permit foreign ownership of locally chartered insurance corporations, while others permit only minority foreign ownership or none at all. Such requirements usually have two principal purposes. First, they prevent alien insurers from dominating the local market and preventing the growth of the local insurance industry. Second, such regulations may be designed to minimize the outflow of funds as a result of foreign insurance and reinsurance transactions. While United States insurers are critical of such practices, it should be remembered that the United States, or at least several of the individual states, adopted such laws in the early 1800s to protect the then infant American insurance industry from competition from the more advanced British industry.

American companies also have criticized the practice in some countries of requiring alien insurers to deposit funds within the country as a condition of licensing. However, this is a common requirement in the United States, not only for companies domiciled in foreign countries, but also for companies domiciled in other states of the United States. It is possible, of course, that some such deposits may be so large as to be prohibitive rather than protective of the public.

Other limitations, such as external currency controls, are less easy to justify. These controls seldom are aimed specifically at insurers but, rather, apply to all kinds of transactions. Currency controls prevent or make more difficult the repatriation of profits or the repatriation of invested capital if the insurer chooses to discontinue its operations in a country.

Discriminatory taxation of alien insurers is also common. That is, alien insurers may be required to pay either higher income taxes or higher premium taxes than domestic insurers. The purpose, again, is to give local insurers a competitive advantage over their foreign competitors.

Some countries prohibit their domestic insurers from purchasing reinsurance abroad or severely restrict their right to do so. In some cases, they are required to buy all of their reinsurance from a governmental reinsurance organization. The principal purpose of such laws is the minimization of currency outflows. However, such restrictions place severe limitations on the ability of the nation's insurance industry to protect the nation against catastrophe by spreading the loss widely over the world's economy rather than over the nation's economy.[35]

CONGLOMERATION OF THE INSURANCE INDUSTRY

Beginning in the decade of the fifties and accelerating into the sixties, a giant tidal wave of mergers swept over the United States economy. It was the third, and by far the largest, wave of mergers in the nation's history.[36]

Factors Leading to the Present Situation

The first great merger wave, in the 1890s, was characterized by *horizontal mergers* in which companies in the same business combined to form great corporations. The second wave, in the 1920s, was dominated by *vertical mergers* in which firms merged with their suppliers, their customers, or both. By the 1950s, the adoption, amendment, and rigid enforcement of antitrust laws had made horizontal and vertical mergers difficult or impossible for many large firms. So the third wave of mergers was characterized by *conglomerate mergers* combining two or more firms in unrelated businesses. In addition to avoiding many of the antitrust pitfalls, conglomerate mergers offered the possibility of combining lines of business that respond in different ways to swings in the economic cycle, thus possibly shielding the firm from economic recessions.

The merger wave of the fifties, like those that preceded it, was caused by an unusual combination of economic circumstances. All of the merger waves have occurred near the end of a long bull market, when high stock prices, heavy stock trading volume, and rising public optimism have made it easy to sell new securities. All have followed major economic changes. The first followed the development of the transcontinental railroad system and the change from an agricultural economy to a manufacturing economy. The second followed the change from the railroads to highway vehicles as the major form of transportation, and the development of advertising mass media, such as the radio and mass circulation magazines.

The third followed the rise of the professional manager who was supposed to be able to manage any kind of business. The prevailing theory was that the skills of the manager and the techniques of management were independent of the kind of business. Competition among mutual fund managers also created a ready and anxious market for the stocks of promising corporations, and the conglomerates were among the ones they favored. This combination led one official of the Securities and Exchange Commission to observe that "the scientific manager, the psychedelic accountant, and the go-go fund"[37] were the driving forces behind the conglomerate merger movement of the fifties and sixties.

In 1967, as the conglomeration movement neared its peak, the conglomerateurs discovered the property and liability insurance industry. A prominent investment brokerage firm released a research report in which it suggested property and liability insurers could, by increasing their premium writings, generate funds to be used in the acquisition of other companies.[38]

A second report, released early in 1968, concluded that many insurers possessed surplus funds in excess of the amount required to support their premium writings and suggested that they be permitted to invest such "surplus surplus" in noninsurance enterprises.[39] Coming as it did from a major state insurance department, the report and its coined phrase "surplus surplus" gave a new air of respectability to the idea of using the policyholders' surplus of a property and liability insurer to finance acquisitions in other industries. Since the conglomerateurs were already hard pressed for funds to continue their company acquisitions, they seized the opportunity readily.

Effect on Capacity

The merger wave moved insurers into conglomerate organizations in two ways. In some instances, insurers were absorbed into existing conglomerates. In other instances, the managers of the insurers established their own conglomerates at least partially to avoid being taken over by other conglomerates. The results of the two approaches were much the same; in most cases, large amounts of policyholders' surplus were siphoned off to be used in acquiring noninsurance operations.

For example, the stockholders of one insurance company formed a holding company to become its conglomerate. Then over $400 million of insurer assets were moved up to the holding company to be used for other acquisitions. Another conglomerate acquired control of a large multiline insurer and caused it to declare a special cash dividend of $171 million to be paid to the conglomerate.[40]

In 1969 alone, almost a billion dollars of assets were removed from the insurance industry to parent noninsurance companies. At least $1.5 billion, and possibly more, were removed in the eight years beginning with 1965.[41]

At first, it did not appear that this outflow of capital was having an adverse effect on the capacity of the insurance industry to provide the protection required by consumers. One study made in 1973 showed that, with a few very notable exceptions, the insurers controlled by conglomerates had increased their premium writings in roughly the same proportion as the rest of the industry.[42] However, by the very nature of insurance capacity, it is apparent that the capacity of the industry has been reduced.

There are two kinds of insurance capacity about which the industry and the public must be concerned: (1) *large line capacity* and (2) *premium volume capacity*. Large line capacity is the ability of an insurer to write a large amount of insurance on a single subject of insurance. Examples are a large fire insurance policy covering a major industrial plant or a liability insurance policy on a Boeing 747 passenger aircraft. The amount of insurance required might be several hundred millions of dollars. Large line capacity, ignoring reinsurance for the moment, is a function of an insurer's surplus to policyholders. Most states have statutory provisions limiting the amount an insurer can write on a single subject of insurance to 10 percent of its surplus to policyholders. However, few insurers would risk that large a percentage even on the safest exposures.

Premium volume capacity also is a function of surplus to policyholders. Traditionally, a property and liability insurer is considered to have overexpanded when its annual net written premiums exceed twice or three times its surplus to policyholders. More recently, premiums equal to three times the surplus to policyholders have been deemed acceptable. At the latter ratio, removal of $1.5 billion of surplus would reduce the industry's premium capacity by $4.5 billion, or about 15 percent of the total industry premiums of $29.2 billion in 1969, at the height of the outflow.

The effect of capital removal on capacity did not become apparent at first. The rising stock market and profits from underwriting and investments provided adequate surplus for a few years. But the poor underwriting results of 1974 and 1975, combined with poor stock market results, made it apparent that the "surplus surplus" of the 1960s had not been as surplus as it then appeared.

Many major insurers, even though not in immediate danger of insolvency, found their premium writings too high for their surplus to policyholders. In a recent analysis, a conglomerate reported that in the ten years ending in 1972 the aggregate policyholders' surplus of its property and liability companies doubled, but all that gain had been virtually wiped out in 1974. The result was that, in 1974, the insurer was equipped only with a 1962 policyholders' surplus to write the enormously increased exposures, both property and liability, of 1974.[43]

While the outflow of capital to conglomerates was only one of several causes of the capacity problem of 1974, the more than $1.5 billion that the conglomerates siphoned off would have supported at least 10 percent of the industry's total premium volume of $45 billion for that year. That 10 percent might well have been the difference between shortage and adequacy of capacity.

As it was, the industry was unable to meet the insurance needs of many consumers. One result was the establishment of captive insurance companies to provide the lacking coverage. Another result was the outflow of much premium to foreign insurers through the surplus lines markets. Also, in order to bolster the surplus account, some insurers were forced to sell stock holdings at depressed prices. Many commercial insureds found self-insurance or retention more attractive because of the difficulty of obtaining insurance and the higher premiums that usually accompany shortages. Much of the business lost during the capacity shortage may never return.

Indications for the Future

The very special conditions which spawned the era of conglomerate mergers have passed into history. The idea that the stock market can move only upward has lost much of its following. Insurers with "surplus surplus" became almost as rare as pterodactyls. It seems unlikely, therefore, that many more insurers will be absorbed by noninsurance corporations in the near future. And one conglomerate that acquired an insurer found it necessary to put capital in instead of taking it out.

The recovery of the stock market in the late 1970s and early 1980s helped the policyholders' surpluses of many insurers. The high investment income resulting from the high interest rates of the late 1970s and early 1980s also helped, as have a few years of underwriting profits during the early part of that period. The increasing profits of insurers may make them attractive to future congomerateurs, but another sustained bull market probably will be needed before a new wave of conglomeration can be launched.

GOVERNMENTAL INSURANCE ACTIVITIES AND THEIR EFFECTS ON MARKETING

Government, both state and federal, has been increasingly active in meeting the insurance needs of the public. One study classified the governmental insurance programs as (1) those which compete with private insurers, (2) those in which the government operates in partnership with private insurers, and (3) those in which the government is exclusive agent or monopolistic insurer.[44] At the federal level, the monopolistic insurance programs usually deal with loss exposures that are considered commercially uninsurable, such as war loss and unemployment. However, several state governments operate monopolistic insurance programs for certain lines of insurance that would otherwise be written by private insurers.

Governmental insurance programs usually are justified by their supporters on several grounds. The first, and most convincing, is the inability or unwillingness of private insurers to provide a form of protection that is necessary for the public welfare. Flood insurance and war risk coverage are examples.

Lower cost to the consumer also seems to be a consideration in the establishment of some governmental insurance plans. Lower cost probably was the major factor in the establishment of the state life insurance fund in Wisconsin and quite possibly in the establishment of state funds for crop hail insurance.

In some cases, the proponents may justify governmental insurance plans on the ground that it is unfair to enrich private insurers by permitting them to profit on insurance that is required by law. This seems to have been a major consideration in the establishment of state workers' compensation insurance funds.

Some governmental insurance programs seem to have been started to promote social, economic, or scientific developments. For example, mortgage guaranty insurance was established, at least in part, to encourage home ownership and to provide financial support to the construction industry. Export credit insurance is provided by a federal agency in order to promote exports and thus to promote a healthy national economy.

Whatever the reasons, a number of governmental insurance programs have been established over the past few decades, and more are under consideration. Other courses in the CPCU program will include a detailed description of the various government programs. The following section is limited to a discussion of the government insurance programs from a marketing standpoint and from the standpoint of private insurer involvement.

Flood Insurance

Private insurers debated the insurability of the flood exposure for many years. It was the prevailing belief within the industry that the flood exposure was not commercially insurable. The principal reasons given for uninsurability were (1) the catastrophic nature of losses, (2) the repetition of claims, and (3) adverse selection—the tendency of those in flood-prone areas to buy flood insurance while those on high ground would not. Consequently, flood insurance was not generally available in the private insurance market. Some commercial and industrial firms could purchase flood coverage under a difference in conditions policy (DIC), but even that was not usually available to firms located in flood plains.

The Housing and Urban Development Act of 1968 provided a federal subsidy for flood insurance. In 1969 the program was expanded to include mud flows. The original enabling legislation required state and local governments to adopt land use control measures to minimize flood damage before they could qualify to participate in the flood insurance program. The program originally was available only to one- to four-family dwellings and small business firms. Later it was expanded to include churches and several other property classes. It presently provides coverage to many types of residences and businesses.

Federal flood insurance is marketed through normal insurance marketing channels. Beginning in 1983, under the new cooperative venture called WRITE YOUR OWN, participating insurers began to write flood insurance under their own name through their normal distribution systems. Under this arrangement, the insurers keep 29.5 percent for expenses, premium taxes, and commissions, with the balance being deposited in a separate account to pay for losses.

Participating insurers have no risk-bearing role in the WRITE

YOUR OWN program. They will be able to draw funds on a letter of credit from the U.S. Treasury when and if they have expended the remainder of the premiums and investments in loss payments and loss payment expenses.[45]

Federal Crime Insurance

The riots and crime wave that accompanied the 1960s made crime insurance very difficult to obtain in many metropolitan areas of the country. As a part of the Housing and Urban Development Act of 1970, Congress authorized the Department of Housing and Urban Development to underwrite crime insurance in those areas in which it was not available.

Crime insurance in the federal program is underwritten by the federal government and sold either directly by the government or through insurance agents and brokers. The program is authorized to insure against robbery, burglary, larceny, and similar crimes. Policies that may be issued include personal theft insurance, mercantile open stock insurance, mercantile robbery and mercantile safe burglary insurance, storekeepers' burglary and robbery insurance, and office burglary and robbery insurance. It is now available in twenty-eight states, the District of Columbia, and Puerto Rico.

The Federal Insurance Administration appoints a private organization to serve as servicing company. The servicing company is responsible for (1) accepting and underwriting applications, (2) issuance of policies, (3) collection and accounting for premiums, (4) adjustment and payment of claims, and similar functions. Any licensed producer can sell the coverage and be compensated by commission for the services rendered.

FAIR Plans

Fair Access to Insurance Requirements (FAIR) Plans, like federal crime insurance, resulted primarily from the riots and crime wave of the 1960s, along with the general deterioration of central city areas. Because of these factors, many people in the central city areas found themselves unable to obtain fire and allied lines coverage for their homes and businesses. A federal study commission suggested, as one method of providing such protection, the establishment of FAIR Plans and federal reinsurance for riot losses.[46]

Both the FAIR Plans and riot reinsurance were authorized by the Urban Property Protection and Reinsurance Act of 1968. FAIR Plans are associations of insurers formed under state law but required to meet certain minimum requirements established by the U.S. Depart-

ment of Housing and Urban Development. Persons who cannot obtain
fire and allied lines insurance in the voluntary market can apply to the
FAIR Plan. Some state FAIR Plans also provide crime insurance. The
FAIR Plan cannot refuse coverage solely because of the location of
property but *can* refuse coverage if the property is in such poor
condition as to be uninsurable and if the insured refuses to restore it to
insurable condition. However, these options have proven to be unen-
forceable in some states. The premiums, losses, and expenses of FAIR
Plans are allocated to participating insurers in proportion to their
property insurance premiums in the state.

In 1983, the riot reinsurance program was terminated. No new riot
reinsurance policies were being issued, and no policies were renewed
after they expired. The FAIR Plans remain unchanged.

Expropriation Insurance

Expropriation insurance protects United States business firms
against loss caused by expropriation of their assets in foreign countries
by the governments or other organizations in those countries. For
example, U.S. firms suffered many millions of dollars of losses when the
Iranian government expropriated their properties in that country in
1979.

Expropriation insurance was originally a governmental monopoly
in the United States. It was written only by the Agency for International Development (AID), a federal government agency of the State
Department established to promote industrialization of underdeveloped
countries. Coverage also was provided for losses from war, revolution
and insurrection, and inability to convert foreign currencies to U.S.
funds due to governmental regulation.

In 1971, the expropriation and war risk programs formerly
managed by AID were transferred to Overseas Private Investment
Corporation (OPIC), another federal agency newly formed for that
purpose. Beginning shortly after its founding, OPIC has purchased
reinsurance from private insurers.

In 1975, a group of private insurers, Overseas Investment Insurance Group, began issuing expropriation and inconvertibility insurance
policies and reinsuring a part of the exposure with OPIC.

In fiscal year 1983, OPIC insured or financed a total of 124 projects
resulting in approximately $4 billion of investments in developing
nations. Total insurance volume amounted to more than $3.9 billion in
1983, a 30 percent increase over the previous year. OPIC's insurance of
bid, performance, and advance payment guarantees posted by U.S.
contractors and exporters developed almost $120 million in coverage
issued on twenty-three projects. OPIC's contractors' program was

expanded to include the additional contracted risks of inconvertibility, expropriation, war, and payment disputes. First made available in 1983, OPIC's new civil strife coverage protects investors against losses due to politically motivated acts of civil strife, terrorism, and sabotage.[47]

Export Credit Insurance

Export credit insurance protects an exporter against loss resulting from inability to collect accounts due from foreign importers. The insured perils are divided into two groups, commercial perils and political perils. Commercial perils include insolvency of the debtor or inability or unwillingness of the debtor to pay for reasons other than those included under political perils. Political perils include war, blocked currencies, and other governmental actions that make payment impossible.

The coverage was written for many years by the Foreign Credit Insurance Association (FCIA), an organization of insurance companies. The Export-Import Bank, an agency of the U.S. Government, reinsured all of the political risks and much of the commercial risks. In 1983, the FCIA ceased operations, so all of the coverage is now provided by the Export-Import Bank. Coverage is available through normal insurance agency and brokerage channels.

Other Government Programs

The foregoing discussion deals with only a few of the government insurance programs now in existence. The federal government writes war risk insurance on aircraft and ships, "all-risks" insurance on crops, deposit insurance for financial institutions, and many other kinds of insurance. Eighteen states have state funds to write workers' compensation insurance for private employers. Six of them (Nevada, North Dakota, Ohio, Washington, West Virginia, and Wyoming) are monopolistic funds writing all of the compensation insurance in the state. The remaining twelve state funds compete with private insurers.

California, New Jersey, New York, Puerto Rico, and Rhode Island have governmental insurers for nonoccupational disability insurance. The Rhode Island program is the exclusive insurer of that coverage in that state. All of the jurisdictions named require employers to provide such coverage for their employees.

Pennsylvania writes insurance against damage to surface property resulting from the collapse of old underground mine shafts.

Several states established government insurers for medical professional liability insurance in recent years because of the unwillingness of private insurers to provide that coverage. Some of the funds write coverage in excess of $100,000 or some other substantial amount.

The Future

In the late 1970s, the expansion of governmental insurance programs seemed very unlikely, but political and economic changes in the early 1980s have slowed the development of such programs substantially. No new governmental programs seem likely unless and until the political and economic outlook changes.

NEW SOURCES OF COMPETITION

One of the principal sources of new competition for property and liability insurers in recent years has been the major life insurers. Producers and insurers alike have been concerned with competition from life insurers but have been concerned even more about potential competition from banks, savings and loan associations, and other financial institutions.

Life Insurers

The movement of the major life insurers into the property and liability insurance business might be viewed as a continuation of a trend, rather than the beginning of one. The trend toward insurance groups offering all lines of insurance, property and liability and life, might be traced back to the latter part of the nineteenth century.

In the late 1950s, when excessive competition and regulation had reduced profit margins in property and liability lines, there was a veritable flood of property and liability insurers into life insurance. One study found that twenty-four property and liability insurers entered the life insurance business in 1957 and 1958, and an additional twenty-eight in 1964 and 1965.[48] By 1973, all of the major property and liability insurer groups had formed or acquired life insurance affiliates.

Life insurers, at least the major ones, were unable to acquire property and liability affiliates during that period because of regulatory restrictions. Specifically, life insurers licensed to do business in New York were prohibited from owning property and liability insurers by the laws of that state.[49]

In 1961, the high court of New York overturned that law insofar as it applied to out-of-state life insurers licensed in New York.[50] In 1962, the law was amended to permit domestic life insurers to enter into such affiliations.[51] Within the next few years, several life insurers acquired property and liability affiliates. However, these acquisitions did not create any new competition, since all of the acquired insurers were established independent agency companies, and all of them continued to operate in their traditional manner, although there may have been an increase in capacity for property and liability operations.

Aggressive competition appeared in 1970, when the Prudential Insurance Company of America announced that it would form a property and liability insurer to sell personal lines insurance through its life insurance agents. Prudential had approximately 25,000 life insurance agents, more than double State Farm's production force of 11,000. In 1982, its thirteenth year of operation, Prudential Property and Casualty Company wrote over $687 million in direct premiums, an indication of the sales power of 25,000 agents, even when only a part of their work time is devoted to property and liability insurance. Prudential Reinsurance Company, founded in 1973, wrote over $337 million of property and liability reinsurance in 1982.

John Hancock Mutual Life Insurance Company entered the property and liability insurance business in 1970 through its subsidiary Hanseco.

Metropolitan Life Insurance Company, with 24,000 agents, entered the property and liability insurance business in 1972. Metropolitan wrote $46 million of premiums in its first full year of operation and had grown to $354 million in direct premiums by 1982.[52] Several other large life insurers also have joined the movement. One survey showed that at least ten large life insurers with a total of over 80,000 agents were selling property and liability insurance in 1975.[53] The life insurers, with their large pools of capital and virtual armies of agents, promise to become major factors in the future of property and liability insurance marketing.

Lending Institutions

The entry of lending institutions into property and liability insurance marketing cannot be called a new phenomenon. In 1810, the Farmer's Bank of Delaware was a major participant in a fire insurance rate war in Philadelphia. However, the Farmer's Bank was an insurer, writing policies for its own account and not representing other insurers. In more recent years, the banks and other lending institutions have acted as agents and brokers rather than insurers. But even that is not a new activity; it has existed at least since 1920.[54]

Producer organizations fear competition from lending institutions through requiring the purchase of insurance as a condition of granting credit. The fear persists in spite of court decisions that such coercion is a violation of federal antitrust laws.

In the 1960s, banks, like insurance companies, turned to the holding company form of organization in order to join the conglomerate movement. Bank holding companies had existed for many years, but there were relatively few of them. The Federal Bank Holding Company Act of 1956 severely restricted the kinds of business in which a multibank holding company, one which owns more than one bank, could engage. However, that law did not apply to a holding company that owned only one bank.

As the loophole became widely known, there was a rush to start one-bank holding companies in order to permit diversification outside the banking industry. In 1954, there were 117 one-bank holding companies in the United States. By 1969, the number had increased to 1,116 and they controlled 32 percent of all U.S. bank deposits.[55]

By 1970, many small business groups, including insurance producers, had become concerned with the potential competition from the bank holding companies. A major lobbying effort was undertaken to pass a federal law restricting the kinds of business in which such organizations could engage. The result was the adoption of the 1970 amendments to the Bank Holding Company Act of 1956.

The 1970 amendments restricted bank holding companies to the transaction of businesses closely related to banking. However, the law did not specify what businesses were closely related but left that decision to the Board of Governors of the Federal Reserve System. The Federal Reserve list of businesses closely related to banking included, among many others, acting as insurance agent or broker in connection with credit extensions.[56] Also, a bank holding company is permitted to engage in the agency or brokerage business in any city with a population of less than five thousand persons.

Following the issuance of the list of closely related businesses, the producer associations entered into litigation before the administrative judges of the Federal Reserve System to oppose the applications of bank holding companies to enter into the insurance agency and brokerage business.

Some of the applications that the producer associations opposed were rejected by the Federal Reserve System; others were approved. Consequently, the associations turned to opposing the holding companies on two new fronts. Their state lobbying was effective in some cases. The Florida insurance commissioner issued a ruling on March 7, 1974, that insurance written by an insurance affiliate of a bank holding company on property of the holding company or insurance related to credit extended by a bank owned by the holding company constituted controlled business. Therefore, a holding company and agency that writes more than 35 percent of its total premium volume in the business of the holding company would be in violation of Florida law.

When the commissioner's ruling is considered together with the Federal Reserve rule that restricts bank holding companies to writing insurance related to credit extensions (except for 5 percent of the agency volume), it is apparent that the two rulings together prohibit bank holding companies from entering the insurance business in Florida. The state regulation says they cannot write more than 35 percent controlled business, and the federal regulation says that they must write at least 95 percent controlled business or no business at all.[57] Legislation specifically prohibiting bank holding companies from entering the agency business has been adopted in several additional states.

In the meantime, the producer associations mounted a campaign at the federal level to persuade Congress to pass additional amendments to the Bank Holding Company Act that specifically prohibit banks from entering the insurance business. They have been joined in this campaign by other trade associations representing other small businesses.

In March 1983, the South Dakota Senate passed Bill 256 which empowered state banks owned by bank holding companies to engage in all facets of the insurance business, including underwriting activities— activities that are prohibited to bank holding companies and national banks by federal law. The federal law prohibiting bank holding companies from selling or underwriting insurance except in very limited cases is the Garn—St. Germain Act of 1982.[58]

Three major bank holding companies immediately made applications to either purchase or establish state-chartered banks in South Dakota. The Federal Reserve Board indicated in January "that it could not approve the proposed bank acquisitions in view of present law and expressions of Congressional intent." The banks then withdrew their applications in order to prevent an adverse ruling. As a result of this decision by the Federal Reserve Board, the entry of bank holding companies into the insurance business is now an issue which must be resolved by the Congress of the United States and will not be determined by state laws such as the new law in South Dakota.[59]

CONSUMERISM

The term *consumerism* is very difficult to define because it seems to mean different things to different people. The term would seem to indicate the protection of members of the public in their roles as consumers—protection against defective products, improper sales techniques, overcharging, and similar matters. However, the consumerist movement has extended well beyond those areas into such distantly related areas as protection of the environment, stockholder relations and corporations, labor union politics, and others.

Organizations and individuals have been concerned with consumer protection for many years. But consumerism, in the form that is now so familiar, stems from 1965. In that year, Ralph Nader's book *Unsafe at Any Speed* was published. Capitalizing on the publicity and the resulting influence with the federal goverment, Nader expanded his activities from his original field of automobile safety into such areas as coal mine safety, private pensions, the performance of federal regulatory agencies, and many others.

Many imitators followed Nader's lead, and the consumerist movement was well under way. Until recently, Nader had not been particularly active in matters directly affecting insurance, though he took an active role in opposing the takeover of the Hartford Fire Insurance Company by the International Telephone and Telegraph Company. However, other persons and organizations have been more active in trying to shape insurance practices to conform with their ideas of the consumer's needs.

For example, the Consumers Union, and many other consumer organizations have lobbied for no-fault automobile insurance legislation at both the state and federal levels. Consumers Union also conducted an extensive survey of its members to determine their experiences with the insurers from which they purchase automobile and homeowners insurance, including such possible problem areas as policy cancellations, claim adjustment problems, rate increases, and others. The results of the surveys were published for guidance in selecting insurers.

Criticisms by consumerists and others have led to many changes in insurer practices. For example, the FAIR Plans were established in response to criticisms of the industry for refusing to provide property coverage in deteriorating urban areas. The joint underwriting associations and reinsurance plans were developed to provide automobile insurance for high risk drivers without the stigma that allegedly was attached to the assigned risk plans that preceded them.

Individual insurers, insurer trade associations, and producer organizations established consumer information offices that consumers could contact to obtain information or make complaints regarding insurance coverage, rates, or practices. Charges of unjustified cancellations and nonrenewals brought both voluntary and statutory limitations on the rights of insurers to terminate automobile, homeowners, and other policies.

Consumerism affects the insurance industry indirectly in many ways, some of them perhaps more important than the direct effects. For example, the consumerist movement, with its frequent allegations of unsafe products, has been a major cause of the increase in products liability claims and of the increasing tendency of courts and juries to find for the plaintiff in such cases.

Class action suits, which were and are vigorously advocated by consumerists, have made it easier to bring products liability and other suits when the amount of loss for any one person would not justify the legal cost of suit. For example, a suit was filed on behalf of all policyholders of a large insurer in one state. The suit alleged that the insurer had added an optional coverage to all of its automobile policies in that state and billed the policyholders for the coverage without the policyholders' consent. The charge to each policyholder ranged from eight to ten dollars per year and would not justify the expense of such a suit. However, the total amount for all policyholders was about $25 million, so that the expense of suit could be justified when a class action suit was brought on behalf of all policyholders.

In October 1980, a new consumerist organization was formed to campaign for changes in the insurance industry. The organization, which has the support of Ralph Nader, is the National Insurance Consumer Organization (NICO). A former head of the Federal Insurance Administration is president of NICO, and two former state insurance commissioners are directors.[60] The president of NICO has stated that the organization will make in-depth studies of rate-making practices, how policies are sold, redlining, and claims settlement practices, among other things. One of the directors of NICO has said that the organization will also develop national consumer cooperatives to sell insurance of all kinds, and that the cooperatives will be under the control of consumers rather than under the control of management.[61]

The first insurance study by NICO was released concurrently with the announcement of its organization. It alleges that the failure to include investment income in automobile insurance rate making has resulted in overcharges to the public totaling $4 billion.[62]

Another consumerist organization that has taken a substantial interest in insurance marketing is Association of Community Organizations for Reform Now (ACORN). With its various affiliates, ACORN is active in nineteen states. Its principal insurance interest has been redlining with regard to homeowners insurance. Redlining is usually defined as the refusal to sell homeowners or other insurance in specified geographic areas, usually the inner city areas. Citizens Action League (CAL), a California affiliate of ACORN, has turned its attention to redlining in automobile insurance.[63]

Increasing Role of Regulators

Consumerists have been quite critical of regulatory agencies in general, both federal and state. Quite naturally, the regulatory agencies have responded to the widely publicized criticisms by taking actions that they hope will be more acceptable to the consumerists.

Consumer Guides Among the most common consumerist activities of insurance regulators has been the publication of booklets intended to assist consumers in purchasing insurance and dealing with insurers. One of the first of the consumer guides was *Georgia Automobile Insurance Rates*, published by the Georgia Insurance Department early in 1969. It listed premiums for all automobile insurers operating in the state for three driver classifications and for two rating territories. It also explained the state's statutory restriction on the cancellation of automobile insurance policies and offered suggestions for those shopping for automobile insurance.

Several other states have published consumer guides on various subjects, but the Pennsylvania Insurance Department seems to have been the most active. Beginning in 1971, it has published a large number of guides on a variety of subjects. Among the subjects are (1) insurance rights of women, (2) automobile insurance, (3) buying insurance, (4) snowmobile insurance, (5) mobile home insurance, (6) homeowners insurance, (7) surgery, (8) dentistry, (9) lawyers, (10) nuclear power, and others. In all, over twenty-five such guides were published by the Pennsylvania Insurance Department, some of them related only remotely to insurance.

The consumer guides generally have stressed price comparisons and rather general suggestions on shopping for insurance. However, the New York Insurance Department took a slightly different approach in one of its guides. It tabulated its policyholder complaints about automobile insurance and published a list showing for each insurer the number of complaints received and the number of complaints per thousand dollars of premiums.

The consumer guides seem to have an effect on insurance marketing. The New York Insurance Department conducted a survey of persons to whom it had sent its automobile and homeowners guides. Of those who responded to the survey questionnaire, 25 percent said they either had changed or planned to change their homeowners insurer, and 20 percent had changed or planned to change their automobile insurer as a result of reading the guides. Additionally 20 percent of the readers of the homeowners guide and 10 percent of the readers of the automobile insurance guide indicated that they had made changes in their policies as a result of reading the guides.

It is apparent that insurers and producers are aware of such changes, and many of them will move to lower prices or otherwise place themselves in better competitive position with regard to the factors publicized in the guides.

The NAIC and Consumerism The National Association of Insurance Commissioners (NAIC) has not been spared the pressure of consumerism. In response to complaints from consumerists, the NAIC invited over three hundred consumer organizations to send representatives to the NAIC meeting in June 1972. Only four consumer organizations accepted the invitations. However, consumer representatives became more active in subsequent years. In 1973, a ten-person committee of consumer representatives was appointed to work with the NAIC on consumer problems.

Consumerism and State Regulatory Authorities Consumer protection is one of the major goals of insurance regulation and has been almost since its inception. However, the ills against which consumers were protected have changed over time. In the early years of regulation, the principal problem was insurer insolvency, which is still a major problem. Prohibition of unfair discrimination in rating became a major phase of insurance regulation and consumer protection around the beginning of this century.

Within the last two decades and primarily since 1965, the emphasis of insurance regulation has been shifting to require the insurance industry to make coverages available and affordable to all who seek such coverages. FAIR Plans, joint underwriting associations, reinsurance plans, and similar programs are examples of such service requirements.

Regulatory authorities have also encouraged consumers to submit complaints, and they have intervened with insurers to resolve justified complaints. Most of the insurance departments have established branches or WATS telephone systems to enable consumers to submit complaints with a minimum of cost and inconvenience.

Consumerism also has been felt in rate regulation. Regulatory authorities have been examining rate filings more thoroughly and resisting rate increases more vigorously.

Changing Coverages and Practices to Meet Consumer Needs

The consumerist movement has brought and is still bringing changes to insurance coverages and practices. One of the most conspicuous changes, though not yet complete, is the development of more readable policies. Over the years, insurance policies had evolved into very complex legal documents as insurers amended them to cope with new laws and court decisions. In fact, they had become all but impossible for a typical consumer to understand. Under pressure from consumerists and regulators, insurers have now started the process of rewriting policies in simplified language easily understandable to most policyholders. In some cases, illustrations are used to make the policies more attractive and possibly to make them more understandable.

Coverages have been modified to meet consumer needs. The uninsured motorist coverage was developed first as a voluntary effort by insurers, though it was later required by law in some states.

When policy terminations became an important concern to consumers, insurers voluntarily inserted policy provisions restricting their right of cancellation. These restrictions became statutory in many states. Also, some insurers developed automobile insurance rating plans intended to enable them to write all drivers in the voluntary market rather than forcing them into assigned risk plans or similar facilities.

SUMMARY AND CONCLUSIONS

Property and liability insurance marketing has been in a state of change for three decades and seems likely to continue to change throughout the foreseeable future. The independent agency insurers have seen their personal lines market share reduced by the other marketing systems. They are now moving to meet the competition through expense reduction methods. The producer's commission, being the largest single item of expense, is especially vulnerable to reduction.

The independent agency companies, being the major writers of commercial lines, also have lost business to captive insurers and self-insurance (retention). Both of these methods of risk handling seem likely to increase in importance in the future. Retention (self-insurance) will become increasingly popular to smaller firms as additional states authorize the establishment of self-insurance trusts under which commercial and industrial firms band together in a joint self-insurance arrangement. Such trusts have been limited to workers' compensation in the past, but Florida authorized them for medical professional liability exposures.

It is still too early to assess the long-term impact of the Risk Retention Act. To date, hardly any risk retention groups have been formed.

The producers of the independent agency system also see themselves threatened not only by direct writers, exclusive agency insurers, and mail order insurers, but also by bank holding companies. The independent agents also are threatened by the large national independent brokerage firms, which have been expanding rapidly.

Differences Disappearing

One of the most striking changes in property and liability insurance marketing is the tendency of the various personal producer marketing systems to draw more closely together. The independent agency and producers are becoming less independent, and the exclusive agency and direct writer producers are becoming more independent.

The signs of lessening independence of the independent producers are (1) the trend, perhaps incipient, toward one-company representation; (2) company purchases of agencies; and (3) company assistance in planning marketing strategy, recruiting new producers, and similar areas.

The exclusive agency and direct writer producers have been demonstrating their increased independence by organizing producer associations and joining labor unions. The companies that employ them have resisted dealing with such organizations, but they have also moved to meet some of the producer demands. Company supervision of exclusive agents and direct writer salespersons is less rigorous than in the past, and some of the insurers have even given their producers a limited form of ownership of expirations. The ownership usually lasts only while the producer is associated with the insurer, but, in some cases, the insurer is required to pay the producer for the expirations when the relationship is terminated.

These developments, when coupled with (1) lower commissions for independent agents, (2) a dual commission scale for new and renewal business for independent agents, (3) entry of independent agency companies into the other marketing systems and (4) recruiting of independent agents by direct writers and exclusive agency insurers, may eventually all but obliterate the distinction between the systems. In fact, the Independent Insurance Agents of America has already explored the possibility of opening membership to exclusive agency producers. The decision was negative, but even consideration of such a move marks a major change in attitude from the past.

Marketing of Services

To provide a new source of income and to compensate for premiums lost to self-insurance and captive insurers, some insurers have started marketing services. Some of the services now sold are (1) loss adjustment services for self-insurers, captive insurers, and other insurers; (2) loss control services; (3) rehabilitation services for injured persons; and (4) management services for captive insurers, and others.

This chapter has outlined many phases of property and liability insurance marketing. The one characteristic that has been conspicuous throughout the discussion is the constancy of change. Insurance marketing reflects the changes in our society and our economy. The pace of change has been rapid in recent years and promises to be equally rapid in the foreseeable future. Those insurers and producers that are able to adapt to the changes will survive; those that cannot are likely to fail or be replaced by other institutions. If the industry as a whole fails to meet the changing needs of consumers, it is likely to be replaced, in whole or in part, by governmental insurers.

The American insurance industry has demonstrated a substantial talent for adapting to change. If that adaptability continues in the future, it is likely that the industry will survive and prosper.

Chapter Notes

---

1. Stuart V. d'Adolf, "Why Allstate Is Appointing Independent Agents," *Independent Agent*, December 1974, p. 26.
2. Robert Catherwood, "Allstate Tries Out Non-Exclusive Agents," *The Financial Post*, 23 March 1974, p. 4.
3. "INA's Exclusive (?) Agency Plan," *Independent Agent*, July 1972, p. 39.
4. "Insurancenter Pilots," *Agents Confidential* (Florida Association of Insurance Agents), 5 December 1980, p. 2.
5. "Florida Agents Support Personal Lines Contract," *Journal of Commerce*, 2 July 1979, p. 8.
6. See, for example, "INA Challenged by Producers," *Journal of Commerce*, 19 July 1972, p. 2; Andrew Leonard, "INA vs. NAIA: Direct-Mail Auto Cover Controversy Continues," *Journal of Commerce*, 27 July 1972, p. 1.
7. "IIAA Raps Hartford's Direct Mail Program," *Independent Agent*, September 1983, p. 39.
8. C.A. Carpenter, "Distribution Guidelines Formulated by IIAA," *Journal of Commerce*, 6 February 1984, p. 7A.
9. The Florida Agents' Manifesto (Tallahasee: Florida Association of Insurance Agents, 1973), Task Force C, Remuneration.
10. E.J. Leverett, Jr., and James S. Trieschmann, "Fees vs. Commissions: Are They Legal?" *CPCU Annals*, December 1974, p. 266; see also "Charging Illegal Fees," *Independent Agent*, September 1975, p. 55.
11. American Insurance Association, Independent Insurance Agents of America, National Association of Casualty and Surety Agents, and Professional Insurance Agents, *Improving the American Agency System* (New York: American Insurance Association, 1979), p. 42.
12. *Improving the American Agency System*, p. 42.
13. "IIR Project Allows Agents to Shop Insurance," *National Underwriter*, Property and Casualty Insurance Edition, 17 October 1980, p. 10.
14. Stuart V. d'Adolf, "The Agency Universe," *Independent Agent*, September 1983, p. 19.
15. Patricia K. Mortenson, "IVANS: Making the Connection," *Best's Review*, Property/Casualty Insurance Edition, September 1983, p. 108. Also see, William H. McCray, "IVANS is Here: The Great Computer Link-up," *The Journal of Insurance*, September/October 1983, p. 33; and David C. Jones, "IVANS on Line, Industry on Hold," *National Underwriter*, Property and Liability Insurance Edition, 9 September 1983, p. 36.
16. Subcommittee on Antitrust and Monopoly, Committee on the Judiciary, U.S. Senate, *Insurance Industry*, Part 18B, pp. 13427-13747.
17. National Association of Insurance Commissioners, *Report of the Special Committee on Automobile Insurance Problems* (Milwaukee: National Association of Insurance Commissioners, 1969), p. 22.
18. Jon S. Hanson and Robert E. Dineen, *The Regulation of Mass Marketing*

in Property and Liability Insurance (Milwaukee: National Association of Insurance Commissioners, 1971).

19. Louis Harris & Associates, *Sentry Insurance National Opinion Study: A Profile of Consumer Attitudes Toward Auto and Homeowners Insurance* (Stevens Point, WI: Sentry Insurance, 1974), p. 55.

20. Louis Harris & Associates, p. 74.

21. J. David Cummins, Dan M. McGill, Howard E. Winklevoss and Robert A. Zelten, *Consumer Attitudes Toward Auto and Homeowners Insurance* (Philadelphia: University of Pennsylvania, 1974), p. 47.

22. *Attitudes Toward Group Automobile Insurance*, p. 9.

23. *Attitudes Toward Group Automobile Insurance*, p. 31.

24. Fortune Market Research, *How Major Industrial Corporations View Employee Benefit Programs* (New York: *Fortune*, 1975), p. 15.

25. Fortune Market Research, p. 15.

26. Fortune Market Research, *How Medium-Size Companies View Employee Benefit Programs*, p. 17.

27. *Attitudes Toward Group Automobile Insurance* (Washington: *U.S. News & World Report*, 1974), p. 38.

28. Ann M. Marin, "Workmen's Compensation Groups Open to Brokers on a Brokerage Basis," *The Broker*, July 1973, p. 3.

29. "Bermuda Insurers Underwrite $6.2 Billion in Gross Premium," *Business Insurance*, 26 September 1983, p. 1.

30. *The Present Status and Future Role of Risk Management*, Risk & Insurance Management Society, 1981, pp. 33-36.

31. Rhonda L. Rundle, "Bermuda Captives Forming Exchange to Trade Risks," *Business Insurance*, 25 July 1983, p. 1.

32. J. William Sherar, "Should You Have a Captive Brokerage Firm?" *International Insurance Monitor*, December 1971, p. 373.

33. *Proceedings of the National Association of Insurance Commissioners*, 1973, Vol. 2, p. 384.

34. Norman A. Baglini, *Global Risk Management* (New York: Risk Management Society Publishing, Inc., 1983), p. 117.

35. For a more complete discussion on restrictions on international insurance, see U.S. General Accounting Office, *International Insurance Trade—U.S. Market Open; Impact of Foreign Barriers Unknown* (Washington: General Accounting Office, 1982).

36. Lewis Beman, "What We Learned from the Great Merger Frenzy," *Fortune*, April 1973, p. 70.

37. Beman, p. 144.

38. Edward Netter, *The Financial Services Holding Company* reproduced in United States Senate, Subcommittee on Antitrust and Monopoly of the Committee on the Judiciary, *The Insurance Industry: Hearings*, part 15, pp. 9573-9591.

39. State of New York, Insurance Department, Special Committee on Insurance Holding Companies, *Report of the Special Committee on Insurance Holding Companies*.

40. "The Billion-Dollar Insurance Caper," *Forbes*, 15 October 1970, p. 66.

41. Richard deR. Kip, "How To Get Capital Out of the Insurance Business," *CPCU Annals*, September 1970, p. 235.
42. Harold H. Seneker, "Examining the Conglomerate Takeovers," *Independent Agent*, December 1973, p. 13.
43. "Reinsurance Leader Predicts One of Worst Capacity Crunches in History," *National Underwriter*, Property and Casualty Insurance Edition, 3 January 1975, p. 18.
44. Mark R. Greene, *Government and Private Insurance* (Chicago: National Association of Independent Insurers, 1975), p. 11.
45. WRITE YOUR OWN, Executive Overview Questions and Answers, revised 17 February 1984. Federal Insurance Administrator, Washington, DC 20472.
46. National Advisory Panel On Insurance in Riot-Affected Areas, *Meeting the Insurance Crisis in Our Cities* (Washington: GPO, 1968). Also see Richard F. Syron, *An Analysis of the Collapse of the Normal Market for Fire Insurance in Substandard Urban Core Areas* (Boston: Federal Reserve Bank of Boston, 1972).
47. *The Overseas Private Investment Corporation Annual Report*, 1983 (Washington, DC: OPIC, 1983), pp. 226-227.
48. Joseph Earnest Johnson, "The Movement of Property-Liability Insurer Groups into Life Insurance" (Ph.D. dissertation, Georgia State University, 1971), pp. 19, 21.
49. Adelbert G. Stroub, Jr., Ed., *Examination of Insurance Companies*, seven volumes, Vol. 2, p. 292.
50. Connecticut General Life Insurance Company v. Superintendent of Insurance, 10 N.Y.2d 42, 176 N.E.2d 63 (1961).
51. 1962 Laws of New York, ch. 627.
52. "Life Companies Pose Threat to P/C Lines," *Journal of Commerce*, 29 September 1975, p. 3A.
53. "Life Companies Pose Threat to P/C Lines," p. 3A.
54. Walter H. Bennett, *The History of the National Association of Insurance Agents* (Cincinnati: The National Underwriter Co., 1955).
55. Charles D. Salley, "1970 Bank Holding Company Amendments: What Is 'Closely Related to Banking'?" *Monthly Review* (Federal Reserve Bank of Atlanta), June 1971, p. 98.
56. Harvey Rosenblum, "Bank Holding Company Review 1973/74," *Business Conditions* (Federal Reserve Bank of Chicago), part 1, February 1975, p. 3; part 2, April 1975, p. 13.
57. *Agents Confidential* (Florida Association of Insurance Agents), 8 March 1974, p. 1.
58. Public Policy Issue Analysis—Financial Services, Alliance of American Insurers, Schaumberg, IL.
59. Joseph P. Decaminada, "Insurance and Banks: Quo Vadis?" *National Underwriter*, Property and Casualty Edition, 23 March 1984, p. 11.
60. Mary Jane Fisher, "Ins. Consumer Watchdog Group Formed," *National Underwriter*, Life and Health Insurance Edition, 3 October 1980, p. 1.
61. Fisher, p. 1.
62. Mary Jane Fisher, "Auto Cover Overpriced by $4 Billion," *National*

Underwriter, Property and Casualty Insurance Edition, 10 October 1980, p. 1.

63. Al Haggerty, "California Citizens' Group Focuses on Auto Redlining," *National Underwriter*, Property and Casualty Insurance Edition, 22 August 1980, p. 5.

CHAPTER 4

Underwriting

INTRODUCTION

Underwriting is defined as the process of hazard recognition and evaluation, selection of insureds, pricing, and determination of policy terms and conditions. Underwriting includes more than mere selection of insureds.

The importance of underwriting to the success of any insurance enterprise cannot be overstressed. Favorable underwriting results are a necessity for the growth and even the survival of the insurance company. While many other insurance company functions, such as marketing, loss control, rate making, and claims, are occasionally subcontracted to outside companies or individuals, underwriting is rarely delegated to others.

Prior to the emergence of the corporate form of insurance entity, the underwriter was also the insurer. This personal "risk-bearing" persists to this day at Lloyd's of London, where each individual "name" at Lloyd's bears whatever portion of a loss he or she has accepted. While the underwriting function in modern insurance corporations has been delegated to specialized underwriting departments, the ultimate underwriters remain the top corporate officers of the insurance company.

The purpose of underwriting is to help the insurer maintain solvency so that coverage and service may be provided to policyholders. An underwriting profit (or a contribution to surplus) should result. To do this, underwriters must avoid adverse selection.

Adverse selection occurs when the applicants for insurance represent a sample of the population that is biased toward those with a greater loss exposure rather than representing a true random sample. In flood insurance, for example, only those persons and businesses with serious flood exposures are likely to purchase flood insurance. Also, adverse selection may result when the premium charged is inadequate for the "risk" involved.

If one insurance company practices selective screening, accepting the best and declining the others, then the other insurance companies must practice selective screening or a poor book of business (all policies in force with an insurer in a particular line of insurance) will result. The rule then is, "select or be selected against!"

Evolution of Underwriting

Prior to the passage of multiple-line rating laws in this country, all coverages were provided through separate lines of business. Underwriting therefore developed along the same lines. An underwriter was trained as a fire underwriter, a marine underwriter, or a casualty underwriter.

The typical career path of the underwriter of forty or fifty years ago was quite different from its modern counterpart. The fire underwriter often began as a "map clerk" after completion of high school. The map clerk worked with the large, leather-bound volumes of the Sanborn Maps then in general use. These maps, which contained scale drawings of all buildings, streets, and fire mains, were maintained by the map clerk, who would paste in any changes such as new construction or occupancy. Then came a long indenture as a junior underwriter or assistant underwriter before the title of underwriter was finally achieved. This training process was similar to that of the medieval guild systems—the apprentice learning from the master.

Describing a typical example of this system in a recent trade publication, it was noted that:

> . . . he knew his craft. He had worked at this desk for 35 years— apprenticed there for 20 of those years at the elbow of a senior underwriter. When his senior retired, he slipped into that slot and, like his former boss, he, too, would retire there. But he wasn't worried about a replacement. For the past eight years a young assistant had worked at *his* side, learning everything there was to know about his particular line of underwriting. In another 10 years or so—maybe more—this lad would be ready to step into his shoes.[1]

This system produced underwriting specialists. They could quote rates from memory and were conversant with all of the intricacies of the contract provisions and coverage for their particular line. The system was disadvantageous for the individual assistant underwriter because promotion was often blocked for many years by senior underwriters. Moving to another line of coverage would mean beginning over again at the bottom of the ladder. This system of producing underwriting specialists is still in use in certain companies at certain line or staff levels and is also in use by some specialty insurers.

Multiple-Line Underwriting

With the passage of the McCarran-Ferguson Act in 1945, the regulatory environment changed. Multiple-line laws appeared in several states, and in the 1950s, insurers began offering package policies that included more than one line of coverage. It soon became apparent that underwriters who were specialists in one line had little or no skills in others, and they now were being called upon to deal with unfamiliar lines in these package policies.

Many insurance companies changed both the structure of their underwriting departments and the training of their underwriters to deal with the multiple-lines innovations. This development, together with an increasing mobility in the insurance labor force, created more flexibility in underwriting organizations. Long apprenticeship programs have given way to modern training programs. Often an underwriter must learn the nuances of several lines of insurance in a relatively short time span. A further complexity is that changes in coverages, hazards, and exposures have become extremely rapid in recent years. Technological advances have introduced both new materials and new industrial processes which have drastically altered the hazards in such lines as commercial fire, commercial liability, and workers' compensation. Changes in the legal environment have had profound effects on products liability and professional liability. These factors, combined with inflation, have placed heavy demands on today's underwriters. Rather than having the benefit of a lengthy apprenticeship in which to learn a single line of insurance in a stable technological, legal, and cultural environment, the modern underwriter must master several lines of insurance in a continually changing environment in a relatively short time period.

Underwriting Developments

Insurance companies have developed a variety of responses to the challenges of modern underwriting. Many companies have developed intensive training programs to provide underwriters with the necessary techniques and knowledge in the shortest possible time. One company has developed a Monte Carlo simulation model for use in training underwriters.[2] This model simulates loss histories of both individual insureds and entire classes of business, shows the effect of loss development delay, and simulates the market's response to pricing decisions. Such training techniques have the effect of synthesizing experience, enabling the underwriter to quickly obtain in the classroom insights that otherwise would be available only after years of experience.

Some insurers are using the computer to replace the traditional paper underwriting file. Some have all of their private passenger auto underwriting file information on magnetic tape in the computer. The underwriter works with a cathode-ray tube (CRT) display unit rather than with a paper file. All policy coverage information, together with claims, billing data, and underwriting information, is stored in the computer and available for instant recall. The underwriting data includes a "flagging" or reminder system for future action to be taken, motor vehicle records or reports (MVR), inspection report information, appraisal data, and a system for automatic reclassification by age. Under this program, the problem of searching to locate a file is eliminated. The program is updated to the close of business of the previous day so that policy coverage information is always current. A similar program for commercial lines is being used by a few insurers, but the greatest potential for computer assistance in underwriting seems to be in personal lines.

Other developments include the advent of "production underwriters" or "account analysts" who have both marketing and underwriting responsibilities. This concept avoids the typical marketing versus underwriting point of view by combining those responsibilities within the same individual. Other insurers have not gone that far but have encouraged their underwriters to make sales calls and inspections with producers. This enables the underwriter to obtain first-hand knowledge of the operations of the applicant and helps the underwriter to develop a better appreciation for the producer's competitive environment.

UNDERWRITING ACTIVITIES

As insurance enterprises have increased in both size and complexity, their organizational structures have changed as well. The manner in which a particular underwriting department is organized reflects a great many influences. The size of the insurer, whether it is national or regional in scope, whether it writes all lines or specializes in one or two, and the type of marketing system used—all have major effects on the organization of the underwriting department.

A large national insurer typically has more levels in its structure than a small regional one. This distinction would not necessarily hold true with regard to a large regional company, of which there are several in the industry. The perplexing question as to the best way to segment the various lines of business is much more relevant to a multiple-lines insurer than to one specializing in one or two lines of business. The effect of the marketing objectives can be seen when the underwriting department is organized in a manner that best meets the needs of its particular producers. Therefore, a direct writer that writes personal lines exclusively will have its underwriting department organized in a different manner from an insurer that specializes in large highly protected risks (HPRs).

Line Versus Staff

The first major dichotomy in underwriting department organization is the distinction between line and staff underwriting activities. In a very small insurance company with only a handful of underwriters, the same individuals probably fulfill both out of necessity. Even in that case, the distinction between line and staff is important. In all but the smallest insurers, these functions are assigned to separate departments.

The definition of the terms *line* and *staff* are complicated by the fact that these terms refer not only to organizational departments but also to authority relationships. The concepts of line and staff were first used in military organizations. Here, the *line* positions have *command* responsibilities, while the *staff* positions are *advisory*. In business organizations one authority notes:

1. The units that are designated as line have ultimate responsibility for successful operation of the company. Therefore the line must be responsible for operating decisions.

2. Staff elements contribute by providing advice and service to the line in accomplishing the objectives of the enterprise.[3]

Staff Underwriting Activities

While staff underwriting activities are usually performed at the home office, some regional underwriting managers have staff assistants. The major staff underwriting activities are:

- Formulation of underwriting policy
- Appraisal of experience
- Research and development of coverages and policy forms
- Review and revision of rating plans
- Preparation of underwriting guides and bulletins
- Conduct of underwriting audits

- Participation in associations and bureaus
- Education and training

Following is a brief overview of each of these activities.

Formulation of Underwriting Policy Continuing research must be done on such fundamental issues as which markets the insurer should attempt to reach. This includes consideration of the addition or deletion of entire lines of business, expansion into additional states or retirement from states presently serviced, and the determination of the optimal product mix (the makeup of the book of business, e.g., general liability, homeowners, etc.). A determination of present and prospective future capacity leads to the setting of premium volume goals. This overall underwriting policy is ultimately communicated to the field through changes in underwriting guides, bulletins to producers, and home office directives. This important function is considered in detail in a later section of this chapter.

Appraisal of Experience The staff underwriting department also reviews the loss and premium data of its own book of business and of the industry by line, class, and territory to discern the presence of trends. This analysis is then used to determine if changes must be made in the company's marketing or underwriting posture. The necessary changes are usually enacted through the underwriting guide, but sometimes special situations are outlined in underwriting bulletins or bulletins sent to the company's producers.

Research and Development of Coverages and Policy Forms As in many other businesses and industries, research and development of new products is vital to continued growth and prosperity. New coverages are developed to meet a changing legal, social, economic, and technological environment such as directors' and officers' liability, products recall, or kidnap/ransom insurance, and satellite insurance. Other staff underwriting development activities include the simplification of language in existing policies and modifications in coverage to meet changes in market conditions or changes in various state statutes.

Review and Revision of Rating Plans As coverages change, the rates and rating plans for those coverages change as well. If an insurer belongs to a rating bureau, much of the rate review will be done by the bureau. Even in this case, there will be some coverages or even entire lines of business in which the bureau does not file rates and the insurance company must develop its own.

In some states, bureau rate making is not permitted, with the bureaus relegated strictly to an advisory role. Rate deviations are often adopted for competitive purposes. An insurance company that has a large book of a certain line of business may develop its own rates if it has sufficient data for credibility. This also serves to differentiate that company in the marketplace, which is an advantage from a competitive standpoint.

Preparation of Underwriting Guides and Bulletins The underwriting guides and bulletins take the broad precepts of underwriting policy and make them more specific by describing practices that carry out the policy. Staff underwriters periodically update the underwriting guides to reflect current underwriting policy. The underwriting guide which delineates acceptable from unacceptable business will be considered in detail later in this chapter.

Conduct of Underwriting Audits Staff underwriters usually have the responsibility for monitoring line underwriting activities to ensure compliance with the company's underwriting philosophy and practices. This is accomplished through statistical analysis of underwriting results by line, class, and territory and by field audits. The typical field audit consists of a staff underwriter, or team of staff underwriters, visiting a branch or regional office and checking individual underwriting files. The audit focuses upon proper documentation, adherence to procedure, and selection decisions that conform to the underwriting guide and bulletins. The audit team may also check on how well the underwriting programs are being managed by visiting some producers in the territory.

Participation in Associations and Bureaus Most insurance companies are members of some associations and bureaus. Staff underwriters participate in the activities of these organizations on behalf of their companies. In addition to rating bureaus, staff underwriters often work with trade associations that represent their members in legislative and other matters, automobile insurance (assigned risk) plans and joint underwriting associations that deal with residual markets and pools for coverage of specialized risks.

Education and Training Staff underwriters usually have the responsibility for determining the educational needs of their underwriters. The resulting training program and continuing educational activities are then implemented through the training department.

Line Underwriting Activities

The principal line underwriting functions are:

- Selection of insureds
- Classification and determination of proper coverage
- Determination of the appropriate rate or price
- Producer and policyholder service

Certain hazardous classes of business or unusually large amounts of insurance often require review by higher underwriting authority. This higher degree of underwriting authority may rest with an underwriting manager in the branch office or regional office or may be centralized at the home office.

In addition to these activities, some line underwriters have additional responsibilities in analyzing insurance needs, designing insurance coverages, rate making, and marketing, including calling on present or prospective clients with producers.[4] Following is a brief overview of each of the major activities of the line underwriter.

Selection of Insureds If the insurance company does not select those applicants it desires to insure, it will have to depend upon prospective insureds to select it. This will quickly lead to adverse selection, with loss-prone applicants most likely to be among those seeking coverage. The selection process enables the insurer to ration its available capacity to obtain the optimum spread of loss exposures by geographic distribution, class, and line of business.

The selection process is an ongoing one. Once an account has been placed on the books, it must be monitored to determine that it *continues* to be acceptable. Corrective action may have to be taken on those with excessive losses or where adverse information has come to light after initial acceptance. While many think of selection of insureds as negative (declination of unacceptable business) the process has its positive side. The creation of risk management and insurance programs that seek out desirable lines and classes of insureds to write is also part of the selection process.

Classification and Determination of Proper Coverage The primary reason for classification is to provide a basis for rating. A secondary reason is to assist in selection. Classification is employed in both personal and commercial lines. In personal lines, a variety of state laws are removing some of the discretion formerly allowed the underwriter in selection. This makes determination of the proper classification for rating purposes even more important.

Another aspect of this function is the determination of the appropriate coverage. This can range from simply ascertaining that the policy is issued with the appropriate forms and endorsements to the drafting of manuscript policies and endorsements for complex or unique risks. An old cliché among underwriters is, "No two insureds (or applicants) are exactly alike." The peculiar characteristics of each submission must be related to policy provisions that deal with these potential loss characteristics.

In addition, producers and insureds look to the underwriter to determine if the policy requested is proper for the applicant. For example, suppose an applicant has requested fire and extended coverage on contents (including stock) at a manufacturing location. Upon reviewing the nature of the applicant's operations in the inspection report, the underwriter may discover a transportation exposure to stock that is not covered by the policy requested. If the transit exposure is acceptable, the underwriter may bring this exposure to the attention of the producer and offer to provide coverage. This type of activity exemplifies the *positive* approach to underwriting.

Knowledge of insurance contracts and the ability to relate contract provisions to individual insureds or applicants are important in another way. Often, producers request broader coverage on a particular applicant than the underwriter is willing to provide. Rather than decline the application altogether, the underwriter may offer a more limited but adequate form of coverage. The producer then has an opportunity to provide some form of protection to the client.

Determination of the Appropriate Rate or Price In some simple personal lines cases, proper classification automatically determines the proper rate. In large commercial lines, this function is much more complex. The underwriter may have a variety of rating plans from which to choose and may have to take the response of competitors into account. In both commercial and personal lines, the appropriate rate is not only the one that attracts the business, but it must also be reasonable enough to permit the insurer to continue to write the business profitably.

A knowledge of rate making, especially the assumptions upon which the rates are made, and an understanding of pricing trends in the market are essential to sound underwriting. This will be discussed in subsequent chapters.

Producer and Policyholder Service The extent of the line underwriter's responsibility for producer and policyholder service varies considerably. Many companies utilizing the independent agency marketing system allow their agents to issue some types of policies and endorsements. Often there is a policyholder service department which handles the issuance of policies and necessary endorsements. In other cases, the underwriter must prepare the file for the policy typist or computer department.

One service performed by all underwriters is the preparation of quotations and assistance with proposals (usually only on commercial lines) for producers. The underwriter is frequently a major source of technical expertise for the producer. The skill and dispatch with which the line underwriters fulfill this function is an important determinant of the company's success in the marketplace.

Centralized Versus Decentralized Underwriting Authority

Insurance organizations vary considerably in the degree to which underwriting authority is decentralized. When most insurers operated out of a single office, underwriting authority was centralized in the home office. As insurers expanded their service areas geographically, some underwriting authority was moved out into regional and branch offices. Further decentralization took place as producers were given underwriting authority.

The degree of decentralization of underwriting authority varies considerably from one insurance company to another and from one line of business to another. Specialty lines, such as surety bonding, aviation, and livestock mortality, have retained relatively centralized underwriting authority. On the other hand, some insurance companies are delegating a substantial amount of underwriting authority to selected producers. These producers operate like managing general agents and have complete underwriting authority for personal lines and some commercial lines. Proponents of this system state that it eliminates duplication and capitalizes on the producers' familiarity with local conditions. A higher commission rate and a larger percentage of profit sharing (contingent commission) are the producers' compensation for the additional expense of issuing policies and handling claims.

Producers' Underwriting Authority The amount of underwriting authority given to producers depends upon the insurer's philosophy, the experience and profitability of the producer, the line of business involved, and other factors. Some insurers permit producers to issue certain personal lines policies and bill the insureds. Here, a considerable amount of underwriting authority has been delegated to the producer, through the agency agreement. Further motivation for proper underwriting may be provided through a contingency commission (profit-sharing) agreement that provides the producer with an additional commission override based upon the loss ratio on the book of business and on the increase in premium volume.

In certain lines of business, the producer may have no underwriting authority. Large amounts of insurance, specialized classes of business, and unusually hazardous classes may also require referral to the company to obtain the necessary underwriting authority.

While most insurance companies do not permit producers to issue policies, varying amounts of underwriting authority are generally granted. Typically, the producer is furnished with an underwriting guide categorizing the types of insurance and classes of applicants where the producer has binding authority, where they must be referred to higher underwriting authority, and where they should be declined. Often the scope of the producer's underwriting authority is determined by his or her experience and areas of expertise. Company policy sometimes governs cases that must be referred by the producer to higher underwriting authority.

Producers favor broad underwriting authority to enhance the service provided to insureds. Rapid answers can be provided on submissions, giving the producer a competitive advantage. On the other hand, since the producer's primary task is marketing, it is difficult for the producer to develop advanced underwriting skills. Each insurer balances these conflicting factors to achieve the optimum degree of decentralization of underwriting authority for its particular production force and mix of business.

ESTABLISHMENT OF UNDERWRITING POLICY

Underwriting policy determines the composition of the book of business of the insurance company. These decisions are made by top underwriting management and reflect the underwriting philosophy of the owners, as communicated to top underwriting management by the board of directors and senior executives. The underwriting policy of a particular company can be visualized in the form of a matrix. There are four major limiting factors: (1) capacity, (2) regulations, (3) personnel, and (4) reinsurance.

These major limiting factors affect the various dimensions along which underwriting policy is structured. This policy is, of course, affected by management objectives in terms of combined loss and expense ratios relative to the firm's growth expectations. The principal dimensions of underwriting policy are (1) lines of business to be written, (2) territories to be developed, and (3) forms, rates, and rating plans.

The first limiting factor—*capacity*—refers to the relationship between premiums written and the size of the policyholders' surplus of the insurer. The amount of business that can be safely written is fundamentally dependent upon the firm's surplus.

The National Association of Insurance Commissioners includes in its early warning system the guideline that written premium be less than three times policyholders' surplus. While a rapid increase in written premium is the most obvious way to attain an unacceptably high ratio, decreases in surplus as a result of underwriting losses or realized or unrealized capital losses in the investment portfolio can also bring on problems.

Increased surplus, and therefore increased capacity, can accrue from underwriting gains, increases in the value of the investment portfolio, or the infusion of additional capital. (An in-depth explanation of capacity and policyholders' surplus is found in CPCU 8.)

The second limiting factor is the series of insurance *regulations* enacted by the several states. Some regulations are concerned with the relationship between capacity and underwriting, while others are concerned with forms, rates, and underwriting practices.

The third limiting factor encompasses the skills and ability of the *personnel* employed by the insurance company. An insurer that foresees a large potential profit in aviation insurance must employ a sufficient number of experienced aviation specialists before venturing into this field.

The final limiting factor is *reinsurance*. The price and availability of reinsurance treaties may set limitations upon what the primary company can write. While reinsurance can be found for virtually any underwriting program, those programs considered too hazardous or poorly structured by the reinsurers will be difficult and expensive to place.

Exhibit 4-1 shows an underwriting policy matrix illustrating the relationship between the limiting factors and the dimensions of underwriting policy. As top underwriting management establishes its underwriting policy, decisions are made concerning each of these major dimensions, subject to the constraints of the limiting factors. The following section lists each dimension or underwriting factor and shows the effect of the limiting factors and the way underwriting policy must be established to deal with them.

Lines of Business

There are thirty separate lines of business listed in the Annual Statement which is filed by all insurance companies with the several states.

Underwriting policy must be established concerning which of these lines of business are to be written by the company and the relative weight each of these lines should have in the mix of business. Another decision that must be made pertains to whether the insurer will write direct business only or accept reinsurance in these various lines of business. In addition, the company must determine the market segments (personal and commercial lines) to which underwriting policy must be directed.

Exhibit 4-1
An Underwriting Policy Matrix

Limiting Factors	Dimensions of Underwriting Policy		
	Lines of Business to Be Written	Territories	Forms and Rates
Capacity			
Regulations			
Personnel			
Reinsurance Markets			

Capacity and Regulation As has been previously noted, the size of the policyholders' surplus determines the amount of written premium volume that can be safely written. The insurer whose premium volume exceeds three times its policyholders' surplus may be scrutinized by insurance regulators. While striving to increase policyholders' surplus through investment gains and underwriting profits as a means of increasing capacity, the volume of business that can be written at any point in time is ultimately determined by the amount of the policyholders' surplus at that time.

Since statutory accounting rules are inherently conservative, capacity may conceivably be increased in the future if regulators will recognize the "equity" in the unearned premium reserve as additional surplus and consider it when comparing the written premium to surplus. This would have the effect of dramatically increasing industry capacity without any infusion of new capital.

For the company writing at a relatively low multiple of its surplus, e.g., 1.5 to 1, this aspect of regulation has little practical effect on underwriting policy. However, when the limit of premium volume is being reached, the allocation of limited capacity becomes a major policy question. It may be necessary to allocate the available capacity across the various lines and territories which make up the book of business. Therefore, it may be decided that fire business will be increased and general liability decreased while keeping the same premium volume goals. Similarly, the decision may be made to stop writing one line of business completely or to add a line not previously written as a means of optimally allocating scarce capacity. This constraint will also have an effect upon production goals and decisions to enter, leave, or emphasize various territories.

Personnel Since most underwriting is done in the home offices and regional or branch offices, the availability of skilled underwriters is a prerequisite for each line of business to be written. In developing underwriting policy, management usually confines its efforts to those lines in which the necessary skilled personnel are available. Therefore, the decision may be made to avoid such specialty lines as ocean marine, boiler and machinery, and aviation. Conversely, when adding a new line of business to the company's writings, the necessary underwriting technicians must be acquired either through training of present personnel or acquisition of additional ones.

In some cases, a company may refrain from adding a particular line to its mix of business because of a lack of skilled personnel in areas other than underwriting. A particular line may require marketing, loss control, or adjusting facilities the company does not possess, such as boiler and machinery.

Reinsurance The availability of adequate reinsurance is an important consideration in the implementation of underwriting policy. Reinsurance treaties that have been negotiated may exclude certain lines or classes of business, or the cost of reinsurance may be prohibitive. This has the effect of increasing the company's retention on those lines to an unacceptable level should those lines be written. For example, some years ago an insurer had a very successful homeowner's program for high-valued properties located in a brush area that was subject to a conflagration (a disastrous fire). The reinsurers announced that they were retiring from this program at the expiration of the treaty. The primary insurer, unable to find other reinsurance at acceptable terms, had no choice but to withdraw the program. Therefore, before any particular line or class of business can be included in the mix of business offered by an insurer, there must be reinsurance available at reasonable cost and on acceptable terms.

Territories

The second major dimension of underwriting policy involves territories in which business is written and serviced. While marketing considerations play an important part in this decision, it is nevertheless a major facet of underwriting policy.

Capacity and Regulation The effect of geography and state regulation is to divide the country into several territories. Top management must decide:

1. In which states shall the insurer be admitted?
2. What relative emphasis should each of these states be given?

Since all insurance companies have a limited capacity, their premium writings must be allocated among the territories as well as across the thirty lines of business. While the lines of business and territory decision may be made simultaneously, for analytic purposes each facet is considered separately.

Other things remaining equal, insurance theory suggests the widest possible territorial distribution of writings in order to obtain the widest possible spread of loss exposures. Cost and policyholder service requirements usually preclude a small insurance company from national operations, since it would be much more efficient operating in a small territory.

For an insurance company that is already admitted in all fifty states and the District of Columbia, the question of territorial allocation of capacity becomes one of emphasis. Conditions in the several states vary considerably both in terms of the physical hazards (catastrophe potential) present in the territory and in the legal and regulatory climate especially. Climatic conditions and rate adequacy are not present to the same degree in all states. Underwriting policy may dictate curtailment of business written in those states with inadequate rate structures, and aggressive marketing efforts in those states with a more favorable regulatory environment. This is an instance of underwriting policy that is influenced by the marketing department.

Personnel   The cost and availability of skilled personnel is an important factor in the determination of the territory to be serviced. A national premium-writing effort usually requires some decentralization of underwriting. This means either the establishment and staffing of regional and branch offices with capable underwriters or the use of managing general agents where premium volume is not large enough to warrant a branch office in a state or territory. Since the managing general agents typically represent several insurance companies in a territory, the cost of the necessary underwriters is spread across a wider premium base.

Reinsurance   Reinsurance is not a very important limiting factor in the decision on the size or relative emphasis of the territory to be serviced. Reinsurance considerations would be a factor in those cases in which a particular territory presented hazards deemed unacceptable by the reinsurers or if the reinsurer had reservations about the primary insurer's ability to service an additional territory.

Forms and Rates

The final major dimension of underwriting policy to be considered is the determination of whether the insurer will utilize bureau forms and rates or file its own. Some utilize rating bureaus in certain lines of business and territories, while making independent filings elsewhere.

Regulation State regulations significantly influence this area of underwriting policy. The filing requirements in some states dictate both the rate and the form to be used, particularly in personal auto insurance. This is discussed further in a later chapter.

Personnel and Reinsurance If a company is a member of a rating bureau, the bureau will perform most of the actuarial functions. This reduces the need for actuarial personnel. The policy determination to use bureau rather than independent filings is affected strongly by the size of the data base usually required for independent filings. Reinsurance has minimal impact on this aspect of underwriting policy.

Other Considerations One of the major reasons for adopting independent rather than bureau forms and rating plans is marketing considerations. By means of independent rating plans and forms, an insurance company frequently may offer a lower price or broadened coverage to enhance its position in the marketplace. A deviation may be based either on a favorable expected loss ratio or on a favorable expense ratio. A company with a lower expense ratio than contemplated in a bureau rate may justify a deviated rate even with a relatively limited data base.

IMPLEMENTATION OF UNDERWRITING POLICY

Underwriting Guides and Bulletins

Once underwriting policy has been set, it must be disseminated and implemented. The instruments used for this purpose in most cases are the underwriting guides and bulletins hereinafter referred to as underwriting guides. Underwriting policy is reflected in a statement of objectives. Underwriting guides specify ways to achieve these objectives. Underwriting guides are usually structured by major line of business and modified to meet changing conditions. They contain criteria for eligibility and acceptability and set forth underwriting authority requirements.

The primary purposes of underwriting guides are (1) provide structure for underwriting decisions, (2) ensure uniformity and consistency, (3) synthesize insights and experience, (4) distinguish routine from nonroutine decisions, and (5) avoid duplication of effort. Each of these purposes requires further amplification.

Provide Structure for Underwriting Decisions The underwriting guides provide structure for underwriting decisions by identifying the major elements that should be considered in each situation. For example, an inland marine underwriting guide under the contractors' equipment floater classification might indicate to the underwriter that the manner in which the equipment is used is of paramount importance in determining acceptability and the premium to be charged. The underwriting guides would point out that two identical bulldozers are exposed to completely different hazards if one is utilized in road construction on flat terrain while the other is used to clear fire breaks in mountainous terrain.

By identifying the principal hazards associated with a particular class of business, the underwriting guide serves to orient an underwriter unfamiliar with the class. It also serves as a memory aid to the experienced underwriter.

Ensure Uniformity and Consistency The underwriting guide provides a means for ensuring that selection decisions are made on a uniform and consistent basis throughout all geographic regions. Ideally, submissions that are identical in every respect should elicit the same underwriting response no matter to which of the company's branch offices it is submitted. While total realization of this goal is quite difficult due to individual underwriter's biases, the underwriting guide reflects underwriting policy. At the extremes, in the cases of those applicants that are clearly acceptable or clearly prohibited, uniformity is easily achieved.

Synthesize Insights and Experience Underwriting guides also serve to synthesize the insights and experience of mature underwriters, assisting those less familiar with each particular line and class. Particularly in commercial lines, each industry and type of industrial process has its own unique set of hazards and exposures. The underwriting guide contains a summary of the most pertinent observations that have been accumulated on the basis of the insurance company's past experience. An overall evaluation of the desirability of each class reflects the company's particular risk-taking philosophy.

In addition to company underwriting guides, there are a few commercial publications containing a wealth of underwriting information, one such publication being *Best's Underwriting Guide*. This guide concentrates on the significant areas of each industrial classification, omitting such universal hazards as slips and falls common to all types of facilities.

Commercial publications are usually used as a supplement to the insurance company's underwriting guide because, although they contain useful underwriting information, they do not reflect the insurer's underwriting philosophy.

Distinguish Routine from Nonroutine Decisions Another purpose of the underwriting guides is to distinguish routine from nonroutine decisions. This enables the routine decisions to be handled at the lowest level of underwriting authority, permitting the more highly skilled underwriters to concentrate their efforts on the more difficult nonroutine submissions. The usual manner in which the distinction is made is in the delegation of authority. The line underwriter is given authority to make selection decisions on routine submissions. The nonroutine submissions must be referred to higher underwriting authority for approval which, in some cases, is the home office.

Avoid Duplication of Effort Many underwriting situations occur repetitively. If the problems inherent in a particular situation have been identified and solved, the solution should be applicable to all identical situations recurring in the future. The underwriting guide contains the information necessary to avoid costly duplication of effort.

Other Functions of Underwriting Guides In addition to fulfilling the foregoing major purposes, underwriting guides also provide information to assist the underwriter in policy preparation. The typical underwriting guide indicates the proper forms and endorsements to be utilized for each particular situation. Rules and eligibility requirements for various rating plans are also included. Specialized information, such as eligibility for experience and retrospective rating together with appropriate rating formulas, is often found in the underwriting guide as well.

Point Evaluation Systems Some companies employ a specialized type of underwriting guide using a point evaluation system in personal lines. Certain attributes of potential insureds are identified and assigned points. The desirability of a particular applicant is determined on the basis of the total number of points generated by the applicant. A typical point evaluation system also determines the appropriate underwriting authority based upon total points of the applicant or insured. Exhibit 4-2 shows an internal underwriting procedure based on this system. A private passenger auto point count chart used in conjunction with this system is shown in Exhibit 4-3.

A point evaluation system permits expeditious handling of underwriting decisions in a personal lines situation where underwriters are handling a large number of similar applications. The system lends itself well to quantification and thus computerization.

Exhibit 4-2
Internal Underwriting Procedure*

New and Renewal	
0 to 3 points	Risk may be approved by underwriter's assistant.
4 to 5 points	Risk must be referred to senior underwriter.
6 points	Risk must be referred to supervising underwriter for decision if not rejected.
over 6 points	If not rejected, risk must be referred to branch manager or regional casualty manager for decision.
	Underwriter's assistant may process renewals 0 to 4 points if no accident record during expiring year.
Policy Issuance	
0 to 3 points	Policy may be issued immediately and report ordered.
4 points	Coverage may be bound—policy issuance after receipt of reports.
5 points and over	If not rejected, coverage is not to be afforded and policy is not to be issued until after receipt of reports.

*Excerpted with permission from Larry D. Gaunt, "Decision-Making in Underwriting: Policyholder Selection in Private Passenger Automobile Insurance" (Ph.D. dissertation, Georgia State University, 1972), p. 262.

Underwriting Audits

The underwriting audit is a management control tool to determine if underwriting policy is being properly implemented in the field. The larger and more decentralized the company's operations, the more difficult the task of achieving uniformity and consistency in underwriting standards and adhering to a particular underwriting philosophy.

The typical underwriting audit in a field office is conducted by an individual or a team of staff underwriters usually from the home office visiting the field office and reviewing selected files. While it is exceedingly difficult to evaluate the quality of underwriting decision making, the underwriting audit can determine if proper procedures and policies are being followed. The simpler the line of business being underwritten, the easier the audit task becomes. In personal lines, where the attributes of desirable insureds can easily be enumerated, the auditing team can identify lack of compliance quickly. Some companies use a point system to grade underwriters, assessing a

Exhibit 4-3
Private Passenger Underwriting Point Count Chart*

Car Year	Vehicle							
	Standard Yr.	Stock Veh.	Convertible or Compact† Yr.	Veh.	Sport Model or High Performance Yr.	Veh.	Sports Car Yr.	Veh.
5 years or less	0	0	0	1	0	2	0	3
6—10 years	1	0	1	1	1	2	1	3
Over 10 years	2	0	2	1	2	2	2	3

†Charge compact points only where credit exists.

Drivers Age	Marital Status (M.S.)			
	Married		Single†	
	Age	M.S.	Age	M.S.
Under 21(M)	3	0	3	2
Under 21(F)	2	0	2	2
21—25	2	0	2	2
26—29	1	0	1	2
30—50	0	0	0	2
51—60	0	0	0	1
61—65	1	0	1	1
66—70	2	0	2	1
71—75	3	0	3	1
75 and over	4	0	4	1

†Clergyman, single because of religious convictions—0 points.

*Excerpted with permission from Larry D. Gaunt, "Decision-Making in Underwriting: Policyholder Selection in Private Passenger Automobile Insurance" (Ph.D. dissertation, Georgia State University, 1972), p. 264.

penalty point for each violation of underwriting standards or procedure uncovered.

Where the personal lines underwriting data have been computerized, computers can be used to evaluate the composition of a book of business to determine if underwriting policy is being properly implemented. Problems identified in this manner can then be explored by the audit teams in the field.

Two major underwriting functions are selection and classification. Misclassification may be uncovered during the underwriting audit. Classification errors can result in a significant loss of premium dollars through undercharging. When the error results in a higher than proper premium charge, the insured will often complain, and may change insurers.

One study shows that quality control techniques can be applied in underwriting audits.[5] These scientific quality control techniques which have long been used in factory production to identify and control defects can be modified to apply to both underwriting selection and classification.

Measuring Underwriting Results

Just as the proof of the pudding is in the eating, the ultimate test of underwriting is in the results obtained. The insurance company's combined loss and expense ratio tends to indicate the effectiveness of its underwriting program. Of course, serious inflationary trends, catastrophic losses, and adverse political and economic trends may distort these ratios in the short run. Evaluation of results by line of business and by territory will identify problem areas. Interpretation of these underwriting results is also affected by the above factors. In addition, the entire insurance industry has proved to be a cyclical one over the years, providing constantly changing industry average performances against which any particular company can be measured.

Insurance Industry Trends Countrywide underwriting results have indicated the presence of a continuing underwriting cycle. Within the last several years there have been extreme periods of both good and poor underwriting results as shown in Exhibit 4-4. Recently, underwriting losses have been offset by investment income.

The exact causal mechanism for this cycle has not been defined. There are certain forces that appear to have had a significant impact. These include inflation, competition, and the effect of regulation. Slow regulatory responses to rate increase requests in the present period of rapid inflation may have been an important determinant of the subsequent unsatisfactory underwriting results. It has been said that the total impact of rate increases which have been delayed, reduced, or denied by regulatory authorities in recent years was to reduce written premiums by hundreds of millions of dollars. Poor underwriting results are hardly surprising because the major components of loss costs are increasing rapidly due to inflationary factors, and the corresponding rate increases are held down by regulators.

Additional factors influencing recent underwriting experience

Exhibit 4-4
Survey of Underwriting Results*

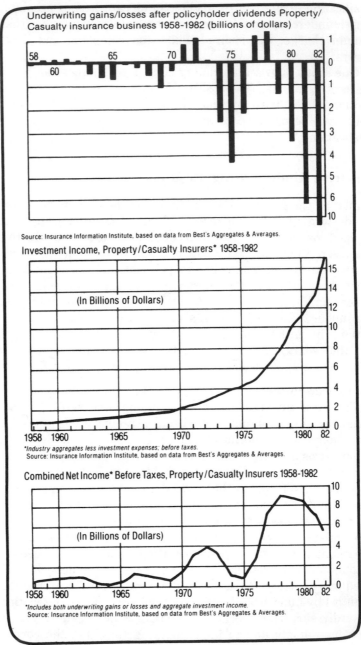

Underwriting gains/losses after policyholder dividends Property/Casualty insurance business 1958-1982 (billions of dollars)

Source: Insurance Information Institute, based on data from Best's Aggregates & Averages.

Investment Income, Property/Casualty Insurers* 1958-1982

(In Billions of Dollars)

*Industry aggregates less investment expenses; before taxes.
Source: Insurance Information Institute, based on data from Best's Aggregates & Averages.

Combined Net Income* Before Taxes, Property/Casualty Insurers 1958-1982

(In Billions of Dollars)

*Includes both underwriting gains or losses and aggregate investment income.
Source: Insurance Information Institute, based on data from Best's Aggregates & Averages.

*Reprinted, with permission, from *Insurance Facts, 1983-84.*

include automobile insurance plans, joint underwriting associations, and similar residual market schemes to solve social as well as insurance problems. Once limited to substandard private passenger auto, residual market plans have expanded to include the FAIR Plans and a variety of joint underwriting associations (JUAs).

Competitive forces may also act to increase the amplitude of these cycles. During periods of seemingly favorable results, insurers try to increase their premium volume. In commercial lines, desirable business may be written at less than manual rates. Contributing to this particular problem is the belief by certain managements that they can write increased volumes of commercial lines at an underwriting loss which can be made up by superior investment results.

Difficulties in Interpretation of Results The evaluation of underwriting results based upon loss and expense ratios is made more difficult by the fact that the ratio's efficiency as a measurement device is reduced by the existence of several complicating factors. The most significant of these factors are (1) premium volume considerations, and (2) loss development delay.

Premium Volume Considerations. There is a direct relationship between premium volume and underwriting policy. Adherence to stricter underwriting standards than those previously employed will usually result in a drop in premium volume. Conversely, a loosening of underwriting standards ordinarily results in an increase in premium volume. The interpretation of the company's combined loss and expense ratio, both on an aggregate basis and by line, must be tempered by consideration of the extent to which the company's premium volume goals have or have not been met. To cite an extreme example, an insurer might adopt a much more stringent underwriting program than in the past, with the result that the combined loss and expense ratio, based on incurred losses and expenses to *earned premium*, is lowered from 102 percent to 96 percent. If *written premium* drops by 25 percent during the same period, then evaluation of the same results using an expense ratio that compares expenses to *written* premiums might well show an actual deterioration of results, with the combined ratio increasing. (In statutory accounting, the loss ratio is constructed with incurred losses to earned premiums, and the expense ratio also relates underwriting expenses to earned premium. The sum of these ratios is the *statutory combined ratio*. The Best's combined ratio, also referred to as the *trade basis combined ratio*, utilizes the same loss ratio but relates underwriting expenses to written premium.)

The rationale for relating underwriting expenses to written premium lies in the fact that most expenses are related to placing business on the books rather than maintaining it. The effect of the trade basis combined ratio is to recognize the "equity" in the unearned premium reserve. There are some limitations to analysis on a trade basis. First, the extent to which expenses are related to written rather than earned premium will vary by line. There are variations in commission and acquisition expenses from line to line. Certain specialty lines such as boiler and machinery have heavy continuing inspection expenses which are actually related more to earned premium. This is also true to a lesser extent in workers' compensation. For this reason, comparisons between insurance companies with different mixes of business on a trade basis may be misleading.

Exhibit 4-5 shows a hypothetical example of an insurer experiencing a 25 percent drop in written premium as a result of following a much more restrictive underwriting policy. Note that on a *statutory basis* the combined results have improved from 102 percent to 96 percent. On a *trade basis*, the company's experience actually deteriorated from 99.9 percent to 102.2 percent. Analysis of underwriting results should be done on both bases in order to properly evaluate the effect of changes in premium volume.

Loss Development Delay. In certain lines of business, particularly the liability coverages, a considerable time elapses between the occurrence of a loss and the final settlement of the claim. While reserves are established as soon as the loss is reported, significant inaccuracy exists in the estimation of ultimate loss costs. This is known as loss development delay or the so-called "long tail," and it has two major components which are (1) changes in the reserves for reported losses and (2) changes in the IBNR (incurred but not reported).

In lines of business written on an occurrence basis, where there is an extended discovery period between the time of the occurrence of the insured event and the discovery and subsequent suit by the claimant, the IBNR greatly affects the accuracy of current reported loss results. The change on the part of many professional liability insurers to a "claims-made" basis is meant to reduce this problem.

If a policy is written on an *occurrence* basis, the underwriter provides coverage on those claims that occur during the policy period even if claims are not actually brought against the insured for years after the coverage has expired. If a policy is written on a *claims-made* basis, the underwriter provides coverage only on those claims made against the insured during the policy period. The difference is that under the claims-made policy underwriters may adjust the renewal premiums to reflect the actual experience of the previous year.

In all liability lines, where several years may elapse between the notification of a claim and the final settlement, changes in reserves occur frequently. Since the incurred losses used in the compilation of

Exhibit 4-5
Underwriting Results—Statutory and Trade Basis

	19X1	19X2
Written premium	$10,000,000	$7,500,000
Earned premium	9,500,000	9,000,000
Underwriting expense	3,990,000	2,790,000
Losses incurred	5,700,000	5,850,000
Statutory Basis		
Loss ratio: $\frac{\text{Incurred losses}}{\text{Earned premium}}$	$\frac{\$5,700,000}{\$9,500,000} = 60\%$	$\frac{\$5,850,000}{\$9,000,000} = 65\%$
Expense ratio: $\frac{\text{Underwriting expenses}}{\text{Earned premium}}$	$\frac{\$3,990,000}{\$9,500,000} = 42\%$	$\frac{\$2,790,000}{\$9,000,000} = 31\%$
Statutory Combined ratio	102%	96%
Trade Basis		
Loss ratio: $\frac{\text{Incurred losses}}{\text{Earned premium}}$	$\frac{\$5,700,000}{\$9,500,000} = 60\%$	$\frac{\$5,850,000}{\$9,000,000} = 65\%$
Expense ratio: $\frac{\text{Underwriting expenses}}{\text{Written premium}}$	$\frac{\$3,990,000}{\$10,000,000} = 39.9\%$	$\frac{\$2,790,000}{\$7,500,000} = 37.2\%$
Trade basis Combined ratio	99.9%	102.2%

loss ratios include both paid losses and loss reserves, the loss ratio as an indicator of underwriting performance relies heavily on the accuracy and realistic evaluation of the reserve estimations. The greater the loss development delay, the less accurate the estimation. Exhibit 4-6 shows an example of loss development delay for a particular group of general liability policies on a calendar-accident-year basis.

Exhibit 4-6
Loss Development Delay—Calendar-Accident-Year Basis*

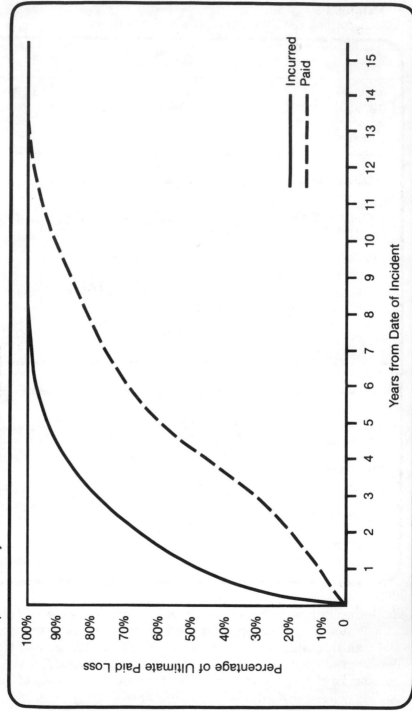

*Reprinted with permission from J. S. Hammond, E. P. Hollingsworth, Jr., and C. Sadler, "Using a Monte Carlo Simulation as a Part of Training Liability Insurance Underwriters," presented at the ORSA/TIMS Conference, San Juan, Puerto Rico, October 1974, p. 4.

Standards of Performance   One technique that can be used to evaluate the performance of an underwriting department is to set standards of performance with respect to several crucial areas of underwriting. These standards of performance include:

1. Selection standards
2. Product mix standards
3. Pricing standards
4. Accommodated risks standards
5. Retention ratio standards
6. Success ratio standards
7. Service to producers standards

While some of these standards by their nature are clearly applicable only to commercial lines underwriting departments, others can be used for both personal and commercial lines.

Selection Standards.   In order to implement this monitoring technique, it is necessary to set up well-defined selection rules in the underwriting guide. These selection rules would define highly desirable, average, and below average types of insureds, and each underwriter, branch, or region should have a goal, a specified balance of the three types. During an underwriting audit or review, the business written by a particular underwriter, branch, or region can be segmented into the various categories and an evaluation made of the percentages of the book of business in each category.

Product Mix Standards.   This monitoring technique requires a statement within the underwriting guide of the desired product mix for new and renewal business. For example, if liability losses are causing an adverse effect on the entire book of business, the product mix standard may call for a reduction in manufacturing classes but a concerted effort to increase the writing in the contractor, service, and mercantile classes. The comparison of the actual book to the desired one provides a straightforward evaluation of performance.

Pricing Standards.   In those lines of business where experience rating, loss rating, and schedule rating plans are available, the relationship between the premium developed by the rates utilized and those that would have been developed at straight manual rates is of great importance. Instances have been found when an insurance company's aggregate book of general liability and commercial auto business is at less than 80 percent of manual rates. The pricing standard consists of a procedure in which all accounts which deviate from manual premium by more than 5 percent are monitored. Records are kept of premium volume above and below manual. The pricing standard consists of setting goals for a branch or region that the entire book should not deviate from manual premium by more than a set allowable range.

"Accommodated Risks" Standards.   This standard of performance requires a log in which all "accommodated risks" are entered together with the full particulars of the reasons for the accommodation. An *accommodation* is usually the acceptance of a substandard exposure in return for more profitable business. During regular underwriting audits and reviews, evaluation of the log can determine if it is being overused and assure that follow-up has been made of the "increased volume" or other promise from the producer.

Retention Ratio Standards.   The *retention ratio* is the percentage of business renewed. An unfavorable percentage of renewals may indicate serious deficiencies, including poor service to producers, uncompetitive pricing, or unfavorable claims service. This standard requires careful monitoring of the renewal rate and evaluation of any trends discerned.

Success Ratio Standards.   The *success ratio* is the ratio of business written to business quoted. This standard is usually employed in commercial lines. Data must be gathered for a large number of quotations to determine the average range for this ratio. Ratios which are either inordinately high or low may require follow-up and further investigation. A high ratio may indicate:

1. easing of competition
2. rate inadequacy
3. unduly broad coverage or form
4. deterioration in selection criteria

Low success ratios may suggest:

1. increasing competition
2. rates that are too high
3. coverages or forms that are too restrictive
4. selection criteria that are too high

Service to Producers Standards.   Since producers rank companies and branch offices on the basis of service received, it is important that the company be able to evaluate its own performance. This standard requires establishment of a set of minimum acceptable standards for certain types of service to producers. Then the actual performance of each underwriter, branch, or region being evaluated is compared with the mandated level of performance. An example of one such standard appears in Exhibit 4-7.

Exhibit 4-7
Example of "Service to Producers" Underwriting Standards

Category	Minimum Acceptable Standard
1. Quotations	3 working days
2. New policies	3 working days
3. Replies to correspondence	2 working days
4. Cancellations, endorsements, certificates	5 working days
5. Direct cancellation notices	Same day service
6. Renewals	No later than 10 days prior to expiration.

THE UNDERWRITING PROCESS

The implementation of underwriting policy takes place when line underwriting decisions are made, either on individual applicants or on an entire book of business. Underwriting has been defined as the process of hazard recognition and evaluation, selection of insureds, pricing, and determination of policy terms and conditions. It should also be noted that the same underwriting process is applied both by the line underwriter making decisions on individual submissions and by the underwriting manager making decisions affecting an entire book of business.

Underwriting is not confined to those individuals whose job description labels them as "underwriters." Producers, although their primary function is marketing, also have an underwriting responsibility. The following section follows the underwriting process from the producer's initial contact with the applicant through the steps that lead to the final decision by the company underwriter and through the monitoring function to the evaluation of that decision.

Field Underwriting

Regardless of the type of marketing system, every producer has some underwriting responsibility. While some producers think of underwriting only in a negative sense, there is a positive, creative aspect to underwriting as well. Effective field underwriting by the producer can lead to more efficient, profitable production.

Evaluation of Applicants Field underwriting begins with the evaluation of applicants. Regardless of the type of marketing system, there are two major aspects to this evaluation. These are (1) the moral quality of the applicant(s) and (2) the applicant's suitability for the producer's available markets.

The Moral Quality of the Applicant(s). There is an old saying that there is no rate adequate to compensate for moral hazard. This is based on two premises. First, insurance contracts are negotiated on a level of *uberrimae fidei* or utmost good faith. When moral hazard is present, the insured may well misrepresent or conceal some material fact or condition. Even if the producer can place the business, insureds of this type do not provide the kind of foundation on which a profitable long-term relationship can be built with the available markets.

Second, the entire insurance rating structure is built on the premise that losses are fortuitous and random. When moral hazard is present, losses may be intentionally caused or increased in severity when they do occur. Business that is unprofitable for the insurance company is also unprofitable for the producer in the long run.

Company underwriters frequently underwrite the producer as much as the insured in a particular submission. If a producer has a reputation for continually trying to market "distress" business, every submission from that producer will be scrutinized in minute detail.

The Applicant's Suitability for the Producer's Available Markets. Virtually every insurer will accept an occasional piece of substandard business as an accommodation to the producer. However, the producer whose every other submission is a request for an accommodation wastes everyone's time. It should be noted that the submission that cannot be placed generates no commission income.

One of the most important assets of a producer is markets. Under an exclusive agency or direct writing marketing system, the producer has only one market. It is necessary only to learn that company's underwriting philosophy and seek to produce only that type of business considered desirable. Trying to slip through the occasional piece of clearly unacceptable business may be counterproductive in that it may lead to tougher underwriting of all future submissions or to dismissal. In most companies, it is appropriate to let the company underwriter decide on those prospective insureds that fall into the many gray areas of possible acceptability. On the other hand, a practice of careful evaluation of applicants, full disclosure, and faithful adherence to the company's underwriting requirements earns a producer the respect and support of underwriters.

The question of suitability for the available markets is more complex for the independent agent, since he or she deals with a variety of insurance companies with differing underwriting standards and philosophy. The proper allocation of above average, average, and below average business among the available markets is one of the most important skills of an independent agent.

In addition to determining that the quality of the business is appropriate to each of the available markets, the producer must also ascertain that the class and line of business is one that can be reasonably placed. It would be an obvious waste of time to develop a prospect for a large, open ocean cargo policy if the producer has no market for this coverage. A further consideration with hard-to-place classes of business is whether the extraordinary amount of time and effort required to place the business is justified by the present and potential future commission income.

Development of the Submission   Once the prospect has been determined to be of suitable quality and a market is available, the next step is the development of the submission. This is a routine activity for most producers, but it should be noted that submission development includes two underwriting activities. These are (1) gathering information to complete the required application(s) and (2) determining the appropriate coverage.

Information Gathering.   In many personal lines submissions, the information-gathering phase may simply consist of completion of an application. On the other hand, a large commercial lines submission may require considerable additional information beyond the applications. Usually, the more underwriting information that can be forwarded along with the submission the better. This means that the producer must be familiar with the information requirements of underwriting for that particular type of coverage. A complete submission adds a professional touch and reduces the time required for a decision.

On commercial line submissions, the additional information requirements may include prior-years' loss figures, financial statements, photographs of large or unusual property exposures, and other items of information.

Determination of Appropriate Coverage.   In personal lines, the determination of the appropriate coverage is relatively straightforward due to statutory requirements or the rules of a mortgagee. However, it is also necessary to determine that the limits of liability or amount of property coverage are adequate for the insured.

In the case of a commercial submission, the producer should also ascertain that the applicant is eligible for the particular coverage and rating plan requested. It may be embarrassing to sell a potential insured on the merits of a package policy or a retrospective rating plan only to discover that the applicant does not qualify.

Evaluating the Submission

When the submission reaches the company underwriter, it must be evaluated and a decision made on its acceptability. As previously noted, underwriting extends beyond selection to include determination of the proper price and coverage. While the producer has presumably field underwritten the submission, the acceptability must be made by the line underwriter.

Underwriting decision making may be viewed as a process involving the following six steps:

1. Gathering information
2. Identifying and developing alternative courses of action
3. Evaluating the alternatives
4. Choosing one of the alternatives
5. Implementing the selected course of action
6. Monitoring the decision[6]

The first step in the decision-making process is gathering information.

External Sources of Information   There are four major external sources of information available to the company underwriter. These are (1) the producer, (2) consumer investigation reports, (3) government records, and (4) financial rating services.

The Producer.   The initial source of information for the company underwriter is the producer. A properly completed application and other relevant information available to the producer are of great assistance to the line underwriter. In most cases, the producer also conveys, either verbally or in writing, his or her recommendation concerning the submission, including the producer's assessment of the insured's personal and business reputation.

The data obtained from the producer is subject to corroboration from other sources. The producer's marketing orientation may lead to a tendency to gloss over some of the more adverse characteristics of the submission while emphasizing the better qualities. The credibility of the information supplied by a particular producer is a function of that producer's reputation for objectivity and frankness.

There is also the tendency on the part of the prospect or applicant to gloss over some of their more adverse characteristics. In addition, the wording of some questions on the application and even the lack of the "right" questions may cause the producer a problem. Producers do not know each prospect intimately enough to ascertain whether or not all their answers are correct or complete.

Consumer Investigation Reports. Several independent reporting services provide background information on prospective insureds. On personal lines coverages such as private passenger automobile, these reports usually include a check of the motor vehicle records for violations, a description of the neighborhood and environment of the applicant, and information regarding both the reputation of the applicant and that of his or her associates. Various types of reports are available for most commercial lines coverages.

Most information sources provide both objective and subjective information. Particularly with respect to consumer investigative reports, it is important that the underwriter make the proper distinction between these two types of information. *Objective* information consists of facts that have been recorded and can be verified. *Subjective* information consists of opinions or personal impressions. It may be damaging to the insured and ultimately to the insurance company if the underwriter acts on the basis of some "fact" as if it were a verifiable bit of objective data when it is actually a subjective opinion. Consumer investigation reports are influenced by various types of consumer protection legislation such as the Fair Credit Reporting Act.

Government Records. Government records provide an important source of objective information. These records include motor vehicle reports; criminal court records; and civil court records including records of suits filed, mortgages and liens, lists of business licenses, property tax records, and bankruptcy filings. Motor vehicle records are a fundamental information source for auto underwriting. A check of property mortgages and liens is useful in commercial property underwriting to assure that there are no unreported encumbrances. An unreported encumbrance may indicate that a particular insured interest was inadvertently omitted, or it may indicate an attempt on the part of the insured to conceal an adverse financial condition.

A review of civil court actions will uncover any outstanding judgments under tort liability, or breach of contract. These data are vital in underwriting general liability and professional liability coverages.

Financial Rating Services. Dun and Bradstreet, Standard and Poor's, and the National Association of Credit Management are some of the major financial rating services. They provide data on the credit ratings of individual businesses, together with industry averages for purposes of comparison. While the use of one or more of these financial rating services is almost universal in surety bond underwriting, the services are also used in many other commercial lines, particularly commercial property insurance. They can be used to verify a financial statement provided by an insured as well as to provide an overall picture of the insured's financial stability and strength. A financially weak business may present an unacceptable moral hazard. Use of the data provided by the financial rating services is greatly enhanced if the underwriter is familiar with financial ratios used to evaluate a firm's liquidity, profitability, and debt structure. In addition, the 10K form filed with the Security and Exchange Commission (SEC) contains a wealth of information on public companies.

Internal Sources of Information There are five major sources of internal information. They are (1) loss experience of insureds, (2) inspection (loss control) reports, (3) field marketing personnel, (4) claims files, and (5) production records.

Loss Experience. Underwriters usually have loss experience on insureds, and also on an aggregate basis by class, line of business, and territory, both for the insurance company and the industry. In commercial lines, the loss experience of the insured may be large enough to have some credibility, while in personal lines it is the loss experience for the class or territory that has more significance.

In analyzing loss data, loss frequency, severity, and the cause or type of loss are all important. The peril causing the loss and the date of loss provide further insights. If one peril causes a majority of the losses, there may be a possibility of either reducing the hazards through loss control measures or adding or increasing a deductible. The date of loss provides information on possible seasonality or trends in loss experience. Results for a given line, class, or territory, as well as insurance industry results, may give indications of rate inadequacy, causing modification of underwriting policy pending approval of higher rate levels.

Inspection Reports. Inspection or loss control reports prepared by loss control personnel provide information on the physical condition of property, the safety of business operations, and the inspector's personal impressions. In a statistical analysis of data gathered from inspection reports of the Factory Mutuals, David C. Shpilberg found that the attribute which had the greatest predictive value was the inspector's overall impression of the risk.[7] These inspection reports had 160 data items reporting on physical hazards, while the inspector's impression of the risk was the only item pertaining to moral or morale hazards. This study reinforces the notion that management attitude and effectiveness as reflected in things such as housekeeping, enforcement of safety rules, and commitment to loss control are highly significant.

Since most inspection reports in commercial lines contain lists of both mandatory and suggested recommendations, a follow-up on the degree of compliance will provide the underwriter with an insight into the attitude of management.

Field Marketing Personnel. In most companies, field marketing personnel (such as field representatives) can provide both specific and general information. Field marketing personnel can frequently obtain information which was omitted from an application or submission from a producer. In territories that are sparsely populated or in other situations in which qualified loss control personnel are not available, many insurance companies utilize field marketing personnel to make simplified inspection reports. The field marketing person can also provide detailed background information on the producer and sometimes on the insured. In some companies, this function is fulfilled by sales managers, managing general agents, or the producer.

Claims Files. An underwriter can often obtain insights into the character and moral tone of the insured by reviewing the insured's claims files. Claims adjusters frequently develop significant underwriting information during the course of their investigations. An adjuster investigating a small fire loss at a machine shop may uncover evidence of poor housekeeping and a disregard for loss control on the part of the insured. Some insurers have an information system whereby claims adjusters notify the underwriter any time they obtain pertinent information on physical, moral, and morale hazards on any insureds. In personal lines, the troublesome characteristic of claims consciousness can often be identified by the adjuster during the course of an investigation. In commercial lines, such as workers' compensation, perusal of claims files may indicate the presence of dangerous conditions requiring loss control engineering.

Often the claims adjuster is the only employee of the company who has an opportunity to make a firsthand appraisal of the locations insured. The value of his or her observation is so great that maximum effort is justified to ascertain that nothing inhibits full communication.

Production Records. Records are usually available on individual producers indicating loss ratio, volume, mix of business, amount of supporting business, length of service, and industry experience. In the case of an independent agent, the company's standing in the agency is also relevant. In auto underwriting, the production records on the mix of business would indicate if a particular producer is submitting an inordinately large percentage of young drivers or drivers with poor driving records. In commercial lines, the production records will indicate the producer's familiarity with complex or unusual classes of business. This may be of concern to the underwriter in the case of a large boiler and machinery application or a complex manufacturing submission. Such a submission from a producer whose book of business is 95 percent personal lines would raise questions in the underwriter's mind about the producer's familiarity with the coverage and his or her ability to service the account properly. In all marketing systems, producer results over a reasonably extended period of time (usually three to five years) are a good measure of his or her capability as the first line underwriter.

Hazard Evaluation Much underwriting information is developed to enable the underwriter to identify and evaluate hazards. Hazards may be classified as being either physical, moral, or morale.

Physical Hazards. Physical hazards are defined as tangible characteristics of the property, persons, or operations to be insured that affect the probable frequency and severity of loss due to one or more perils. They may be attributes of the applicant, the property to be insured, or of the environment in which the property is located.

Moral Hazards. Moral hazard is defined as a condition that exists where a person may try to cause a loss, or may exaggerate a loss that has occurred. While most information on moral hazard is subjective in nature, there may be objective data available, such as a history of past financial difficulties or a criminal record. Potential indicators of moral hazard include weak financial condition, undesirable associates, and poor moral character.

WEAK FINANCIAL CONDITION. The owners of a financially weak company may intentionally cause a loss in order to obtain desperately needed cash. Ocean marine underwriters are particularly aware of the possibility that during periods of overcapacity the owners of an idle or obsolete vessel may try to "sell it to the underwriters" by intentionally sailing it aground or scuttling it. Since the financial condition of a business can change quickly, the detection of this hazard requires constant monitoring. Changes in consumer tastes or innovation by competitors can leave a business with a sizable obsolete inventory. Economic downturns may cause postponement of essential maintenance to vital services such as electrical, plumbing, and heating systems.

UNDESIRABLE ASSOCIATES. Association of the insured with unlawful individuals in the community is another indicator of potential moral hazard. A business that is frequented by members of the underworld or other undesirable individuals in the community does not reflect well on the moral tone of the proprietor.

POOR MORAL CHARACTER. Moral hazard may arise from the poor moral character of the insured even when the financial condition is sound. Previous questionable losses, a criminal record, or evidence of moral turpitude may indicate the presence of moral hazard. A reputation in the community for unethical or illegal business practices on the part of the insured is also an indicator of moral hazard. The combination of an insured of poor moral character and overinsurance is an ominous one.

Morale Hazards. Morale hazard is a condition that exists when a person is less careful than he or she should be because of the existence of insurance. It arises out of carelessness or indifference to loss and is usually more subtle and difficult to detect than moral hazard. Morale hazard might better be termed "motivation hazard" because it exists in insureds that are poorly motivated to avoid and minimize losses. Morale hazards may be indicated by poor personality traits or poor management.

POOR PERSONALITY TRAITS. Personality traits such as carelessness and thoughtlessness are indications of morale hazard. Careless individuals do not mean to cause a loss intentionally, but they may exhibit a cavalier attitude toward valuable possessions, increasing the likelihood of loss. An individual who thoughtlessly leaves the keys in his or her car exhibits the presence of this hazard. Pride of ownership is the attribute desired; its lack may indicate the existence of morale hazard.

POOR MANAGEMENT. Poor or inefficient management may also indicate morale hazard. Slovenly housekeeping and indifferent bookkeeping are overt manifestations of this condition. Indifference to loss may result in the neglect of maintenance of fire extinguishers and other safety devices. Poor or nonexistent internal control systems invite theft and embezzlement on the part of employees. Failure to comply with recommendations or to cooperate with loss control personnel is a further indication of morale hazard.

Identifying, Developing, and Evaluating the Alternatives

After all the essential information on a particular submission has been gathered, the underwriter is ready to make a decision. The underwriter must identify and develop the alternatives available with respect to the submission and, after careful evaluation of each of them, choose the optimal one under the circumstances.

Two alternatives are easily identified. The underwriter may accept the submission as is or reject the submission entirely. In addition, the underwriter may accept that submission subject to certain modifications. Determining the appropriate modification to best meet the needs of the insurer, producer, and insured is a challenge to the creative ingenuity of the underwriter.

There are four major types of modifications that can be made: (1) adoption of loss control programs or devices, (2) change in rates or rating plans, (3) amendment of policy terms and conditions, or (4) the use of facultative reinsurance.

Acceptance with Modifications

Adoption of Loss Control Programs or Devices. One alternative available to the underwriter for a submission that would otherwise be unacceptable is to reduce the hazards. Such loss control programs as the installation of sprinklers, addition of guard service, and improvements in housekeeping and maintenance are means of reducing physical hazards. Further examples are the requirement of clear space for insureds in brush or wooded locations or the installation of machinery guards to reduce employee injuries. Some of these programs are relatively inexpensive and simple to implement, while others, such as sprinklers, require considerable capital investment.

From the insured's viewpoint, insurer recommendations to reduce hazards may have a very positive, long-term effect on the ultimate costs of doing business or they may be viewed as wholly unnecessary expenses. A significant function of underwriting is the making of sound recommendations accompanied by well-reasoned and convincing explanations to the insured.

Change in Rates or Rating Plan. A submission that is not acceptable at the rate requested might be desirable business at a higher rate or on a different rating plan. In private passenger auto, for example, a submission may not be eligible for the "safe driver" program for which it is submitted but might qualify for inclusion in another program at standard rates.

The rate modification is not always negative. A producer might submit an account that is particularly desirable, and the underwriter might suggest a rate deviation to increase the producer's likelihood of obtaining the account. Particularly in the *"A" rated* general liability area, proper pricing of submissions is crucial to the attainment of satisfactory underwriting results. *"A" rated* general liability policies are those classes in which the size and variability of the accounts within the classes are such that the underwriter is given a great deal of pricing flexibility. Pricing modifications also play a key role in judgment-rated lines such as inland and ocean marine.

Amendment of Policy Terms and Conditions. A problem submission may be made acceptable by modifying the policy form to exclude certain perils or to add or increase a deductible. Particularly in small commercial accounts where a large number of small losses may have caused unsatisfactory experience in the past, a deductible may greatly improve the viability of the coverage.

There is considerable variation in the degree of flexibility available to the underwriter from one line of business to another. In those situations where the coverage forms have been filed subject to approval by state regulatory bodies, coverage modifications are seldom possible. Even in these cases, it may be possible to suggest an entirely different coverage form.

The Use of Facultative Reinsurance.   In some submissions where there exists a large concentration of values, the submission may be acceptable only if facultative reinsurance can be obtained. An alternative to the purchase of facultative reinsurance is to suggest that the producer divide the insurance among several insurers. This approach has the advantage of reducing reinsurance expense but also the disadvantage of losing ceded reinsurance commissions.

Choice of One of the Alternatives

The selection decision involves the determination of whether it is best to accept the submission as offered, accept it with some modification, or reject it. While rejection is sometimes unavoidable, underwriters should adopt a positive approach since one of the insurer's goals is the production of profitable business. Rejections develop neither premium nor commission. There are five areas which must be considered in arriving at the selection decision. These are the (1) amount of underwriting authority required, (2) presence of supporting business, (3) mix of business, (4) producer relationships, and (5) regulatory constraints.

Amount of Underwriting Authority Required   Prior to accepting an applicant, an underwriter must determine that he or she has the necessary amount of underwriting authority. The underwriter's task differs in those cases where there is sufficient authority to make the final decision and other cases where the underwriter prepares the file for submission to higher underwriting authority. As Chester I. Barnard noted in *The Functions of the Executive,* "The fine art of executive decision consists in not deciding questions that are not now pertinent, in not deciding prematurely, in not making decisions that cannot be made effective, and in not making decisions that others should make."[8] Thus, the underwriter should check the underwriting guide before promising a producer a quick answer on a submission since referral to higher underwriting authority is often time consuming. Axiomatic to determining authority is the willingness to accept the authority granted rather than always looking to higher authority.

Presence of Supporting Business An individual application that is marginal on its own may become acceptable on an account basis if the rest of the account is desirable. Premium volume alone may not be sufficient since five separate pieces of marginal business do not aggregate to an acceptable account. On the other hand, the prospect of obtaining some above-average business in other lines may make a marginal submission viable if the supporting business is profitable enough to subsidize the marginal business.

In account underwriting, all of the business from a particular insured is evaluated as a unit which must stand or fall on its own merits. The account underwriting approach, by looking at both the submission and its supporting business or at the aggregate of submissions, minimizes poorly considered acceptances.

Mix of Business The mix of business is the distribution of individual policies comprising the book of business of a producer, territory, state, or region among the various classifications. Underwriting policy, as set forth in the underwriting guide, frequently will indicate company goals regarding the mix of business. Particular classes, such as youthful drivers in private passenger auto, or restaurants in property fire coverage, may be over-represented in the present book of business. The effect of this is either to raise the criteria for acceptability in these classes or to prohibit new business in some of these classes.

Producer Relationships Often an underwriter is pressured by an important producer to accept a piece of marginal business as an accommodation. Usually there is an assurance of a *quid pro quo* that the producer will respond with some outstanding business later. Some underwriters keep accommodation files to enable them to detect excessive requests for accommodations and to determine if the promised business does materialize.

The relationship between the company and the producer should be based upon mutual trust and respect. Differences of opinion are common, particularly since some of the goals of the producers and the underwriters are in conflict. The long-run goals of the producers and the insurers are in growth and profit. Mutual accommodation and willingness to see the other's viewpoint are essential to building a satisfactory working relationship.

Regulatory Constraints The underwriter's freedom to decline or refuse to renew an applicant has been inhibited increasingly by state regulatory authorities. Particularly in private passenger auto and such property programs as the FAIR Plan, declination or refusal to renew is restricted by regulation. Regulatory constraints are the controlling consideration on those classes of business to which they apply. Where cancellation or refusal to renew is limited by regulation, the selection decision on new submissions should be very carefully evaluated.

Privacy legislation and unfair trade practices acts will impact on underwriting, especially in personal lines.

Implementing the Decision

Implementing underwriting decisions generally requires three steps. The first is communication of the decision to the producer, if necessary, and to other company personnel. If the decision is to accept with modifications, the reasons must be clearly communicated to the producer or insured. If the decision is to reject, the underwriter must sell the negative result. Effective communication contributes to the education of the producer with respect to future submissions.

The second step in implementing the decision is the establishment of a claims information system to assist in monitoring. The purpose of the claims information system is to alert the underwriter to claims activity during the policy period. A claims referral system may immediately refer the file to the underwriter if the frequency of losses exceeds a predetermined limit or if a severe loss occurs.

The third step is the execution of the appropriate documentation. Binders may need to be issued or a policy worksheet sent to the policywriting department. In some lines of business, certificates of insurance must be prepared and filings made with appropriate authorities, such as the Interstate Commerce Commission (ICC).

Monitoring

After an underwriting decision has been made on a submission or renewal, the underwriter's task is not completed. It is necessary that the business be monitored to achieve satisfactory results.

Monitoring refers to two different but related activities. These are:

1. Follow-up on individual policies to assure compliance with recommendations and to determine that there have been no changes in hazards.
2. Review of a book of business to determine that underwriting policy is being complied with and to detect changes in the type, volume, and quality of business which may require corrective action.

While monitoring individual policies is an important part of the line underwriter's task, the form which the monitoring takes varies considerably, depending upon the line of business. The following section concentrates upon the considerations involved in monitoring a book of business.

Linkage Between Decisions and Outcomes Monitoring the quality of decisions affecting a book of business is greatly complicated by the fact that the linkage between underwriting decisions and results is not direct. Since underwriting decisions are made under conditions of uncertainty, it is quite possible to make a good decision that results in a poor outcome. An underwriter can accept a perfectly "clean" application, only to suffer a major loss. On the other hand, an underwriter might make a poor decision, such as accepting a substandard insured, and have no losses. Over the long run, however, the better the quality of the underwriting decisions, the better the results.

Monitoring a Book of Business When monitoring the results for a book of business, the relationship between loss ratio and premium volume should be considered. Often there is a trade-off in that premium volume can be increased at the cost of an increase of a few points in the loss ratio. If such a decision were made, it would be pointless later to criticize the underwriting department for the rise in the loss ratio. Conversely, overly restrictive underwriting may result in an excellent loss ratio but a premium volume too small to cover the fixed costs of underwriting and other overhead expenses.

A book of business in a particular major line such as fire or marine can be subdivided by:

1. class of business
2. territory
3. producer

An analysis of a book of business on the basis of rating class or category of business will determine if there are any imbalances in the book of business. A book of private passenger auto insurance can be examined to determine if there is a disproportionate number of young drivers in the insured's book of business relative to their proportion of the driving population as a whole.

Evaluation of the classes by premium volume can be followed by analysis of the classes with respect to loss ratio. Classes with poor or deteriorating experience can be identified and corrective action taken.

Next, the book of business can be arrayed by geographic territory to determine the spread of business by area. A comparison of the spread of business by territory in the current year with respect to the preceding year provides evidence of shifts in business on a territorial basis. In property insurance, concentration in a particular area may result in an unanticipated conflagration hazard. The amount of business written in hurricane-prone coastline areas should be carefully monitored. In auto insurance, the amount of business written in high density urban areas should also be monitored.

Another aspect of monitoring the book of business by territory is consideration of the volume of business written within rating jurisdictions where the rate levels are felt to be inadequate and where immediate rate relief cannot be obtained due to the regulatory climate. Efforts addressed to increasing premium volume in such territories would seem to be counter-productive.

When analyzing the book of business by producer, the data runs should provide the premium volume and loss ratio for each producer. Other aspects of each producer's book of business which should be monitored are the mix of business between personal lines and commercial lines and the rate of growth of each component. For larger producers, analysis of the book of business with respect to both class of business and territory can provide useful insights into the direction of the producer's efforts.

Evaluation of a Class of Business. Underwriting management periodically reviews loss and expense ratios on a companywide basis by class of business. Changes in technology introducing new materials and types of operation can drastically change the desirability of a particular class of business. Changes in the social and legal climate can have even greater impact as has recently occurred in professional liability and products liability. In addition to evaluation of the entire book of business, the lines and major classes are also reviewed by territory or region to detect regional differences.

Evaluation of a Territory. In review of a particular line or class of business within a particular territory, the reason for any deviation from the national average is sought. A territory may include a state, a group of states, or even a single major urban area. In view of the differences in state regulation, the state is a convenient unit for territorial analysis.

There are often physical differences in terrain, degree of urbanization, and type of operation from one state to another. For example, building construction workers are subject to different climatic conditions in New England than in Southern California. These regional differences might significantly change the desirability of a particular class of business from one area to another.

Insurance regulations vary greatly from one state to another. A class of business that develops an adequate rate in one state may have a seriously inadequate rate in another. Restrictions on selection may also hamper underwriting results in a given state. Finally, there are both legislative and judicial differences among the several states. Comparative negligence is the rule in some states and contributory negligence in others. The differences in the legal environment affecting insurance company operations are legion. The total impact of all these considerations must be determined when evaluating a territorial book of business.

Evaluation of a Producer. The book of business of individual producers is also periodically reviewed. The producer's premium volume and loss ratio are evaluated both on an overall basis and by line and class of business. In independent agency companies, the company's ranking in the agency is also a factor. In addition to loss ratio considerations, the mix of business being produced is analyzed.

One major problem in the evaluation of the loss ratio of a particular producer is statistical credibility. If the producer does not generate sufficient volume, the loss ratio in a particular line, or even in the entire book, may lack credibility.

However, full statistical credibility, while desirable, is not essential for the analysis of a particular producer's book of business. When statistical credibility is lacking, statistical tools, with their analytic power, cannot be used. This often means that the book of business will have to be painstakingly dissected, sometimes loss by loss. It must be determined whether the losses represent unfortunate outcomes on good business, or whether the business itself is substandard. A shock loss on a "clean" piece of business can happen to anyone. A pattern of marginal business and less than full disclosure is another matter.

Chapter Notes

1. "Is Underwriting a Lost Art?" *Producer*, Crum and Forster Insurance Companies, Winter 1976, p. 13.
2. John S. Hammond, E. P. Hollingsworth, Jr., and Carl Sadler, "Using Monte Carlo Simulation as a Part of Training Liability Insurance Underwriters," presented at the ORSA/TIMS Conference, San Juan, Puerto Rico, 16-18 October 1974.
3. Louis A. Allen, "Improving Line and Staff Relationships," *Studies in Personnel Policy*, No. 153, National Industrial Conference Board, Inc. (1956), p. 76.
4. For an in-depth discussion of this topic see J. J. Launie, J. Finley Lee, and Norman A. Baglini, *Principles of Property and Liability Underwriting*, 2nd ed. (Malvern: Insurance Institute of America, 1977), Chapter 1.
5. J. J. Launie, "An Insurance Underwriting Quality Control Model," *Proceedings and Abstracts*, American Institute for Decision Sciences, Sixth Annual Meeting, Western Regional Conference, Phoenix, Arizona, March 1977, pp. 217-219.
6. J. J. Launie, J. Finley Lee, and Norman A. Baglini, *Principles of Property and Liability Underwriting*, Chapter 2.
7. David C. Shpilberg, "The Probability Distribution of Fire Loss Amount," paper presented at the American Risk and Insurance Association Annual Meeting, Newton, Massachusetts, August 1976.
8. Chester I. Barnard, *The Functions of the Executive* (Cambridge, MA: Harvard University Press, 1938), p. 194.

CHAPTER 5

Underwriting Property Insurance

FIRE INSURANCE UNDERWRITING

Introduction

Whether written separately or as part of a package, fire is generally the most important peril to underwrite in property insurance. Fire insurance is one of the oldest types of property coverage, dating back to the seventeenth century. Fire insurance was an outgrowth of destructive conflagrations such as the fire of London in 1666. Early fire insurance contracts were written on property at a fixed location and provided little off-premises coverage and few, if any, additional perils. While loss frequency for a given insured is usually low and most losses that do occur are partial losses, fire always contains a total loss potential, which greatly influences underwriting practices. Historically, the keystone of fire underwriting has been the *fire line*, which is defined as the maximum dollar limit to be written on a particular insured or class. This practice of limiting the amount subject on a particular insured is in sharp contrast to the inland marine insurance practice of writing gross lines.

Writing a *gross line* means that the insurer writes the entire value of the property insured and utilizes its reinsurance treaties to lower its retention. Since fire lines also utilize reinsurance, the difference is one of degree. The total loss potential that clearly exists in fire insurance on properties at a fixed location exists to a much smaller degree, or not at all, in many inland marine coverages.

Unlike liability insurance, which deals primarily with third-party claims, fire insurance is a first-party coverage, and losses are payable directly to the named insured. The nature and extent of the insured's insurable interest is of great significance. Since the vast majority of all real property is encumbered by mortgages and other liens, the interests of mortgagees and loss payees must also be protected. Both the probable maximum loss (PML) and the maximum possible loss (MPL) can be more easily estimated in fire insurance than in liability coverages. This is because liability coverages, in particular, are subject to losses whose frequency and severity exhibit wide variations. The *probable maximum loss* is the largest loss that the underwriter considers likely to occur based on experience and judgment. The *maximum possible loss* is the "amount subject" or the total amount insured that is exposed to a covered peril. Liability loss severities are "open ended" in that judgments may run into millions of dollars. The loss is subject to policy limits, of course, but writing high limits is common in liability insurance.

A fire line is usually set on the basis of a single fire division. A *fire division* is defined by Holtom as "a portion of a building which is so protected from other portions that a fire will be restricted from spreading from one to another."[1] This protection is usually accomplished by means of fire walls. If a particular building has no fire walls, the entire building is one fire division.

The analysis of the hazards affecting a particular fire insurance submission focuses first on the physical hazards. These are categorized as COPE: construction, occupancy, protection, and exposure.

Construction

The Insurance Services Office divides building construction into six classifications:[2]

1. fire resistive (Code 6)
2. modified fire resistive (Code 5)
3. masonry noncombustible (Code 4)
4. noncombustible (Code 3)
5. joisted masonry (Code 2)
6. frame (Code 1)

These classifications are based on (1) the materials used for the bearing portions of the exterior walls, (2) the materials used in the roof and floors of the building, especially the supports for the roof and floor, and (3) the fire resistance rating of the materials used in the building construction.

Fire Resistive Fire-resistive construction is not a modern innovation. Old mission buildings in Florida dating back many centuries have been discovered with walls of lime, burned shells, and clay (known as "tabby"), and roofs of arched, interlocked stones. In the United States, the first fully fire-resistant (inaccurately labeled "fireproof") building was erected in Charleston, South Carolina, in 1823.[3]

A fire-resistive building must be constructed of any combination of the following materials:

Exterior walls or exterior structural frame

- solid masonry, including reinforced concrete
- hollow masonry not less than 12 inches in thickness
- hollow masonry less than 12 inches, but not less than 8 inches in thickness, with a listed fire resistance rating of not less than two hours
- assemblies with a fire resistance rating of not less than two hours

Floors and roof

- monolithic floors and roof of reinforced concrete with slabs not less than 4 inches in thickness
- construction known as "joist systems" with slabs supported by concrete joists spaced not more than 36 inches on centers with a slab thickness of not less than $2\,^3/_4$ inches
- floor and roof assemblies with a fire resistance rating of not less than two hours

Structural metal supports

- horizontal and vertical load-bearing protected metal supports (including pre-stressed or post-tensioned concrete units) with a fire resistance rating of not less than two hours.[4]

Fire resistive construction is the best from an underwriting standpoint. The construction materials are either noncombustible with a fire resistance rating of at least two hours or they are protected through the use of a noncombustible covering such as plaster or gypsum to obtain such a rating.

Modified Fire Resistive A modified fire-resistive building has bearing walls (walls supporting the upper floors and roof) and columns of masonry or reinforced concrete construction, just as in the fire-resistive category. However, the fire resistance rating of the materials is less than two hours but not less than one hour.

Masonry Noncombustible In the masonry noncombustible class are buildings with exterior walls of fire-resistive construction with a rating of not less than one hour or buildings of masonry construction. Roof and floors must be of noncombustible or slow burning materials.

The typical masonry noncombustible building has a masonry nonbearing wall surface, a cement floor, some type of metal deck roof, and an unprotected steel webbing supported by unprotected columns and roof members. Low initial cost and low maintenance have made this type of construction extremely popular.

Noncombustible A noncombustible building is a building with exterior walls, roof, and floor constructed of and supported by metal, asbestos, gypsum, or other noncombustible materials. While these buildings are noncombustible, they are not fire-resistive. If this type of building is filled with combustible contents, structural failure is extremely likely in the event of a serious fire. The unprotected steel structural supports in this type of building will twist and bend when subjected to extreme heat.

Joisted Masonry Joisted masonry construction is also referred to as *ordinary construction*. The joisted masonry class includes buildings with exterior walls of fire-resistive construction (not less than one hour) or of masonry construction. The interior framing and floors are of wood or other combustible material.

Ordinary construction is also referred to as "brick," "wood joisted," or "brick joisted." An example of ordinary construction is shown in Exhibit 5-1.

Ordinary constructed buildings are found in most of the major metropolitan areas in the northern states. They are infrequently over three stories high, since the exterior walls must be bearing walls. The great majority of these were built prior to World War II. Consequently, underwriters are presented with the potential problems of age, deterioration, and determining proper insurance-to-value.

Frame A frame building is one which has exterior walls constructed of wood or other combustible materials (see Exhibit 5-2). Buildings of mixed construction, such as wood frame with brick veneer, stone veneer, aluminum siding, or stucco, are generally classified as frame buildings. A great many dwellings as well as small mercantile buildings are frame. The desirability of frame construction varies somewhat by geographical area. In some parts of the country, the better class of home is of joisted masonry construction. In areas where earthquakes are frequent, such as California, most dwellings are of frame construction with stucco. Frame is superior to masonry in its resistance to earthquakes.

Mill Construction This term originated in New England over a century ago when cotton and woolen mill owners developed a new type of heavy construction to reduce their fire losses. A mill-constructed building has masonry walls. The primary difference between an

Exhibit 5-1
Ordinary Construction*

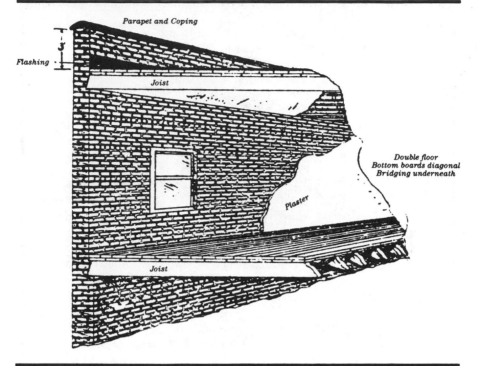

*Reprinted with permission from Charles C. Dominge and Walter O. Lincoln, *Building Construction as Applied to Fire Insurance*, 4th ed. (Philadelphia: Chilton Co., 1949), p. 32.

ordinary masonry building and mill construction is in the interior framing and floors. In ordinary masonry construction, light joists are employed. A mill-constructed building has interior framing and floors of timber arranged in heavy solid masses with smooth flat surfaces eliminating concealed spaces which may not be easily reached by fire fighters. The heavy timber beams used in mill construction resist fire so readily that even an intense fire will only char the surfaces. This type of construction is particularly desirable when protected by sprinklers.

Mill construction has two characteristics of interest to the underwriter: (1) the heavy floors constitute a fire stop retarding the spread of fire. This means that, to be effective, there can be no unprotected openings, stairwells, or shafts. (2) The heavy timbers of the beams and columns give the building great structural strength, reducing the likelihood of collapse.

Exhibit 5-3 shows some of the details of mill construction. These

Exhibit 5-2
Example of Wood Frame Platform Construction*

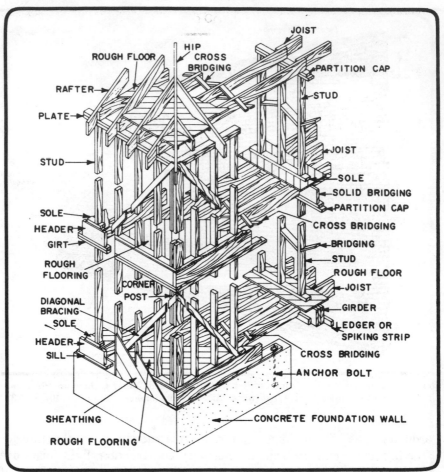

*Reprinted with permission from Gordon P. McKinnon, ed., *Fire Protection Handbook*, 14th ed. (Boston: National Fire Protection Association, 1976), p. 6-21.

construction details are of interest to producers and underwriters alike because insureds sometimes will represent a building as having mill construction when it is actually of ordinary construction.

Construction Materials[5]

Interior Finish. The interior finish of a structure has a definite effect on underwriting acceptance. For example, assume that a structure is of superior fire-resistive construction, with building members rated at three hours fire resistance, with a light hazard occupancy such as an apartment or office. However, it might have an

Exhibit 5-3

Details of Mill Construction*

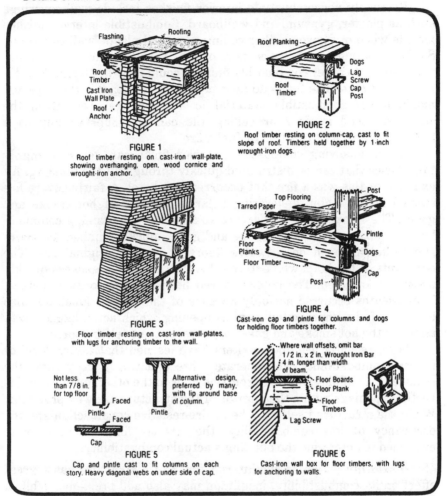

FIGURE 1
Roof timber resting on cast-iron wall-plate, showing overhanging, open, wood cornice and wrought-iron anchor.

FIGURE 2
Roof timber resting on column-cap, cast to fit slope of roof. Timbers held together by 1-inch wrought-iron dogs.

FIGURE 3
Floor timber resting on cast-iron wall-plates, with lugs for anchoring timber to the wall.

FIGURE 4
Cast-iron cap and pintle for columns and dogs for holding floor timbers together.

FIGURE 5
Cap and pintle cast to fit columns on each story. Heavy diagonal webs on under side of cap.

FIGURE 6
Cast-iron wall box for floor timbers, with lugs for anchoring to walls.

*Reprinted with permission from Charles C. Dominge and Walter O. Lincoln, *Building Construction as Applied to Fire Insurance*, 4th ed. (Philadelphia: Chilton Co., Inc, 1949), p. 67.

interior finish of a highly combustible nature with hazardous characteristics. The characteristics of interior finishes which are most relevant to fire problems include their ability to:

1. spread fire,
2. contribute fuel to the fire, and
3. develop smoke and noxious gases when burning.

Any of these three characteristics has an effect on the overall property loss potential as well as affecting the safety of the occupants.

Relatively noncombustible interior finishes include wall coverings such as plaster, gypsum, and wallboard. Combustible interior finishes include wood or plywood, fiber ceiling tiles, and plastic wall coverings. Surface coatings such as certain paints, varnishes, and wallpapers when added to other combustible finishes could contribute significantly to the *fuel load.* The fuel load (also called the fire load) is the expected maximum of combustible material in a given fire area. Even the adhesives used in floor or ceiling tile can add substantially to a building's capacity to sustain or fuel a fire.

A fire involving combustible interior finish can generate highly toxic gases that can be distributed quickly throughout the building. An example of this was a fire that occurred in a hotel. A fairly severe fire started in the lobby, generating a large quantity of hot smoke and gases. The smoke and gases seeped to a stairwell containing combustible interior materials. The smoke and gases quickly climbed the stairs and found an open door twelve floors above the original fire. The occupants of the hotel who entered this twelfth floor area were quickly overcome and died. The hotel suffered little damage to its structure. These deaths occurred not only because of the interior finish but also because of the unprotected vertical opening which acted like a stack, allowing the hot smoke and gases to travel to the twelfth floor.

More recently fire underwriters have learned that a high level of interior combustibility can generate a fire that will literally climb the outside of a building, moving from one floor to the other, even when the vertical openings within the interior of the structure are well protected. While the structure itself may be of fire-resistive construction and the occupancy of low combustibility, the interior finish must also be examined to determine the building's actual combustibility.

Insulation. Just as the interior finish of a structure has a great effect on its combustibility, insulation may also add problems. While a common form of insulation is glass fiber it is, unfortunately, usually bound by a combustible membrane. Insulation material may also include combustible substances such as wood chips formed into fiber board or recycled paper. Insulation is used not only for heat conservation but as a sound barrier. Therefore, combustible insulation can be found in the interior walls of otherwise highly fire-resistive buildings.

Whether the insulation is installed for the conservation of heat or the suppression of sound, an attempt should be made to determine its flame spread, fuel contribution, or smoke contribution characteristics. If this information is unavailable, the material should be viewed with suspicion.

Energy costs have led to renewed interest in heat conservation and sometimes additional insulation is added to a structure. If a roof and wall structure were designed and originally constructed in accordance with a standard fire rating, a severe problem might occur if additional combustible insulation is added. This insulation, if improperly installed, could have the adverse effect of holding the heat being generated by the fire within the structure, concentrating it on the building members and possibly weakening them to the point of collapse.

Roofing. The exterior surface of a roof is used for two basic purposes. The first is as a weather seal. Secondly, the surface of a roof is a barrier against external fire. In its role as a protection barrier, it should be as noncombustible as possible.

Roofs are subject to attack from two sides: sparks and embers falling from outside fires, and heat from inside fires. Therefore, the combustibility of both sides is important. Untreated wooden shingles invite spread of exposure fires. Resistive coverings are classified as A (safest), B, and C (some fire resistance). Treated cedar shingles and zinc sheets over asphalt-saturated organic felt are C. Other metal roofs and various combinations of asphalt, felt, and gravel in layers range from C to A. Concrete, tile, and slate are A. But tile and slate are subject to other damage such as wind damage.

Asphalt shingles are probably the most common roof covering. While they are somewhat combustible, they act as an excellent barrier from severe fire exposures when properly constructed and installed. Conversely, combustible materials such as wood shake shingles or tar paper afford almost no protection. In the presence of high winds, a wood shake roof may send fire brands as much as a mile downwind.

Other Construction Considerations

Age. The following are underwriting considerations with respect to older buildings:

1. a different building code in force at the time of construction;
2. possible obsolescence of heating and electrical systems;
3. possible changes in occupancy relative to the originally intended use for the building, especially conversion and remodeling which may result in concealed spaces through which a fire may spread;
4. potential indirect increases in losses imposed by current building codes; and
5. possible deterioration or erosion by dry rot, rust, termites, settling, or excessive wear.

While proper maintenance will mitigate the effects of age and deterioration, all buildings will eventually wear out. The degree of obsolescence or deterioration is directly related to the type of construction, the occupancy, physical abuse of the building, and the quality of the owner's maintenance.

A frame structure, for example, will normally show its age faster than a joisted masonry building. However, it must be noted that an office occupancy in a frame structure with good maintenance may be preferable to a fire-resistive building occupied by a drop forge operation with minimal maintenance.

The methodology of constructing buildings and the style of their construction materially changes with the passage of time. Building materials that were in use in the 1920s or 1930s have long been abandoned. Electrical systems of forty, fifty, and sixty years ago were designed primarily for lighting while modern wiring systems are designed to accommodate space heating, computer systems, and heavy appliances.

A building that was designed for a dry-goods retailing occupancy fifty years ago might be wholly inadequate for a laundry, a printer, or a beverage distributor today. Weight loadings for machines and bottled goods may exceed the original specifications. Machine demands for electricity have increased greatly. In addition to these occupancy increases in hazard, the structural integrity of the building probably has deteriorated over time from its original strength.

High-Rise Buildings. In recent years structures have been built that are beyond the capabilities of municipal fire protection. Buildings such as the Sears Tower, the twin towers of the World Trade Center, or the Canadian National Tower in Toronto, Canada, which rise in excess of 1,000 feet above street level present unique problems. Usually a municipal fire department is not capable of handling a fire from the exterior of a property in excess of 100 feet. A building 100 feet tall would have eight or nine floors.

In a high rise, the fire department would have to attack the fire from inside. This may result in a time delay in fire fighting response. Therefore, the fire-resistive characteristics of the structure and the presence or lack of approved horizontal and vertical barriers that would confine the fire to its area of origin must be considered. For example, a high rise with heating and air conditioning ducts that penetrate vertical and horizontal barriers can aid in the spread of fire unless equipped with automatic shutoffs. Standpipes and hoses must also be provided.

Structures of such great height require control of heavy combustible loads. The occupancy should not contain high fire hazards as a result of the tenants' operations or high fuel loads due to storage. Normally, high-rise structures are office occupancies and these are usually light hazard exposures. However, most offices have storage areas, duplicating areas, and data processing equipment, all of which contain a high level of combustibility. Therefore, the potential for a severe fire might exist in what are normally light hazard areas.

High rises sometimes have restaurants or bars located on the upper floors to take advantage of attractive views. In this location, restaurants are a hazardous occupancy. Without adequate control or private protection they constitute a significant hazard.

Coupled with these factors are the characteristics of a fire at an extended elevation. As soon as a fire occurs, the windows are normally vented. This limits the buildup of toxic gases. But while the wind at the street level may be minimal, it is oftentimes very severe fifty or more floors above the ground.

More important than property damage in a high-rise building is life safety. A structure of 100 stories in height might have as many as 25,000 occupants. If a severe fire occurs on the fiftieth floor, on the average over 12,000 people may be located above the fire and therefore subjected to potential injury from flame, smoke, and gas. Again, emphasis on integrity of the structure is important since these persons may not be able to pass through the fire area unless the structure is equipped with high-level evacuation facilities.

Fire Divisions. A different type of problem may be found in large horizontal structures. Structures with a total horizontal area approaching 1 million square feet are becoming more common. While the solution to many high-rise structure fire problems is vertical integrity, a corresponding solution for large horizontal areas is fire divisions.

A fire division restricts the spread of fire. Fire walls are essential to fire divisions. Such partitions must be relatively fire resistive or very slow-burning. They must not stop short of the ceiling or floor; nor must they interfere with the safe exit of the building occupants. A stream of superheated gas may pour through a one-inch opening like a blow torch. Generally, a wall must be at least eight inches of masonry material to be classified as a fire wall. The adequacy of fire walls is determined by the combustibility of the contents of the building. What is adequate for a school building may not be adequate to prevent fire spread in a heavy industrial plant, such as a paper mill. In a fire-resistive building, all interior walls which extend from floor to ceiling should be of sufficient fire-resistive quality to be called fire walls.

In a masonry or frame building, a fire wall must extend beyond the roof line in order to be effective. Since fire can spread via the roof in such buildings, these fire wall extensions, or *parapets*, must extend at least twenty-four inches above the normal roof line.

A special class of fire wall is known as a *definite fire-stop*. This type of wall is of substantial construction. As a minimum, such wall must meet or exceed the following construction criteria:

- twelve-inch solid masonry,
- twenty-four-inch parapet,
- no openings, even if protected,
- free standing,
- not broken by building or service lines, and
- minimum fire resistance rating of four hours.

Building Openings. Building openings may affect fire underwriting adversely. The construction type may appear to be excellent and appropriate for the intended occupancy. However, during the construction process, the subcontractors, such as electricians, heating contractors, and air conditioning contractors, have installed equipment throughout the structure. This equipment is designed to pass heat, electrical energy, or air conditioning throughout the premises. It is possible that vertical and horizontal fire-stops may have been violated by these subcontractors.

An example of this was a loss involving a high-rise structure near completion in New York City. The structural members of this building were of a noncombustible nature and originally had been adequately protected to afford a minimum of two-hour fire rating. This protection was diminished by some installation work by subcontractors. The effect was to lay bare the structural steel members. The completion of the structure did not include resurfacing these structural members with a protective coating. A subsequent fire weakened the steel to the point at which it had to be removed before the structure could be occupied. While the damage to these members was minimal and their original cost was not inordinate, the replacement of major building supports within a structure nearing completion resulted in a multimillion dollar loss.

In addition to the other ducts and passageways that might be present within a structure, buildings are often equipped with door openings between fire divisions and floor openings for stairs between floors. In addition, elevators, dumbwaiters, conveyor belts, and air and light shafts are often present. All of these violate the basic integrity of a fire division. Some of these openings in certain rare instances cannot be protected, although most can be corrected with approved fire doors.

A fire door in a fire wall should be capable of withstanding the same fire as the wall itself. A vertical opening is corrected only when it is wholly segregated into a separate fire division. Therefore, elevators and stairwells, when properly constructed, constitute a building within a building. The theory is that the fire must pass horizontally from one floor through a barrier and into the stairwell, up the stairwell, and through a second barrier door.

Fire doors are "approved" when they meet design specifications of the National Fire Protection Association. Manufacturers of fire doors have their products tested by Underwriters' Laboratories, Inc. or the Factory Mutuals. An approved door is granted a seal which is usually placed on its edge indicating its rating.

Fire doors are rated, in descending order of fire resistance, *A* through *E*. (Class A have a three-hour rating; Class E have a forty-five-minute rating.) These ratings measure the door's ability to prevent passage of heat, smoke, and other products of combustion. The rating may vary depending upon the occupancy and the location of the door within the building.

An approved fire door obviously is useless if propped open. Therefore each door must be automatically self-closing and unobstructed. Doors that must be left open to permit efficient industrial operations are fitted with fusible links that permit automatic self-closing when activated by heat.

Sources of Construction Information Specific data on the construction of a particular building is available from:

1. applications;
2. rate cards and manuals;
3. bureau reports (such as ISO);
4. inspection reports and accompanying diagrams;
5. local building codes;
6. local contractors;
7. original blueprints or specifications; and
8. independent appraisals

Occupancy

Occupancy greatly affects the likelihood of a fire loss. Some aspects of occupancies increase loss frequency while others affect the severity of a loss which has occurred. The factors varying from one occupancy to another can be grouped under three headings. These are (1) ignition sources or fire causes, (2) combustibility of contents, and (3) damageability of contents.

Ignition Sources The principal ignition sources include:

1. open flames and heaters: smoking, torches, lamps, furnaces, ovens and heaters, welding and cutting;

2. friction: hot bearings, rubbing belts, grinding, shredding, picking, polishing, cutting, and drilling;
3. electricity: arcs and sparks, including lightning and static, overloaded circuits, worn wiring; and
4. chemical reactions.[6]

Ignition sources or causes provide the means for fires to start. While certain industrial occupancies present obvious hazards with respect to ignition sources, others are more subtle. Smoking and the hazards of cigarettes are related to the number of people passing through a premises. Hotels are particularly vulnerable to this ignition source.

Combustibility The combustibility of contents depends upon the speed of ignition of the materials, the rate at which a fire will spread, and the intensity or amount of heat generated when fire does take place. Gasoline, for example, is easily ignited since it has a very low flash point. Gasoline spreads fire with great speed and burns with explosive intensity.

The major classifications of materials that are highly combustible include:

1. light combustible materials: thin plywood, shingles, shavings, paper, cotton, and other fibers;
2. combustible dusts such as those produced when refinishing bowling alley lanes;
3. flammable liquids;
4. combustible gases such as hydrogen;
5. materials subject to spontaneous heating; and
6. explosive materials, acids, and oxidizing agents.[7]

Damageability The size of a particular loss will be greatly affected by the damageability of contents. Even a small and quickly extinguishable fire can result in a severe loss to highly damageable contents, such as expensive clothing, so the damageability of contents is important in estimating the probable maximum loss to contents in the event fire should occur.

Common Hazards[8] Physical occupancy hazards may be separated into two categories, *common hazards*, which are present in virtually every occupancy, and *special hazards*, which are found in a particular occupancy.

These are broad categories developed for convenience in analysis but they are not truly mutually exclusive. The circumstance in which a hazard occurs in a particular occupancy may take what is normally considered a common hazard and endow it with unique or special characteristics. An example is housekeeping. This is of concern for all occupancy classifications, but it can range from a minor concern in an office occupancy to a major consideration in the case of sawdust and woodchips in a furniture manufacturing occupancy.

Common hazards include:

1. housekeeping, including trash disposal;
2. heating and air conditioning equipment;
3. common electrical equipment and lighting; and
4. smoking materials.

Housekeeping. Every type of occupancy involves waste and trash. There are three parts of the exposure: uncollected litter, storage, and disposal.

UNCOLLECTED LITTER. Waste and trash in the form of uncollected litter can make a significant contribution to spread of fire. Particularly hazardous common types include oily or greasy items, paper and packing materials, small pieces of all kinds of combustibles, and discarded smoking materials.

In machining and many other industrial operations, lubricants must be widely used so wastes and litter are often oily. Many janitorial cleaning functions involve oily substances or take place where oil or grease is present. Accumulation of greasy soot in vents and flues, particularly over cooking stoves, is a significant hazard.

The most common form of waste and litter is paper, which is especially combustible in litter form. Packing materials from incoming items are a major source of waste materials in stores and similar types of businesses. Such materials tend to be concentrated in limited areas. Piled up loosely or haphazardly they are ideal fuels for the growth and spread of fire.

STORAGE. Most commercial and institutional occupancies involve some storage of wastes. This means concentration of the material in a limited space. Depending on the material and the nature of the storage, such concentration and confinement may increase or decrease the hazard. Paper and cardboard, neatly stacked and enclosed, resists total burning better than the same quantity of material piled haphazardly and loosely. On the other hand, oily materials left undisturbed in a confined space may produce spontaneous ignition.

One problem with some storage is that different materials are mixed together with deleterious interaction. Common examples include putting unextinguished cigarettes in general trash bins and mixing oily wastes with quantities of dry combustibles.

Trash and waste storage should be in adequate noncombustible containers. Apart from small quantities such as one wastebasket size, the storage should be well separated by adequate space or noncombustible barrier from all other exposures, especially sources of heat. Specially hazardous materials such as combustible metal shavings or powders and flammable liquids should be kept isolated from other waste.

DISPOSAL. When ultimate disposal of waste is on the premises, special precautions need to be taken. Disposal by incineration means creation of another heat source. Sparks and products of incomplete combustion are a common problem from burning of wastes. These are controlled by proper design and operation of the incinerator.

Mixtures of wastes present special problems. Common items such as aerosol cans and mercury batteries explode when burned. Some industrial wastes give off seriously toxic gases when burned; others produce extremely high temperatures or explode; some react violently with other materials that may be found in trash.

Heating. Furnaces and other equipment for providing heat are a potential source of fire. The hazard centers in the burners or heating elements of the equipment. The equipment itself and the pipes, ducts, and flues leading from it also get hot. The pipes and flues that conduct combustion wastes to the outside, such as smokepipes or chimney flues, get extremely hot. The piping and ducts that spread heat throughout the interior of the building typically operate at temperatures that present less hazard; however, under some circumstances they can cause fires.

Electrical Equipment. The National Fire Protection Association reports that most of the fires that are started by electrical motors and appliances are due to careless use, improper installation, or poor maintenance. Fires from electrical distribution come principally from arcs or sparks from damaged or defective components.[9] It is clear that the care and reliability of management are major factors in fire loss prevention.

Smoking. Control of fire by smoking and matches has two principal parts: prohibition in areas not designed for safety of smoking materials, and proper design and attendance of equipment such as ashtrays and butt and waste cans in areas where smoking is allowed. Control of smoking areas because of possible health hazard may also reduce fire loss depending on care taken with the areas into which smoking is concentrated. Management attitude, procedures, and practices constitute the essential ingredient in the control of the smoking hazard.

Special Hazards Each occupancy class has its own special hazards. Examples of special hazards are cooking in a restaurant and the use of volatile chemicals in a manufacturing plant. The list of occupancy classes is too long for discussion here, but a brief look at the special hazards of mercantile and service occupancies will illustrate their importance to underwriting.

Mercantile Occupancies. This category includes retail stores such as department stores, clothing stores, hardware stores, and specialty shops and grocery stores. A rapidly growing segment of this category is shopping centers, particularly those with covered malls.

According to the National Fire Protection Association, three forms of heat of ignition accounted for the majority of the fires in this category.[10] These are electrical arcs or overload, heat from smoking materials, and open flames or sparks. Clearly, control of smoking and the condition of electrical wiring are major underwriting concerns for this occupancy category.

In mercantile occupancies the combustibility of the contents varies depending upon the merchandise being sold. Usually the entire inventory is susceptible to fire, smoke, and water damage.

Many mercantile operations carry highly combustible items in inventory or as operating supplies. A sporting goods store usually stocks ammunition, fuel for camping stoves, and portable lanterns. Hardware stores stock paints, varnishes, solvents, and other combustible liquids. A fast growing variation of the hardware store is the home center which, in addition to the items just enumerated, stocks lumber and building supplies. A furniture store has refinishing chemicals and polishes as operating supplies. The store may also provide upholstering service. Even the appliance and television retailer may operate a repair service using combustible liquids.

In a retail operation, shelving, showcases, displays on the selling floor, and adequate storage facilities off the selling floor must be provided. Unless proper care is taken, the operation can become congested with accumulations of cartons, excelsior, and other debris. Proper containers and storage facilities should be provided for highly combustible items. The public should be prohibited from entering storage and service areas, and smoking should not be permitted in these areas.

Most stocks of merchandise are subject to water damage and smoke. Women's clothing is especially subject to severe loss from smoke and water damage. The stock of a hardware store will rust from the water used in fighting a fire. Residual damage such as smoke and water, therefore, can turn a small fire into a large loss.

Food in the neighborhood store or supermarket usually will be destroyed by health authorities should there be a fire and smoke damage on the premises. In this class a small fire can result in a large loss.

Service Occupancies. This category includes dry cleaners, laundries, and automobile service stations. Another segment of this category incudes upholstery shops and furniture and appliance shops. One fire source that is common to many service industries is the ignition of flammable liquids such as gasoline in service stations and solvents in dry cleaners.

In both dry cleaners and laundries, lint escapes from drying units and settles on machinery, motors, and equipment. Lint accumulation presents both a fire and explosion hazard, which is compounded in a dry cleaning operation by the accumulation of vapors from the solvents that permeate the premises. Therefore, housekeeping is of prime importance. Timely cleaning of the lint traps and the removal of lint from machinery is essential. Proper ventilation to remove lint and accumulated vapors from the air is required.

The quality of storage provides an indication of the overall quality of housekeeping. The inventory should be stored in a manner that is prescribed for the type of commodity. Flammable items such as solvents, fluids, and paints should be stored in metal enclosed lockers. Metal containers with self-closing lids should be used for trash, and trash and rubbish should be routinely removed to an outside storage area away from the building.

Solvents, oils, paints, and grease are highly combustible. Due to the combustibility of solvents, dry cleaning operations should be done in a separate area. This area should be well ventilated, all equipment should be grounded, and lighting and other switches should be explosion proof. To reduce the possibility of fire or explosion, most cleaners use a standard solvent with a flash point comparable to that of kerosene.

Repair shops use flammable paints, refinishing fluids, and cleaning solvents which should be used with care in a well ventilated area.

Service stations, in addition to gasoline, oil, and other flammable liquids, may have acetylene tanks to provide gas for welding and cutting. Gasoline spillage, welding, and cutting in rooms where vapor from flammable gases exists is an extreme hazard. Spray painting is also hazardous unless the station is kept very clean, ventilated, and the hazard is properly controlled. The best control is to limit welding, cutting, and spray painting to an approved paint booth isolated from gasoline and vapors.

Dry cleaners and laundries require a sizable boiler which should be in a separate room fully isolated from the rest of the premises. In addition, hand irons, dryers, mangles, and presses are all heat-generating equipment. Electrical equipment should have "on-off" warning lights, be adequately grounded, and have master cutoff switches. Steam pipes from the boiler should be insulated and combustibles should not be stored close to the pipes.

Soldering irons in television and appliance shops should have "on-off" lights and be used on a metal table with a metal resting stand.

Although the refrigeration unit may not be thought of in terms of a heating process, the motors will generate heat. Motor installation has a grill or screen permitting air circulation. Blockage of this ventilation will cause the motor to run hot, constituting an ignition source.

Protection

Fire protection is of two types: *public* or municipal protection provided by towns and cities, and *private* protection provided by the property owner. Private and public protection alike consist of three elements: (1) prevention, (2) detection, and (3) extinguishment. The quantity and quality of fire protection available to particular properties vary widely. Although these are some exceptions, dwellings and small commercial buildings depend almost entirely on public protection, while the larger commercial buildings supplement public protection with their own fire protection systems. Public protection is covered in Chapter 10.

Private Protection   The existence of private protection systems is an important factor in underwriting. While all three elements of prevention, detection, and extinguishment are vital, this section will focus on detection and extinguishment. Prevention will be covered in the section on loss control.

Detection.   There are two approaches to detection of fire. The first approach utilizes a guard, while the second approach depends upon some type of automatic device. The major detection systems include (1) private patrol service, (2) guard service with clock, (3) supervised guard service, (4) automatic local alarm, and (5) automatic central station alarm. In addition, certain sprinkler systems include an alarm that is triggered by water flow within the system.

A private patrol service is often employed by small merchants or businesses. The business is visited several times during the night to determine that all doors and windows are secure and that fire has not broken out. The disadvantages of this system are obvious. While it is better than nothing, the patrol is unlikely to discover a fire on a timely basis. Patrols tend to be more useful for burglary protection.

A guard service depends upon the alertness of the guard. A clock system requires that certain key recorders be punched in sequence as the guard makes rounds. If the guard is delayed, disabled, or asleep, the fact will be known only on perusal of the tape of the next day. This shortcoming of the guard system can be overcome by tying the key recorders into a central station. If a guard fails to punch in on time, a messenger is dispatched to determine the cause. These systems are quite expensive although the "tour system" where every tenth box is wired to the central station reduces the cost somewhat.

An automatic local alarm system is one in which a type of fire or smoke detector triggers a local gong or buzzer alarm. Smoke detectors are now being sold for use in private dwellings. Widespread use of smoke detectors in the home could greatly reduce the loss of life by providing early fire warning. In commercial districts, local alarms are somewhat less effective. There is a widespread tendency for people to ignore fire or burglar alarms that go off in commercial or industrial districts. Passersby either "don't want to get involved" or conveniently assume that an alarm has been triggered by a stray cat. Since it is impossible to distinguish between a local fire alarm or burglar alarm by its sound, citizens are reluctant to investigate for fear of interrupting an irritable burglar. From an underwriting standpoint, while a local alarm system is better than nothing, it falls far short of solving the problem in commercial firms.

An automatic central station alarm, with or without sprinklers, provides a far better solution to the commercial firm's fire detection problem. The additional expense of these systems should be outweighed by the fact that they greatly increase the likelihood of rapid response to an outbreak of fire and should greatly reduce both insured and uninsured losses. Automatic alarm systems eliminate the human factor to the highest possible degree. While anything mechanical can fail, these systems have an enviable record of reliability.

Extinguishment. Private fire extinguishment falls into four categories. These are (1) portable extinguishers, (2) standpipes and hoses, (3) automatic sprinkler systems, and (4) private fire departments.

Almost every business location and a great many private dwellings have some type of portable extinguisher available. The care and maintenance of this equipment and the familiarity of personnel with its use vary drastically. Exhibit 5-4 shows some of the equipment that is available and its ratings. The number in the classification column indicates the number of extinguishers of that type required to constitute one fire unit. The letter indicates the class of fire for which the extinguisher is suitable. For extinguishment purposes, fires are divided into the following classes:

Class A—wood, paper, and textiles
Class B—flammable liquids, greases, and waxes
Class C—electrical equipment
Class D—flammable metals

Exhibit 5-4
Type, Size, and Classifications of First-Aid Fire Extinguishers*

Type	Size	Classification
Chemical solution	2½ gal.	A1
(soda acid)	1¼-1½ gal.	A2
Water	2½ gal. (stored pressure cartridge)	A1
	5 gal. (pump)	A1
	50-gal. cask with 3 pails	
	(25, 35, and 40 gal.)	A1
	Bucket tanks (6 pails)	A1
	2½ gal. (pump)	A2
	12-qt. pail	A5
Antifreeze solution	2½ gal. (stored pressure cartridge	
	and internally generated pressure)	A1
	5 gal. (pump)	A1
	50-gal. cask with 3 pails	
	(25, 35, and 40 gal.)	A1
	Bucket tanks (6 pails)	A1
	2½ gal. (pump)	A2
	12-qt. pail	A5
Foam	2½ and 5 gal.	A1, B1
	1¼-1½ gal.	A2, B2
Loaded stream	1¾ and 2½ gal.	A1, B1
	1 gal.	A2, B2
Vaporizing liquid	1 gal., 2 gal., and 3 gal.	B2, C1
(carbon tetrachloride)	1 qt., 1¼ qt., 1½ qt., and 2 qt.	B2, C2
Carbon dioxide	15 and 20 lbs. of carbon dioxide	B1, C1
	7½ lbs.[†] and 10 lbs.[†] of carbon dioxide	B2, C2
	4 lbs. of carbon dioxide	B2, C2
	2 lbs. of carbon dioxide	B4
Dry compound	12 and 20 lbs. of dry chemical	B1, C1

[†]With 24-inch cone.

*Reprinted with permission from John V. Grimaldi and Rollin H. Simonds, *Safety Management*, 3rd ed. (Homewood, IL: Richard D. Irwin, 1975), p. 552.

It is not sufficient merely to have fire extinguishers readily available. They must be carefully checked to determine that they are in working order, but most important of all, there must be personnel who know how to use them and what type of fire they can be used for. The use of a water extinguisher on an electrical fire can lead to a workers' compensation loss in addition to the fire. Particularly in large commercial accounts, the underwriter should determine the amount of fire training given to plant personnel.

Standpipes and hoses should be periodically checked and certified. Plant personnel should be familiar with their location and use.

Automatic sprinkler systems are either of the *wet* or *dry pipe* variety. If the sprinkler system is located in an area where no freezing weather is anticipated, then a wet system may be used with water at the sprinkler head. Otherwise, the dry pipe system is employed in which pipes are filled with air under pressure. When a sprinkler head opens, water then flows through the system. In those situations where water is not an appropriate extinguishing material, such as restaurant kitchens where grease fires are likely, dry powder or carbon dioxide systems are used. An alarm is an important part of a sprinkler system because once a sprinkler is opened, it will continue to discharge water until shut off. A small fire extinguished rapidly by one or two sprinkler heads might cause heavy damage if the fire occurs at night and is not discovered until morning. Another problem with sprinkler systems occurs when a system must be shut down for maintenance. In some cases, the insurance company must be notified and appropriate action taken whenever the system is to be shut down.

Private fire departments are found only in the largest commercial businesses. From an underwriting standpoint, these fire departments should be evaluated as public fire departments. The underwriter should develop information on the number and training of personnel as well as on the amount and type of equipment and its location within the industrial complex. Some large resort hotels located in rural areas have their own fire departments.

Exposure

Individual dwellings and commercial buildings are subject to loss from *external exposures*—those outside the area owned or controlled by the particular insured. These exposures fall into two categories: (1) single-occupancy exposures, and (2) multiple-occupancy exposures. Each of these categories presents different underwriting problems.

Single-Occupancy Exposures When the property being underwritten consists of a single building, fire division, or group of buildings, all owned or controlled by the insured, a single-occupancy exposure exists. The external exposures in this case come from buildings that expose the insured property to loss, or from the proximity of fire fuel such as brush, woodlands, or trash. Exposure hazards differ in one significant characteristic from those previously considered. Deficiencies in construction, occupancy, and private protection can be corrected to some degree by means of loss control recommendations. By their very definition, external exposures are factors that are usually outside the control of the insured. There is often little that can be done in an engineering sense to reduce or minimize external exposures. In some cases, however, there are certain external preventive measures such as outside sprinklers and fusible linked opening closures that are available to protect buildings from external exposures.

Exposing Buildings. A building may be considered exposed by another if fire in the other building significantly increases the probability of fire in the first building. Consider a building that is so located that it has no external exposing buildings. From an underwriting standpoint, this building is independent of all others. Fire, if it occurs, would have to be the result of internal causes or external exposures other than buildings (such as lightning.) When this situation is contrasted with a congested urban area with buildings close together and mutually exposing their neighbors, the increase in hazard can easily be visualized.

When determining whether adjacent buildings constitute an exposure, the following factors must be considered:

1. clear space;
2. construction and combustibility of walls and roofs of exposed and exposing buildings;
3. size, number, and protection of openings in the walls of the exposed building;
4. height of both the exposed and exposing buildings; and
5. occupancy of the exposing buildings.

Adequate clear space will enable fire fighters to properly respond to a fire in an adjoining building as well as reduce the likelihood of sufficient heat being generated to ignite the exposed structure. Clear space should be free of fire fuel. An alley filled with trash would not provide the advantageous clear space.

Construction materials used in the walls and roofs of both the exposed and exposing buildings greatly affect the exposure. The worst situation is one in which both buildings are of frame construction. Masonry walls provide some protection, but wooden sills or eaves may ignite. If the roof of the exposed building is of wooden shingles, it may easily be ignited by sparks. Similarly, if the exposing building has a wooden roof, it can create flaming brands that may carry as far as one mile in the wind.

A masonry or fire-resistive wall is only as effective as its weakest opening. Unprotected openings, such as windows with ordinary glass, will readily transmit fire from an exposing building. The underwriter should endeavor to have all openings, fire doors, and parapets carefully evaluated by an on-site inspection.

The height of the exposed and exposing buildings is also significant because fires travel upward very rapidly. A tall building exposed by shorter ones may have fire transmitted to its upper windows and other openings. A building that is shorter than neighboring buildings may be ignited by falling debris, and the possibility of the collapse of the walls of the adjoining buildings must be considered. In buildings of equal height, parapets are important because parapets reduce the chance of fire spreading from one roof to another. They also provide some protection for fire fighters.

The final factor to be considered is the occupancy of the exposing buildings. An explosives manufacturer or a mattress factory provides much greater exposure to surrounding buildings than would an office building.

Other Exposures. There are a variety of other exposures that can markedly increase the likelihood of a fire loss such as exposing lumber yards, gasoline storage tanks, brush, or woodlands. When brush is dry, humidity is low, and high winds occur, the stage is set for a fire that can spread very rapidly. Buildings with wooden shake roofs are particularly vulnerable to loss under these conditions, since sparks can travel up to one mile. Exhibit 5-5 shows some of the major losses that have occurred. Not all of these losses were brush fires—a severe hazard in Southern California. Some of these fires were forest fires, with the Peshtigo, Wisconsin fire resulting in the highest loss of life in United States history. The Bar Harbor fire in 1947, which started on the mainland and then spread onto Mount Desert Island, forced the evacuation of some of the residents by boat.

From an underwriting standpoint, it should be remembered that one of the assumptions of an insurable risk is independent, homogeneous exposure units. The existence of brush or woodlands may eliminate the independence of the separate structures and present the potential of a catastrophic loss. Building codes that require fire-resistive materials on roofs and other exterior areas can reduce the hazard. Another hazard reduction technique is to provide a clear space free of dry grass or brush around the dwelling or structure.

Logging risks are particularly susceptible to surrounding brush or woodland fires. Cold decks, which are piles of large logs, should have ample clear space to prevent ignition from the surrounding wooded area.

Multiple-Occupancy Exposures A multiple-occupancy exposure occurs whenever other portions of the same fire division are owned or controlled by persons other than the insured. If the insured in

Exhibit 5-5
Major Brush and Woodland Fires*

Date	Location	Property Damage	Deaths
1871	Peshtigo, Wisconsin, and environs	unknown	1,152
1947	Bar Harbor, Maine	$ 7,000,000	0
1961	Los Angeles, California	25,000,000	0
1967	Orange, California	5,000,000	0
1974	Cloudcroft, New Mexico	16,000,000	0
1977	Santa Barbara, California	20,000,000	0
1977	Los Alamos, New Mexico	24,800,000	0
1978	Los Angeles, California	38,166,000	1
1979	Los Angeles, California	9,840,600	0
1980	San Bernardino, California	38,031,400	N/A
1981	Saint Helena, California	35,666,500	N/A
1982	Los Angeles, California	8,990,000	N/A

*Based on information in *Insurance Facts* (New York: Insurance Information Institute. 1976, 1979, 1980, 1981-2 Ed. p.47, 1982-3 Ed. p. 51 and 1983-4 Ed. p. 61.

question occupies part of a building which is divided from the rest of the building by an approved fire wall, this is considered a single-occupancy exposure. In this case the rest of the building is treated as an exposing separate building. On the other hand, if the insured occupies part of a building with combustible walls separating the other occupancies, a multiple-occupancy exposure is created. Multiple-occupancy exposures fall into two categories: (1) dwelling units, or (2) commercial and industrial units.

Multiple-Occupancy Dwelling Units. The typical multiple-occupancy dwelling unit is a duplex apartment building or condominium in which units are not separated by approved fire walls. Other things remaining equal, the more units within a single fire division, the more ignition sources. That is, as the number of units increases, so does the number of kitchens, heating appliances, and potential smokers. In urban areas, there are mixed occupancies where dwelling units are located over stores or other commercial occupancies. These represent a considerably different loss potential from that of the typical dwelling.

Multiple-Occupancy Commercial Units. The first underwriting consideration in a multiple-occupancy commercial location is the occupancy class of the other building occupants. In a typical commercial shopping center of ordinary construction, a dry goods store may be exposed by a hardware store or a paint store in adjacent portions of the same fire division.

The next consideration is the amount of protection available against fire originating in other occupancies. By definition, a multiple-occupancy unit stipulates that approved fire walls do not exist between the occupancies. On the other hand, there could be a noncombustible wall that provides considerable protection but is deficient as a fire wall either due to unprotected openings, insufficient parapets, or other construction defects. This is to be contrasted rather strongly with the situation where there is a multiple-occupancy building with combustible walls and thin partitions. Basements and attic spaces can easily provide areas for transmission of fire and should be inspected. In older buildings that have been remodeled, there may be sizable concealed spaces which extend throughout the entire structure.

In multi-story buildings, stairwells and elevator shafts become chimneys for fire; therefore, proper fire doors and other fire barriers are essential. Ventilators, furnaces, and air conditioning systems should be equipped with automatic closing devices to prevent smoke and flames from exposing occupancies. The possibility of water damage from a fire in other occupancies is greater in a multi-story building than in a single-story structure.

There is one final consideration in multiple-occupancy commercial buildings that is present to a lesser degree when a single occupancy is exposed by other buildings. Careful underwriting can determine the extent of moral and morale hazard in the particular occupancy that is being insured. In most cases, this same investigation cannot be undertaken with regard to the other occupancies in the same building.

The Human Factor—Moral and Morale Hazards

Construction, occupancy, protection, and exposures constitute the physical hazards in fixed location property insurance. The human factor is also important. Moral hazard (or dishonesty) indicates that there is a possibility that the insured will deliberately cause a loss (arson). Morale hazard, which is more subtle, arises out of carelessness, indifference to loss, or inattention to hazardous conditions. It is also significant in fire insurance underwriting.

Moral Hazard Moral hazards were previously viewed as falling into three general categories: (1) weak financial condition, (2) undesirable associates, and (3) poor moral character. The categories are repeated at this time to emphasize the manner in which these conditions may result in arson.

While arson continues to be the primary cause of nonresidential fires and dollar losses, there is some progress being made in an ongoing campaign to reduce arson. A report by the National Fire Protection Association (NFPA) noted that the number of fires of incendiary or suspicious origin declined 16.5 percent from 154,500 in 1981 to 129,000 in 1982, and that the resulting property damage dropped about 3.3 percent to just over $1.6 billion. The number of civilian deaths attributed to such fires increased 11 percent, however—from 820 in 1981 to 910 in 1982.

The insurance industry for several years has worked closely with federal, state, and local authorities in the effort to combat arson. An industry-supported measure to assure a more effective accumulation of arson statistics by the Federal Bureau of Investigation was enacted and signed into law in 1982. As of 1983, all states except South Carolina had enacted arson reporting immunity laws which grant insurers civil (and in most cases, criminal) immunity from lawsuits when they share arson-related information with law enforcement officials.[11]

Incendiary and suspicious fires tend to increase in a cyclical fashion during recessions as more and more businesses fall into weakened financial condition. To the underwriter and producer this means that up-to-date financial statements and reports from financial rating services are essential to sound property underwriting.

Morale Hazard Morale hazards fall into two general categories which are (1) poor personality traits and (2) poor management. In both personal and commercial fire lines, careless smoking and thoughtless handling of flammable liquids can frequently be found as a major cause of loss. Smoking-related losses continue to be the leading cause of residential fire deaths and injuries. The careless parent is also unlikely to prevent children from playing with matches, another important cause of fires.

In commercial locations, the carelessness evidenced by reckless disposal of cigarette butts is usually a symptom of overall poor management. Other evidences of poor management practices include accumulations of trash, greasy floors and machinery, and poor house-keeping. This type of management is unlikely to maintain fire extinguishers even if their presence is mandated, and the equipment is virtually useless unless personnel are trained to use it.

While deficiencies in physical hazards are usually reflected in the rates, moral and morale hazards usually are not. In both class rates and individual (specific or schedule) rates, there is little provision in the rating structure for morale hazard, or management attitude, and nothing at all for moral hazard. There is no rate at which moral hazard is acceptable, and morale hazard is not much easier to deal with by means of a rate increase.

Homeowners and Dwelling Underwriting

An important fundamental in homeowners and dwelling underwriting is insurance to value. Most insurers prefer to have cutomers insure to 100 percent of replacement cost under coverage A (dwelling). While insurance to 80 percent of replacement cost meets minimum requirements, this can rapidly become inadequate due to constantly increasing building costs.

The hazards in homeowners underwriting can be considered under two headings, the applicant and the property. With respect to the applicant, attitude toward the property as evidenced by the exterior maintenance of the dwelling is an important consideration. Other vital attributes of the applicant include personal characteristics and attitudes, claims history, occupation, and employment record.

Attributes of the property that are important include characteristics of the construction of the dwelling, its age, the type and quality of public protection, and the location of the dwelling. Certain locations present serious windstorm exposures in addition to the perils of fire and theft. A final consideration is the presence or absence of such private protection devices as smoke alarms, fire extinguishers, dead bolt locks, and burglary alarms.

UNDERWRITING OTHER PERILS

Windstorm

The major peril causing loss among the extended coverage perils is windstorm. Since most dwelling and commercial fire policies include extended coverage, windstorm must be considered from an underwriting standpoint for virtually all property insurance submissions.

In addition to high winds occurring during cyclonic storms, which often strike in the winter, there are two major sources of windstorm damage—hurricanes and tornadoes.

Hurricanes

Few natural events can approach the destructive power of the hurricane which has caused as many as 300,000 deaths in a single storm and property damage approaching $1 billion. The National Weather Service utilizes the Saffir/Simpson scale to classify hurricanes and to provide a continuing assessment of the potential wind damage. This scale has gradients from 1 to 5. Scale 1 begins with hurricanes that have sustained wind speeds of at least 75 miles per hour or a storm surge of tidal waters 4 to 5 feet above normal. Scale 5 applies to storms with maximum sustained winds of 155 miles per hour or more. These scale numbers provide estimates of what a hurricane would do to a coastal area if it were to strike without change in size or strength. It is most useful in assessing potential hurricane damage for underwriting purposes. The Saffir/Simpson scale is shown in Exhibit 5-6.

Hurricane Paths Hurricane tracks exhibit a certain uniformity. However, each particular storm evidences its own peculiarities. Hurricanes strike the coast either as penetrating storms or raking storms.[12] A *penetrating storm* occurs when the hurricane track strikes the coastline at approximately a right angle and moves directly inland. With this type of storm, once the eye of the hurricane is over land, the hurricane decreases in intensity very quickly, only to increase rapidly after the eye moves on. A *raking storm* occurs when the hurricane track parallels the coast. A raking storm can maintain its intensity for a long time if the eye remains over the ocean.

Construction Considerations As high winds blow against a building, positive pressure is exerted on the windward side while the other sides experience a partial vacuum.

Roofs with a slope of more than thirty degrees will also have an area of positive pressure on the windward slope and a partial vacuum on the leeward slope. The forces acting on the roof in these circumstances can be quite similar to the forces acting on an airplane wing; lift is created which can jeopardize the roof surface and in extreme cases the roof itself. Overhanging eaves can provide pockets in which considerable pressure can be built up. Such projections should be avoided where possible or designed to resist the forces to which they may be subjected. Roof coverings of all types are susceptible to wind damage from both the direct wind force and the partial vacuum created on the lee side of sloping roofs. The greatest damage occurs when these coverings are not installed to the manufacturer's specifications and shortcut construction methods are employed.

Flying debris or the force of the wind itself frequently will break a window on the windward side of a structure exposing the interior to the full force of the wind. The interior not only can be exposed to wind-driven rain, but the wind also can exert positive pressure within the structure. This pressure, in combination with the external suction pressure, may lift off the roof or cause a lee wall to fail and collapse outward.

Storm Surge and Heavy Rainfall Storm surge is a combination of higher than normal tides and huge hurricane-induced waves which can pound the shoreline and move inland flooding low ground. Structures built near the waterfront can be flooded or undermined by

Exhibit 5-6
Saffir/Simpson Hurricane Scale*

Scale No.	Wind (MPH)	Surge (Feet)	Damage
1	74—95	4—5	Damage primarily to shrubbery, trees, foliage, and unanchored mobile homes. No real damage to other structures. Some damage to poorly constructed signs. And/or:low-lying coastal roads inundated, minor pier damage, some small craft in exposed anchorage torn from moorings.
2	96—110	6—8	Considerable damage to shrubbery and tree foliage, some trees blown down, major damage to exposed mobile homes. Extensive damage to poorly constructed signs. Some damage to roofing materials of buildings. And/or: coastal roads and low-lying escape routes inland cut by rising water 2 to 4 hours before arrival of hurricane center; considerable damage to piers; marinas flooded; small craft in unprotected anchorages torn from moorings; evacuation of some shoreline residences and low-lying areas required.
3	111—130	9—12	Foliage torn from trees, large trees blown down. Practically all poorly constructed signs blown down. Some damage to roofing materials of buildings; some window and door damage. Some structural damage to small buildings. Mobile homes destroyed. And/or: serious flooding at coast and many smaller structures near coast destroyed; larger structures near coast damaged by battering waves and floating debris; low-lying escape routes inland cut by rising water 3 to 5 hours before hurricane center arrives. Flat terrain 5 feet or less above sea level flooded inland 8 miles or more. Evacuation of low-lying residences within several blocks of shoreline possibly required.

4	131—155	13—18	Shrubs and trees blown down, all signs down. Extensive damage to roofing materials, windows and doors. Complete failure of roofs on many small residences. Complete destruction of mobile homes. And/or: flat terrain 10 feet or less above sea level flooded inland as far as 6 miles; major damage to lower floors of structures near shore due to flooding and battering by waves and floating debris; low-lying escape routes inland cut by rising water 3 to 5 hours before hurricane center arrives; major erosion of beaches; massive evacuation of all residences within 500 yards of shore possibly required, and all single-story residences on low ground within 2 miles of shore.
5	Over 155	Over 18	Shrubs and trees blown down, considerable damage to roofs of buildings; all signs down. Very severe and extensive damage to windows and doors. Complete failure of roofs on many residences and industrial buildings. Extensive shattering of glass in windows and doors. Some complete building failures. Small buildings overturned or blown away. Complete destruction of mobile homes. And/or: major damage to lower floors of all structures less than 15 feet above sea level within 500 yards of shore; low-lying escape routes inland cut by rising water 3 to 5 hours before hurricane center arrives; massive evacuation of residential areas on low ground within 5 to 10 miles of shore probably required.

*Adapted from Paul J. Herbert and Glen Taylor, "Hurricane Experience Levels of Coastal County Populations—Texas to Maine" (Washington: U.S. Department of Commerce, National Oceanic and Atmospheric Administration, National Weather Service).

this surge. Low-lying structures inland are also subject to flooding since the water levels may increase to eighteen feet or more above mean low water. Further damage can be caused by the six to twelve inches of rainfall that often accompany a hurricane. The ensuing flood damage is often greater than the damage from wind alone.

Tornadoes

Tornadoes are capable of causing almost as much damage as hurricanes, though they are smaller in size. Tornado winds usually attain speeds in excess of 200 miles per hour, considerably higher than those of hurricanes.

Tornadoes are intense local storms of short duration. They have winds rotating at very high speeds around a vortex in a counter-clockwise direction in the Northern Hemisphere. As the vortex, in which a partial vacuum has been produced, comes into contact with the ground, the storm draws dust and debris into the funnel, causing it to darken. The Oklahoma Turnpike contains signs saying, "Do not drive into smoke!" since that is what a tornado looks like to the uninitiated.[13]

The destructive power of a tornado is fantastic. This destruction comes partly from the high velocity of the winds and also from the sudden drop in atmospheric pressure caused when the vortex passes over a building. The near vacuum in the vortex causes buildings to explode from overpressure within the building.

Tornado Incidence While tornadoes occur in virtually all parts of the United States, their greatest incidence is across the great plains of the Midwest and Southwest. Although they occur at any time of the year, April, May, and June are the peak months. The incidence of tornadoes during the period 1955 through 1982 is shown in Exhibit 5-7.

Wind-resistant construction is important to minimize damage in areas with high tornado frequency. The past loss history of a community is an important underwriting consideration. Due to the randomness of tornadoes, the basic property underwriting principle of spread of risk and dispersion of exposures is one of the most reliable tools in dealing with this peril.

Hail

Destructive hail falls almost exclusively during violent thunder-storms. Hailstones have attained a size of more than five inches, weighing over one and one half pounds. The damage from hail can be severe to auto and home windows, neon signs, and fragile structures

Exhibit 5-7
Tornadoes in the U.S.—1955-1982*

Year	Tornadoes	Deaths	Year	Tornadoes	Deaths	Year	Tornadoes	Deaths
1955	593	126	1964	704	31	1973	1,102	87
1956	504	83	1965	906	296	1974	947	361
1957	856	192	1966	585	98	1975	920	60
1958	564	66	1967	926	114	1976	835	44
1959	604	58	1968	660	131	1977	852	43
1960	616	46	1969	608	66	1978	788	53
1961	697	51	1970	653	72	1979	852	84
1962	657	28	1971	888	156	1980	866	28
1963	464	31	1972	741	27	1981	772	24
						1982	1,033	64

*Reprinted with permission from *Insurance Facts*, 1980-81 (New York: Insurance
Information Institute), 1981, p. 52, 1981-2 Ed. p. 53, 1982-3 Ed. p. 57, 1983-4 Ed. p. 67.

such as greenhouses. Certain growing crops are particularly susceptible to hail damage, accounting for nearly 80 percent of all hail losses.
Auto damage in a severe hailstorm can include dents in the sheet metal
and chipped metal as well as window damage.

Structural damage to buildings can include damage to shingles,
roll roofing, and aluminum roofs. Wooden siding can be stripped of
paint and even split.

Hailstorms are seasonal in nature, beginning in January and
February in the Gulf states and reaching peak frequency in the
remainder of the country in June.

Explosion

The generally accepted definition of explosion states that it must
involve a sudden, violent, bursting, breaking, or expansion caused by an
internal force or pressure with material going away from the center of
the occurrence and usually accompanied by noise. Explosions generally
occur either in confined spaces or pressure vessels. Each of these
situations will be considered separately.

Confined Spaces A confined space, such as a compartment,
room, or building, may contain flammable dust, vapor, mist, or gas
which, when mixed with air under certain conditions, can ignite and
burn with sufficient speed to generate high pressure, resulting in an
explosion. Flammable liquids produce vapors at their surface which can
burn. Often these vapors sink to the floor and concentrate in low spots

such as basements, furnace pits, and switching equipment shafts. Ignition can be caused by the spark of a closing electrical switch or furnace start-up. Gases may leak from pipes through poorly maintained connections, joints, and valves. Most finely divided combustible materials are dangerous. When combustible dust is suspended in air and ignited, the result can be a severe explosion. Grain elevator explosions are examples of this.

The basic approach in the prevention of explosions is to contain gases, exclude oxygen, reduce or vent vapors, and reduce dusts. Another important aspect is removal of the ignition source.

Pressure Vessels Pressure vessels may be found in homes, processing and manufacturing operations, service businesses, and offices. Heating system boilers and pressure tanks for water circulation are examples of common pressure vessels. These vessels may fail when pressure exceeds safe levels. Often there is a failure of a poorly maintained pressure relief safety valve. Age, corrosion, and heat are factors which can weaken the walls of a pressure vessel, resulting in an explosion. Regular inspections of pressure vessels by experienced engineers should be conducted to minimize the potential exposure.

Sprinkler Leakage and Water Damage

Sprinkler leakage losses, while relatively infrequent, can result in severe damage. One of the most common causes of sprinkler leakage losses is freezing. Mechanical injury—damage from fork-lift trucks, for instance—is another common cause of loss. Sprinklered warehouses using fork-lift trucks should have guards over all sprinkler heads, and both the pipes and risers should be protected from accidental rupture. Other causes of loss include improper installation and maintenance, overheating due to high ceiling temperatures, and industrial operations that create a corrosive atmosphere.

The underwriting of sprinkler leakage insurance concentrates on two elements: (1) the damageability of the contents with respect to water and (2) the physical condition, maintenance, and design of the sprinkler system itself.

When the contents of the structure protected by a sprinkler system are highly susceptible to water damage, sprinkler leakage may result in a total loss. The condition, maintenance, and design of sprinkler systems should be determined by inspection at frequent intervals. Sprinkler systems that do not have alarms are much more likely to have a substantial loss from sprinkler leakage than those equipped with alarms.

Water damage is a covered peril under many forms of coverage.

Direct damage caused by accidental discharge, overflow or leakage of water or steam from plumbing, heating, and cooling systems is frequently covered. Most of these losses are due to lack of maintenance.

Underground water is frequently excluded from coverage, but this exclusion has resulted in some difficult litigation. Courts have generally held that when the coverage for accidental discharge from plumbing systems is included as a named peril, loss from a broken underground sewer line on the premises is generally covered. On the other hand, if the coverage is on an "all-risks" form, with the usual exclusions, the exclusion of underground water is more likely to prevail.

Vandalism or Malicious Mischief

Most vandalism is committed by children and young adults. Police authorities estimate that 75 to 80 percent of all vandalism is committed by persons under twenty-five years of age. Schools, churches, parks, playgrounds, and youth centers are examples of properties with the possibility of vandalism exposure. Since groups of children are more likely to commit vandalism, areas with large child populations such as urban areas are likely to have a higher incidence of vandalism.

Other types of vandalism can occur during labor disputes or when an organization becomes the target for violence as the result of some type of social protest. Violent protest has caused vandalism damage to home offices of multinational corporations, major banks, offices of foreign airlines, and the homes of public officials. While some large corporations seem to attract attention and draw more than their fair share of vandalism, it is virtually impossible to underwrite this exposure. Corporations that are highly visible and tend to attract protestors should evaluate their exposures and endeavor to adopt reasonable loss control methods to minimize losses. Many large corporations carry high deductibles and should have contingency plans to keep their vandalism losses to a minimum.

Earthquake

Earthquake underwriting is difficult since this peril is subject to natural adverse selection. It is important that underwriters control their total earthquake writings in order to protect against a catastrophic loss. The underwriting analysis of earthquake considers three major areas: (1) the distance of the site from the epicenter, (2) the soil conditions, and (3) building design, construction techniques, and materials.

Exhibit 5-8

Seismic Risk by Geographic Area*

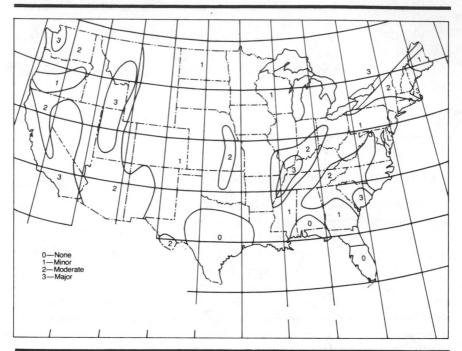

0—None
1—Minor
2—Moderate
3—Major

*Reprinted from National Oceanic and Atmospheric Administration and National Ocean Survey, *Seismic Risk Studies in the United States* (Washington: U.S. Department of Commerce).

Areas of Earthquake Activity Most earthquakes occur on the west coast of the United States from Alaska to California. While 90 percent of all earthquakes within the United States occur in California and western Nevada, the New Madrid, Missouri quake of 1811 was the largest ever recorded.

Seismic risk for each area of the country has been charted by the United States Office of Science and Technology. The country is divided into four zones, designated from 0 to 3. Earthquake risk is almost nonexistent in Zone 0. In Zone 1, minor damage from earthquakes of Modified Mercalli Scales V and VI may occur. This scale is presented in the next section. Zone 2 is exposed to moderate damage, with damage from quakes of a magnitude of VII on the Modified Mercalli Scale recorded. Zone 3 represents areas of significant damage potential with earthquakes of VIII and greater in intensity recorded. The map of seismic risk is shown in Exhibit 5-8.

The Modified Mercalli Scale   While the more familiar Richter Scale measures the magnitude of an earthquake in terms of total energy released, the Modified Mercalli Scale measures *intensity*. This scale measures the degree of damage caused by an earthquake to people, structures, and the earth's surface. Due to its focus on damage, the Modified Mercalli Scale is extremely useful for earthquake underwriting. This scale is shown in Exhibit 5-9.

Soil Conditions   Since earthquake waves travel at small amplitudes in bedrock, structures built on bedrock or supported on piling driven into bedrock are less susceptible to earthquake damage than other structures on less secure foundations. *Consolidated soil* of long standing (thousands of years) such as limestone and some clay will stand up better than *unconsolidated soil* such as sand, gravel, silt, and some clays. Filled land, common in many large cities, represents a particularly hazardous type of unconsolidated soil from the standpoint of earthquake. Unconsolidated filled land (as well as certain other types of unconsolidated soils) is subject to *liquefaction* during an earthquake, becoming so unstable that it acts like a liquid.

Building Design   Nonseismic building construction concentrates principally on the vertical loads a structure must bear. An earthquake causes horizontal stresses which weight-bearing columns and walls may not have been designed to bear. An earthquake-resistant building has all its structural members tied together securely so that the entire building moves as a single unit when subjected to earthquake forces. Walls designed only to withstand vertical stresses, such as those found in ordinary masonry construction, may simply move out from under the floors and roof they are supporting, causing collapse.

Construction   Ordinary construction—that is, unreinforced masonry—is particularly susceptible to earthquake damage. On the other hand, frame construction is quite resistant to earthquakes. A masonry building is rigid and subject to structural failure during earth movements. A frame building, on the other hand, is relatively flexible and will "give" during earth movement, often sustaining relatively minor damage such as cracked plaster. Brick, or other stone veneer, and tile roofs often sustain earthquake damage. Tilt slab construction which is sometimes found in light industrial buildings and warehouses is also susceptible to earthquake damage. Fire-resistive construction, particularly where there is a strong earth safety code, will survive most earthquakes with slight damage.

Exhibit 5-9
The Modified Mercalli Scale

I. Not felt except by a very few under especially favorable circumstances.

II. Felt only by a few persons at rest, especially on upper floors of buildings. Delicately suspended objects may swing.

III. Felt quite noticeably indoors, especially on upper floors of buildings, but many people do not recognize it as an earthquake. Standing motor cars may rock slightly. Vibration like passing truck. Duration estimated.

IV. During the day felt indoors by many, outdoors by few. At night some awakened. Dishes, windows, doors disturbed; walls make creaking sound. Sensation like heavy truck striking building. Standing motor cars rocked noticeably.

V. Felt by nearly everyone; many awakened. Some dishes, windows, etc., broken; a few instances of cracked plaster; unstable objects overturned. Disturbances of trees, poles, and other tall objects sometimes noticed. Pendulum clocks may stop.

VI. Felt by all; many frightened and run outdoors. Some heavy furniture moved; a few instances of fallen plaster or damaged chimneys. Damage slight.

VII. Everybody runs outdoors. Damage negligible in buildings of good design and construction; slight to moderate in well-built ordinary structures; considerable in poorly built or badly designed structures; some chimneys broken. Noticed by persons driving motor cars.

VIII. Damage slight in specially designed structures; considerable in ordinary substantial buildings, with partial collapse; great in poorly built structures. Panel walls thrown out of frame structures. Fall of chimneys, factory stacks, columns, monuments, walls. Heavy furniture overturned. Sand and mud ejected in small amounts. Changes in well water. Disturbs persons driving motor cars.

IX. Damage considerable in specially designed structures; well designed frame structures thrown out of plumb; great in substantial buildings, with partial collapse. Buildings shifted off foundations. Ground cracked conspicuously. Underground pipes broken.

X. Some well built, wooden structures destroyed; most masonry and frame structures destroyed with foundations; ground badly cracked. Rails bent. Landslides considerable from river banks and steep slopes. Shifted sand and mud. Water splashed over banks.

XI. Few, if any, (masonry) structures remain standing. Bridges destroyed. Broad fissures in ground. Underground pipelines completely out of service. Earth slumps and land slips in soft ground. Rails bent greatly.

XII. Damage total. Waves seen on ground surfaces. Lines of sight and level distorted. Objects thrown upward into the air.

UNDERWRITING TIME ELEMENT COVERAGES

Types of Time Element Coverages

Time element coverages provide indemnity for *indirect* or *consequential losses* caused by an insured peril. In personal lines, the major time element coverage is additional living expense (also called loss of use in some policies) which is found in the homeowners policy and in the dwellings and contents broad form policy. This coverage provides for payment of additional expenses of meals, motel accommodations and other additional living expenses while the insured's home is uninhabitable due to damage by an insured peril. Additional living expenses are those costs over and above usual living expenses.

The major indirect insurable property losses to which business firms are exposed include:

1. loss of earnings (all income arising out of business operations) due to property damage to buildings, equipment, or inventory;
2. extra expense due to extraordinary expenses incurred in continuing to operate after damage to an operating facility; and
3. contingent losses due to the interruption of production or sales caused by direct damage to a contributing or recipient subcontractor, supplier, or customer.

In commercial lines, the most common time element coverages are (1) business interruption, (2) extra expense, (3) rents insurance, and (4) leasehold interest. The first three are similar in that they provide indemnity during the time period necessary to restore the building or operation, using due diligence and dispatch. However, they differ in the type of coverage they provide and in the determination of amounts of loss. Leasehold interest, on the other hand, provides compensation for the loss of a favorable lease due to the occurrence of an insured peril.

Underwriting the Gross Earnings Form

One of the problems encountered when dealing with the gross earnings form is that it is necessary to make two separate evaluations of the amount of insured exposure. It is necessary, first, to make an estimate of the probable maximum loss and, second, to estimate the amount of insurance required to comply with the coinsurance clause in the policy. Calculation of the amount of insured exposure in both cases involves four steps:

1. analysis of the firm's current gross earnings for the preceding twelve months, including an analysis by month to pinpoint seasonal fluctuations.
2. a projection of the firm's gross earnings for the next twelve to twenty-four months, also pinpointing fluctuations.
3. an estimation of the probable period of maximum interruption (this involves determining the probable time to rebuild a damaged facility, or in the case of a manufacturer, the time it takes to return the goods in process to their pre-loss level.
4. a determination of whether or not to cover ordinary payroll and an identification of all charges and expenses that would not necessarily continue after loss occurs.

Each of these steps involves projections and estimates. The range of possible error is quite wide.

Analysis of Current Gross Earnings   The most recent year-end financial statement is one source for this analysis. If the fiscal year has ended more than six months previously, an evaluation of the most recent twelve months of earnings would be in order. Since the recent past is some indication of the short-term future trend for sales and earnings, an analysis of current gross earnings is a necessary step before making the projection of future gross earnings.

Obviously, significant seasonal fluctuations in sales and/or earnings will have a direct bearing upon the calculation of not only the proper amount of insurance needed to cover the probable maximum loss but also the amount of insurance required to comply with the coinsurance clause.

In order to encourage insurance to value and to simplify rate making, business interruption gross earnings forms contain a coinsurance clause that operates essentially the same as the coinsurance clause in direct damage property insurance policies. Older policies used the term "contribution clause," but most now use the term "coinsurance clause." The insured may choose 50, 60, 70, or 80 percent coinsurance.

Three important points must be remembered about the business interruption coinsurance clause:[14]

1. *The coinsurance percentage does not apply to the maximum loss exposure.* The coinsurance percentage in the *gross earnings* form applies instead to the *"gross earnings"* that probably would have occurred during the twelve-month period following the beginning of the shutdown.
2. *The coinsurance clause may require an insured to purchase more business interruption insurance than seems necessary*

for a maximum loss. It might seem most logical if the coinsurance percentage applied to " 'gross earnings' less continuing expenses." Those who drafted the contract language, however, recognized that estimates of noncontinuing expenses are difficult to make before a loss occurs, and such a requirement might make it difficult to comply with the coinsurance clause. Furthermore, the disadvantage of buying more insurance than may be needed is offset by lower insurance rates.

3. *The coinsurance clause applies to "gross earnings," not in the past or present, but in the future.* Specifically, it applies to the "gross earnings" the company probably would have achieved in the twelve-month period *starting at the beginning of the loss.* This approach arises because the insurance is intended to "do for the insured what the business would have done" if there had been no loss.

Projection of Gross Earnings   The projection of gross earnings may be performed by utilizing standard financial techniques such as linear extrapolation of the trend of past sales. Sales data should be examined on a quarterly or monthly basis to determine seasonal fluctuations. In extreme cases, 75 to 80 percent of sales may occur within a single quarter, raising the possibility that a three-month shutdown might cause an 80 percent loss of annual sales.

Determination of the Probable Period of Interruption   The probable period of interruption for a nonmanufacturing insured is the time to rebuild a similar structure, install fixtures, restock, orient new employees, and prepare for reopening. This assumes a total loss of the existing structure or damage so severe that demolition of the existing structure is necessary. In the case of older buildings, this may be complicated if the structure does not meet present codes or zoning. In the case of a manufacturing insured, in addition to the preceding steps, the manufacturing process must be brought up to the point reached at the time of the loss. In the case of a manufacturer with an extended time period for the completion of a manufactured item, this may considerably extend the period of interruption.

The time to rebuild depends on the following factors:

- type of construction, whether frame or fire-resistive
- size and number of floors in the building
- grade of construction and unusual features
- degree of traffic congestion at the building site
- time to obtain necessary permits
- weather factors including severe winters

- changes in the local building code since the building was initially constructed

Identification of Noncontinuing Expenses While the gross earnings form limits expenses which may be deducted in the determination of gross earnings to payroll and a few other categories, there are a number of other expenses that will not continue in the event of a shutdown. Identification of these expenses and estimation of their probable amount is necessary in order to estimate the probable maximum loss.

Other Underwriting Considerations Whether the business interruption is written on the gross earnings form or on the earnings form with no coinsurance clause, factors that may increase the severity of a given business interruption loss must be considered. These factors include the seasonality and rebuilding time previously discussed, as well as bottlenecks and lengthy production processes. The presence or absence of a proper disaster contingency plan may greatly affect the desirability of a particular applicant or insured.

Manufacturing and mining insureds are particularly susceptible to bottlenecks. Alistair MacLean's novel *Athabasca* has as its plot the threat by terrorists to extort vast sums of money from an oil tar sands production facility. The threat was that the terrorists would destroy key production machinery which would take many months to replace. This novel makes disturbing reading for both risk managers and underwriters.[15] A bottleneck occurs whenever a particular machine, process, structure, or building is essential for the continued operation of the business. A small fire in a single machine which takes six months to rebuild may shut down an entire business as completely as a total loss.

An example of such a bottleneck is shown in Exhibit 5-10. The bottleneck occurs in process AB, in the fifth stage of production. The entire manufacturing flow includes this process. If that unit is destroyed, all production ceases.

Disaster Contingency Plans

For a business of any size, a disaster contingency plan can reduce the length of interruption. Such a plan includes detailed written plans for the restoration of the operation in the event of destruction of part or all of the buildings and equipment. In addition to expediting the return to operation, a disaster contingency plan can determine whether business interruption, extra expense, or a combined form is the proper coverage for the business. The disaster contingency plan will provide a

Exhibit 5-10
A Manufacturing Bottleneck*

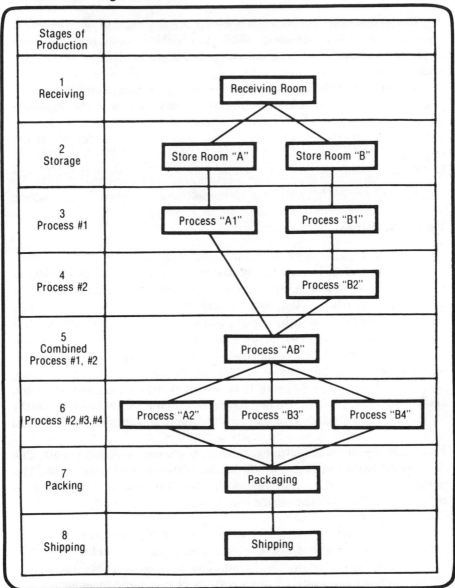

Stages of Production	
1 Receiving	Receiving Room
2 Storage	Store Room "A" Store Room "B"
3 Process #1	Process "A1" Process "B1"
4 Process #2	Process "B2"
5 Combined Process #1, #2	Process "AB"
6 Process #2,#3,#4	Process "A2" Process "B3" Process "B4"
7 Packing	Packaging
8 Shipping	Shipping

*Reprinted with permission from Matthew Lenz, Jr., *Risk Management Manual* (Santa Monica: The Merritt Company, 1976), p. 18.

means for checking the adequacy of the requested amount of extra expense coverage. Insureds with no contingency plans and vague estimates of anticipated costs should be carefully underwritten.

UNDERWRITING CRIME INSURANCE

Crime insurances represent an important segment of both personal and commercial lines business. While much crime insurance is written as part of a package policy, the crime perils in particular require careful underwriting.

Whether burglary, robbery, or theft coverage is written on a personal or commercial lines basis, moral hazard is a primary underwriting consideration. While moral hazard is particularly troublesome with respect to money and securities, it is a problem for all crime coverages. Crime insurance by its very nature is susceptible to fraudulent claims, intentionally caused losses, and losses in which the severity is artificially inflated.

Personal Lines

Most personal lines crime insurance is written in conjunction with a homeowners policy. Paradoxically, the greatest underwriting problems occur at the extremes of the socio-economic scale. In poverty-stricken areas, particularly in the urban core areas, the crime rates are extremely high. In wealthy neighborhoods, at the other end of the scale, burglaries may occur with high frequency and severity because residents in this income class often travel extensively, leaving an unoccupied dwelling which is attractive to burglars.

The peril of theft, which is covered under all homeowners contracts, is one of the most frequent causes of loss under these policies. Theft coverage tends to be unattractive from an underwriting standpoint because theft is so easily committed in today's mobile world. Electronic equipment, jewelry, and appliances readily available in American homes can be easily stolen and quickly converted to cash or personal use by a thief. Further, a theft loss is difficult to validate or refute due to the fact that there is no injured third party or no partially destroyed property to examine.

There are factors which increase the probability of a theft loss.[16] A concentration of high-valued contents increases the likelihood that a thief will be attracted to the home. The degree of police protection affects both the likelihood of theft and the chances of apprehension if a theft is committed. Of course, some apartments or condominium complexes have private security services which act as deterrents.

Occupancy affects theft potential. An unoccupied home increases the likelihood of theft. Many underwriters become concerned when asked to insure a residence which is always unoccupied during the day.

An isolated location is more susceptible to theft than a location where neighbors are likely to notice and report suspicious activities.

Certain protective measures can be taken by the insured and may, occasionally, be recommended by an underwriter. Burglar alarms are the most obvious such measures. Double-cylinder dead-bolt locks make it more difficult for a burglar to enter or escape. (Dead-bolt locks are not spring-loaded; a double-cylinder lock requires a key to lock or unlock from inside or outside.) Common sense dictates many other theft protection measures—locking all doors and windows not in use, keeping bicycles and other personal property locked in a garage or basement while unattended, and so on.

Homes temporarily unoccupied when the residents are vacationing pose a special problem. Here again such common-sense measures as operating a light on a timer, notifying police and neighbors, hiring someone to keep the grass mowed, and so on, can reduce the likelihood of a loss.

Commercial Lines

Coverage for open stock burglary, safe burglary, and inside and outside robbery may be written either separately or as part of a package policy. When these coverages are written as part of a package, it is important that proper underwriting attention be given to the loss potential of these perils and to the reduced premium from what would have been charged if written separately.

Commercial crime policies include mercantile open stock burglary, mercantile robbery, safe burglary, money and securities broad form, fidelity bonds, the 3-D, and the blanket crime policy. Since these coverages are analyzed in CPCU 3, this section will concentrate on the underwriting of the coverages.

Whether provided on a single coverage or a package basis, most of these commercial crime coverages are of a premises nature in that most of the coverage is provided at the insured premises. The exception to this is the off-premises robbery coverage provided in specific mercantile robbery policies and those package policies providing robbery coverage off-premises. Even with respect to off-premises robbery coverage, the location of the premises affects the probability of loss since most trips with money to other locations originate at the insured premises.

The key underwriting considerations for commercial crime insurance are type of business and location of the premises. The congested urban core areas of major cities often have a prohibitively high rate of burglaries and robberies. Suburban shopping centers may often have high crime rates because police coverage in these areas is often poor due to manpower limitations.

The next underwriting consideration is the physical loss control devices at the insured premises designed to reduce the incidence of crime losses. Crime loss control devices include such items as money chests and safes, locks and bars on doors, windows, and skylights, and private alarm systems. The protective devices employed by a particular business should be consistent with the quantity of money and property being protected and the attractiveness of the merchandise to criminals. An important factor for premises robbery coverage is the hours of operation for the business. Such business establishments as gas stations, small convenience grocery stores and liquor stores that remain open in the late evening hours are particularly susceptible to robbery. Many gas stations in urban areas reduce the robbery exposure by accepting only exact change or credit cards after certain hours. The exact change is placed by the attendant in a slot in a vault which cannot be opened by the attendant. A mercantile firm which has a high robbery exposure also has a high exposure to serious workers' compensation losses due to robbery related violence to store employees.

A final underwriting consideration for commercial crime insurance is moral and morale hazard. This is often difficult to assess adequately; however, the following characteristics should be carefully analyzed:

1. the experience, longevity, and cooperation of ownership, and the responsibility of management;
2. the financial and moral reputation of the firm in the community; and
3. loss experience.

UNDERWRITING OCEAN AND INLAND MARINE INSURANCE

The Marine Concept

Ocean marine is one of the oldest forms of insurance stemming back to the bottomry bonds of the Mediterranean nations more than a thousand years ago. Ocean marine underwriters have historically insured both oceangoing hulls and their cargoes. The "warehouse-to-warehouse" clause added land transportation as well. Inland marine insurance, which is peculiar to the United States, grew out of a willingness of ocean marine underwriters to provide coverage for goods and equipment in transit within the North American continent. Using the marine tradition of broad insuring agreements, inland marine coverages grew rapidly, cutting into traditional fire and casualty writings. This led to the adoption of the *Nation-Wide Marine*

Definition in 1933, amended in 1953 and 1976, which defined those areas within which inland marine coverage could be afforded.

Ocean Marine

Ocean marine is divided into the following four major categories: (1) yachts, (2) commercial hulls, (3) protection and indemnity, and (4) cargoes.

There are some differences between the underwriting considerations for yachts and those for commercial hulls and cargoes. While the term yacht usually brings to mind a 70-foot trawler, all sailboats and inboard powered boats fall within the definition.

Yachts Underwriting considerations for all yachts from 20-foot sailboats to 100-foot oceangoing powerboats can be grouped under three headings: (1) age, manufacturer, construction, equipment and maintenance of the vessel; (2) area of navigation and time of year of use; and (3) experience of the operators.

Construction, Equipment, and Maintenance. Fiberglass has greatly changed construction techniques in the last decade. Virtually all new yachts of less than fifty feet are being constructed of this material, which greatly decreases the required maintenance relative to wooden boats and makes older fiberglass yachts more likely to be seaworthy with only routine maintenance. There are great differences in construction techniques, and the fact that a yacht has been built of fiberglass does not automatically guarantee that it will be seaworthy, even for the most limited use. Since most yachts used throughout the year are hauled annually for new bottom paint, an out-of-the-water survey (inspection) is prudent.

The engines, electronics, and other equipment of the yacht should be appropriate for the use for which it is intended. A sixteen-foot hull with a 200-horsepower inboard engine is not really suited for anything but racing. It is not appropriate for waterskiing. For oceangoing yachts, minimum navigation equipment would be a compass and radio direction finder or fathometer. Recently, in a sudden fog bank at Marina del Rey, California, on a Sunday afternoon, over a dozen "Sunday sailors" put their boats on the beach in a 500-yard stretch because of lack of navigational instruments. Even a one-hour sail can result in a beaching if the yacht is poorly equipped.

The Area and Time of Year of Use. The use of a *trading warranty* on the yacht policy has traditionally been a major tool of marine underwriting. The trading warranty restricts coverage to the area for which the yacht, equipment and the experience of the operator are appropriate. The hazards of the seas differ greatly from one area to another and from one season to another within the same area. Putting to sea during the hurricane season in the Caribbean or during the winter in Maine waters is less than prudent.

The increase in the size of trailerable yachts has led to many underwriting problems. A person can now place a 25-foot yacht on a trailer and navigate lakes, rivers, and oceans from one coast to another. Frequently, this results in the owner sailing in waters where he or she is unfamiliar with the weather conditions and dangers such as reefs and shallows.

A great many sailboats are used for racing. While racing sailors often strain their equipment to its utmost, local and medium-distance ocean racing is generally not an underwriting problem. Racing sailors are usually more skilled and experienced than those who do not race, their boats are better maintained and equipped, and the crew can often deal quickly with emergencies that do occur. However, long distance races such as the Trans-Pac and the Trans-Atlantic Race do present the possibility of heavy weather damage to both boats and equipment.

The Experience of the Operator. An experienced operator is an extremely important underwriting consideration. Many insurance companies give credit for completion of Power Squadron or Coast Guard Auxiliary courses. Yacht owners who belong to organized yacht clubs generally have more experience, training, and dedication to their sport than those not so affiliated. The finest construction and equipment are useless unless the operator possesses sufficient seamanship to use the vessel properly.

Commercial Hulls Commercial hulls require consideration of some of the same basic types of information as yachts; the construction of the ship, its equipment and maintenance, the area within which it is used, and the expertise of the master and mariners are all important. While similar in kind, commercial hull underwriting differs in the sources of information. There are various registers of shipping that give the physical characteristics of the vessel. The "flag" or nation in which the ship is registered will determine the safety regulations under which the ship is operated and the frequency of inspections. An inspection should determine the state of maintenance.

In commercial hulls the cargo is a major consideration. Some cargoes, such as oil, chemicals, and coal, present serious hazards to the hull.

Protection and Indemnity Protection and indemnity coverage is a special type of legal liability insurance. It covers the legal liability of the vessel owner for bodily injury, illness, death, and damage to the property of others arising out of the ownership, use, or operation of the vessel. Admiralty law sets certain limits on the liability of vessels when the owner does not have privity to its operation. This limitation is usually applicable in commercial hull situations but seldom applies to yachts whose owners are usually on board.

Protection and indemnity (P & I) coverage includes:

- *Loss of Life and Bodily Injury.* This applies to persons injured aboard the vessel or elsewhere, including members of the crew if such injury is deemed to be the responsibility of the insured.
- *Property Damage.* This covers the owner's liability for loss of, or damage to, the property of others aboard the owner's vessel, fixed objects, and other vessels and property on board them (insofar as the collision clause in the hull policy does not apply).
- *Other Coverages.* A vessel owner whose craft sinks in private waters or obstructs a channel or otherwise constitutes a menace to navigation may be faced with the legal responsibility of marking or removing the wreck, or destroying it. Insofar as the expense of this procedure constitutes a legal liability of the owner, it is covered by P & I.
- *Sudden and Accidental Pollution.* Accidental discharge of fuel oil or other pollution-like substances into the water, or other violations that may be subject to fines or other penalties, unless as a result of the lack of due diligence on the owner's part.
- *Defense Costs.* The cost of litigation, including necessary bonds for release from court seizure, is covered whether against the vessel (*in rem*) or against the owner (*in personam*).[17]

Small outboard motorboats and small sailboats are usually insured for liability under a homeowners policy. Protection and indemnity provides liability coverage beyond that provided by the "running down clause" which gives only property damage liability for other vessels struck by the insured vessel. The running down clause is part of the hull coverage.

One serious area of exposure under the P & I coverage is pollution from oil tankers. The tanker *Argo Merchant*, which finally broke apart on Nantucket shoals on December 22, 1976, caused millions of dollars of pollution losses. The explosion of the *Sansiena* broke windows twenty-one miles away and caused nine deaths and approximately $12 million of property damage.

Cargo Insurance While commercial hulls are usually written only in seacoast cities, ocean cargo policies may be written any place in the country. Many firms today import components, raw materials, and finished goods from overseas, and still more firms are involved in export. All these firms are prospects for ocean cargo insurance. By use of the "warehouse-to-warehouse" clause, ocean cargo coverage will also include land transit from the originating warehouse to the dock and from the dock at the port of destination to the consignee's warehouse, involving, in many cases, land transit of thousands of miles. When underwriting cargo insurance the quality of the assured and his or her business reputation are of utmost importance. He or she must have as a primary interest the safe arrival of the product at destination. An insured who cuts corners in packing and shipping practices cannot be profitably underwritten.

Underwriters are asked to insure a wide variety of commodities. Commodities such as ingots of pig iron offer a very low susceptibility to loss or damage while others, such as fine glassware and china, are very easily damaged. Shipments of fishmeal or burlap can present extraordinary fire hazards. Auto parts and liquor are very attractive to thieves. Any bulk shipment or any shipment of raw materials will present its own unique problems. An unusual or sophisticated manufactured product will require a detailed explanation of the effects which its special characteristics will produce in the event of loss. There are chemicals which become worthless if they are exposed to air. There are electronic devices which require expensive recalibration in the event of the slightest damage. A few commodities and special hazards associated with them are shown in Exhibit 5-11.

The ports between which the goods will be shipped and the land transportation that will be used from "warehouse-to-warehouse" also are major underwriting concerns. In some ports, ships must be unloaded by a lighter, increasing the probability of damage to the cargo. Excluding bulk shipments, much of today's cargo is shipped in large enclosed metal boxes known as *containers*. These are similar to the semi-trailers we see on the road every day without their chassis. They can be "stuffed" at the original point of shipment and unloaded at destination, thus eliminating extra handling at the port. Much of the most recent tonnage has been vessels constructed solely to transport containers.

Containerization may be an answer to pilferage and fresh water damage provided the container is watertight and carries the merchandise warehouse to warehouse. Since at least one-third of containers are shipped on deck, however, the risk of exposure to heavy weather and washing overboard is greatly increased. The threat of a hijack of an entire shipment and the danger of breakage due to shifting of cargo within the container are additional serious perils.

A final but important point is the location of the goods on the ship. Deck cargo is subject to wind and wave damage to a much greater extent than that shipped below decks. Certain cargoes such as rough lumber are usually unaffected by deck shipment.

Exhibit 5-11
Some Commodity Characteristics*

Automobiles	Marring, denting, and scratching
Auto parts	Pilferage and theft in certain areas of the world where new cars are not readily available
Canned goods	Rusting, denting, and theft
Chemicals in paper bags	Shortage and contamination from torn bags
Fishmeal	Highly susceptible to heating damage and fire
Fine arts	Handling damage and theft
Fresh fruit	Extremely sensitive to temperature change and difficult to keep from spoiling
Glass	Breakage and staining
Grain	Shortage and weevil damage
Household effects	Breakage, marring, chipping, scratching, shortage, and water damage
Liquids in bulk	Leakage, shortage, and contamination
Lumber (cut)	Shortage, staining, and handling damage
Machinery	Rust and breakage of parts
Paper in rolls	Chafing, cutting, and water damage
Rags	Fire and shortage
Refrigerators and stoves	Marring, scratching, chipping, and denting
Scrap metals	Alleged shortage due to difference in scale weights at origin and destination
Steel products	Rusting, bending, and twisting
Television sets	Breakage of tubes
Textiles	Hook damage, theft, and water damage

*Reprinted with permission from *Commercial Property and Multible-Lines Underwriting* by E.P. Hollingsworth Jr., and J.J. Launie, (Malvern: Insurance Institute of America, 1978), p. 453.

Inland Marine

In terms of forms and rates, inland marine policies are divided into two categories—filed and nonfiled. Those classes in which the major rating bureaus have developed rates, rules, and forms for their member companies are defined as *filed*. *Nonfiled* classes are developed and rated in accordance with the underwriting practices of an individual insurance company. Most filed policies are relatively inflexible in terms of coverage or rates and are generally those for which there are a large number of similar exposures needing similar coverage.

Many loss exposures covered by inland marine insurance are handled on nonfiled forms. Insurers have forms they use for certain common classes of business, such as the contractors' equipment floater. Their use may vary substantially from one insurer to the next. Depending on company practice, any of these forms may be freely modified at the option of the underwriter. In many circumstances, it is necessary to design a "manuscript" policy to cover an unusual or one-of-a-kind exposure.

Because inland marine policies in nonfiled lines may be extensively modified or manuscripted, there is a great deal of flexibility in providing coverages for such exposures.

Inland marine may be grouped for study into the following classifications: (1) transportation, (2) instrumentalities of transportation and communication, (3) floaters, (4) miscellaneous coverages, including outboard motors and boats, and (5) bailee coverages.

Transportation   Goods shipped by truck, air, rail, and mail are eligible for coverage on some type of inland marine policy or as an extension to coverage in a multiple-lines policy.

The first point to emphasize with respect to underwriting goods in transit is that the perils insured against may differ markedly from those same perils at a fixed location. In transit insurance, coverage is routinely afforded for the perils of flood and earthquake. The difference stems from three facts:

1. The amount of insurance on goods in transit is small relative to the amount of insurance at a fixed location, such as a warehouse.
2. Goods in transit can be moved by their very nature; therefore, the likelihood of saving the goods from a flood is good.
3. During the course of transit, it is unlikely that the goods will *continually* be in areas threatened by flood or earthquake.

The underwriting of goods in transit on land includes the same basic types of considerations that apply to ocean cargo insurance.

There is one major difference. In land transit, the legal liability of the various types of carriers varies widely. This will affect the subrogation possibilities when insuring goods for the shipper's interest. When goods are shipped by common carrier, there is some possibility of subrogation, but there obviously can be no subrogation for goods shipped on the owner's vehicles.

Instrumentalities of Transportation and Communication

The principal instrumentalities of transportation and communication include bridges; tunnels; pipelines; wharves, docks, and piers; radio and TV towers and stations; and dry docks and marine railways and cranes. While much of inland marine insurance concerns itself with property in transit or capable of being transported, these subjects of insurance are *related* to transportation. Instrumentalities of transportation and communication are fixed location structures and present many of the same hazards as any other type of real property. In addition, due to their specialized nature, these structures are subject to some unique hazards.

When underwriting any of these instrumentalities, primary areas of concern include the construction of the structure, its maintenance, and any unique hazards or exposures that may exist. Bridges and tunnels, for example, may be exposed by trucks carrying gasoline or explosives. Television towers are susceptible to ice buildup in severe winter storms, increasing the likelihood of failure in high winds. Pipelines are particularly susceptible to earthquakes. Wharves, docks, and piers may be damaged by high waves as well as ship collisions.

Floaters

Floaters include both personal and commercial line coverages. The most familiar inland marine floaters are the personal articles floaters covering jewelry, furs, cameras, silverware, musical instruments, and fine arts most often attached to a homeowners policy. The major underwriting considerations on this type of coverage are accurate and timely appraisals and careful assessment of moral hazard.

In terms of premium volume, the largest classes of commercial floaters are the contractors equipment floater, motor truck cargo floater, and miscellaneous dealer floater. The primary underwriting concerns in these floaters are the financial stability of the owner or operator of the property insured, the use of the property, the area in which it is located, and the past loss experience.

Miscellaneous Coverages

While there are numerous miscellaneous coverages, such as rain insurance, often included in inland marine insurance, the principal miscellaneous coverages are the jewelers' block and the furriers' block policies. Both of these policies require extremely careful underwriting and should be declined at the first hint of moral hazard. They both have a formal, written application in which the declarations of the insured become warranties. This application must be carefully completed to avoid unintended breaches of warranty. The valuable nature of the property requires strong security measures, and central station alarm systems are virtually mandatory. In addition to the crime exposure, it should be remembered that these coverages provide fire insurance as well, and all fire underwriting considerations apply.

Bailee Coverages   Bailee coverage is provided in many inland marine policies, either as a section of coverage in a policy providing other coverage, such as the jewelers' block, or as a separate policy. The cleaners and dyers customer's policy generally provides bailee coverage only. This policy provides direct damage coverage for the customer's goods that the cleaner or dyer has in bailment, with all losses by insured perils being covered whether or not the insured was legally liable for the loss. In this way, bailee's insurance goes beyond any type of legal liability coverage. Bailee insurance also serves to close a gap in coverage which otherwise would be created by the common wording in legal liability policies excluding coverage for the property of others in the insured's "care, custody, or control."

Chapter Notes

1. Robert B. Holtom, *Commercial Fire Underwriting* (Cincinnati: The National Underwriter Company, 1969), p. 21.
2. Insurance Services Office, *Commercial Fire Rating Schedule* (New York, 1983), pp. 3-4.
3. Charles C. Dominge and Walter O. Lincoln, *Building Construction as Applied to Fire Insurance* (Philadelphia: Chilton Co., Inc., 1964), p. 82.
4. Insurance Services Office, *Commercial Fire Rating Schedule* (New York, 1983), p. 3.
5. This section is drawn from E. P. Hollingsworth, Jr. and J. J. Launie, *Commercial Property and Multiple-Lines Underwriting* (Malvern, PA: Insurance Institute of America, 1978).
6. *NFPA Inspection Manual,* ed. Charles A. Tuck, Jr., 4th ed. (Boston: National Fire Protection Association, 1976), p. 20.
7. *NFPA Inspection Manual,* p. 20.
8. This section is drawn from E. P. Hollingsworth, Jr. and J. J. Launie.
9. *Fire Protection Handbook,* 14th ed. George P. McKinnon and Keith Towers, eds. (Boston: National Fire Protection Association, 1976), pp. 1-26, 1-28.
10. Gordon P. McKinnon, ed., *Fire Protection Handbook,* 14th ed. (Boston: National Fire Protection Association, 1976), p. 1-33.
11. *Insurance Facts,* 1983-84 Edition, p. 58.
12. E. P. Hollingsworth, Jr. and J. J. Launie, p. 113.
13. E. P. Hollingsworth, Jr. and J. J. Launie, p. 118.
14. William H. Rodda, James S. Trieschmann, Eric A. Wiening, and Bob A. Hedges, *Commercial Property Risk Management and Insurance,* 2nd ed. (Malvern, PA: American Institute for Property and Liability Underwriters, 1983), pp. 258-259.
15. Alistair MacLean, *Athabasca* (Garden City: Doubleday & Co., 1980).
16. G. William Glendenning and Robert B. Holtom, *Personal Lines Underwriting,* 2nd ed. (Malvern, PA: Insurance Institute of America, 1982), pp. 240-241.
17. E. P. Hollingsworth, Jr. and J. J. Launie, pp. 431-432.

CHAPTER 6

Underwriting Liability and Multiple Lines Insurance

UNDERWRITING AUTOMOBILE INSURANCE

The Regulatory Environment

In the United States, most people regard driving an automobile as a right rather than a privilege. In some parts of the country where public transportation facilities are poor or nonexistent, driving an automobile is a virtual precondition for employment. For this reason, powerful public pressure is brought to bear on any institution or system that would limit the ability of a person to own and operate a motor vehicle.

At the same time, motor vehicles result in the death and disability of thousands of people each year. If, as a result of an accident, the head of a household is killed or disabled, his or her dependents will suffer serious economic loss. If insurance is not available to meet these losses, the innocent victims must look to the general welfare system. These two facts, the public's demand for unlimited access to the automobile and the automobile's well demonstrated capacity for mayhem, have combined to place great pressure on automobile underwriting.

The automobile underwriting task is bounded by myriad regulatory restrictions, particularly with respect to private passenger automobiles. Some underwriters feel that the trend in the regulatory environment is becoming so restrictive that it eventually will preempt the underwriting selection process in private passenger automobile insurance.

Attempts to Provide Universal Coverage A number of attempts have been made to provide universal coverage of all motor vehicles by some type of insurance that would compensate the innocent victims of automobile accidents. In the following section, three aspects of this approach are discussed: (1) compulsory automobile insurance, (2) financial responsibility laws, and (3) automobile insurance plans.

Compulsory Automobile Insurance. One of the earliest attempts to deal with the "innocent victim problem" by assuring universal automobile insurance coverage was instituted by the Commonwealth of Massachusetts in 1929. Massachusetts adopted a plan of compulsory bodily injury liability insurance, with limits of $5,000 per person and $10,000 per accident. Property damage liability was not made compulsory. This system reduced uninsured motorists to less than 1 percent by making some bodily injury insurance available to all motorists.

The Massachusetts system required a massive compliance mechanism. Every motorist was required to have an application for motor vehicle registration stamped by an insurance company. The insurance company was then required to provide compulsory coverage for that vehicle as long as the license plates were on the vehicle. To facilitate enforcement, all policies were effective January 1 and had a common expiration date of December 31. The Registry of Motor Vehicles Department was staffed with its own law enforcement personnel to police the system.

The major problem with the Massachusetts compulsory system was the high incidence of exaggerated and frivolous bodily injury claims that resulted. If the at-fault vehicle in an accident had a Massachusetts license plate, the owner of the other vehicle knew that at least $5,000/$10,000 bodily injury coverage was available. Property damage liability coverage might or might not be in effect. Many motorists filed bodily injury claims for alleged injuries which, although often groundless, were difficult to disprove. In 1970, this system was replaced by a no-fault statute. The no-fault concept makes first-party coverage for medical costs and loss of wages available to all motorists involved in an accident without determination of fault. There is usually a *threshold* (a dollar amount or specification of certain types of injuries) which, when exceeded, permits access to the usual tort remedies of suit for damages.

Financial Responsibility Laws. Some form of financial responsibility laws are in effect in all states and the provinces of Canada. The laws require the owner or operator of a motor vehicle to show proof of financial responsibility up to a certain minimum dollar amount in certain situations. The financial responsibility laws usually require such proof in one of three instances:

1. after an automobile accident involving bodily injury or property damage greater than a specified dollar amount;
2. after conviction for such offenses as reckless driving, driving under the influence of alcohol, or leaving the scene of an accident; or
3. after failure to pay a final judgment arising from an automobile accident.

The intent of the financial responsibility laws is to require motorists to have access to sufficient liquid assets up to a specified amount to compensate the victims of any accident in which they might be involved. Some states have a *security type law* which deals only with the *current* accident, while others have a *security and proof law* which requires evidence of solvency for *future* accidents as well as for the current one.[1] The advantage of the financial responsibility laws is that they increase the number of insured motorists without the heavy enforcement costs inherent in compulsory insurance regulations. The filings required after conviction for serious offenses place a burden on the reckless but solvent motorist, which, of course, is desirable.

Both types of financial responsibility laws suffer from the defect that the laws come into operation only *after* the motorist has been involved in a serious accident or traffic violation. While insurance is the usual mechanism for assuring financial responsibility, this type of law falls far short of the goal of universal coverage.

Another defect of the financial responsibility law approach is that there is little or no effective enforcement mechanism. It is very difficult to remove the irresponsible driver from the road, even after the driver's license has been suspended or revoked. If this person continues to drive, unlicensed and uninsured, the financial responsibility system provides no assistance to any future innocent victims.

Underwriting is affected by financial responsibility laws through the requirement of filing proof of the existence and amount of liability insurance in effect. In most noncompulsory insurance states, if the owner or operator appears to be at fault in an accident, the underwriter may have to file a form verifying that the owner or operator who had the accident and was without insurance at the time now has insurance coverage. The underwriter filing the form declares that insurance is in effect until a notice of termination is filed. Another effect is that under financial responsibility laws, insurance is provided to all vehicles, whether declared on the application or not.

Automobile Insurance Plans. Legislation has been passed in a number of states requiring insurers operating in the state to form an Automobile Insurance Plan (formerly called Assigned Risk Plan). Insurers in other states have voluntarily set up similar plans.

The Automobile Insurance Plan provides a market for those unable to obtain insurance in the voluntary market. These plans vary considerably from state to state, but generally, applicants are shared on some equitable basis by all insurers writing automobile insurance in the state.

Some Automobile Insurance Plans set criteria for admission to the plans, while others admit anyone with a valid driver's license. Other variables include the availability of premium financing and whether the plan permits higher limits than those required by the state's financial responsibility laws. Those insured in the plans pay higher rates than are available in the standard voluntary market.

An alternative approach used in some states is to establish a reinsurance pool to which an insurer can transfer an insured who would otherwise be placed in an Automobile Insurance Plan. Eight states use a reinsurance facility or joint underwriting association instead of an automobile insurance plan. The approach in Maryland is unique in that a state fund was established whereby a driver who cannot obtain insurance in the voluntary market is accommodated by an "insurance company" operated by the state. —

Restrictions on Cancellations In most states, there are restrictions on cancellation that apply to private passenger automobiles, but a few states include commercial automobiles as well. The public pressure that led to the passage of these laws was focused primarily on the private passenger sector.

The statutes usually set forth a minimum amount of notice that must be given prior to nonrenewal. Often the reason for nonrenewal must either be given in writing or available upon request of the insured.

It should be noted that in an environment when cancellation and nonrenewal are both inhibited by regulation, careful underwriting of new business submissions is extremely important. Once a poor driver has been put on the books, it is much more difficult to remedy the situation under present conditions than it was in the past. The industry is faced with the dilemma that tight underwriting in the voluntary market increases the size of the involuntary market which the insurance companies share on a pro-rata basis.

The Legal Environment

A major modification of the legal environment of automobile insurance underwriting in recent years has been the adoption of no-fault statutes in several states. There have been other changes in the legal environment which may also affect automobile underwriting.

No-Fault Legislation No-fault auto insurance represents a modest departure from and addition to the tort system. The majority of the states with "no-fault" laws require first party and liability insurance and restrict in some way the right of an injured party to sue. The remaining states have no restrictions on lawsuits and vary as to whether the insurance is compulsory.

The no-fault idea was introduced in a book by law professors Keeton and O'Connell in 1965.[2] While there are a variety of no-fault plans presently in effect, the typical plan provides first-party medical coverage and loss of earnings coverage for automobile accident victims in all cases below a *statutory threshold*.

A statutory threshold can be either a monetary threshold or a verbal threshold. A *monetary* threshold is a dollar amount of medical costs or other specific economic damages that must be exceeded before a claim for pain and suffering may be filed. On the other hand, a *verbal* threshold is measured by the seriousness of the injury as expressed in words such as "permanent disfigurement."

Like financial responsibility laws, no-fault laws are difficult to enforce. Some car owners purchase no-fault insurance only to obtain a vehicle registration and promptly cancel no-fault insurance thereafter.

From an underwriting standpoint, no-fault statutes do not change the existence of hazards. Moreover, underwriting practices in no-fault states have not been noticeably changed. There are two primary reasons for this.[3] First, no-fault laws do not affect potential accident *frequency*, a major underwriting factor. Second, in many states the insurer retains the right of subrogation, thus making little change in the ultimate costs of losses. (When an insurer pays an insured for a loss, the insurer takes over the insured's right to collect damages from any other person responsible for the loss.)

Private Passenger Automobile Underwriting Factors[4]

Since private passenger automobile underwriting is virtually class underwriting, the preparation of the underwriting guide to indicate the relative desirability of the various classes is of great importance. In Chapter 4, a point evaluation system was described. While there are many types of systems used to evaluate attributes of private passenger automobile applicants with regard to loss potential, the major underwriting factors considered in most private passenger automobile underwriting guides are (1) age of operators, (2) age and type of automobile, (3) use of the automobile, (4) driving record, (5) territory, (6) sex and marital status, (7) occupation, (8) personal characteristics, and (9) physical condition.

Exhibit 6-1
Accidents by Age of Drivers, 1982*

Age Group	Number of Drivers	Percent of Total	Drivers in All Accidents	Percent of Total	Drivers in Fatal Accidents	Percent of Total	Accident Involvement Rate All[1]	Fatal[2]
Under 20	14,700,000	9.9	4,200,000	13.8	8,300	13.8	29	56
20-24	17,800,000	11.9	5,500,000	18.0	12,500	20.7	31	70
25-29	18,000,000	12.1	5,600,000	18.4	8,800	14.6	31	49
30-34	17,200,000	11.6	4,400,000	14.4	7,600	12.6	26	44
35-39	14,200,000	9.5	2,200,000	7.2	4,500	7.5	15	32
40-44	12,000,000	8.1	2,000,000	6.5	4,500	7.5	17	38
45-49	11,200,000	7.5	1,500,000	4.9	3,200	5.3	13	29
50-54	11,800,000	7.9	1,200,000	3.9	2,400	4.0	10	20
55-59	10,300,000	6.9	1,200,000	3.9	2,300	3.8	12	22
60-64	7,800,000	5.2	900,000	3.0	2,000	3.3	12	26
65-69	6,600,000	4.4	900,000	3.0	1,400	2.3	14	21
70-74	4,500,000	3.0	300,000	1.0	1,100	1.8	7	24
75 and over	3,000,000	2.0	600,000	2.0	1,700	2.8	20	57
Total	149,100,000	100.0	30,500,000	100.0	60,300	100.0	20	40

1. Drivers in all accidents per 100 drivers in each age group.
2. Drivers in fatal accidents per 100,000 drivers in each age group.
   Source: National Safety Council.

*Reprinted with permission from *Insurance Facts* (New York: Insurance Information Institute, 1983-4 Edition), p. 76.

Age of Operators Historical loss data contain strong evidence that the age of the operator is an important determinant of the likelihood of loss. Drivers under the age of thirty are involved in a disproportionately large number of accidents. In 1982, drivers in that age group represented 33.9 percent of the driving population but were involved in 50.2 percent of all accidents and 49.1 percent of fatal accidents. The relationship between accident frequency and age is shown in Exhibit 6-1.

While the rating plans in virtually all states take age explicitly into account, charging considerably higher rates for young drivers, it remains an underwriting judgment to determine the extent to which the higher rate offsets the increased loss potential.

Age and Type of Automobile The age of an automobile may be used as a rough indication of its mechanical condition. While there are some old automobiles that are in outstanding mechanical condition, there is a correlation between age and mechanical condition.

The type of automobile also has a bearing on underwriting

Exhibit 6-2
Collision Coverages Relative Average Loss Payments Per Insured
Vehicle Year by Car Size and Body Style Group, 1982 Models*

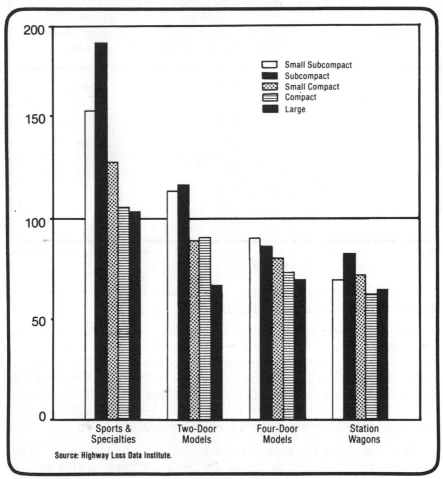

Source: Highway Loss Data Institute.

*Reprinted with permission from *Insurance Facts*, 1983-84, p. 80.

acceptability. Sports cars and high performance cars tend to produce higher loss costs than standard sedans. The damageability and cost of repair of the automobiles should be reflected in the physical damage premium. To the extent that the premium structure does not account for damageability, the desirability of that type of automobile is affected. Numerous studies have been made of the cost of repairing various makes and models of automobiles.

Exhibit 6-2 shows the relative average loss payments for collision coverage for 1982 models. In all size groups, sports and specialty cars had the worst experience while station wagons had the best of the 1982

Exhibit 6-3
Number of Convictions vs. Accident Rate—Three-Year Period*

Number of Convictions	Relative Increase in Accident Rate Over "0" Convictions (Times-As-Many Factor)	Percent of "Accident Free" Drivers
0	1.00	89.44%
1	1.95	80.09
2	2.70	73.74
3	3.54	66.81
4	3.98	64.44
5	5.17	57.75
6	5.34	55.95
7	6.72	48.12
8	8.11	44.94
9+	9.03	39.56

*Reprinted from *The California Driver Fact Book*, State of California, Department of Motor Vehicles, July 1981, Report No. 29, p. 5.

model year cars during their first year of availability, according to the Highway Loss Data Institute (HLDI).

Use of Automobile Other things being equal, the longer the automobile is on the highway the greater the probability of an accident. Long commuting distances or business use of the automobile will result in high annual mileage. As is the case with most of these characteristics, rates attempt to reflect the increased loss potential. The underwriter must determine whether the particular driving mileage indicated is excessive in view of the rate that will be obtained.

Driving Record Both prior accidents and prior moving violations are considered vitally important in the evaluation of a private passenger automobile applicant. The prior loss history of the drivers may indicate poor driving habits, recklessness, or simply lack of skill. Certain moving violations are an indication of a disregard for safety, while others indicate carelessness.

At least one study suggests that the probability of an accident for a particular driver is directly related to the past driving record. This is shown in Exhibit 6-3.

Territory The principal place of garaging is an indication of the probability of both liability and physical damage losses. Congested urban areas, with parking on the streets, provide high incidence of theft and vandalism. Cars parked on the street are vulnerable to being struck by passing automobiles, often with a hit-run resulting. Congestion also increases the probability of bodily injury and property damage liability claims which are related to traffic density.

There are other territorial variations unrelated to population density. Some areas of the country have severe winter weather causing dangerous icing conditions. In other areas, sandstorms frequently cause comprehensive losses to paint and windshields.

It is important that underwriters understand the particular perils present in the various territories being underwritten. If there is a particularly hazardous area in a neighboring territory, the possibility that the insured may be commuting there should be investigated.

Sex and Marital Status Sex and marital status have long been factors considered by underwriters. However, the value placed on them has varied considerably by the age of the applicant involved. For example, young female drivers were generally considered to be better than young male drivers. For many years young female drivers paid the same premiums as adult drivers. However, in recent years, young females have paid more than adult drivers in most states, but still considerably less than young males.

Marital status is recognized in both rating and underwriting, especially at the younger ages. Married male drivers under thirty usually pay less than their single counterparts. This recognizes the fact that, generally, married persons at these ages tend to be more mature and responsible than single persons of the same age, and also that their marital situation tends to result in more time being spent at home.

Marital status and sex are two of the underwriting factors about which some states have legislated. In effect most states do not permit the rejection of an applicant on the basis of sex or marital status. In some states, the rejection is not permitted if an applicant's sex or marital status is the *sole* reason for rejection. In others, sex or marital status cannot be used at all—either alone or in conjunction with other factors—in making an underwriting decision. Additionally, a few states are now trying to prohibit price discrimination on the basis of sex or marital status.

Occupation The relationship between the occupation of the drivers and driving habits is quite controversial. Some underwriting guides make distinctions on this basis; others do not. Certain occupations, such as traveling salespersons, require extensive driving and increase the probability of loss. This should be accounted for in the rates reflecting use of the vehicle.

Personal Characteristics Consumer investigation reports are often ordered to provide information on the personal characteristics of the insured and other drivers. This information is subjective and must be carefully evaluated. Financial instability and emotional or marital problems may lead to poor driving habits. Association with criminal

Exhibit 6-4
Traffic Accidents in the United States, 1955-1982*

Year	Accidents[1]	Deaths[2]	Injuries[3]	Economic Loss[1]
1955	11,516,000	38,426	2,158,000	$ 5,400,000,000
1960	11,429,000	38,137	3,078,000	10,211,000,000
1965	14,733,000	49,163	3,982,000	14,177,000,000
1970	22,116,000	54,633	4,983,000	23,549,000,000
1975	24,887,000	45,853	4,978,000	36,058,000,000
1976	25,439,000	47,038	5,269,000	40,889,000,000
1977	26,716,000	49,510	5,575,000	47,710,000,000
1978	27,742,000	51,500	5,798,000	52,622,000,000
1979	26,669,000	51,900	5,681,000	56,371,000,000
1980	24,100,000	52,600	5,230,000	57,519,000,000
1981	28,342,800	51,500	5,019,000	58,744,140,000
1982	28,501,500	46,000	4,490,000	60,189,000,000

Sources: [1]Insurance Information Institute.
[2]National Safety Council (1979 figure is preliminary estimate).
[3]Prior to 1965, The Travelers Insurance Companies; 1965 to present,
Insurance Information Institute.

*Reprinted with permission from *Insurance Facts* (New York: Insurance Information Institute, 1982), p. 53; 1982-3, p. 54; 1983-4, p. 69.

elements or a criminal record may also indicate a worse-than-average loss potential.

Physical Condition Physical impairments may be a problem if allowances for the impairment have not been made. Modifications of the car to accommodate an impaired driver and demonstrated mastery of the vehicle usually make the applicant acceptable.

Private Passenger Automobile Loss Control

There is little or nothing that can be done on an individual basis for loss control in private passenger automobile underwriting. Loss control measures in private passenger automobiles must be addressed to the public at large. The automobile accident problem is a complex one. The design of automobiles, highway design, licensing and automobile inspection by the several states, and more rigorous enforcement of drunk-driving laws are all elements of the automobile loss control situation.

The magnitude of the problem can be seen in the data contained in Exhibit 6-4. Although the number of traffic deaths in the United States declined dramatically in 1982, economic losses growing out of those accidents continued to rise as a result of steady increases in the costs of automobile repair and medical and hospital care. The economic loss figure increased 2.1 percent from $58.7 billion to $60.1 billion. The economic loss data reflect the cost, both insured and uninsured, of paying for property damage and legal, medical, and funeral bills, along with loss of income from absence from work and the administrative costs of insurance.[5]

Commercial Automobile Underwriting Factors

In commercial automobile underwriting, a combination of class underwriting and individual risk underwriting is employed. Some commercial automobile policies are routinely class underwritten much in the same manner as private passenger automobile policies. Other commercial automobile fleets are individually underwritten if they develop sufficient premium to make this feasible.

When underwriting a large commercial automobile fleet, the territory or radius of operation and the type of business are of major importance. Some fleets haul only their owners' goods as would be the case with a manufacturer who used company trucks to deliver goods to distributors. A common carrier's fleet would present different exposures since these trucks would be hauling a variety of goods between various points on a regularly scheduled basis. Common carriers (those that hold themselves out to transport persons or goods of all who choose to employ them) present additional liability exposures because they are liable for damage to the cargoes they carry.

Analysis of a commercial automobile account requires the following information: (1) number, type, and age of the vehicles in the fleet; (2) radius or area of operation, whether local, intermediate, or long haul; (3) experience and financial stability of management; (4) type of cargo hauled; (5) age and experience of drivers; (6) maintenance and repair facilities; (7) loss experience; (8) weight of vehicles; and (9) use of vehicles.

The weight and type of vehicle is a consideration that is not as important in private passenger automobile underwriting as it is in commercial automobile underwriting. The damage resulting from an accident is related to the size, or weight, and speed of the vehicles involved. Commercial tractor-trailer rigs can weigh 80,000 pounds or more when loaded and often travel at the maximum legal speed. No comparison needs to be shown as to how much more damage could be done by one of these rigs in a fifty-five-mile-per-hour collision than by a compact car. Large trucks are also very difficult to maneuver in heavy traffic or on small inner-city streets. The vehicle weight and type are reflected in the primary rating classifications of commercial vehicles.

Commercial vehicles vary significantly in the intensity of use as well as how they used. Some may be used almost continuously in hauling goods while others may be used only to travel to and from a job site, remaining parked most of the time. Each of these factors is usually reflected in the primary and secondary class to which the vehicle is assigned.

Public attitudes toward commercial automobiles also differ from those toward private passenger automobiles. The public has learned that virtually all commercial firms carry insurance with high liability limits. The presence of the insurance and its normally high limits may tend to increase the number of claims made and the size of the claims, given a similar accident involving a personal automobile.

There are two alternative courses of action available to the underwriter of a commercial automobile fleet that would normally not be present with respect to private passenger automobiles. These are: (1) modify the rate by applying debits or credits or by the imposition of a larger deductible, and (2) modify the hazards through a loss control program such as driver training, improved hiring practices, increased frequency of inspection and maintenance, the installation of monitor logs in the trucks, or other similar techniques.

Commercial Automobile Underwriting Characteristics Summarized

The following is an outline of underwriting characteristics for commercial auto risks.[6] Exhibit 6-5 categorizes these underwriting characteristics by major secondary classification from the commercial auto manual. The letters in the body of Exhibit 6-5 refer to the subheadings under each major characteristic.

1. Possibility of inadequate rates caused by:
    a. delivery to or servicing of new customers,
    b. delivery to more distant locations because of price advantages,
    c. pickups of raw materials at more distant sources,
    d. lack of expertise of producer in providing complete information to assure proper classification, and
    e. difficulty in determining place of principal garaging.
2. Excessive speed resulting from:
    a. meeting schedules,
    b. bonuses paid to drivers to minimize trip times, and
    c. hauling perishables.
3. Extensive mileage expected:
    a. as a result of use of sleeper cabs and two-man crews, and
    b. because of wages based on the number of miles driven or paid per trip.
4. Driver characteristics including:
    a. training in special skills may be necessary;
    b. salaries not competitive to attract and retain those who are experienced, thus causing turnover and unknown (to the underwriter) drivers;

    c. unfamiliarity with changing routes;

    d. drivers who are poorly educated and make poor witnesses in court;

    e. casual or pickup type labor, frequently unknown to the insurer, and

    f. driver fatigue.

5. Automobiles:

    a. maintained improperly,

    b. not available for periodic servicing,

    c. loading and unloading,

    d. operated over narrow, substandard roads, and

    e. operated in areas of dense traffic or numerous pedestrians.

6. Goods being transported:

    a. bulky, high center of gravity, contributing to upset;

    b. large loads that obscure driver vision;

    c. spillage, causing a frequency of property damage claims;

    d. shifting preventing proper automobile control;

    e. flammables or explosives contributing to severity of liability claims, especially in congested areas such as cities, tunnels, and so on;

    f. heavy loads that damage bridges, overpasses, curbs, sidewalks, driveways, and roads;

    g. high loads damaging overpasses, wires, signs;

    h. overloading that makes a trial defense more difficult;

    i. acids, corrosives, pollutants; and

    j. unpleasant cargo to handle, attracting less desirable drivers.

7. Management:

    a. lack of profits that requires expense economies and a tendency toward inadequate automobile maintenance,

    b. use of independent contractors who might be uninsured and who cannot be adequately supervised or controlled,

    c. establishment of unreasonable time schedules,

    d. improper driver selection and training,

    e. lack of cooperation with insurer and disinterest in safety,

    f. transportation of employees in vehicles that are unsafe for that purpose,

    g. inadequate records,

    h. involvement in labor disputes, and

    i. inability to closely supervise drivers due to nature of the business.

8. Laws:

    a. lack of traffic law enforcement, and

    b. filings creating a situation where policy conditions cannot be used to deny a claim for which the insured is liable.

Exhibit 6-5
Summary of Underwriting Characteristics*

Factors to Consider	Secondary Classification						
	Manufacturers	Truckers	Food Delivery	Specialized Delivery	Waste Disposal	Farmers	Dump and Transit Mix Trucks and Trailers
1. Possibility of inadequate rates caused by	a,c	a,d,e	a	a	a	a,b	a,c
2. Excessive speed resulting from	a,b	a,b,c	a,b,c	a,b	a,b	a,c	a,b
3. Extensive mileage expected	a,b	a,b	a	—	b	—	b
4. Driver characteristics including	a,e,f	a,b,c,f	b,c,e,f	a,b,c,f	a,f	b,d,e	a,f
5. Autos	a,c	a,d	a,c,d,e	a,e	a,e	a,c,d	a,d
6. Goods being transported	a,j	a,j	d,h	d	a,d,h,j	a,d,h,j	a,c,d,f,h,j
7. Management	a,i	a,e,g, h,i	a,c,d, e,i	a,e,h,i	a,c,d, ei	a,d,e, f,i	a,e,i,
8. Laws	—	b	—	b	—	a	—

*Reprinted with permission from Larry D. Gaunt, Numan A. Williams, and Everett D. Randall, *Commercial Liability Underwriting* (Malvern, PA: Insurance Institute of America, 1982), p. 156.

Commercial Automobile Loss Control

Loss control is an important underwriting tool in commercial automobile insurance. A loss control program can make both drivers and management more safety conscious and systematize vehicle inspection and maintenance, thus reducing accidents.

Commercial automobile loss control programs emphasize the following areas: (1) driver selection and training, (2) equipment inspection and maintenance, and (3) management support for safety programs.

Driver Selection and Training   It has been estimated that 85 percent of all automobile accidents result from the unsafe acts of drivers.[7] This means that any fleet loss control program must focus on driver selection and training. Improved screening techniques, including both physical and psychological tests, can be effective in reducing accidents. In addition, most state motor vehicle departments require that truck drivers pass a special test. The Interstate Commerce Commission (ICC) also sets standards for drivers that come under that agency's jurisdiction.

Driver selection should include determination that the employee has the right class of license for the type of vehicle to be driven. If a driver is involved in an accident and does not have the proper license to operate the vehicle involved, defense of the lawsuit will become much more difficult.

Also important in driver selection is a complete medical examination of the prospective drivers. It is a good idea to give periodic examinations to current drivers as well. The extent of the examination will be determined primarily by the type of driving to be done. Driving a tractor-trailer rig from New York to Chicago would logically require more physical effort than driving a company car to the post office to pick up mail.

When allowed by law, driver selection should include a check of the applicant's Motor Vehicle Record (MVR). There should be a standard of how many and what type of violations or accidents will be allowed when hiring a driver. Periodically, new MVRs should be obtained on current drivers. There should be a procedure to follow in cases where the driver is to be removed from a driving position. Action may vary from transfer to a nondriving position to termination of the driver's employment.

Equipment Inspection and Maintenance   Proper inspection and maintenance of such items as tires, brakes, and electrical systems is essential for proper fleet operation. A loss control program can be devised to assure that all vehicles are regularly inspected and any indicated maintenance promptly done. A poorly maintained fleet is unlikely to have satisfactory loss experience.

Management Support for Safety Programs   Management support must be obtained if any loss control program is to be effective. Many large fleets have dramatically reduced losses by introducing safety programs and contests. Such items as recognition of years of accident-free driving, posters, films, and lectures on safety all contribute to fleet loss control. Some companies have found that awards of money, merchandise, and extra vacation time to drivers with accident-free records have been very effective. If management does not take an active role in the program, or similarly, if it does not encourage vehicle maintenance, employee morale is affected. An employee may ask, "Why should I be worried about maintaining the vehicle if management is not concerned?" This lax attitude on the part of management can create dangerous conditions in vehicles and may cause serious accidents.

Management's lack of concern for vehicle maintenance and safety programs may also be reflected by the drivers in a lack of concern for vehicle safety rules and traffic laws. It is important for the insurer to point this out to the insured and to show how this may affect the premium and, in many cases, the availability of coverage through a standard market.

ICC Regulations on Commercial Automobiles

The Bureau of Motor Carriers of the Interstate Commerce Commission (ICC) requires truckers to carry bodily injury and property damage liability insurance. The regulations require truckers to file a certificate indicating that appropriate limits of coverage have been obtained from an approved insurance company. The trucking company must also have cargo insurance covering its legal liability as a common carrier.

This certificate modifies the liability of the insurance company in two significant ways. First, the ICC endorsement makes the insurance company liable with regard to successful claims against the trucker, regardless of policy language to the contrary. Second, the ICC endorsement modifies the cancellation clause of the policy in that cancellation may occur only after thirty days have elapsed after notice of cancellation is received in writing at the office of the ICC.

Since the insurance company must pay all claims for which the trucker is liable, even those not covered under the policy, the policy becomes in effect a bond. As is true with other surety bonds, the insurance company may recover from the insured all amounts paid beyond the policy coverage. It is here that the thirty day cancellation restriction becomes important. If a motor carrier becomes insolvent, there may be a large number of overage, shortage, and damaged cargo claims which have been pending. Since the insurance company cannot cancel for thirty days, these claims would have to be paid. The insolvency of the motor carrier usually makes any attempt by the insurance company to recover for payments made above the policy a futile exercise.

The cancellation provision of the ICC endorsement is an important regulatory restriction in commercial automobile underwriting. The financial capacity and stability of the insured become as important as the loss history and MVRs of the drivers.

WORKERS' COMPENSATION UNDERWRITING

Workers' compensation was introduced in this country in 1911 as the first social insurance program of its kind. The concept of workers' compensation originated in Germany in the 1880s. The workers' compensation concept replaces the tort system of employers' liability. Under a compensation system, when a worker is injured or becomes ill in the course of employment, he or she is entitled to the benefits specified in the workers' compensation statutes without the necessity of proving fault on the part of the employer. In a sense, workers' compensation was the first no-fault insurance system adopted in this country.

Over the years, workers' compensation insurance has changed in many ways. In most states, coverage has been broadened by legislation extending coverage to almost all workers and increasing benefits to be received by injured workers. The definition of a compensable injury or illness has been broadened both by legislation and by judicial rulings. An example of the broadening of the definition of compensable injury or illness is found in the case of *continuous (or cumulative) trauma* where an employee is eligible for benefits, not as the result of a particular accident or acute illness, but as the result of a physical condition which has developed over a period of years of working at that particular occupation.

Another recent development has been recent judicial interpretations which have had the effect of making many additional workers eligible for coverage under the United States Longshoremen's and Harbor Workers' Compensation Act, even if their employment is only slightly related to the waterfront. The United States Longshoremen's and Harbor Workers' Compensation Act generally provides broader benefits than those of state workers' compensation laws, which could render the premium inadequate if it were predicated on the basis of state benefits rather than federal benefits. The underwriting of workers' compensation requires knowledge of state or federal legislation, together with an awareness of the effect of recent court decisions affecting eligibility for benefits.

The Evaluation of Workers' Compensation Submissions

The evaluation of workers' compensation submissions requires an analysis of the following underwriting factors: (1) management attitude and capability, (2) on-premises hazards, (3) off-premises hazards, and (4) potential for hazard modification through loss control.

Management Attitude and Capability A successful workers' compensation insurance program requires active cooperation between the management of the insured firm and the insurer. The underwriter must determine the willingness and ability of management to cooperate in the effort to minimize hazards and reduce losses.

If the firm does not have a safety program, or if the program exists only on paper with no management effort directed toward its implementation, managerial indifference may usually be assumed.

Employee morale and claims consciousness are often reflections of both management attitude toward workers' compensation and industrial safety on the one hand and the degree of managerial skill on the other hand. A poorly managed firm is unlikely to have above average workers' compensation loss experience. If the employee morale is low, grievances against management may motivate workers to file false or exaggerated claims for workers' compensation as a means of escaping from an unpleasant work environment.

On-Premises Hazards There are a variety of on-premises hazards, some of which are found in virtually all occupations, while others are peculiar to a particular operation or industry. From an underwriting standpoint, these hazards must be evaluated with regard to their loss-causing potential. In a very general sense, workers' compensation losses fall into the following categories: (1) industrial accidents, (2) occupational disease, and (3) continuous (or cumulative) trauma.

General On-Premises Hazards. All premises should be evaluated with respect to two general on-premises hazards which could exist in all workplaces regardless of the type of employment. These are housekeeping and maintenance.

HOUSEKEEPING. From an underwriting standpoint, housekeeping refers to the quality of planning for the workplace, cleanliness, and efficiency of operation. This includes such factors as the arrangement of machinery, the placing and adequacy of aisles, the marking and cleanliness of stairs and freight elevator openings, and general overall cleanliness.

MAINTENANCE. Poorly maintained machinery is inherently dangerous. A good program of plant and machinery maintenance is an indicator of a positive management attitude toward work safety, while the absence of such a program indicates a lack of awareness, or carelessness, which can have a severe impact on future work injuries. A firm in shaky financial condition may postpone or ignore necessary maintenance, greatly increasing the hazard from this source. Underwriters should keep currently aware of the financial condition of the firm since a firm that formerly had a good maintenance program might drop it under severe financial pressure.

Specific On-Premises Hazards. While the preceding general hazards are present in all types of firms, there are specific hazards which may be present in a particular firm due to the type of machines, equipment, materials, and processes used in their operation. These specific hazards require specific controls such as machine guards, exhaust systems, and materials handling devices designed to meet the requirements of the particular situation.

The specific hazards vary widely but can be categorized under the following headings:

1. machinery and equipment hazards;
2. material-handling hazards;
3. electrical hazards;
4. occupational hazards;
5. fire and explosion hazards;
6. slips, falls, working conditions;
7. burns, heat, chemicals and dangerous processes;
8. flying and falling materials, resulting in eye and head injuries; and
9. miscellaneous hazards resulting in cuts, punctures, bumps, bruises, and abrasions.

Hazard Analysis of On-Premises Hazards. One type of hazard analysis consists of taking each of the National Council classifications and identifying the type of injury most likely to occur in that classification. The National Safety Council has identified the following ten principal causes of injuries:

1. striking against objects (cuts, slivers, punctures);
2. struck by objects (falling, flying, moving objects);
3. caught in, on, or between objects;
4. fall on the same level;
5. fall to different level;
6. slip or overexertion (hernias, strains);
7. temperature extremes (burning, scalding, frostbite, etc.);
8. inhalation, absorption, or ingestion (occupational disease, poisoning, dermatitis, including cumulative effects);
9. contact with electric current (i.e., shock); and
10. miscellaneous or other causes.[8]

Exhibit 6-6
Analysis of Injuries and Hazards by Classification*

Classification	Injury Type	Occupational Hazards
Abrasive paper or cloth preparation	2,6,8	Dust, housekeeping, occupational disease
Acid manufacturing	6,7,8	Fumes, dermatitis, burns, explosives, housekeeping
Bakeries (commercial)	1,4,6,7,10	Dermatitis, fires, strains, burns, auto exposure
Bookbinding	1,4,6	Improper lifting, stacking of paper, cutting tools

*Reprinted with permission from Larry D. Gaunt, Numan A. Williams and Everett D. Randall, *Commercial Liability Underwriting*, 2nd ed. (Malvern, PA: Insurance Institute of America, 1982), p. 390.

Each injury type is identified utilizing the National Safety Council causes of injuries identified by number. Any special occupational hazards may also be noted. An example of this approach is shown in Exhibit 6-6.

Another method of analysis is to list each of the specific hazard categories listed above and indicate for each of these categories whether the hazards are *remote, common,* or *constant* for each of the occupational classifications.

These terms are defined as follows:

- remote: neither regular nor frequent
- common: regular but not frequent
- constant: both regular and frequent

Regular is defined as occurring or functioning at regular or uniform intervals while *frequent* is defined as happening at short intervals. Therefore, *constant* hazard may result in a loss on a recurring or uniform basis at short intervals, while a *common* hazard is capable of producing loss on a recurring or uniform basis but not at short intervals. *Remote* hazards may result in an infrequent loss that will not occur at uniform intervals.

Based on reference material or knowledge of the hazards normally present in a particular classification, assignment of one of these categories is made. Exhibit 6-7 is a chart which may be used in this type of evaluation.

INDUSTRIAL ACCIDENTS. Most accidents occur either as a result of an unsafe act or an unsafe condition. Unsafe acts or practices on the part of employees include such things as disregard for hard hats in

Exhibit 6-7
Workers' Compensation Hazard Analysis*

Code			
Hazard Source	Remote	Common	Constant
Machinery and equipment			
Material handling hazards			
Electrical hazards			
O. D. hazards			
Fire and explosion hazards			
Slips, falls, collision, etc.			
Flying material—eye injuries			
Burns—heat, chemicals, etc.			
Miscellaneous—cuts, punctures, bumps, bruises, etc.			

*Reprinted with permission of Allstate Insurance Company.

construction areas or disregard of safety devices such as goggles when their use is indicated. The management of the firm, by their hiring policy, safety program, and enforcement of safety regulations, can influence employee behavior. Premises inspections can indicate the extent to which these unsafe actions appear to be tolerated. Unfortunately, there is always the danger that employees may act differently during the inspection than on other occasions, or that supervisors may not enforce safety rules continuously.

Unsafe conditions are generally easier to identify than unsafe acts. In an office, there is usually a minimum of dangerous conditions such as those involving machinery, chemicals, and similar hazards. Depending on the premises, there may be some potential for slips and falls and even back strain from improper lifting of files, boxes of paper, and similar heavy objects.

In a factory, the manufacturing process utilized and the type of materials used are important. The loss history of the insured firm and others in the same industry provides information on the types of losses that might occur. In woodworking, for example, sharp cutting tools operating at high speeds can result in serious lacerations. In other processes, the potential for burns is inherent in the operation.

The rating structure takes into account the differences in relative hazards among occupational classes. It is clear that a machine shop is more hazardous than an office, for example. What is significant is that the underwriter must attempt to determine to what extent the insured is typical of its class. The machine shop must be evaluated relative to some guidelines which indicate the conditions to be found in a typical machine shop. The presence of additional hazards not found in other machine shops or the heightening of normal hazards due to poor maintenance or housekeeping would indicate a substandard exposure.

OCCUPATIONAL DISEASE. Predicting the frequency and severity of occupational disease is more difficult than for work-related accidents. This is because accidents are easily identified, while exposure to unfavorable work conditions does not always cause occupational disease. Coverage of occupational disease has been broadened by changes in the state workers' compensation statutes and by more liberal interpretation of compensable diseases by state workers' compensation commissions and the courts.

Some of the occupational diseases covered by the various state workers' compensation laws are silicosis (exposure to silica dust), asbestosis (caused by inhalation of asbestos fibers), radiation (including ionizing radiation), tuberculosis, pneumoconiosis (black lung) and heart or lung disease for certain groups such as police or fire fighters.

In an industrial setting, hazard analysis involves monitoring the working environment for the presence of industrial poisons. These poisons may enter the body by ingestion, inhalation, or absorption through the skin. Analysis of the toxicity of the various chemical compounds used in a particular process provides a means of evaluating the occupational disease hazards due to this source.

CONTINUOUS (OR CUMULATIVE) TRAUMA. The most difficult type of hazard to evaluate is continuous or cumulative trauma. In continuous trauma cases, the injured worker maintains that the stress and strain of the occupation eventually resulted in a disability. In most of these cases the claim is for permanent total disability.

Examples of continuous trauma include deafness as a result of a long exposure to high noise levels or kidney damage from a lifetime of jolting in the cab of a truck.

Industrial noise that can lead to workers' compensation losses can also be evaluated on a straightforward basis by observing the ambient noise level in the industrial plant. Various techniques, including the use of sound absorbing materials and ear protection devices, can be utilized to mitigate this problem.

The more difficult occupational illnesses to evaluate are those related to physical and emotional stress. In some cases, heart attacks, ulcers, and nervous disorders have been determined to be compensable occupational illnesses. In some jurisdictions, the courts have ruled that any heart condition suffered by a police officer or fire fighter is *presumed* to be work related and therefore compensable. An air traffic controller who works under great stress is subject to hypertension, heart disorders, and ulcers as occupational illnesses.

Off-Premises Hazards Individual firms differ in the extent to which they present off-premises hazards. In some firms, the employees carry out all their employment duties on the premises. In other firms, there is a great deal of travel in the course of employment. There are two elements to the off-premises hazard: (1) the duration of travel and the mode of transportation, and (2) the types and extent of hazards at the remote job sites.

As an example of the first type of off-premises hazard, consider two accounting firms with identical payrolls. In Firm A, the accountants do all their work on the firm's premises. In Firm B, which does a great deal of auditing for firms in the construction business, the accountants travel much of the time in the course of employment. This travel is done in private automobiles as well as in commercial and corporate aircraft. Traffic accidents or plane crashes could result in serious workers' compensation losses for Firm B from this off-premises exposure which is not present in Firm A. If the accountants are present at hazardous remote job sites exposed to falling building materials and similar hazards, then the second element must also be considered.

Corporate aircraft may result in a multiple-fatality worker's compensation loss in the event of a crash. The potential for multiple losses is also present when several employees share the same car or truck when traveling on the business of their employer.

The same techniques previously mentioned to evaluate on-premises hazards may be used for off-premises hazards. The separate evaluation of off and on premises is necessitated by the fact that the number of workers exposed to off-premises hazards may be only a small fraction of the total work force.

Potential for Hazard Modification Through Loss Control A loss control program may reduce workers' compensation losses if successfully implemented. Since individual firms vary in the degree to which hazard reduction through loss control is possible, this is an important underwriting variable. It is the task of the underwriter to evaluate any existing loss control program and to estimate the extent to which additional loss control efforts will change the desirability of the insured.

Exhibit 6-8
A Safety Management Control System*

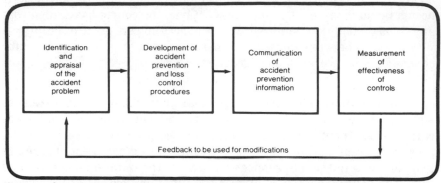

Identification and appraisal of the accident problem → Development of accident prevention and loss control procedures → Communication of accident prevention information → Measurement of effectiveness of controls

Feedback to be used for modifications

*Reprinted with permission from "Scope and Functions of the Professional Safety Position" (Chicago: American Society of Safety Engineers, 1966).

The following are the basic principles of an effective loss control program.[9]

1. An unsafe act, an unsafe condition, an accident: all these are symptoms of something wrong in the management system.
2. Certain sets of circumstances can be predicted to produce severe injuries. These circumstances can be identified and controlled.
3. Safety should be managed like any other company function. Management should direct the safety effort by setting achievable goals, and by planning, organizing, and controlling to achieve them.
4. The key to effective line safety performance is management procedures that fix accountability.
5. The function of safety is to locate and define the operational errors that allow accidents to occur. This function can be carried out in two ways:
   a. by asking why—searching for root causes of accidents and
   b. by asking whether or not certain known effective controls are being utilized.

The management control system that should be applied in safety programs can be visualized as an ongoing process whereby each accident situation is analyzed to evaluate the effectiveness of present loss control techniques. This is shown in Exhibit 6-8.

Occupational Safety and Health Act

The Occupational Safety and Health Act was passed by the U.S. Congress in 1970, effective in 1971. The purpose of the act was to provide all workers with safe and healthy working conditions and to preserve our human resources. This act set safety standards for employers and imposed penalties for violations of the standards.

The Department of Labor has the task of enforcing the act. Safety inspectors may enter the working premises at any reasonable time to inspect the premises, equipment, and environment of the work force. When a violation is detected, a citation is issued describing the exact nature of the violation. The employer has fifteen working days after receiving written notice of the violation to notify the Department of Labor that either the citation or the penalty assessed will be contested.

Any willful violation that results in an employee's death is punishable by a fine of up to $10,000, or imprisonment of up to six months. The second conviction carries double penalties. From an underwriting standpoint, any indication that an employer has received a serious OSHA citation should call for a thorough underwriting review.

While OSHA is a step in the right direction, the resources of the federal government and those states that have passed similar legislation are quite limited. OSHA safety inspections are no substitute for underwriting inspections of the various locations. Rather, they should be viewed as a source of additional data and inspection assistance. The desirable workers' compensation insured undertakes a safety program because it makes good economic sense, not because of the coercion of possible federal or state criminal fines and penalties. Unfortunately, some insureds will respond to no other means of persuasion.

UNDERWRITING GENERAL LIABILITY LINES

The hazards and underwriting approach used in general liability lines differ markedly between personal lines coverages on the one hand and commercial lines on the other.

Comprehensive Personal Liability

Most comprehensive personal liability coverage is currently written in conjunction with the homeowners coverage. There are two major areas of hazard within the comprehensive personal liability coverage: (1) residence premises liability, including new residences in the process of construction, and (2) sports liability.

Residence Premises Exposure A great many residence premises losses are due to an attractive nuisance on the premises. An *attractive nuisance* is an alluring or unusual object or structure (usually man-made) that may entice young children. Neglecting to properly fence a swimming pool may allow young children to fall into it and drown. A tree house or similar structure may also be an attractive nuisance. These hazards are in addition to the basic premises hazards of uneven or icy sidewalks, poorly maintained steps and porches, and poorly lighted hallways. The use of large plate glass sliding doors has produced substantial losses when guests have walked or run through them. Residence liability losses are low in frequency but may be severe and therefore difficult to accurately predict except for large books of business.

The recent increase in crime has led to two developments that may increase residence liability losses. Many householders are buying guns for home protection. A person who is unfamiliar with the proper care and storage of firearms and ammunition may leave a weapon where children or others can reach it with serious consequences. Some homeowners have purchased large dogs for premises protection. While these dogs may reduce residence burglaries, they may increase premises liability claims if they attack innocent persons.

Sports Liability Exposure Typical sports liability hazards are golf balls and watercraft. There is little that can be done about the golf exposure from an underwriting standpoint. Questions about the accuracy of a golfer's drives might irritate even the best-humored insured. Where there is a watercraft exposure, information about the age, experience, and training of boat operators can indicate the severity of the hazard. Organizations such as the Power Squadron, Coast Guard Auxiliary, and local yacht clubs offer training courses in seamanship and navigation which can greatly reduce the hazard for those insureds with the benefit of this training. Additional sports exposures are found in hunting, fishing, and skiing. Hunting accidents are often fatal, and a skier moving at a high rate of speed can cause serious injury to others.

Loss Control Whether written alone or as part of a package policy, personal liability coverages do not usually generate sufficient premium to make insurance company inspections feasible. Therefore, any loss control program is difficult to institute on an individual insured basis.

Loss control efforts for personal lines must rely upon education and local ordinances to improve residential premises safety. Safety education programs may be conducted in the schools and supplemented by advertising campaigns utilizing the mass media. The entire community benefits as a result of these programs although they are not aimed at improving the physical condition of a particular insured.

Similarly insurance industry support can lead to the passage of local ordinances dealing with such areas as fencing of swimming pools, requiring that doors be removed from all discarded refrigerators, and similar ordinances banning various types of attractive nuisances. An ordinance banning exotic pets in a city will reduce the incidence of losses due to bites by ocelots, cougars, and other types of animals.

General Liability

There are three major facets of exposure for commercial insureds that are underwritten under the heading of general liability: (1) premises and operations exposure, (2) independent contractor exposure, and (3) products and completed operations exposure.

These areas of exposure are often referred to as "hazards" in the sense that the premises exposure of a particular commercial insured presents the "hazard" of possible tort action. The liability exposures of commercial firms are covered in a variety of policies such as the comprehensive general liability policy. These coverages are analyzed in detail in CPCU 4—*Commercial Liability Risk Management and Insurance.*

Premises and Operations Exposures Premises hazards may exist inside the building or may emanate from the areas surrounding it, such as parking lots and sidewalks. Typical losses occurring inside the building are slips, falls, cuts, tears, and burns. The underwriter must analyze these losses to determine the underlying causes. Some of the hazards or conditions that increase the likelihood of loss include uneven stairs, torn carpets, poor lighting, congestion, poor housekeeping, or poor heating and electrical equipment. Some types of businesses present other hazards, such as sharp objects, flammable liquids, explosives, and toxic or infectious gases. The frequency of loss from premises is affected by the amount of pedestrian traffic.

Typical losses occurring outside the building may be caused by broken sidewalks, broken or uneven surfaces in the parking lot, and outside signs. Mobile equipment, such as forklift trucks, may be a cause of loss.

The operations exposure includes injuries and damages resulting from the insured's activities and operations wherever they occur. Service companies, such as plumbers and electricians, have few premises exposures but serious operations exposures. Liability losses from operations generally involve damage to property. A plumber may damage the customer's home with equipment or solvents or cause a water damage or a fire loss from careless use of welding equipment. Building contractors may damage vehicles in parking lots or injure pedestrians. The nature of the business suggests the common types of exposures to expect, but each insured firm must be carefully evaluated to determine the variations in these common exposures to loss.

Sufficient information must be developed concerning the insured's operations to permit proper evaluation of the potential hazards. The classification of the business given on an application or submission may cover only the primary aspect of the business. There may be subsidiary operations or divisions with quite different hazards.

Checklists and questionnaires on hazard analysis are usually included in company underwriting guides, manuals, or bulletins. Some commercially distributed underwriting guides are also available. It is important to note, however, that any guide lists only those hazards that are common to or typical of a certain type of operation. It does not list all of the hazards in a particular firm. These must be obtained from an inspection report.

Premises and Operations Loss Control The purpose of loss control is to reduce loss frequency or loss severity or both. Loss control services usually concentrate on physical hazards because these are more easily recognized and dealt with than moral and morale hazards. It is also easier for the insured to see the positive results of efforts to reduce physical hazards. Loss control implementation must be cost effective. It may be that certain hazard minimization techniques may be too expensive for the insured to adopt. If that is the case, the underwriter must decide if the firm is insurable without the benefits of the loss control procedures.

The starting point for a loss control program for the premises and operations exposures of a particular firm is an inspection made by the insurance company or a preliminary survey made by the producer. This inspection should detail the hazardous areas where claims are likely to occur, and recommendations can be made to improve these physical conditions.

In a premises liability situation, typical recommendations will call for improved housekeeping, improved lighting in areas frequented by the public, the installation of guard rails where required, and upgrading of the condition of the surface of sidewalks and parking lots.

A description of the operations of the insured will provide a basis for recommendations to reduce claims incidence. For example, if a security guard firm is causing claims resulting from excessive or improper use of force on the part of its guards, a training program for the guards may be an essential part of any loss control program.

Loss control programs are an important underwriting tool in

general liability since an effective program can greatly improve the desirability of a particular firm. While the physical conditions are important, the attitude of management toward loss control is even more vital.

Insurance Company Loss Control Reports. A loss control report based on a physical inspection can provide the following assistance to the general liability underwriter:

1. confirm the classification and rating information,
2. determine whether the firm is representative or "average" for the class,
3. discover unknown exposures,
4. make loss control recommendations, and
5. provide a source of information for schedule rating (discussed in Chapter 10).

The underwriter can greatly increase the efficiency of the work of the loss control representative by providing full and complete instructions on the inspection request. The underwriter should advise the loss control representative of the nature of the account to be inspected, including any unusual features of which the underwriter is aware. Underwriters should also provide full classification and rating data so that loss control representatives are aware of what data should be verified.

The inspection report can also provide the underwriter with certain types of information which can indicate the presence or absence of moral or morale hazards in addition to the more obvious physical hazards. Managerial attitudes and abilities are aspects of a firm which may lead to serious moral or morale hazards. The inspection report can provide some information in this area by indicating the condition of the firm with respect to the following elements:

1. quality of housekeeping;
2. quality of general premises maintenance;
3. knowledge of management in safety areas;
4. cooperation of management with loss control efforts; and
5. overall attitude of management.

Pre-Loss Controls. Exposure to loss can be affected by controlling the degree to which the public is subjected to the insured's operations. Fencing can be utilized to protect pedestrians from a construction site, or people can be protected from hazardous operations by prohibiting public access to the area. Danger to the public can be further reduced by controlling the physical hazard involved. Machines can be guarded;

Exhibit 6-9
Loss Control Techniques—Tripping *

	Occurrence	Engineering Approach	Human Behavior Approach
Source	Torn carpet in lobby	Repair carpet	Train employees in procedures in handling customers' injuries
Initial or operating subject	High heel of customer catching in tear	None	Direct customers away from lobby where tear is present
Damage or injury spread	Arm, leg, back injury from fall	None	First aid; immediate attention; ambulance service
Insured loss effect	Medical expense, disability, possible pain and suffering expenses	Ambulance transportation	Quick treatment; courteous service to injured customer

* Adapted with permission from Larry D. Gaunt and Numan A. Williams, *Commercial Liability Underwriting* (Malvern, PA: Insurance Institute of America, 1978), p. 241.

safety nets can be used in blasting operations; and spilled liquids on supermarket floors can be mopped up.

One of the most common losses encountered in a hotel is tripping and falling. Exhibit 6-9 shows an analysis of this type of loss and possible engineering and human behavior solutions.

In the hotel classification, fire presents a more severe loss exposure as was graphically illustrated by the fires at the MGM Grand Hotel and the Las Vegas Hilton. A similar analysis of this loss exposure is contained in Exhibit 6-10.

A loss control representative could recommend loss control procedures, as shown in Exhibits 6-9 and 6-10, for most of the exposures encountered in a hotel. For each, the hazard must be evaluated first, and the engineering or human behavior solutions then identified and recommended. Engineering solutions control losses by manipulating *things* while human behavior solutions control losses by modifying human *behavior*. A follow-up check will determine if the recommendations have been properly implemented by the insured.

A business such as television repair has off-premises property damage losses as a major exposure. Exhibit 6-11 contains a loss control analysis of this exposure, utilizing the same format. This table indicates that a number of these losses cannot be controlled by the engineering approach. The human element is a major factor determining whether a

Exhibit 6-10
Loss Control Techniques—Fire *

	Occurrence	Engineering Approach	Human Behavior Approach
Source	Smoldering cigarette	None	No smoking signs; special smoking areas with receptacles
Initial or operating subject	Flammable contents	Possible use of nonflammable materials	None
Damage or injury spread	Fire division	Adequate exits, clear stairways, automatic sprinklers, fire extinguishers	Training of employees for emergency; alarms; evacuation
Insured loss effect	Burns, smoke inhalation, death	Emergency vehicles	First aid equipment; emergency procedures

* Reprinted with permission from Larry D. Gaunt and Numan A. Williams, *Commercial Liability Underwriting* (Malvern, PA: Insurance Institute of America, 1978), p. 241.

loss of this type will occur and the severity of those losses that do occur.

Post-Loss Controls. In general liability underwriting, post-loss controls can be quite significant. After a person has been injured by tripping on a torn carpet, post-loss controls can help to minimize the severity of the loss. A medical facility or first aid availability could provide immediate treatment to the injured customer, and this could reduce the physical injury. Quick treatment often eliminates expensive complications, infection, or shock. Quick, efficient, and courteous handling of such an injury may result in goodwill which will affect the customer's attitude toward the insured and may reduce the likelihood of a suit being filed.

The courtesy, training, and supervision of employees in the prompt reporting of occurrences and the proper handling of injured customers will have an important effect on claim costs. If the claims adjuster is also efficient and courteous, losses can be reduced.

The operations of independent contractors doing work for the insured are often referred to as owners' and contractors' protective (OCP) liability or the independent contractors' coverage. Through the legal doctrine of *respondeat superior*, the employer is responsible for

Exhibit 6-11
Loss Control Techniques—TV Repair, Off-Premises Losses *

	Occurrence	Engineering Approach	Human Behavior Approach
Source	Soldering iron	None	Worker trained in use of soldering iron
Initial or operating subject	Customer's carpet	Asbestos mat in work area	None
Damage or injury spread	Burn in carpet	None	Careful work habits
Insured loss effect	Expenses to repair or replace carpet	None	Good relations with customer

* Reprinted with permission from Larry D. Gaunt and Numan A. Williams, *Commercial Liability Underwriting* (Malvern, PA: Insurance Institute of America, 1978), p. 242.

the actions of employees. Similarly, a principal is responsible for the actions of agents even though they are not employees of the principal. The liability is imputed because the agent is acting on behalf of and for the benefit of the principal.

Independent Contractor Exposure The exposure to loss caused by independent contractors is quite obvious in the case of a general contractor, but this exposure goes far beyond that classification alone. Most businesses employ independent contractors to a greater or lesser degree. Since the principal may be held liable for the torts of the independent contractor, this loss exposure warrants close underwriting attention.

Analysis of this exposure may focus on two points.

1. How frequently are independent contractors employed and in what capacity?
2. Does the firm require evidence of insurance coverage on its independent contractors? If coverage is required, what is the nature of the coverage? What are the limits of the coverage?

Often a large firm will hire relatively small independent contractors for such tasks as building maintenance and repair or for small construction projects. The independent contractor may have limits of liability that are much lower than those of the principal. In one instance, a large manufacturing firm hired a small contractor to dig a new sewer line. The contractor's backhoe severed a phone line carrying computer data to a nearby space project. The line, which was leased for thousands of dollars a minute, was not repaired for eighteen hours. The claim ran well over the contractor's limits of liability, exposing the principal to a major loss.

Products and Completed Operations Exposure Products liability losses have increased steadily over the past decade. This is partially due to changes in the legal environment as manifested by court decisions that have had the following effects:

1. diminution of the right of privity of contract
2. increased application of strict liability
3. increased filing of class action suits

Today, it is generally held that a manufacturer has a duty to exercise reasonable care in the manufacture, design, and packaging of its product. This duty extends to anyone who may come in contact with the product, not merely the consumer or purchaser. The parties to a contract are said to stand in *privity* with each other, and the relationship between them is termed *privity of contract.* Formerly, manufacturers could avoid product liability suits from persons other than the consumers of their product on the grounds of the lack of privity. Courts today increasingly take the view that the duty to exercise reasonable care extends to everyone and that lack of privity is not a bar to recovery.

The doctrine of *strict liability* in tort holds most sellers or manufacturers liable for injuries caused by defective and dangerous products. Under this doctrine, the injured person is not required to prove negligence of the seller or manufacturer or to prove breach of warranty, either express or implied. The injured person must show that the product was defective when it left the control of the seller or manufacturer, that the defect made the product dangerous, and that the product was the ultimate cause of injury. Since the seller or manufacturer still has some defenses against such claims, including the defense that the product was improperly used, strict liability is not the same as absolute liability. Under absolute liability, if the product is the proximate cause of the loss, there are no defenses for the seller or manufacturer. Under recent court decisions, the trend appears that few defenses are effective under strict liability leaving a result close, if not the same, as that under absolute liability.

A *class action* suit is an action that may be brought in either state or federal court when a group of claimants have a similar or identical cause of action against a defendant. A class action may be brought against a manufacturer on behalf of all the consumers of a defective product. This has the effect of enabling consumers to afford to bring an expensive legal action against a manufacturer due to the size of the damages for the aggregate of the class when the damages for each individual member of the group might be relatively small. If a manufacturer has sold a defective product which results in damages to each individual consumer of $150, the expenses of a legal action would be prohibitive and the consumer would be unlikely to be able to obtain redress through the courts. If the consumer is a member of a class of one million similarly situated claimants, the action can now be brought for $150 million, which justifies considerable legal expense on the part of the plaintiffs' attorneys.

Both the federal and state court systems have rules under which class actions may be brought. The class must be clearly defined. Generally the class must be so numerous that the joinder of all such persons is impractical. There must be a well-defined community of interest in the questions of fact and law affecting the parties in the class. It must be possible to prove a common or single state of facts to establish the right of each member of the class to recover.

In a class action, a named member of the class is set forth as the plaintiff for itself and all other members of the class. The named member of the class must be representative of the class as defined. Class actions in the product liability area represent an important liability exposure. A relatively small amount of damages per claimant can become a huge loss if the class size is large. Defense costs in class action suits are often considerable due to the large potential exposure. The recent trend in both the federal and state courts is toward making it easier to file a class action case.

Manufacturers are finding that they are being sued for alleged defects of products that were manufactured thirty or forty years earlier and have changed hands a number of times. Many of these products were not expected to be used even half that length of time. In addition, manufacturers are finding situations where a person purchased the item for scrap or show purposes but, upon finding it in workable condition, began to use it in a business. Understandably, the original warnings, warranty, or instructions for use were destroyed or lost. Also, many parts have been replaced with inappropriate new parts since the old parts are no longer made. Safety devices may have been removed sometime during the life of the product. Yet, despite all these changes and modifications, the original manufacturer is being held liable in some cases today.

In view of the current trends, it is not always a valid defense that the manufacturer used all quality control techniques and installed all safety devices available and customary at the time. As new safety devices are invented, the public comes to expect all products to have the safety device, even if the product was manufactured prior to the development of it. Some courts and juries are asking if it was technically possible to have had the device earlier, and making decisions and judgments on that basis.

The Consumer Products Safety Act of 1972 was intended to aid the consumer primarily through the removal of unsafe products from the market. It may be found that the Act will aid the manufacturer also. If a government agency or similar organization examines a product, conducts extensive tests on it, and finds nothing wrong with the product, the manufacturer will almost certainly use this in its defense if a suit is brought against the manufacturer regarding that particular product. Whether this will be a valid defense, some defense, or no defense at all is a matter for each court to decide.

Another area that underwriters and manufacturers must be aware of is in the purchase of one firm by another. Traditionally, under common law, a firm does not assume the liabilities of another firm when it buys that firm unless one or more of these four conditions are present: (1) there is an express or implied agreement to assume the liabilities; (2) the transaction is essentially a merger; (3) the purchasing corporation is in essence a continuation of the seller; and/or (4) the transfer of assets is for fraudulent purposes. Thus, if the original firm is a corporation that dissolves after the sale of its assets, the injured consumer may have no one to sue if one or more of the above exceptions are not present. However, courts have held that if the firm purchasing the equipment uses it to manufacture essentially the same product, often under the same brand name, it may be responsible for claims made against the defunct corporation that manufactured the product. The fifth exception would now seem to be whether the purchaser "is an integral part of the overall producing and marketing enterprise that should bear the cost of injuries resulting from defective products."[10]

To look into the products liability problem, the federal government established the Interagency Task Force, which is one of many groups set up to study the problem and the proposed solutions. Some of the solutions which are proposed include:

1. one statute of limitations to run from the date of purchase and one to run from the date of the accident;
2. reinsurance by the federal government;
3. captive insurers;
4. nonliability when the product is altered in an unforeseen manner;
5. coordination of benefits between workers' compensation and products liability insurers; and
6. abolishment of punitive damages.

Products recall is another area of great concern. Products recall insurance provides coverage for all reasonable and necessary expenses to withdraw or recover a potentially dangerous product from use of from the channels of distribution. Coverage applies when a recall is made because the insured determines that the use of these products will cause bodily injury or property damage due to a fault in the manufacture or as a result of a mistake in the design, formula, plan, specification, advertising material, instructions, or labeling of the product. Products recall coverage is not provided by standard comprehensive liability policies—it must be added by endorsement or a separate policy must be purchased.

The efficiency of the firm in being able to recall its products promptly may determine if few or many claims are filed. The insurer should take a direct interest in the measures the insured has taken so that products needing recall can be identified, located, and recalled as soon as possible. Record keeping is very important in the recall process. The records are also important in showing what quality control and safety precautions were taken to make the product safe. This may help to defend a suit successfully when it is claimed that the manufacturer should have discovered a defect in the product before it was sold.

Since virtually any product or completed operation may lead to a loss, previous loss history is an important guide to the evaluation of hazards. For large insureds, the insured's own loss history will give an indication of the efficiency of the quality control and inspection program. For smaller insureds, only the loss history of the entire classification in which the insured falls is likely to have any credibility. Inspection of the insured's premises is necessary to evaluate the quality control program and procedures for minimizing product liability losses.

Sources of Underwriting Information for Products Liability. The application is the first source of underwriting information with respect to products liability or completed operations. The nature of the product determines the type and quantity of information required by the underwriter. Exhibit 6-12 indicates the type of products liability information required by one insurance company on its comprehensive general liability policy application.

Items 1 and 2 of the application in Exhibit 6-12 cover the nature of the products and the scope of the exposure. Item 3 deals with quality while item 4 covers record keeping and traceability. Items 5 and 6 develop information on past and future products. The nature of the ultimate product and whether it is a component is covered in items 7 and 8. Items 9, 10, and 12 deal with quality control. Finally, item 11 develops information on the scope of other operations whether related to product manufacture or not. These twelve questions represent only

Exhibit 6-12
Products Liability Questions from CGL Application *

IF PRODUCTS LIABILITY INSURANCE DESIRED, PLEASE COMPLETE THE FOLLOWING (IF APPLICANT IS CONTRACTOR, COMPLETE COMPLETED OPERATIONS SECTION INSTEAD):

1. Please list below all products which applicant manufactures or handles

NAME AND DESCRIPTION	MFR. OR DISTR.	YEARS ON MARKET	HOW SOLD BULK PKGE.	ANNUAL SALES VALUE	UNITS

2. Totals for past 3 years: Value _____ Units _____

3. Does applicant manufacture a price ☐ or quality ☐ product?

4. Which of the above products bears applicant's name, label or serial number? _____

5. Describe any other products applicant has manufactured or sold within the past 5 years? _____

6. Describe any new products applicant may place on market soon _____

7. Which of applicant's products are sold for further processing? _____

8. Which of applicant's products have been sold for further processing? _____

9. Which of applicant's products have been tested by Underwriters Laboratories or other recognized testing bureau? _____

10. Brief description of method of inspecting products for quality or purity before being shipped _____

11. Percent of service or installation to total operations. _____ %

12. Does applicant make express warranties regarding the quality, safety or performance of your products? _____ If yes, please attach samples of warranties.

*Reprinted with permission from Larry D. Gaunt, Numan A. Williams and Everett D. Randall, *Commercial Liability Underwriting*, 2nd Ed. (Malvern, PA: Insurance Institute of America, 1982), p. 293.

the beginning of the underwriting process for a products liability submission and serve to direct the underwriter to those areas where more information must be developed in order to properly assess the exposure.

Many insurance companies use preinspections for businesses with significant products liability exposures. Some have developed special inspection forms to produce the detailed information required for underwriting hazardous products. A loss control inspection form for product liability may include the following:[11]

1. List all products manufactured and/or distributed by the risk, including any private label products.
2. What are the typical applications for these products?
3. How can these products cause injury or property damage through product failure or misuse?
4. What type of quality control organization is employed? Include description of incoming, in-process, and finished product inspection.
5. Are any products labeled by a recognized testing lab such as Underwriters Laboratories? What industry standards do products comply with?
6. What type of labels, warnings, or precautionary statements are provided on the product?
7. Describe the instructional materials or manuals provided with the product to inform the user of the proper use and maintenance of the product.
8. Is there a formal product safety program in operation?
9. What type of engineering procedures does the firm utilize to anticipate potential product safety problems?
10. What type of testing is performed during the design and development of the products?
11. What types of safety features, devices, or precautionary markings are designed into the product as a result of the engineering procedures in (9) above?
12. Briefly describe how the products are distributed.
13. What types of record are kept of design tests, quality control inspections, sales, customer complaints, and product failure reports and analyses?
14. Describe previous claims and type of corrective action or product changes that have been implemented due to these claims.

Loss Control.   While nothing constructive can be done with regard to products manufactured in previous time periods from the standpoint of loss control, an effective program is essential to reduce the incidence of claims on products presently being sold and manufactured.

The loss control program will vary in detail depending upon the type of product manufactured and the size of the firm. A multi-plant manufacturer producing a variety of products for different markets requires a much more extensive program than a single-plant, single-product operation. There are common elements to all programs. Following is a description of a model products loss control program:[12]

1. The organization should be efficient and have full top-management backing.
2. Research and design controls should be used so that products are developed with the safety of the consumer in mind.
3. Written quality control procedures with regular report files must be maintained.
4. Installation and owner's manuals must be carefully prepared and reviewed by competent legal counsel.
5. Advertising and sales material must present a true picture of the product and should be reviewed by the legal staff.
6. Warning and instruction labels must be clear and unambiguous.
7. Packaging and shipping procedures must take into account any product peculiarities or unusual hazards.
8. All complaints and alleged accidents resulting in injury or damage must be promptly and adequately investigated and written reports filed.
9. Appropriate written records must be maintained throughout the entire manufacturing process and any subsequent investigation documented and filed.

However, the underwriter must recognize that unless endorsed to the contrary, the policy covers all past products of the insured if the loss-causing event *occurs* during the policy period. Therefore, a large part of the exposure stems from the insured's *past* operating practice, regardless of what is presently being done in terms of inspection and quality control.

Professional Liability

A "professional" is one who possesses the special knowledge and skill necessary to render a professional service. Typically, the special knowledge and skill result from a combination of the person's education and experience in a particular branch of science or learning. For tort law purposes, those whom the law has recognized as professionals include physicians, surgeons, dentists, attorneys, engineers, accountants, architects, insurance agents and brokers, and many others.[13]

Professional liability, by its nature, is subject to large and relatively infrequent claims. Additionally, these claims are usually filed and settled many years after the date of the event from which the claim arose. Thus, it is often difficult to determine if this line of business is profitable until many years after the premium has been collected. To alleviate this problem, some professional liability policies have been changed from an occurrence basis to a claims-made basis. If a policy is written on an *occurrence* basis, coverage is provided on those occurrences that happen during the policy period, even if claims are not actually brought against the insured for years after the coverage has expired. If a policy is written on a *claims-made* basis, the underwriter provides coverage on only those *claims made* against the insured during the policy period.

Under the claims-made form, the insurance company knows at the end of the year the claims it will be expected to defend, even if it does not know the exact amount it will have to pay. The claims-made policy will affect underwriting in that the insurer may pay some claims that occurred during a previous policy period. Similarly, some claims for occurrences under the present policy will not be made during the current policy period. The underwriter must adjust the pricing to reflect these situations.

In the past, professional liability policies almost always included a condition that required the insured (the professional) to consent to any out of court settlement. Before an out of court settlement was possible, the insurer needed the permission of the insured.

The trend is away from this rule. In most areas of professional liability, claims have become so large and so serious that insurance companies insist on the right to settle out of court without the consent of insureds. At present, some professional liability policies contain the traditional condition and some do not. Obviously the difference is significant to the underwriter.[14]

It is usually best for one insurer to write both the premises and professional liability on hospitals or institutions such as nursing homes. If a person falls out of a hospital bed, there may be some question as to whether this is a premises claim due to a faulty bed or a professional liability claim due to the failure to use the necessary restraints on the patient to prevent the fall. If one insurer has both coverages, it will defend in either case. If two separate insurers are involved, there may be some question as to who should defend the suit.

The legal environment of professional liability has greatly changed in recent years. Both claims frequency and severity have increased as courts have held professionals liable for damages in a wide variety of circumstances.

The medical professional liability exposure is not limited to doctors in private practice, hospitals, and clinics. Many manufacturing plants have first aid facilities, nurses, or even doctors in attendance. While these facilities improve the account from a workers' compensation standpoint, the presence of these medical facilities should not be overlooked when surveying the professional liability exposure of the firm. Other professional liability exposures found in many industrial and commercial firms are directors' and officers' errors and omissions and fiduciary liability for pension plan administrators.

When underwriting physicians' professional liability, the type of specialty practiced by the particular physician is important. Those generally considered in the high risk category are anesthesiologists, neurosurgeons, plastic surgeons, and cardiovascular surgeons. The general practitioner has much less exposure, particularly if surgery is not performed.

When evaluating a physician's professional liability submission, the important attributes to consider include degrees and/or licenses held, professional organizations in which membership is held, certification, recertification (continuing education), years in practice, type of clientele, associates (i.e., fellow workers), and whether the physician practices as an individual or as a member of a professional association. All of these give some indication of the doctor's position within the medical community, which will often play a major role in the defense of suits. This is not to say that a well-known doctor will be found innocent because he or she is popular with other doctors; but it should be recognized that the professional reputation of the doctor will be quite important in malpractice cases, and the insurer is looking for other doctors to speak on behalf of the doctor's professional competence.

Exhibit 6-13 summarizes medical malpractice claims of a leading insurer by categories.

The principle that exposure is related to areas of specialty extends to lawyers' professional liability as well. A law office that specializes in corporate practice involving many complex cases at one time has much more exposure to loss than a firm dealing in small probate and real estate work exclusively. Once again, the consequences of a mistake must be considered.

This analysis of the clientele of the professional may be extended to insurance agents' errors and omissions, real estate brokers' errors and omissions, and accountants' and auditors' errors and omissions as well. Several large accounting firms have had losses that occurred as a result of the accounting firm's certification of the annual statement of a

Exhibit 6-13

Causes of Malpractice Claims by Allegation—1979-1983*

Allegation	Number of Claims	Percent of Claims	Average Cost
1) Surgery — Postoperative complication	2,456	12.0%	$27,792
2) Improper treatment — Birth related	1,103	5.4	70,997
3) Surgery — Inadvertent act	1,012	4.9	27,460
4) Failure to diagnose — Fracture or dislocation	895	4.4	17,305
5) Failure to diagnose — Cancer	692	3.4	41,883
6) Surgery — Inappropriate procedure	666	3.2	28,263
7) Improper treatment — Fracture or dislocation	661	3.2	19,528
8) Improper treatment — Lack of supervision	570	2.8	20,523
9) Improper treatment — Drug side effect	568	2.8	29,989
10) Failure to diagnose — Pregnancy problems	482	2.3	30,585
11) Improper treatment — Infection	480	2.3	16,669
12) Improper treatment — During examination	470	2.3	16,704
TOTAL	10,055	49.0%	

This data provides an overview of medical malpractice claims against physicians insured by The St. Paul and the average cost of those claims. The top 12 allegations account for almost half of the total claims filed during the five-year period from 1979 through 1983. The figures are useful for physicians and hospitals as a basis for claims prevention programs.

*Reprinted with permission from The St. Paul Insurance Companies.

publicly held company. The auditing process which preceded the certification was held by the courts to be negligent and resulted in losses to stockholders and others. This exposure is certainly greater for a firm auditing large public companies than for one keeping the books for a number of small privately held firms.

Underwriting Umbrella and Excess Liability Policies

Umbrella Policies Umbrella liability insurance, both commercial and personal, is designed to cover large, infrequent losses. It does not provide primary insurance; nor does it cover all losses.

Umbrella policies are not standardized. The contract language and underwriting rules and guidelines vary from one insurer to another. In most cases umbrella policies have three basic characteristics. Umbrellas are:

1. designed to provide excess liability limits above all specified underlying policies,
2. designed to provide coverage when the aggregate limits of the underlying policies have been exhausted; and
3. designed to cover gaps in coverage in the underlying policies.

The umbrella policy requires as a condition of coverage that agreed limits of liability be maintained on the underlying policies. If this is not done, then the umbrella excludes coverage for the difference between the limits maintained and those required.

Underwriting umbrella policies for commercial businesses requires careful analysis of the exposures covered by all the underlying policies. Due to the excess nature of this insurance, loss frequency is not a problem, but loss severity must be carefully evaluated. The limits of liability on umbrella policies are usually quite high, and severe losses can result.

Personal umbrella liability policies are usually purchased by individuals with higher than average income who may present an adverse selection with respect to high liability judgments due to their prominence in the community. Because of the aggregate excess nature of this coverage, it is important that the policy term of the underlying coverage and the umbrella be the same.

Excess Policies The first distinction between specific excess insurance and umbrella coverage is that while the umbrella is written over *all* underlying liability coverage, specific excess is written only to increase the limits of liability on a particular policy. Excess insurance is frequently written on a layered basis, with several policies utilized to provide very high limits.

As in the case with umbrella policies, loss frequency is not a problem with specific excess insurance, but severity is a potential problem. This is usually dealt with by reinsurance for both umbrella and specific excess policies. Specific excess policies are seldom under-written in the sense of traditional risk analysis, but pricing is important. The philosophy is usually that if the primary insurance is acceptable, then the excess is acceptable also. Obviously, the excess insurer is relying upon the underwriting judgment of the primary insurer.

UNDERWRITING FIDELITY AND SURETY BONDS

Fidelity Bonds

There have been many attempts to estimate how much employers lose every year through dishonesty of employees. The overall economic impact of embezzlement is almost incalculable simply because such a large amount of the overall loss is undetermined. However, it is estimated that employee dishonesty is a factor in one-third of all business bankruptcies. The intent of fidelity bonds is to indemnify an employer for loss due to dishonesty of employees; therefore, this type of protection is often referred to as "dishonesty insurance."

A review of fidelity claim files reveals literally hundreds of ways of stealing from an employer. Dishonest employees take advantage of oversights and other faults in the firm's operations, such as neglected trash barrels, employee parking areas that are too close to receiving areas, and exits that are not supervised.

In the office area of the business, pilfering of petty cash, "kiting" in the accounts receivable, overextension in cash returns, falsification of records on accounts payable, and other forms of embezzlement are common. The following claims should illustrate the variety of losses covered by fidelity bonds.[15]

- A bookkeeper falsified payroll records and altered checks, such as raising the amount of a valid check so that it became a draft for $1,161.00 rather than $161.10 (total amount of losses $77,183.84).
- A dispatcher and a truck driver converted merchandise to their own use by falsifying or destroying freight bills to conceal the shipment they had sold to "fences" (amount of loss $18,000).
- A treasurer for a credit union embezzled money over a seven-year period by failing to record share payments received from members, writing checks and charging them to various members' accounts, making unauthorized share withdrawals, and carrying share balances forward on a new ledger card for a lesser amount than shown on the prior card (amount of losses $169,000).

Loss control is the key to underwriting employee dishonesty insurance. Loss control is best achieved by minimizing one or all of three factors: (1) temptation, (2) opportunity, and (3) motive. Financially troubled employees with access to valuable property or money may be tempted to steal, and poor management of valuable property creates the opportunity for such theft. The most difficult element to deal with is motive. Employees may be motivated to steal by events in their personal lives or developments on the job. A frustrated employee who sees a raise or promotion go to another who is considered less deserving may feel that the company "owes me something" and may set about to obtain it. New employees may bring larcenous intentions with them. A few years ago, some New York stock brokerage houses were experiencing so much theft of stock certificates that they suspected infiltration of their operations by organized crime.

The firm most vulnerable to employee dishonesty is one that has recently experienced extremely rapid growth. Often this requires the hiring of many new employees who may not be properly screened. Another type of firm that may experience employee dishonesty problems is a conglomerate that has made many recent acquisitions. If it unknowingly acquires a firm previously owned by an unscrupulous individual, tight internal controls are necessary. Often the former owner of an acquired firm is retained under a management contract for a year or more. If this individual wishes to steal or embezzle, a conspiracy may be organized involving employees with loyalty to the individual rather than the conglomerate.

New employee screening has been made more difficult by new governmental regulations restricting the questions that can be asked of job applicants. This means that the necessary underwriting information will have to be revised to reflect what information is available.

The accounting and finance departments of the firm whose employees are bonded must play a major role in the loss control program. There is no substitute for well-designed internal control systems. Any abnormality, whether it is an inventory shortage, increase in cash sales, increase in petty cash disbursements, or other change, should be carefully investigated. Company checks and check writers should be tightly controlled.

A particularly troublesome area to control is computer crime, which can range from unauthorized access to the computer to schemes to divert large amounts of cash and property. A brilliant but unethical teenager developed a scheme that enabled him to telephone into the computer that controlled supplies for a large utility. He misappropriated hundreds of thousands of dollars of goods before being discovered. Computer programmers with control over inventory or cash functions are in a sensitive position. Careful supervision is necessary. One control technique is to shift individuals around from job to job so that one individual does not have the sole access to any sensitive program over a long period of time.

Employers should institute procedures that will permit detection of dishonest acts as soon as possible. For example, a credit manager should not be permitted to receive money and at the same time be in charge of posting and deposits. These functions should be performed by different employees.

Shipping and receiving should be two completely separate operations if possible, with two individuals having to submit individual returns to the accounting office. Collection receipts and bank deposits should be verified as to their individual entries by someone other than the person preparing the statement.

Spot checks, audits, and inventories should be made frequently and on a surprise basis. There should also be periodic revisions of auditing and security measures to avoid a pattern that can be easily detected.[16]

Surety Bonds

Underwriting surety bonds is somewhat different from underwriting property and liability insurance. This is due in part to the well-established fact that surety bonds are not insurance policies. Suretyship is a technique used to provide assurance to one party, called the obligee, that another party, called the principal, will fulfill an obligation he or she has undertaken to perform. Surety bonds may guarantee (1) honesty or faithful performance, (2) financial strength, or (3) ability or capacity to perform.

Unique Features of Bonds Unlike insurance, bond underwriters do not anticipate any serious losses. The principal is primarily responsible to fulfill the contractual obligation—not the surety. Since insurance contracts are between two parties, either may cancel unilaterally. But surety bonds are written for the benefit of a third party to the bond and may be terminated only with the consent of the obligee. Thus, the initial surety underwriting decision must reflect this situation. Surety bonds are often written for an indefinite period, and there is little rate flexibility in some types of bonds. If the surety pays a loss, the principal is usually legally liable to reimburse the surety for the loss, but underwriters must be concerned with the ability of the principal to meet this financial obligation.

Underwriting Contract Bonds The knowledge of financial analysis is of paramount importance in the underwriting of contract bonds. Audited statements for at least the last two years provide a starting point; and if the latest statements are more than six months old, an interim statement may be requested. In addition, the following underwriting factors should be carefully evaluated:

1. Business Experience of the Contractor. This should include the experience of the owners before their association with the firm as well as the business experience of the firm itself.
2. Performance Record. The size and growth pattern of individual jobs must be checked. A contractor that is growing too rapidly or is bidding on a job that is much larger than his customary work must be carefully scrutinized.
3. Plant and Equipment. The need for a plant may be nonexistent for a road contractor, but an extensive sheet metal shop is essential for an air conditioning contractor. The age and condition of equipment may be determined by a physical inspection.
4. Financial Resources Not Included in Financial Statements. The status of work in process (or work on hand) is not truly reflected in the financial statements. The profit (or lack of it) from these incompleted projects is not shown and requires further investigation. The terms and conditions of the line of credit available from banks should also be investigated.

One study revealed a statistical analysis of common underwriting measures utilized by surety underwriters. The study found that analysis of six variables was 88 percent accurate in predicting whether a particular construction company would fall into the claim category. These six variables are (1) Dun & Bradstreet rating, (2) sales growth ratio, (3) rate of return on net worth, (4) trade payment rating, (5) experience of the construction firm, and (6) bank credit line/net worth ratio.[17] The results of this study indicate that careful attention should be paid to these six variables when underwriting contract bonds.

PACKAGE AND ACCOUNT UNDERWRITING

In both personal and commercial lines, package policies and account selling are increasingly common. From the standpoint of the insured, the package policy offers an opportunity for discounts, reduces the number of policies, reduces the likelihood of gaps and overlaps in coverage, and often simplifies the insurance program. From the standpoint of the producer, package policies and account selling (where not all coverages can be packaged) increase the commission income per account, provide a means of combining all the insurance coverage for a particular insured, and provide techniques to ensure common renewal dates to reduce expenses. From an underwriting standpoint, package policies and account selling reduce expenses by cutting policy writing and renewal costs and making it possible to combine property and liability inspections in a single visit. However, there are underwriting problems that accompany the package and account selling approach.

Interaction of Multi-Line Hazards

When all the insurance for an account is carried in a single insurance company, a single loss may affect many lines of coverage. An explosion at an insured's plant may cause property damage, a business interruption loss, damage to third parties under the comprehensive general liability policy, and a workers' compensation loss. This accumulation of coverage reduces spread of risk to a certain extent. This disadvantage may well be offset by competitive advantages and expense savings, but its existence should be recognized. To a certain extent, this accumulation of coverage can be offset by reinsurance.

The most difficult underwriting problems for both package policies and account selling occur when an applicant presents above-average and desirable exposures for most lines but has a substandard exposure for a single line or a part of a line. A firm that is extremely desirable from the standpoint of fire, transportation, workers' compensation, commercial automobile, and premises and operations liability exposures may present a substandard products liability exposure. When this firm is presented to the underwriter on a package basis, the substandard coverage is often written to "get the business." Even worse is the submission where there are three above-average lines and three marginal lines of business presented as a package.

It is also important that a package policy where much of the coverage is in a single line not be underwritten on the basis of that line alone and the other coverage ignored. An example of this is the homeowners policy. This is largely a property policy, but there are important liability exposures in every policy written, and often there are inland marine exposures as well. These other exposures should be underwritten with as much care as the property portion of the submission.

Pyramiding Limits of Liability

Whether written as a package or written on a single-line basis within the same company, package policies and account selling have the effect of pyramiding limits of liability. A simple case is the homeowners policy. A dwelling insured for $75,000 is often considered by the producer and underwriter alike as a "$75,000 homeowners." When considering the extent to which reinsurance treaties may be exposed, or making decisions considering the maximum exposure at one location, it is misleading to consider this as a $75,000 homeowners exposure. Since total loss for a dwelling is not an improbable event, the maximum possible loss for this policy is not $75,000 but $127,500 which consists of $75,000 on the dwelling, $37,500 on the contents, and $15,000 additional living expense. If one has a $127,500 loss after assuming the maximum loss to be $75,000, there will be many explanations needed.

For large commercial and municipal risks, this pyramiding of limits of liability can produce severe capacity problems. The County of Los Angeles, which has over $1.6 billion in property, has no single building valued at over $40 million. When analyzing the potential loss for a single earthquake at a location, the exposure increases rapidly if the workers' compensation and general liability exposures are included. In the event of the total collapse of a $40 million building, losses from workers' compensation and general liability could reach $100 million.[18] It should be noted that in the 1947 Texas City explosion, which virtually destroyed a large chemical plant in addition to two ships, some docks, and much of the rest of the city, workers' compensation losses were *greater* than the property damage. There were 468 dead, 100 missing, 3,500 seriously injured, and close to $100 million property damage.[19]

Pyramiding of limits can occur when property insurance, inland marine, automobile liability, general liability, and workers' compensation coverages are simultaneously involved in a catastrophe at a particular location:

- Direct damage to building
- Direct damage to contents
- Business interruption
- Additional expense
- Bailee's coverage on customers' goods
- Transportation coverage on goods still covered under transit policies
- Bodily injury to customers, employees of others, and passersby
- Property damage to adjacent locations
- Injury and death of employees
- Physical damage to fleet vehicles

Where a package policy or account selling results in large pyramiding of limits on a single location, careful analysis of the available reinsurance should be made.

Other Underwriting Considerations[20]

Underwriting decision making is simple on a submission with no adverse exposures. Likewise, the decision is clear if the submission has no redeeming values. The decision becomes difficult when part of the package is acceptable but the balance is not. Perhaps the property loss exposures of a small manufacturer are minimal due to loss control devices but the products liability exposure may be great due to the nature of the product. Or, the premises and operations liability exposures of a dry cleaner may be excellent as demonstrated in its loss-free history, but the property exposure may be questionable due to the use of a solvent with a low flash point.

In these cases, the underwriter must weigh the strengths against the weaknesses, identify any appropriate alternatives and choose the best one. To do this, an underwriter may ask questions such as:

1. What are the respective *limits of liability* of each of the sections of the package policy?
2. What are the respective *premiums* for each policy section? (This question is inappropriate if the package policy has an indivisible premium, thus complicating the underwriter's decision.)
3. What are the respective *frequencies* of loss for each major policy section?
4. What are the respective *severities* of loss for each major policy section?

Interrelating and sometimes conflicting exposures are those in which a low hazard for one line of coverage increases the hazard of another coverage. This may be compounded by the fact that an underwriter may wish to offer suggestions to further lower the exposure in the first category which will increase the exposure in the second line of coverage. An example of this problem is a large building with only one entrance. This arrangement will reduce the hazards of burglary and theft since only one door opening must be monitored and secured. The lack of alternate openings, however, increases the fire hazard since it limits the access to the building. It also increases the hazard of third-party liability in preventing good egress from the building for personnel if a fire or other emergency were to occur.

The underwriter must therefore approach hazard control across all lines of coverage as well as consider the public. How does the underwriter decide in which direction to go? First, loss severity and frequency must be considered and, second, the desirability and cost of providing additional protection for one line of coverage to compensate for the reduction in hazard in another must be considered. Can the underwriter sell additional doors and windows in the blank walls of a building to allow fire department access and emergency egress with the burglary protection needed for these new openings in an occupancy vulnerable to a crime exposure? And if he or she can, is the increased access worth the additional cost to the insured, the resulting increased crime hazard, and the chance of losing the account to a competitor? The interrelation of hazards must be evaluated on an overall basis.

In addition, the underwriter must determine if the premium for the low hazard exposures compensates for the inadequate premiums of the higher hazard exposures. Most rating plans contain minimum rates and/or minimum premiums by coverage for low hazard risks. They have been developed to cover the expenses of underwriting and issuing a policy which may account for the majority of the cost in some instances. When a number of coverages are combined into a single package, the minimum rates, being primarily for expense purposes, may provide more than adequate premium when added to other line premiums.

In indivisible premium policies, the underwriter must use imagination to identify unusual exposures for which an indivisible "class rate" does not develop sufficiently. For example, one such package provided "all-risks" coverage on liquor stores at a premium less than that for mercantile open stock alone.

Package underwriting also provides the opportunity to investigate the management abilities and techniques as they relate to the total loss control of the account. Management will influence all areas of loss potential to assure the continuing profitability of the operation and the development of programs for the recognition and control of loss exposures. The package policy analysis, because it has more expense dollars available from the larger premium enables the underwriter to look more closely at many aspects of management including their ability to make a profit. A profitable operation will have both the resources to invest in loss control as well as the desire to do so to remain in operation and continue to make money.

Chapter Notes

1. *FC&S Bulletins* (Cincinnati: The National Underwriter Co.), Auto (Casualty) Fri-2, Fri-3.
2. Robert E. Keeton and Jeffrey O'Connell, *Basic Protection for the Traffic Victim* (Boston: Little, Brown and Co., 1965).
3. G. William Glendenning and Robert B. Holtom, *Personal Lines Underwriting* (Malvern, PA: Insurance Institute of America, 2nd ed., 1982), p. 151.
4. This section is based on Chapters 2 and 3 of *Personal Lines Underwriting* by Glendenning and Holtom, 2nd ed. (Malvern, PA: Insurance Institute of America).
5. *Insurance Facts*, 1983-4 ed. (New York: Insurance Information Institute), p. 76.
6. Larry D. Gaunt, Numan A. Williams, and Everett D. Randall, *Commercial Liability Underwriting* (Malvern, PA: Insurance Institute of America, 2nd ed., 1982), pp. 153-155.
7. John V. Grimaldi and Rollin H. Simonds, *Safety Management*, 3rd ed. (Homewood, IL: Richard D. Irwin, 1975), p. 559.
8. Gaunt, Williams, and Randall, p. 389.
9. Dan Petersen, *Techniques of Safety Management*, (New York: McGraw-Hill Book Co., 1971), pp. 19-22.
10. Ray v. Alad Corp., 136 Cal. Rptr. 574, 560 P 2d 3 (1977).
11. Gaunt, Williams, and Randall, pp. 295-296.
12. A. E. Thompson, "Underwriting Products Liability," *The Journal of Commerce* (19 February 1969).
13. Gaunt, Williams, and Randall, pp. 157-158.
14. Gaunt, Williams, and Randall, p. 443.
15. "The Forty Thieves" (Baltimore: USF&G Co., 1970), pp. 11, 12, 19.
16. "The Forty Thieves," p. 6.
17. Richard W. Filippone, "A Statistical Analysis of Some Common Underwriting Measures Used by Contract Surety Underwriters," *Best's Review*, Property/Casualty Insurance Edition (December 1976), p. 22.
18. *Minutes*, Los Angeles County Risk Management Advisory Committee, 6 April 1977.
19. Robert I. Mehr and Bob A. Hedges, *Risk Management in the Business Enterprise* (Homewood, IL: Richard D. Irwin, 1963), pp. 191-192.
20. E. P. Hollingsworth, Jr. and J. J. Launie, *Commercial Property and Multiple-Lines Underwriting* (Malvern, PA: Insurance Institute of America), pp. 515-516.

CHAPTER 7

Reinsurance

INTRODUCTION

An insurance company, like any other business firm, insures those loss exposures which are too great to retain. This is true of all of the insurer's loss exposures, whether they be the exposures inherent in its own business operations, such as fire damage to the home office building, or loss exposures of others assumed under insurance contracts. This chapter will deal with the insurance of the latter class of loss exposures, those assumed under insurance contracts. The practice is known as *reinsurance*, or sometimes *reassurance*. (This latter term is more commonly identified with life insurance.)

Reinsurance may be defined as a contractual arrangement under which one insurer, known as the ceding company, transfers to another insurer, called the reinsurer, some or all of the losses incurred by the ceding company under insurance contracts it has issued or will issue in the future. The ceding company is sometimes referred to by other terms, such as the primary insurer, cedent, direct writer, direct insurer, the reinsured, and so forth. In the interest of clarity and consistency, the terms *ceding company* and *primary insurer*, depending on context, will be used here to denote an insurer that provides insurance to the general public rather than to other insurers. However, it should be recognized that not all insurers and not all purchasers of reinsurance are companies.

Reinsurers also may reinsure some of the loss exposures they assume under reinsurance contracts. Such transactions are known as *retrocessions*, and the insurer or reinsurer to which the exposure is transferred is known as a *retrocessionaire* and the ceding reinsurer is called the *retrocedent*. However, retrocession agreements do not differ greatly in detail from reinsurance agreements, and they will not be discussed in detail here.

In most cases, the reinsurer does not assume all of the liability of the ceding company. The reinsurance agreement usually requires the ceding company to hold a part of its liability. That part is known as its *retention* and may be expressed as a dollar amount, a percentage of the original amount of insurance, or a combination of the two. Also, there usually is an upper limit on the reinsurer's liability.

PURPOSE AND FUNCTION OF REINSURANCE

At first, it may seem odd that an insurance company would go to the trouble and expense of selling a policy and then pay a reinsurer to relieve it of some or all of the exposure assumed. There are several logical reasons why an insurer may find itself in that position. The functions of reinsurance will be discussed in some detail, along with the benefits of reinsurance to the ceding company.

The functions or puposes of reinsurance are:

1. risk sharing and reciprocity,
2. stabilization of loss experience,
3. increased capacity,
4. surplus relief,
5. catastrophe protection,
6. underwriting assistance, and
7. retirement from a territory or class of business.

Risk Sharing and Reciprocity

As noted in the chapters on rate making, the mathematical basis for insurance is the law of large numbers. Simply stated, that law says that the accuracy with which losses can be predicted increases as the number of exposure units increases, assuming that all else remains constant. This is especially true if the loss exposures are homogeneous, or nearly homogeneous, in size and kind.

Reinsurance helps the functioning of the law of large numbers in two ways. First, by reinsuring a part of large loss exposures, the ceding company increases the size homogeneity of the loss exposures it retains for its own account. Consequently, its loss experience cannot be distorted unduly by one or a few large losses. To illustrate this concept with an extreme example, assume that the Matchless Fire Insurance Company (MFIC) insures 10,000 dwellings and small mercantile structures, each valued at from $25,000 to $100,000. In addition, MFIC insures one automobile manufacturing plant for $50 million. It is apparent that a total loss at the automobile plant would be painful, if not fatal, to MFIC. However, the financial strain could be avoided or reduced by reinsuring most of the automobile plant exposure. The exact amount to be retained by MFIC would depend on its financial strength, premium volume, and other considerations. Of course, few insurers would permit themselves to be placed in the extreme position of the foregoing example, but very few insurers are able to achieve satisfactory size homogeneity without the benefit of reinsurance.

Another way to achieve size homogeneity would be to restrict the amount to be insured on any one exposure (a loss limit). For example, MFIC could tell the automobile manufacturer that it would provide only $100,000 of coverage on the factory; but if all insurers took that position, the manufacturer would be required to buy 500 separate policies to fully insure the factory. If other insurers were willing to write the entire amount, MFIC would probably not succeed in writing any of it.

There are also other valid reasons an insurer may find it desirable to write more coverage than it can safely retain for its own account. A workers' compensation insurer must accept all or none of the coverage for a particular work place. There is no legal provision for an insurer to limit its coverage to some maximum amount. The same is true of those automobile no-fault insurance laws which provide unlimited medical benefits. Also, an insurer that cannot write reasonably large lines may find it difficult to obtain and keep good producers.

The second way in which reinsurance can help to reinforce the law of large numbers is by enabling an insurer to increase the number and geographic spread of its insured loss exposures. For example, an insurer that writes homeowners coverage only in New England might decide to reinsure a part of the homeowners business of an insurer which operates only in the Southwest, or each of the insurers could reinsure a part of the business of the other. By the latter method, known as *reciprocal reinsurance* or *reciprocity*, both insurers could increase the number and geographic spread and decrease the effective size of the insured exposures. Thus, they would reinforce the law of large numbers in three ways: (1) by writing a larger number of exposures, (2) by improving geographic spread, and (3) by reducing the effective size of the exposures insured. Although reciprocity is still common in Europe, it is rarely practiced in the United States.

Stabilization of Loss Experience

An insurance company, like any other business firm, must have a reasonably steady flow of profits in order to attract and retain capital and, in fact, increase its capital and surplus to support growth. However, insurance losses sometimes fluctuate widely because of demographic, economic, social, and natural forces, as well as simple chance. Smoothing the peaks and valleys of the loss experience curve is a major function of reinsurance. This function of reinsurance is closely related to risk sharing and reciprocity and to some other functions that will follow. As noted above, reciprocity tends to stabilize an insurer's loss experience. However, reinsurance agreements may stabilize loss experience more directly also.

Reinsurance is sometimes compared to a banking operation. The ceding company borrows money from the reinsurer in the years when the ceding company's loss experience is unfavorable and pays back the loan in the years when its loss experience is good. In fact, one form of reinsurance agreement works almost exactly in this manner. It is known as a *spread-loss treaty*, or sometimes as a Carpenter treaty after its supposed inventor. Under a spread-loss treaty, the reinsurance premium is calculated as a moving average of the losses under the treaty for a specified number of years, frequently five, plus an expense loading, but subject to a minimum and a maximum. Under such an arrangement, an insurer would, in fact, pay back all claims collected from the reinsurer provided the agreement remains in force for a sufficiently long period of time and provided the maximum premium is high enough. In the meantime, however, the reinsurance agreement will have served its purpose of leveling the loss experience of the ceding company. Even aside from the spread-loss treaty, it is well established in reinsurance that the ceding company should pay its own way over the long run. A ceding company cannot expect to make a profit at the expense of its reinsurer over any prolonged period.

The function of catastrophe protection, which is discussed later, is also closely related to stabilization of loss experience, since catastrophes are an important factor in loss fluctuations.

Increased Capacity

There are two kinds of capacity in property and liability insurance: large line capacity and premium capacity. *Large line capacity* refers to an insurer's ability to provide a large amount of insurance on a single loss exposure. For example, an insurer may be called upon to write $40 million of coverage on a large factory, or the physical damage (hull) coverage on one airplane may amount to $30 million or more. The liability coverage on a large passenger airplane may exceed $100 million. Few American insurers could write such a large amount of insurance on a single loss exposure without reinsurance because of regulations which prohibit an insurer from writing net for its own account an amount of insurance in excess of 10 percent of its surplus to policyholders on any one loss exposure. However, an insurer may write a large line by keeping its retention within a reasonable relationship to its capital and surplus and reinsuring the balance.

The second kind of capacity, *premium capacity*, simply refers to the aggregate premium volume an insurer can write. That concept and its relationship to reinsurance are discussed in the section that follows.

Surplus Relief

There is a limit to the amount of premiums an insurer can write. The limit for a given insurer is a function of its surplus to policyholders. The exact theoretical relationship between premium volume and surplus to policyholders is open to debate. However, as a practical matter, an insurer is likely to be considered overextended if its net written premiums, after deduction of reinsurance premiums, exceed its surplus to policyholders by a ratio of more than 3 to 1. That is, a ratio *below* 3 to 1 would be favorable.

However, a growing insurer may find it difficult to maintain an acceptable ratio because the premium-to-surplus ratio of a rapidly growing insurer is somewhat like a candle burning at both ends. As the premium volume grows, it causes the surplus to shrink. The shrinkage results from the prepaid expense portion of the unearned premium reserve, such as agents' commission and policy issuance, being charged against surplus.

In American insurance accounting, an insurer must establish an initial unearned premium reserve equal to the total premium for the policy. However, it must pay out most of its expenses at the inception of the policy also. Therefore, it must take money from surplus to pay these initial expenses. A somewhat simplified example will illustrate the problem.

Assume that Quaking Casualty Company opened for business on December 31, 19X1. On that date, it had $2 million of paid-in capital and surplus but no premiums. On January 1, 19X2, it wrote and collected $5 million of premiums on one-year policies. Its initial expenses for the policies were $1.5 million for producer commissions, premium taxes, underwriting expenses, policy writing, billing and collection, and so forth. However, Quaking Casualty also had to establish an unearned premium reserve, a liability, equal to the total amount of premium, $5 million. Consequently, the money for the expenses must be taken from surplus, leaving surplus to policyholders of only $500,000. Exhibit 7-1 shows Quaking Casualty's balance sheet as it appeared on December 31, 19X1, before writing the premiums, and on January 1, 19X2, after

Exhibit 7-1
Balance Sheets for Quaking Casualty Company—December 31, 19X1 and January 1, 19X2

	12/31/X1	1/1/X2
Assets		
Cash	$ 500,000	$4,000,000 [†]
Investments	1,500,000	1,500,000
Total Assets	$2,000,000	$5,500,000
Liabilities		
Unearned Premium		
Reserve	$ 0	$5,000,000
Total Liabilities	$ 0	$5,000,000
Surplus to Policyholders		
Capital	$ 500,000	$ 500,000
Surplus	1,500,000	0
Total Surplus to		
Policyholders	$2,000,000	$ 500,000
Total Liabilities and		
Surplus to Policyholders	$2,000,000	$5,500,000

[†] The cash for 1/1/X2 was calculated by adding the premiums collected ($5,000,000) to the cash for 12/31/X1 ($500,000) and subtracting the expenses paid ($1,500,000).

writing the premiums and paying the initial expense resulting from them.

As can be seen from Exhibit 7-1, the shrinkage of the surplus to policyholders caused the ratio which originally seemed to be 2.5 to 1 ($5 million of premiums to $2 million of net worth) to become a ratio of 10 to 1 ($5 million of premiums to $500,000 of net worth). This is an extreme example, of course, but it does illustrate the problems that can be encountered by a rapidly growing insurer.

Some forms of reinsurance can relieve the unearned premium problem in three ways. First, the premiums-to-surplus ratio is calculated on the basis of net premiums, after deduction of premiums for reinsurance ceded. Second, the unearned premium reserve also is calculated on the basis of net premiums. Finally, in some forms of reinsurance the reinsurer pays a ceding commission to the ceding company to cover the ceding company's expenses in selling and issuing the business. Thus, while the ceding company takes credit for the full reinsurance premium in calculating its unearned premium reserve, it

Exhibit 7-2

Balance Sheet for Quaking Casualty Company, January 1, 19X2—Net After Ceding 50 Percent of Premiums and Receiving 30 Percent Ceding Commission

Assets	
Cash	$2,250,000
Investments	1,500,000
Total Assets	$3,750,000
Liabilities	
Unearned Premium Reserve [†]	$2,500,000
Total Liabilities	$2,500,000
Surplus to Policyholders	
Capital	$ 500,000
Surplus	750,000
Total Surplus to Policyholders	$1,250,000
Total Liabilities and Surplus to Policyholders	$3,750,000

†50% of written premiums

actually pays out only the net amount after deducting the ceding commission.

Exhibit 7-2 shows the balance sheet of Quaking Casualty Company on January 1, 19X2, as it would have appeared if Quaking had ceded half of its premiums to a reinsurer and had received a 30 percent ceding commission on the reinsurance premium.

Note that Quaking Casualty's premiums-to-surplus ratio has fallen from 10 to 1 in Exhibit 7-1 to 2 to 1 in Exhibit 7-2, solely through the use of reinsurance. First, the written premiums dropped from $5 million to $2.5 million because of the reinsurance cession. Second, the surplus to policyholders increased from $500,000 to $1.25 million because of the reduction in the unearned premium reserve reflected by the ceding commission. That is, the $1.25 million is the result of the recapture of $750,000 of prepaid expense via 30 percent commission on the $2.5 million of written premiums ceded.

Exhibits 7-1 and 7-2 illustrate the financing function of reinsurance—the reduction of surplus drain resulting from the method of calculating the unearned premium reserve. This function is so important to poorly financed insurers that a special kind of reinsurance, sometimes called surplus-aid reinsurance, was offered in the past to insurers with inadequate surplus. A surplus-aid reinsurance agreement appeared on superficial examination to be a typical reinsurance contract, but it usually contained an agreement requiring the ceding company to reimburse the reinsurer for any claims paid under the reinsurance contract. The ceding company would take credit for the reinsurance in setting its unearned premium reserve, even though no reinsurance protection was actually provided. A similar device involved purchasing a normal treaty near the end of the year and canceling it early in the following year, so it would be in force on December 31 for annual statement purposes. Fortunately, these devices for thwarting solvency regulation have largely disappeared. Reputable reinsurers do not engage in such questionable practices, and reputable insurers no longer initiate requests for such schemes. [1]

A different form of reinsurance that provides surplus relief has received considerable attention recently, although it has been used on a limited scale for many years. It is sometimes called *loss portfolio reinsurance*. Loss portfolio reinsurance involves the reinsurance of past losses rather than the future losses reinsured under the other contracts discussed herein.

The effectiveness of this form of reinsurance in providing surplus relief stems from statutory insurance accounting rules used in this country. Insurers operating in the U.S. are required to establish a liability, called claims or loss reserves, equal to the amount they expect to eventually pay out on claims that have occurred but have not been paid. Although there may be a delay of many years between the occurrence of the loss and the payment, insurers are not permitted to "discount" the claim or loss reserves to reflect the interest earned during the delay period. Discounting loss reserves would result in showing a reserve less than the amount that will eventually be paid. The difference between the initial reserve and the eventual payment would be made up by the investment income or the assets counterpart to the reserve during the period from the date of the accident until the date of payment. Reinsurance of loss reserves has been used by some insurers to gain substantially the same effect as discounting loss reserves.

Perhaps an example will help to clarify this rather elusive concept. Exhibit 7-3 shows the balance sheet of Quaking Casualty Company on December 30, 19X1, one day before its annual statement date for 19X1. At this point in time, Quaking Casualty had only $1 million in policyholders' surplus to support its premium volume of $6 million.

Quaking negotiates an agreement with Matchless Fire Insurance Company under which Matchless reinsures $4 million of Quaking's outstanding losses. Matchless estimates that there will be an average delay of seven years in the payment of the claims ceded to it by Quaking. After reflecting the investment income it expects to earn during that period, Matchless is willing to assume the $4 million in claims for a reinsurance premium of $1.6 million. Exhibit 7-4 shows Quaking's balance sheet on December 31, 19X1, one day after the

Exhibit 7-3
Balance Sheet for Quaking Casualty Company, December 30, 19X1

		Handwritten margin notes
Assets		
Cash	$ 2,000,000	400,000
Investments	12,000,000	
Total Assets	$14,000,000	12,900,000
Liabilities		
Unearned premium reserve	$ 3,000,000	3,000,000
Loss and loss expense reserves	10,000,000	6,000,000
Total Liabilities	$13,000,000	9,000,000
Surplus to policyholders		
Capital	$ 500,000	400,000
Surplus	500,000	3,000,000
Total Surplus to Policyholders	$ 1,000,000	3,400,000
Total Liabilities and Surplus to Policyholders	$14,000,000	12,400,000,

balance sheet in Exhibit 7-3 and after entering into the reinsurance agreement. Quaking Casualty's surplus to policyholders has increased from $1.0 million to $3.4 million solely because of the reinsurance agreement. Since its net written premiums were $6 million in both cases, its ratio of premiums to policyholders' surplus has fallen from an unacceptable 6-to-1 to a very acceptable 1.76 to 1.

In a few instances, contracts reinsuring loss reserves have included provisions requiring the ceding company to reimburse the reinsurer if the total amount required to settle the reinsured claims exceeds the reserves in effect at the inception of the reinsurance contract. The inclusion of such a provision leaves substantial doubt that the parties intended to enter into a valid reinsurance agreement, and places such contracts in a category with the surplus relief contracts mentioned above, which are entered into primarily to make the ceding company's surplus or profit look better than it actually is.

Reinsurance of loss reserves may have an adverse effect on the ceding company's income tax liability. The reduction in loss reserves, to the extent that it exceeds the reinsurance premium, results in an increase in the ceding company's underwriting profit (or a reduction in its underwriting loss), with a resulting increase in its income tax liability. In one instance, two large insurers entered into a contract for the reciprocal reinsurance of loss reserves. As a result, one of the insurers increased its reported profit by $66 million and the other by

Exhibit 7-4
Balance Sheet for Quaking Casualty Company, December 31, 19X1

Assets	
Cash	$ 400,000[†]
Investments	12,000,000
Total Assets	12,400,000
Liabilities	
Unearned premium reserve	$ 3,000,000
Loss and loss expense reserves	6,000,000
Total Liabilities	$ 9,000,000
Surplus to policyholders	
Capital	$ 500,000
Surplus	2,900,000
Total Surplus to Policyholders	$ 3,400,000
Total Liabilities and Surplus to Policyholders	$12,400,000

[†]$1.6 million of cash was used to pay the reinsurance premium.

$76 million.[2] Other insurers are believed to have entered into such contracts.[3]

Catastrophe Protection

Property and liability insurers are subject to major catastrophe losses from earthquakes, hurricanes, tornadoes, industrial explosions, plane crashes, and similar disasters. These events may result in large property and liability claims to a single insurer. Total industry losses have reached as high as $750 million in one hurricane, and losses in excess of $100 million are not uncommon.

Special forms of reinsurance, to be discussed in a later section of this chapter, have been developed to protect against the adverse effects of such catastrophes. This purpose of reinsurance is, of course, closely related to the purpose of stabilizing loss experience, since catastrophes are major causes of instability of losses.

Underwriting Assistance

Reinsurers deal with a wide variety of insurers in many different circumstances. Consequently, they accumulate a great deal of information regarding the experience of various insurers with particular coverages and the methods of rating, underwriting, and handling various coverages. This experience can be quite helpful to ceding insurers, particularly relatively small insurers or even larger insurers planning to enter a new line. For example, one medium-sized insurer reinsured 95 percent of its umbrella liability coverage over a period of years and relied heavily upon the expertise of the reinsurer in rating and underwriting the policies.

This service of reinsurers probably has been more important in life reinsurance than in the property and liability field. However, it can be quite important in property and liability insurance as well. Of course, reinsurers must be careful in offering advisory service to be sure that they do not reveal or use proprietary information obtained through confidential relationships with other ceding companies.

Retirement from a Territory or Class of Business

Occasionally, an insurer will decide to withdraw from a territory or a class of business, or perhaps to go out of business entirely. There are two ways to achieve that end. The insurer could merely cancel the unwanted policies and refund the unearned premiums to its insureds. However, that process is unwieldy, expensive, and likely to create ill will among insureds, producers, and regulatory authorities. An alternative method is to reinsure the unwanted business with another insurer. This method not only avoids the ill will resulting from cancellation, but it is quite possible that the cost of reinsurance may be less than the cost of processing and paying return premiums on canceled policies.

The process of insuring an entire class, territory, or book of business is known as *portfolio reinsurance*. It is an exception to the statement above that reinsurers usually do not assume all of the liability of the ceding company. In the absence of fraud, the portfolio reinsurer does not normally have any recourse against the ceding company if the loss experience on the business does not turn out as expected.

THE INSURED AND REINSURANCE

Reinsurance is a contractual relationship between two insurers. The persons or firms insured by the ceding company are not parties to the contract and usually have no rights under the reinsurance contract. For example, assume that the Wittle Widget Company insures its factory for $1 million with the Matchless Fire Insurance Company, and that Matchless reinsures 90 percent of the exposure with Solid

Reinsurance Company. The factory is destroyed by fire, but Matchless is insolvent and unable to pay. Wittle Widget cannot collect directly from Solid Re. Solid Re pays its share of the loss to the receiver of Matchless, and it is distributed proportionately to all creditors of Matchless. Wittle Widget gets only its proportionate share as one creditor of Matchless.

There is one exception to the general rule that the insured has no direct right of action against a reinsurer. Occasionally, a reinsurer will authorize a ceding company to attach to its policies an endorsement, executed by the reinsurer, called an *assumption certificate*, or sometimes a *cut-through clause or endorsement*. The assumption certificate provides that in the event of the insolvency of the ceding company the obligation under the policy becomes a direct obligation of the reinsurer. The assumption certificate usually is attached to fire insurance or homeowners contracts because a mortgagee has refused to accept the ceding company's policies without it. On less frequent occasions, it is attached at the request of the risk manager of a commercial or industrial firm.

There are some other minor exceptions to the rule that the ceding company's insured does not have a right of direct action against the reinsurer. For example, Section 315(1)(a) of the New York Insurance Law does not permit the ceding company to take credit for surety and fidelity reinsurance unless the reinsurance agreement permits direct suit by the obligee against the reinsurer. New York courts have held that this law section creates a direct right of action by the obligee.[4] On the other hand, a recent case decided in Puerto Rico casts some doubt on the value of an assumption certificate, at least in that Commonwealth. The Supreme Court of Puerto Rico has held that assumption certificates (or cut-through endorsements) are contrary to public policy, and that the reinsurance proceeds should be paid to the liquidator of the insolvent insurer in spite of the existence of the assumption certificate.[5] This ruling is contrary to several other decisions that have upheld and enforced such contracts.[6]

The fact that the policyholders of the ceding company do not have the right of direct action against the reinsurer does not mean that they receive no benefit from the reinsurance. They may, in fact, receive several benefits. The availability of reinsurance may make it possible for them to obtain all of their insurance from one insurer instead of buying it in bits and pieces from several insurers. This simplifies the problems of buying insurance, loss adjustment, and other phases of their insurance programs. Also, the availability of reinsurance helps to maintain the solvency of insurers, with obvious advantages to policyholders. Finally, reinsurance makes it possible for small insurers to compete effectively against larger ones, thus increasing the options available to buyers of insurance. Of course, reinsurers may, in some cases, lessen price and coverage competition, since their rating and underwriting practices influence the rates and policy forms used by their ceding companies.

TYPES OF REINSURANCE

Several different kinds of reinsurance have developed over the years to serve the various functions listed in the first section of this chapter. No single kind of reinsurance serves all of the purposes effectively.

The paragraphs that follow discuss several forms of reinsurance as though they are standardized contracts. While that method of presentation is necessary for clarity, it should be noted that each reinsurance contract is tailored to the specific needs of the specific ceding company and the reinsurer. Consequently, a given treaty may include combinations of the reinsurance forms discussed here, or it may bear only a superficial resemblance to any of these forms.

Reinsurance contracts may be categorized in several ways. The first major categorization is between *facultative* and *treaty* reinsurance. In facultative reinsurance, the ceding company negotiates a separate reinsurance agreement for each policy it wishes to reinsure. The ceding company is not under any obligation to purchase reinsurance on anything it does not wish to reinsure, and the reinsurer is not obligated to accept any business it does not want.

In treaty reinsurance, on the other hand, the ceding company agrees in advance to cede certain classes of business to the reinsurer in accordance with the terms and conditions of the treaty, and the reinsurer agrees to accept the business to be ceded. While the ceding company may have some discretion in ceding individual policies, it is expected that substantially all of the policies which come within the terms of the contract will be ceded to the reinsurer as provided in the treaty.

It should be noted that, having made this seemingly clear-cut distinction between facultative and treaty reinsurance, one may sometimes encounter documents called *facultative treaties*.

One authoritative source defines a facultative treaty as:

> A reinsurance contract under which the ceding company has the option to cede and the reinsurer has the option to accept or decline individual risks. The contract merely reflects how individual facultative reinsurances shall be handled.[7]

On rare occasions, one may encounter an *obligatory facultative*, *automatic facultative*, or other treaty with mixed nomenclature. These may provide that the ceding company has the option of ceding specified classes of business and the reinsurer is obligated to accept any exposure the ceding company elects to cede. Because of the obvious opportunities for adverse selection, reinsurers are quite careful in selecting the insurers for which they write obligatory facultative treaties.

Information regarding the relative importance of facultative and treaty reinsurance within the portfolios of reinsurers is somewhat limited. Some reinsurers specialize in facultative covers, while others prefer treaty business. A survey of 125 reinsurers conducted by the Reinsurance Association of America (RAA), found that 63, or approximately half, wrote some facultative covers. For all of the companies included in the survey, facultative business accounted for 14 percent of premiums, and treaty business accounted for 86 percent. The RAA cautions that "the writings of several reinsurers known to have substantial facultative operations are not included. This will result in an understatement of the proportion of facultative business."[8] The magnitude of the understatement is not known.

Another system for categorizing reinsurance depends upon the manner in which the obligations under contracts are divided between the ceding company and the reinsurer. Under *pro-rata reinsurance*, which is sometimes called proportional reinsurance, the amount of insurance, the premium, and the losses are divided between the ceding company and the reinsurer in the same agreed proportions. That is, if the reinsurer gets 35 percent of the coverage under a given policy, it also gets 35 percent of the premium and pays 35 percent of each loss under the policy, regardless of the size of the loss. Under pro-rata reinsurance treaties, the reinsurer usually pays a ceding commission to the ceding company to cover the ceding company's expenses and possibly an allowance for profit.

Under *excess reinsurance*, sometimes called nonproportional reinsurance, no amount of *insurance* is ceded. The treaty does not come into play until the ceding company has sustained a *loss* which exceeds the ceding company's retention under the contract. Both facultative reinsurance and treaty reinsurance may be written as pro rata or excess or a combination of the two. Exhibit 7-5 shows the specific kinds of reinsurance which fall under the two categories. Each of the forms of reinsurance listed in Exhibit 7-5 will be discussed in detail in the paragraphs that follow.

Treaty Reinsurance

Most insurers depend more heavily on treaty reinsurance to provide the reinsurance protection they need because it provides

Exhibit 7-5

Kinds of Reinsurance Contracts—Treaty or Facultative

Pro Rata (proportional) Reinsurance
    Quota Share
    Surplus Share

Excess (nonproportional) Reinsurance
    Per Risk Excess
    Per Occurrence Excess (catastrophe treaty)[†]
    Aggregate Excess (also Stop Loss or Excess of Loss
    Ratio)[†]

[†]These two forms cannot be written on a facultative basis because they relate to a class of business, a territory, or the ceding company's entire book of business rather than a specific policy or a specific loss exposure.

several advantages over facultative reinsurance. The reinsurer is obligated to accept all cessions of business which fall within the terms of the treaty. Consequently, the ceding company can underwrite, accept, and cede such business without prior consultation with the reinsurer on each pending application. Also, since prior negotiation is not required for each exposure ceded, the handling expense is less under a treaty than in the facultative market. Whether an insurer chooses to use a pro-rata or an excess treaty is determined by the kind of exposures to be ceded, the financial needs of the ceding company, and other factors.

Pro-Rata or Proportional Treaties   Pro-rata reinsurance is the traditional reinsurance form for property insurance, though it has been losing ground rather rapidly to excess reinsurance in recent years. Pro-rata reinsurance is also the choice for an insurer that is thinly financed, since it is more effective than excess coverage in providing surplus relief. Its greater effectiveness in that respect stems largely from the practice of paying ceding commissions under pro-rata treaties, a practice not common under excess treaties. Also, the premium for a pro-rata treaty is likely to be a larger percentage of the original premium than is the case with an excess treaty.

The two kinds of treaties in the pro-rata category are quota share and surplus share (sometimes simply called surplus). The principal difference between them is the way in which the ceding company's retention is stated. Here, the term "surplus" should not be confused with the policyholders' surplus of the insurance company.

Quota Share. Under a quota share treaty, the ceding company cedes a part of every exposure it insures within the class or classes subject to the treaty. Even the smallest loss exposures are reinsured.

The ceding company's retention is stated as a *percentage* of the amount of insurance, so that the dollar amount of its retention varies with the amount of insurance. The reinsurer assumes all of the amount of insurance except for the ceding company's retention, up to the reinsurance limit. The reinsurer receives the same percentage of the premium (less the ceding commission), as it does of the amount of insurance and pays the same percentage of each loss.

To illustrate the application of a quota share treaty to varying situations, assume that Matchless Fire Insurance Company has purchased from Solid Re a quota share treaty with a retention of 25 percent. Matchless Fire has written three policies. Policy A insures Building A for $10,000 for a premium of $100, with one loss of $8,000. Policy B insures Building B for $100,000 for a premium of $1,000, with one loss of $10,000. Policy C insures Building C for $150,000 for a premium of $1,500, with one loss of $60,000. Exhibit 7-6 shows how the insurance, premiums, and losses under these policies would be split between the ceding company and the reinsurer. Note that in each case the ceding company retains 25 percent of the insurance and the premium and pays 25 percent of the losses. However, the dollar amount of its retention increases as the amount of insurance increases.

Quota share treaties can be used with either property or liability coverages, but property quota share treaties are much more common. They have the advantage of being simple to rate and simple to administer, since the reinsurer receives the agreed percentage of all covered premiums. The principal disadvantage is that a quota share treaty results in ceding a large share of presumably profitable business. Because of this disadvantage, quota share reinsurance has been declining in popularity. However, it is still widely used, especially by small insurers and insurers that need to increase surplus by reducing the unearned premium reserve. Quota share is the most effective treaty for that purpose.

Quota share treaties are only modestly effective in stabilizing loss experience and in coping with catastrophes, since they do not affect the ceding company's loss ratio. Of course, a favorable ceding commission may have an effect on the ceding company's combined ratio, since reinsurance commissions received are credited against direct commissions paid in the ceding company's annual statement. Over a period of many years, one company showed a negative expense ratio on its annual statement because its ceding commissions on its reinsurance treaties were greater than all of its expenses paid. Of course, a

Exhibit 7-6

Division of Insurance, Premium, and Losses Under
Quota Share Treaty with 25 Percent Retention and
$250,000 Limit

	Matchless Fire	Solid Re	Total
Policy A			
Insurance	$2,500	$7,500	$10,000
Premium	25	75	100
Loss	2,000	6,000	8,000
Policy B			
Insurance	$25,000	$75,000	$100,000
Premium	250	750	1,000
Loss	2,500	7,500	10,000
Policy C			
Insurance	$37,500	$112,500	$150,000
Premium	375	1,125	1,500
Loss	15,000	45,000	60,000

reinsurer must anticipate an extremely low loss ratio in order to pay such a high ceding commission.

A quota share treaty can be reasonably effective in improving the ceding company's large line capacity, depending upon the percentage retention required. However, it is not as effective in that regard as surplus share and per risk excess treaties.

Quota share treaties are effective in risk sharing, and they can be effective in reciprocity. For example, an automobile insurer active only in the United States recently negotiated a reciprocal quota share treaty with another automobile insurer active only in Canada. The U.S. insurer reinsures, on a quota share basis, 30 percent of the direct business written by the Canadian company, and the Canadian company reinsures 80 percent of the direct business written by the U.S. company. Because of the difference in the sizes of the companies, the dollar amounts of insurance exchanged are approximately equal. However, each insurer has increased both the number and the geographic spread of the cars insured. Such an arrangement should help to stabilize the loss experience of both insurers.

Surplus Share. Surplus share treaties, like quota share treaties, are pro-rata or proportional reinsurance. That is, the ceding company and the reinsurers share the insurance, the premium, and the losses in the same percentage. The difference between them is in the way the retention is stated. While the retention under a quota share treaty is stated as a *percentage* of the amount insured, the retention under a surplus share treaty is stated as a *dollar amount*. However, the ceding company may elect to retain more than the minimum retention stated in the treaty if it wishes to do so. If the amount of insurance under a given policy is less than the retention amount, no coverage under the policy is reinsured. If the amount of insurance under a policy exceeds the retention amount, the amount of insurance over and above the retention is ceded to the reinsurer, subject to the reinsurance limit and possibly other limitations of the treaty. The reinsurer receives the same percentage of the premium as it does of the insurance and pays the same percentage of each loss regardless of size. Therefore, the major difference between quota share and surplus share is that while the same *percentage* of reinsurance applies to all eligible policies under quota share, the percentage *varies* from policy to policy in a surplus share treaty, depending on policy size, and other conditions in the reinsurance agreement.

To illustrate the working of a surplus share treaty, assume that Matchless Fire Insurance Company has purchased from Solid Re a surplus treaty with a retention of $25,000 and a limit of $250,000. This would be referred to as a "ten-line surplus treaty," since the reinsurer will accept coverage up to ten times the retention amount. Exhibit 7-7 shows how this treaty would apply to the same three policies used in Exhibit 7-6 to illustrate the application of a quota share treaty. Note that under a quota share treaty (Exhibit 7-6) the percentage retention remains constant while the dollar amount of retention increases as the amount of insurance increases. Under a surplus share treaty (Exhibit 7-7), the dollar amount of retention remains constant while the percentage retention decreases as the amount of insurance increases. This is the major difference between quota share and surplus share treaties.

Surplus share treaties are sometimes built up in layers, with a different reinsurer for each layer. For example, if Solid Re had been unwilling to provide the full $250,000 of coverage that Matchless Fire wanted, Matchless might have built up the required coverage in the following three surplus share treaties:

Reinsurer	Retention	Reinsurance Limit
Solid Re	$ 25,000	$100,000
Super Re	125,000	100,000
Jumbo Re	225,000	50,000

For Policy B in Exhibit 7-7, the coverage would have been split $25,000 for Matchless Fire and $75,000 for Solid Re. Policy C would

Exhibit 7-7

Division of Insurance, Premium, and Losses Under
Surplus Share Treaty with $25,000 Retention and
$250,000 Limit*

	Matchless Fire	Solid Re	Total
Policy A			
Insurance	$10,000	$0	$10,000
Premium	100	0	100
Loss	8,000	0	8,000
Policy B			
Insurance	$25,000	$ 75,000	$100,000
Premium	250	750	1,000
Loss	2,500	7,500	10,000
Policy C			
Insurance	$25,000	$125,000	$150,000
Premium	250	1,250	1,500
Loss	10,000	50,000	60,000

*This example assumes that MFIC always retains its maximum net line.
This is common, but most treaties permit smaller retention as long as the
line limit is not violated. For example, Policy B could involve a retention
of any amount between $9,091 and $25,000.

have been split $25,000 for Matchless Fire, $100,000 for Solid Re and
$25,000 for Super Re. Jumbo Re would not become involved until the
amount of insurance on one loss exposure exceeds $225,000. Losses and
premiums would still be shared pro rata between Matchless Fire and all
reinsurers that provided coverage on the particular loss exposure which
sustained loss. Jumbo Re would not contribute to any of the losses in
Exhibit 7-7 because none of the amounts of insurance exceeded the
retention under its treaty. Super Re would be involved only with
respect to Policy C.

In the example above, Solid Re's treaty would be referred to as the
first surplus because it would come into play at the lowest amount of
insurance. Super Re's treaty would be the second surplus, and Jumbo
Re's treaty would be the third surplus. As in Exhibit 7-7, it is assumed
that policy limits are spread so as to fill the ceding company's retention
first, then its first surplus, and so on. This is not usually a treaty
requirement, and in the interest of providing better balance (relation of
treaty capacity to premium volume), the ceding company may decide to

place a part of each ceded policy in all its surplus share treaties, or any combination of them.

Surplus share reinsurance has been a common form of reinsurance for property insurers, though it has been losing ground to excess reinsurance in recent years. It has seldom, if ever, been used for liability insurance.

The principal advantage of surplus share treaties over quota share treaties is that surplus share treaties, because of their fixed dollar retentions, avoid ceding reinsurance on loss exposures which are so small that the ceding company can afford to retain them. Consequently, it not only effects some saving in reinsurance premiums but also reduces the processing of reinsurance claims. It also provides a more logical approach to reinsurance, because no reinsurance is purchased unless the loss exposure is beyond the capacity of the ceding company to absorb.

The principal disadvantage of surplus share treaties in comparison with quota share is the increased administrative expense. Since not all loss exposures are reinsured, the ceding company must maintain a record of those that are reinsured and furnish a report of them to the reinsurer each month or at such other frequency as they may agree upon. The listing of reinsured exposures, which usually includes premium and loss information, is known as a *bordereau,* for which the plural is bordereaux. Only a loss bordereau would be necessary under a quota share treaty, since the reinsurer receives a fixed percentage of all covered premiums.

The chief disadvantage of a surplus share treaty in comparison with an excess treaty is the fact that a larger amount of presumably profitable premium is ceded. There is also a loss of investment income on the premium ceded. Then, too, the administration cost is greater for surplus share than for excess because of the necessity for bordereaux.

Surplus share treaties are comparable to quota share in providing surplus relief, though the fixed dollar retention may result in slightly less relief because no reinsurance is ceded on the smaller exposures under a surplus share treaty.

A surplus share treaty is superior to a quota share treaty in providing large line capacity. Under a quota share treaty, the ceding company's dollar retention increases as the amount insured increases. The dollar retention remains constant under a surplus share treaty. Consequently, a ceding company can write a larger line without having its retention go beyond the amount it can safely bear, assuming that the reinsurers are willing to take all of the excess.

Unlike the quota share treaty, which has the same loss ratio as the net retention on policies to which it applies, loss experience of a surplus share treaty may be different from that of the net retention. This is because the surplus share treaty does not participate at all in the smaller policies, and it participates to a greater extent than the ceding company's retention on the larger policies. As a consequence, surplus share treaties tend to have larger capacities and lower premiums than the net account. Obviously, this makes them more vulnerable to large individual losses. Thus, loss experience of a surplus share treaty is expected to be somewhat more volatile than that of a quota share, and it is slightly more effective in stabilizing loss experience.

Like the quota share treaty, the surplus share is not designed to protect the ceding company from catastrophe loss occurrences. This function of reinsurance is satisfied by excess treaties described later. It is important to note that *pro-rata treaties have no occurrence limit.* For example, a regional insurer may write primarily large property exposures within a one or two state territory, and use surplus share as its major form of reinsurance. A severe earthquake might damage or destroy many of the ceded exposures, resulting in a very large loss to the reinsurer.

Excess or Nonproportional Treaties Excess treaties, frequently referred to as nonproportional treaties, differ from pro-rata, or proportional, treaties in that the ceding company and the reinsurer do not share the amount of insurance, premium, and losses in the same proportion. In fact, *no insurance amount is ceded under excess treaties, only losses.* The reinsurance premium usually is stated as a percentage of·the ceding company's premium income for the covered lines of business, but the percentage is subject to negotiation and will vary by line and from one insurer to another. Generally, commissions are not paid to the ceding company under excess treaties, though exceptions are known to occur.

There are three general classes of excess treaties: *per risk excess, per occurrence excess* (also known as per loss excess), and *aggregate excess.* They differ substantially in operation, and are discussed separately below.

Per Risk Excess. The retention under a per risk excess treaty is stated as a dollar amount of *loss* (not an amount of insurance), and the reinsurer is liable for all or a part of loss to any one exposure in excess of the retention and up to the agreed reinsurance limit. In some cases, the reinsurer may agree to pay only a stated percentage, such as 90 percent or 95 percent, of the loss in excess of the retention, though this provision is more common to per occurrence excess and aggregate excess treaties.

The retention amount under a per risk excess treaty usually is set at a level to exclude a large majority, by number, of expected claims. This is consistent with the theory that excess treaties are intended to

Exhibit 7-8

Division of Losses Under Per Risk Excess Treaty with
$25,000 Retention

	Matchless Fire	Solid Re	Total
Policy A Loss	$8,000	$0	$8,000
Policy B Loss	$10,000	$0	$10,000
Policy C Loss	$25,000	$35,000	$60,000

protect the ceding company against unusual loss situations. However, the retention is sometimes set low enough so that reinsurance claims occur frequently. Treaties with such low retentions frequently are referred to as *working covers* or *working excess treaties*. The spread loss treaty is especially suitable for a working cover because the premium is calculated by adding an expense loading to the average amount of losses under the treaty for some period of years, usually three.

It should be noted that the retention under a per risk excess treaty *applies separately to each subject of insurance.* For example, if Matchless Fire Insurance Company insured the Sheer Hosiery Company at 1110 Main Street and the Desiccated Sprinkler Company next door at 1112 Main Street, and they both burned, the retention under a per risk excess treaty would apply separately to each. As will be shown later, this is quite different from the other forms of excess treaty.

Unlike pro-rata treaties, excess reinsurers do not participate in all losses, but only in those which exceed the ceding company's retention, and then only in the part in excess of the retention. This difference is emphasized here because it is a frequent source of confusion among persons who are not familiar with reinsurance practices. Exhibit 7-8 shows how Matchless Fire and Solid Re would split the losses in Exhibit 7-7 under a per risk excess treaty with a retention of $25,000. The amount of insurance and the premium for each policy are not mentioned in Exhibit 7-8, as they were in Exhibit 7-7, because they are not material to the division of losses under an excess treaty. The division of losses in Exhibit 7-8 should be compared carefully with Exhibit 7-7 and the reasons for the differences understood.

The principal advantage of a per risk excess treaty in comparison with pro-rata treaties is the fact that less premium is ceded to the reinsurer. This permits the ceding company to earn income on the investment of these funds. Administration costs are also lower, since fewer reinsurance claims are processed. Also, it is not necessary to keep track of the loss exposures reinsured, in the same manner as under a surplus share treaty. The excess treaty is concerned only with losses.

Because the reinsurance premium is lower than for pro-rata treaties and because commissions normally are not paid to the ceding company, excess treaties are not effective in providing surplus relief.

Per risk excess treaties are very effective in providing large line capacity, since they absorb the large losses that make large lines hazardous to the direct insurer. They are much more effective in this regard than quota share treaties, and somewhat more effective than surplus share treaties, particularly if the reinsurance premium cost is considered.

Per risk excess treaties are very effective in stabilizing loss experience because they lessen the impact of large losses, which contribute disproportionately to fluctuations of loss experience. The loss experience of the reinsurer need not be the same as that of the ceding company in any given year, and normally would not be. However, over the long run, each ceding company should expect to pay its own losses plus the reinsurer's operating expenses. That is, the ceding company gives up a part of its profits in the good years in order to transfer its losses to the reinsurer in the bad years, thus stabilizing its loss experience over time.

Per risk excess treaties are helpful in catastrophes, since they pay the amount in excess of the ceding company's retention on each individual claim. However, they are far less effective in this regard than per occurrence excess treaties, especially since many of them contain a limitation on losses recoverable for any one loss occurrence such as hurricane, tornado, or earthquake.

Per Occurrence Excess. Although casualty (liability) excess reinsurance closely resembles per risk coverages, it is technically an occurrence form.

A casualty excess treaty is extremely important because most casualty (liability) insurers buy it, and the limit requirements are very high. Even companies writing modest amounts of workers' compensation, for example, may feel that $5 million, $10 million, or more of reinsurance protection is advisable.

The distinguishing feature of casualty excess is that it is possible that auto liability, general liability, workers' compensation, umbrella and perhaps other coverages can combine to form a single excess claim, and there may also be multiple claimants.

Another feature materially different from the property classes is the length of time required for the full development and settlement of all losses. The time between date of loss and notice to excess reinsurers may be several years. Final settlement of known losses may require many more years. In some cases there may be questions raised as to the time of the occurrence, as in the case of carcinogenic exposures which may not manifest themselves for decades.

Inflation and the late development of claims make this a difficult class to underwrite.

Property insurers are especially subject to large accumulations of losses arising from a single occurrence, such as a hurricane, which damages many insured properties. Most of the individual claims are relatively small, but the accumulated amount can be staggering. Per occurrence excess treaties, sometimes called catastrophe treaties, are designed especially to cope with this problem, though some catastrophe excess treaties may also be applicable to a large loss arising from damage to a single subject of insurance or a single large liability claim.

Like the per risk excess treaty, the retention under a per occurrence treaty is stated as a dollar amount. However, unlike the per risk excess, all of the losses arising from a single occurrence are totaled to determine when the retention has been satisfied. The reinsurance limit also applies to the aggregate amount of losses from one occurrence. Consequently, the definition of occurrence becomes quite important.

One catastrophe treaty defines an occurrence as follows:

The words "loss or disaster" as applied to the hazards of tornado, cyclone, hurricane, windstorm and/or hailstorm shall be construed to mean the sum total of all the Company's losses occurring during any period of 72 consecutive hours occasioned by tornadoes, cyclones, hurricanes, windstorms and/or hailstorms and arising out of the same atmospheric disturbances, and the Company may elect the moment from which the aforesaid period of 72 consecutive hours shall be deemed to have commenced, not within the period of any previous elected 72 consecutive hours, the Underwriters hereon being responsible only for their proportion of the loss sustained during the said elected 72 hour period.

The words "loss or disaster" as applied to earthquake shall be construed to mean the sum total of all the Company's losses occurring during any period of 72 consecutive hours arising out of or caused by one or a series of earthquakes, and the Company may elect the moment from which the aforesaid period of 72 consecutive hours shall be deemed to have commenced, not within the period of any previous elected 72 consecutive hours, the Underwriters hereon being responsible only for their proportion of the loss sustained during the said elected 72 hour period.[9]

The word "company" in the foregoing quotation refers to the ceding company, and the word "underwriters" refers to the reinsurers. The treaty quoted above did not cover flood damage, but another treaty used a similar definition applicable to flood. It used a period of hours similar to the above and specified that the flood damage must occur in "the same river basin (river basin being defined as the basin of a river including the basin of all of the tributaries of said river, which flows directly into an ocean, bay or gulf, or one of the Great Lakes of the United States)."[10]

This definition of occurrence is very important because it controls the application of the retention and the reinsurance limit. The retention would apply separately, but only once, to each occurrence, as would the reinsurance limit. For example, if a hurricane should travel up the East Coast and cause wind damage over a period of three days, all of the damage would be from a single occurrence. Consequently, the ceding company would be required to absorb only one retention and the reinsurer's liability could not exceed the amount stated in the treaty. On the other hand, if the storm lasted longer than seventy-two hours, it would be two occurrences. Therefore, the ceding company would be required to absorb up to twice the stated retention and the reinsurer would pay up to twice its treaty limit, since catastrophe treaties typically provide for one full reinstatement of cover following a loss.

If the same hurricane brought heavy rains which caused flooding in one river that drained into the Atlantic Ocean and another that drained into the Gulf of Mexico, a not uncommon occurrence, the floods in the two rivers would be two separate occurrences by the above definition. Consequently, the retention and the treaty limit would apply separately to each river, even though both floods originated from the same storm system.

The definitions quoted are merely illustrative. Different definitions may be used by different reinsurers, or even by the same reinsurers in different treaties.

Catastrophe treaties are very effective for the purpose for which they were designed, smoothing the fluctuations in loss experience to the extent that such fluctuations result from an accumulation of losses from catastrophes. Such treaties do not contribute significantly to the ceding company's premium capacity (except to the extent that they stabilize loss experience), since they are not designed to cover individual losses; nor do they contribute to large line capacity unless written to cover for a single large loss as well as an accumulation of losses. Catastrophe treaties do not provide significant surplus relief, since the reinsurance premium is a relatively small percentage of the direct premiums and the reinsurer usually does not pay a ceding commission.

Catastrophe treaties usually provide that the reinsurers will pay up to a stated percentage, i.e., 90 or 95 percent, of the loss in excess of the retention. Therefore, not only does the ceding company pay the losses up to the retention, but they also participate in the loss above the retention. There are two reasons for this: (1) reinsurers do not maintain large claim departments and therefore are not equipped to handle a large number of losses; and (2) it encourages the ceding company to settle losses economically, since they will be participating in the loss even though the retention is exhausted.

Catastrophe treaties also differ from per risk excess of loss contracts in that they are usually written for a specific period of time (twelve months) and usually are noncancellable by either party.

Aggregate Excess or Excess of Loss Ratio. Aggregate excess treaties, sometimes called excess of loss ratio or stop loss treaties, are less common than the other forms of excess treaties. However, they have been used with some frequency in connection with crop hail insurance and for small insurers in other lines.

Under an aggregate excess treaty, the reinsurer begins to pay when the ceding company's claims for some stated period of time, usually one year, exceed the retention stated in the treaty. The retention may be stated in dollars, as a loss ratio percentage, or as a combination of the two. The size of the retention is subject to negotiation between the ceding company and the reinsurer, but it usually would not be set so low that the ceding company would be guaranteed a profit. Also, the reinsurer normally does not pay all losses in excess of the ceding company's retention, but only a percentage of the excess, usually 90 percent or 95 percent. This last feature is intended to discourage the ceding company from relaxing its underwriting or loss adjustment standards after its retention has been reached.

The insuring clause of one aggregate excess treaty for crop hail insurance is as follows:

> 3. The Reinsurer shall not be liable for any loss or damage unless the Ceding Company has paid or has become liable in any one calendar year for a net amount of loss or damage in excess of $_____, and then the Reinsurer shall be liable only for 90% of the amount of such loss or damage but in no event to exceed $_____ in any one calendar year, the amount of this contract.
>
> 4. It is warranted by the Ceding Company that 10% of its net hail loss liability on growing crops in excess of its retention together with its

net retention as specified in Section 3 shall be retained by the Ceding Company at its own risk and not reinsured in any way.[11]

Another treaty, in which the retention is stated as a loss ratio, reads in part:

> . . . the Reinsurer hereby agrees for the consideration hereinafter appearing that they will indemnify the Ceding Company in respect of 90% (the balance of 10% together with the underlying 65% being warranted retained net by the Ceding Company for its own account without benefit of any reinsurance, excess of loss or otherwise) of the amount by which the "Loss Ratio" of the Ceding Company . . . exceeds 65%, provided always, however, that the maximum amount recoverable hereunder shall be limited to $2,500,000 in the aggregate.[12]

As might be expected, the reinsurance premium for an aggregate excess treaty is likely to be larger than that for a per risk or per occurrence excess cover. Consequently, such treaties are used only if the potential loss fluctuations are sufficiently large in relation to the ceding company's surplus to policyholders to pose a threat of insolvency. For that reason, aggregate excess treaties are purchased most often by small property insurers.

Since the aggregate excess treaty puts a cap on the ceding company's losses (or loss ratio), it would appear that no other reinsurance would be needed. In fact, both of the treaties quoted above prohibited reinsurance on the ceding company's retention. However, it is common to have other treaties, either proportional or excess, in conjunction with aggregate excess treaties. In some cases, the reinsurer may insist on other treaties as a condition of providing the aggregate excess cover. In those cases, the other treaties would be written for the benefit of both the ceding company and the aggregate excess reinsurer. That is, the ceding company's retention and the aggregate excess reinsurer's liability would both relate to the net loss after the proceeds of all other reinsurance had been deducted.

The aggregate excess treaty is the most effective of all forms of reinsurance in stabilizing the underwriting results of the ceding company, particularly if the cost of reinsurance is ignored. It is also effective in providing large line capacity and coping with catastrophes, since the cap it puts on losses would apply equally to large individual claims and an accumulation of claims from a catastrophe.

However, an aggregate excess treaty usually does not involve a ceding commission. Therefore, it does not provide significant surplus relief or premium capacity. Logically, it should increase premium capacity because the ceding company would need less surplus to absorb the remaining fluctuation in loss experience. However, current regulatory techniques are not sufficiently sophisticated to adjust premium-

Exhibit 7-9
Functions of Reinsurance by Type of Reinsurance

	Surplus Relief	Capacity	Catastrophe Protection
Quota Share Must all	Yes	Yes	Yes, but not purchased for this purpose
Surplus Share	Yes	Yes	Probably some, but not purchased for this purpose
Per Risk Excess	No	Yes	Possibly to some extent, but not purchased for this purpose
Catastrophe	No	No	Yes, sole purpose

to-surplus ratio requirements to reflect the greater loss stability provided by aggregate excess covers.

A summary of the functions or purposes of reinsurance and how well each type of reinsurance serves those purposes is shown in Exhibit 7-9.

Facultative Reinsurance

It is difficult to make specific statements about facultative reinsurance because each item of coverage is negotiated separately and can be of almost any form and at almost any rate which is agreeable to both parties. In the past, facultative reinsurance on property was almost always written on a pro-rata basis. More recently, facultative excess coverage has become readily available, and appears to be growing in usage.

Regardless of the form, excess or pro-rata, the approach to underwriting facultative reinsurance is quite different from that for treaties. In underwriting a treaty, the principal emphasis is on the management of the ceding company, the classes reinsured, the geographical spread, and the ceding company's historical loss experience for the lines of insurance covered by the treaty. The reinsurer does not underwrite individual loss exposures under the treaty.

Under facultative reinsurance, the reinsurer underwrites each loss exposure individually as it is submitted for consideration. The ceding company is required to furnish detailed information on each exposure, essentially the same information that a prudent primary insurer would obtain for its own underwriting function.

The facultative reinsurer is not bound by the rates quoted or charged by the ceding company. It may, if it chooses and if the ceding company is willing, charge a higher rate for the reinsurance than was charged on the direct policy. For this reason, primary insurers who expect to be heavily dependent on facultative reinsurance frequently obtain a reinsurance commitment before they quote a premium to their prospective insureds. Of course, this precaution is taken only partly because of rates and partly to be sure that reinsurance will be available.

In view of the uncertainty and handling burden of facultative reinsurance, one may wonder why a primary insurer would use it. Why not rely solely on treaties? There are several reasons.

First, treaties have exclusions. Property treaties, for example, usually exclude reinsurance coverage for a list of so-called "target risks," such as large art museums, major bridges, tunnels, nuclear generating facilities, and other properties of high value. These properties are excluded primarily because their large values require them to buy insurance from a number of primary insurers. If they were not excluded in treaties, a reinsurer might find, after a loss, that its accumulated loss through several ceding companies exceeded the amount it deemed prudent to accept. It would not know of such an exposure before a loss because the reinsurer does not underwrite each individual exposure under a treaty. Treaties may also exclude certain hazardous operations, either for property or liability lines. If an exposure is excluded under the primary insurer's treaties, it must turn to facultative reinsurers for protection.

Second, a ceding company may use facultative coverage to protect its treaties, to protect a favorable commission allowance under its treaties, or to protect a profit-sharing agreement. A favorable reinsurance treaty is a valuable relationship for a ceding company, facilitating its operations and contributing to its profits. However, the continuation of the treaty on favorable terms, or perhaps on any terms, depends on the quality of business ceded under it. The rates or ceding commission under treaties are determined by loss experience under the treaty. Some treaties include retrospective rating plans or profit-sharing commission plans which tie the rates or commission directly to loss experience. The rates or commissions under other treaties are negotiated on the basis of loss experience. If a primary insurer finds it necessary to write coverage on a loss exposure it thinks might have an adverse effect on its treaty relationships, it may elect not to reinsure it under the treaties, but to reinsure it facultatively instead. Since each facultative submission is an independent transaction and is underwritten separately, a loss under one facultative agreement has little or no effect on the terms or rates under subsequent transactions.

Another reason for using facultative reinsurance is to cover a loss exposure which exceeds the limits under the applicable treaties. The limit under a reinsurance treaty is one of the major determinants of reinsurance costs. Consequently, a ceding company should set the limit at an amount which is adequate for the vast majority, say 98 percent, of the loss exposures it insures, and rely on facultative coverage for the excess over treaty limits for the unusually large exposures.

There is one exception to the statement that each facultative submission is separately and independently underwritten. Reinsurers sometimes enter into what is called an *obligatory facultative treaty*. Under such a treaty, the primary insurer is not required to cede any exposures, but the reinsurer is obligated to accept any business the direct insurer elects to cede provided only that it is within the class of business covered by the treaty. Under an obligatory facultative treaty, the reinsurer underwrites the management of the ceding company at least as carefully as under the more common treaties, and possibly more carefully.

Obligatory facultative treaties are not common because of the opportunity for adverse selection against the reinsurer. Nonobligatory facultative treaties are slightly more common. Such treaties merely set forth the conditions under which business will be ceded and accepted if the primary insurer elects to cede and the reinsurer elects to accept. However, the ceding company is not required to cede, and the reinsurer is not required to accept.

Pro-Rata Facultative Reinsurance Facultative reinsurance for property exposures traditionally has been written on a pro-rata basis, though excess reinsurance has made some inroads in recent years. Pro-rata facultative reinsurance functions quite similarly to a surplus share treaty except, of course, each facultative agreement relates to a single subject of insurance.

As an illustration, assume that Matchless Fire Insurance Company has received an application from one of its producers to write $1 million of fire and extended coverage insurance on the Pigiron Foundry Corporation. Matchless has established its net retention limit on foundries at $100,000. In addition, it has automatic surplus share treaties which will cover five lines, or, in this case, $500,000. The surplus reinsurers pay Matchless a 35 percent ceding commission under the treaties.

Matchless then approaches the facultative department of Coral Rock Re with a request for $400,000 of pro-rata facultative reinsurance. After Coral Rock Re reviews all of the information furnished by

Exhibit 7-10

Insurance, Premium, and Loss Division Through Surplus Share and
Pro-Rata Facultative Reinsurance

	Insurance	Premium	Loss	Ceding Commission to Matchless
Matchless Fire	$ 100,000	$ 3,000	$ 2,000	$ 0
Surplus Share Reinsurers	500,000	15,000	10,000	5,250
Coral Rock Re (Facultative)	400,000	12,000	8,000	3,600
Totals	$1,000,000	$30,000	$20,000	$8,850

Matchless, it agrees to provide the $400,000 of coverage, for which it will receive 40 percent of the direct premium and will pay Matchless a 30 percent ceding commission. The direct premium charged to Pigiron by Matchless Fire is $30,000.

Having obtained the necessary reinsurance, Matchless issued the policy to Pigiron Foundry. A $20,000 loss occurred shortly thereafter. The insurance, premium, and loss were divided as shown in Exhibit 7-10.

Agency reinsurance is a form of pro-rata facultative reinsurance which was widely used in the past but is less common at present. Agency reinsurance was used by independent agents and brokers to enable them to issue a single policy to an insured instead of issuing several policies with several different insurers. As will be seen, this method generally would not be available to exclusive agents or direct writer producers because they represent only one insurer or group of insurers under common ownership and management.

To illustrate, assume that Independent Agency, Inc., represents Matchless Fire Insurance Company, Quaking Casualty Company, and the Inimitable Mutual Fire Insurance Company, all of which are licensed to write fire insurance. Independent Agency wants to write $100,000 of fire insurance on an unprotected frame woodworking factory, but Matchless will accept only $50,000 of the coverage and each of the other insurers refuses to write more than $25,000. Independent Agency could write three separate policies to provide the coverage, but chooses instead to issue one policy through Matchless Fire for the entire amount and to reinsure $25,000 each with Quaking Casualty and Inimitable Mutual.

The agency reinsurance was not a matter of great consequence in the foregoing example because only three policies would have been needed in the absence of the reinsurance. However, the author is familiar with one case in which over 150 policies covering an unprotected frame fishmeal factory were combined into a single policy through the use of agency reinsurance. Obviously, the insured found it more convenient to deal with a single insurer than with 150 insurers.

Excess Facultative Reinsurance In contrast to treaty reinsurance, there is only one form of facultative excess reinsurance. Only per risk excess is possible on a facultative basis. Catastrophe and aggregate excess must apply to an entire book of business; they are meaningless in the context of a single loss exposure.

Facultative excess reinsurance operates just like a per risk excess treaty. That is, the ceding company pays all losses equal to or less than its agreed retention. The reinsurer is involved only if the loss exceeds the ceding company's retention, and then it pays only the amount in excess of the ceding company's retention, up to the reinsurance limit.

Excess reinsurance has been the traditional form of facultative reinsurance for liability and workers' compensation coverages. It has been used with increasing frequency for property insurance.

For liability insurance, the reinsurance premium usually is based on the increased limits factors used by the primary insurer. However, the reinsurance premium may be higher or lower than the primary insurer's increased limits premium, depending upon the facultative reinsurer's judgment as to the adequacy of that premium for the particular exposure being ceded.

It is difficult to specify a method for rating excess facultative coverage for property insurance. The rate would depend largely on the judgment of the facultative underwriter, reinforced to the extent possible by statistics from the reinsurer's past experience with similar exposures, guides such as Lloyd's first loss scale and Chubb deductible tables, and competition.

Direct Excess Many facultative reinsurers also engage in one line of business which is, in effect, half way between direct insurance and reinsurance: that is, the providing of excess of loss coverage to large business firms and governmental agencies that are otherwise self-insured.

For example, a large employer might elect to qualify as a self-insurer for workers' compensation. The employer might then buy excess of loss coverage to protect against shock losses or an unusual accumulation of smaller losses. That is, it would use excess coverage to stabilize its loss experience, much as an insurer uses reinsurance. However, the direct excess coverages do not qualify as reinsurance under the definition used here, because they are not purchased by an insurance company.

The retention under direct excess covers may apply (1) per claim (per item for property insurance), (2) per occurrence, or (3) aggregate. These are roughly comparable to the per risk, per occurrence, and aggregate bases discussed in connection with excess reinsurance treaties.

To illustrate, assume that Pigiron Foundry is self-insured for workers' compensation and that an explosion has injured three employees. The benefits for the three employees are (1) employee A, $10,000; (2) employee B, $75,000; and (3) employee C, $300,000.

If Pigiron had an excess cover with a retention of $25,000 per claim, it would have been required to retain a total of $60,000, the sum of $25,000 for each of B and C and $10,000 for A. Under a per occurrence coverage with a $25,000 retention, Pigiron would have retained only $25,000, since all three employees were injured in the same occurrence. Under an annual aggregate coverage with a $25,000 retention, the claims from the explosion would be combined with all other claims for the year, and Pigiron would retain a total of $25,000 for all of the claims for the year.

Similar excess coverages are available for property exposures. However, the per claim excess becomes a per item excess. If the insured owns three buildings, the retention would apply separately to each and, quite possibly, separately to the contents of each building.

Extensive statistics have been collected to assist underwriters in setting the rates for direct excess coverages. However, the judgment of the underwriter based on experience with similar exposures is still a major factor in rating, along with the underlying rating methods of the ceding company.

Functions of Facultative Reinsurance The principal functions of facultative reinsurance, whether pro-rata or excess, are to provide large line capacity, to cover those exposures excluded from treaties, or to protect treaties from unusual or hazardous exposures. Facultative reinsurance may also be used to achieve a better spread of risk, for reciprocity, and to secure a "second opinion" from the facultative reinsurer as to acceptability, price, policy terms, and conditions. Since facultative coverage must be negotiated separately on each subject of insurance, it is not likely to provide significant surplus relief unless a very large number of facultative covers are purchased. The same characteristic prevents facultative reinsurance from effectively coping with catastrophes. It does help smooth the fluctuations in loss experience, however, by providing a means of leveling the tops of large losses.

REINSURANCE THROUGH POOLS

Although there may be some fine distinctions among pools, syndicates, and reinsurance associations, the three will be discussed together here, and no distinction will be made between them. A reinsurance pool (or syndicate or association) is an organization of insurers banded together to underwrite reinsurance jointly. Some pools may write reinsurance only for member companies of the pool. Others may write coverage only for nonmember insurers, while still others may write coverage for both members and nonmembers.

Some reinsurance pools may restrict their operations to relatively narrow classes of business, such as fire and allied lines coverages on sprinklered properties. Others may write a wide variety of coverages.

The initiative for the organization of a reinsurance pool may come from any of several sources. Several pools were organized because groups of relatively small insurers wanted to increase their capacity to write high-value properties. None of the insurers operating alone had sufficient skill and capacity, but the group could provide the needed capacity and hire technicians by combining their financial resources through a reinsurance pool. Oftentimes, such pooling results in a lowering of total expenses. Examples of such pools are the Industrial Risk Insurers (IRI) formerly known as the Factory Insurance Association and the United States Aircraft Insurance Group (USAIG).

Governmental pressure or suggestion has been the initiating force in the formation of some pools. Among them are the nuclear energy pools and the reinsurance plans and joint underwriting associations which function in some states to provide automobile, fire, and workers' compensation insurance for those who cannot obtain coverage in the voluntary market.

A reinsurance broker, sometimes called an intermediary, may organize a pool as a means of providing reinsurance to clients of the brokerage firm. Such pools are likely to be somewhat fluid, with old member firms departing and new member firms entering on a fairly frequent basis. Needless to say, the broker would need to have some inducement to offer in order to entice an insurer to participate. The inducement may be an established book of desirable business, some special expertise on the part of the broker, or some similar benefit to the insurer. Although many broker-initiated pools have operated successfully over many years, a few have failed, with rather severe results for the participating companies.

It should be noted that pooling, by itself, does not necessarily improve the underwriting results of the pooled business. Poor business placed in the pool simply develops poor pool results.

The operating methods of reinsurance pools vary as widely as their purpose of organization, or perhaps more so. The operating methods of several pools will be discussed briefly.

Joint Underwriting Associations

The automobile assigned risk plans (or automobile insurance plans) in several states have been replaced by joint underwriting associations or reinsurance plans. The purpose of these newer organizations is the same as that for the assigned risk plans—to make automobile insurance available to persons who are unable to obtain it in the voluntary market. However, the newer plans operate quite differently from the assigned risk plans they replaced.

Under an assigned risk plan, each applicant for insurance in the plan is *assigned* to a specific insurer. The proportion of applicants assigned to a given insurer usually is determined by its proportion, by exposure units, of the automobile insurance written in the state. After assignment, the assigned insured is handled as any other insured of the insurer, except that the assigned insured may not be able to obtain all of the coverages desired. That is, the insurer issues its policy to the assigned insured, adjusts claims under the policy and performs the other services that it performs for its "voluntary" insureds. The assigned exposure is reinsured, if at all, under the insurer's normal reinsurance agreements applicable to its voluntary business.

Under the joint underwriting associations and reinsurance plans, applications are not assigned to specific insurers by the plan, as is done in the assigned risk plans. Instead, each applicant is insured by an insurer represented by the producer who accepted the application, and that company issues the policy, collects the premium, adjusts the losses and provides other necessary services, just as it does for its other business. However, the insurance for applicants the insurer considers to be ineligible for its voluntary coverage is reinsured, in whole or in part, through the joint underwriting association or reinsurance pool. Each member of the association or pool is credited with its share of the premiums and debited with its share of the losses, based on its share of the voluntary automobile business in the state. The company that writes the policy receives its share of the premiums and pays its share of the losses like any other member, but it also receives a fee, comparable to a ceding commission, for the services it provides. It is apparent from the foregoing description that the reinsurance protection provided under the automobile joint underwriting associations and reinsurance pools is pro-rata reinsurance, comparable to quota share reinsurance.

Up to this point, it would appear that there is no significant difference between joint underwriting associations and reinsurance plans. In fact, the difference is rather minor. Under a joint underwriting association, a limited number of insurers are authorized to issue policies on behalf of the association. These insurers, called servicing carriers, receive a fee for issuing the policies and providing the necessary services. Fourteen insurers were originally authorized to act as servicing carriers for the Florida association (the number of servicing carriers has declined in recent years), and every producer is licensed to act on behalf of one servicing carrier.

Under a reinsurance plan, every member company is authorized and required to provide insurance to any qualified applicant, so one might say that all member companies are servicing carriers. The member companies may be able to cede all of the eligible coverages to the plan or, as has been the practice in Canada, may be required to retain a percentage of the coverage under each policy. Of course, even if the entire coverage is ceded, the insurer must take its share as a member company of the pool.

The principal reason for changing from an assigned risk plan to a joint underwriting association or reinsurance plan is to remove or minimize the perceived stigma associated with assigned risk plans, the stigma of having to be assigned to an insurer because no insurer is willing to provide coverage voluntarily. It was hoped that the drivers in the newer plans would not be aware that they were singled out for special treatment. The success of the plans in this respect is uncertain.

However, they have succeeded in spreading the cost of less desirable drivers over the entire automobile insurance system in a more equitable manner. Under an assigned risk plan, one insurer might have worse (or better) experience on assigned business than another, due solely to the luck of the draw. Under the newer plans, all insurers have the same percentage loss experience, though their dollar losses may vary because of differences in market share.

The reinsurance plans and the reinsurance phase of the joint underwriting associations perform some of the functions by which other forms of reinsurance have been judged here. However, they cannot be judged solely on the performance of the traditional functions of reinsurance. The reinsurance plans and joint underwriting associations were formed primarily for a social purpose, rather than the financial purpose of traditional reinsurance techniques. Consequently, they must be judged primarily on their success in serving their social purpose. However, a detailed discussion of their success in serving that purpose is beyond the scope of this chapter.

Nuclear Energy Pools

The atomic bombs of World War II left the people of the world firmly impressed with the power of nuclear reaction and perhaps overly impressed with the dangers of nuclear radiation. As nuclear reaction was converted from weapons use to providing electric power for civilian use, there was a clamor for very high limits of liability coverage for the nuclear power plants. Also, special property insurance forms were needed, since insurers had modified their traditional property insurance policies to exclude loss from nuclear reaction and nuclear radiation. In addition, the high limits of property insurance for nuclear power plants were beyond the then available capacity of the insurance industry.

To provide the necessary protection, three insurance pools were formed. Stock insurers formed the Nuclear Energy Liability Insurance Association (NELIA) and the Nuclear Energy Property Insurance Association (NEPIA), which were merged at a later date to form the Nuclear Energy Liability-Property Insurance Association (NEL-PIA) now known as American Nuclear Insurers (ANI). The mutuals formed the Mutual Atomic Energy Reinsurance Pool (MAERP), which provided both property and liability coverages. All three of the pools were formed in 1956.

At the time it was formed, NELIA had 138 member insurers and an underwriting capacity of $46.5 million for one power plant. There were 189 participating insurers in NEPIA, with underwriting capacity of $50 million for one plant. The mutual pool had 105 members and capacity of $13.5 million for liability and $10 million for property per plant. Combined, the pools could issue $60 million of coverage for liability and the same amount for property coverage on one nuclear facility.[13] By 1984, the combined capacity of the two surviving pools had increased to $585 million for property, $160 million for liability, and $30 million for contingent liability.

Nuclear energy policies for the two surviving pools may be issued either by a single insurer or by several insurers subscribing to the same policy, depending upon the pool involved. In either case, the coverage is fully reinsured by the pool.

The forms and rates used by both pools are identical. If both pools issue policies on a single nuclear facility, the losses are shared pro rata. In addition, each pool reinsures a part of each exposure written by the other, with each pool assuming a part of the coverage roughly in the proportion that its underwriting capacity bears to the total capacity of the two pools combined. Because of this pro-rata reinsurance arrangement, the loss experience on domestic business has been substantially the same for both pools over the years.

The pools also buy reinsurance from nonmember insurers, and reinsure pools in other countries. Pool reinsurance is provided by Lloyd's and alien insurers not operating on a direct basis in this country. This reinsurance also is pro rata, and accounts for about one-half of the underwriting capacity of the pools. Reinsurers domiciled in Europe, South America, and Asia have participated.

In addition to the insurance provided by the nuclear energy pools, the federal government, under the Price-Anderson Act of 1957, has agreed to indemnify operators of nuclear facilities for their liability to others for damages arising from the nuclear facility. While a small charge is made for the indemnity agreement, it is not actually insurance but is a subsidy to encourage the development of nuclear energy. The insurance pools are not directly involved in the governmental program (except for the adjustment of losses on behalf of the government under a service contract), and the indemnity under the Price-Anderson Act is excess over the coverage provided by the pools.

Only one major nuclear incident (Three Mile Island in 1979) has occurred to date in the commercial use of nuclear energy, and, as a result, the amounts paid out by the pools have been substantially less than contemplated in the original rates. Rates have recently been increased for the first time since they were first adopted in 1956, and substantial dividends have been paid to policyholders as a result of the favorable experience. The favorable past experience may or may not indicate that the initial rates were too high. Nuclear energy insurance is potentially subject to very severe catastrophes. It is not certain whether past experience is a good indicator of the probability of such catastrophes or whether the near absence of severe losses in the past twenty years is due solely to chance.

American Nuclear Insurers also acts as a reinsurer for nuclear energy insurers in Canada and other foreign countries. In 1980, ANI's underwriting capacity on foreign business was $69.4 million for each nuclear facility, but consideration was being given to increasing that capacity to $80 million per facility.

THE REINSURANCE MARKET

The boundaries of the reinsurance market are difficult to define. It is a surprisingly international market, and a single large loss may be paid by insurers throughout the noncommunist world. In a few cases, reinsurers from the communist countries may participate in the reinsurance of business originating in the noncommunist world.

International Market

The international nature of reinsurance is emphasized by the statistics published by the U.S. Department of Commerce showing reinsurance transactions between United States insurers and alien insurers. Exhibits 7-11 and 7-12 show some figures excerpted from these reports.

To put the figures in Exhibits 7-11 and 7-12 into perspective, the 1982 reinsurance premiums ceded abroad were about 2 percent of the net written premiums for property and liability insurance in the United States during that year. However, they equal almost 20 percent of the estimated reinsurance premium volume for the United States.

A comparison of Exhibits 7-11 and 7-12 shows that the United States is a net importer of reinsurance. That is, U.S. insurers buy more reinsurance abroad than they sell abroad. However, the balance had been improving throughout the early part of the period covered by the exhibits. In 1960, premiums on reinsurance purchased abroad exceeded premiums on reinsurance sold abroad by a ratio of 4.70 to 1. By 1975, the ratio had fallen to 1.20 to 1. However, the ratio increased after 1975, reaching 2.2 to 1 in 1982. Most of the increase results from transactions with reinsurers in Western Hemisphere countries other than Canada. A substantial portion probably involves fronting operations of American insurance companies shown as reinsurance with captive insurers in Bermuda and the Caribbean.

In 1982, Bermuda accounted for 85.5 percent of all reinsurance purchased by U.S. insurers from reinsurers within the Western Hemisphere (including Canada, but excluding U.S. reinsurers). It accounted for 35.7 percent of all U.S. purchases of reinsurance abroad. Bermuda was not listed separately in the 1960 tables, but all Western Hemisphere countries combined accounted for only 2.4 percent of U.S. purchases of foreign reinsurance in that year.

The international transaction of reinsurance is in the best interest of all parties. One of the major purposes of reinsurance is to spread the financial consequences of fortuitous losses as widely as possible, and international reinsurance transactions increase the spread substantially. This spreading of losses is especially important with regard to major catastrophes, and catastrophe reinsurance constitutes a large part of total international reinsurance transactions.

Statistics for the world reinsurance market are not readily available. However, one further indication of the international nature of reinsurance is given by a listing, by nationality, of the world's largest reinsurers. Such a listing is shown in Exhibit 7-13. Lloyd's, which would rank not lower than third, and perhaps higher, if it had been included in Exhibit 7-13, is not included because it is not a

Exhibit 7-11
Net Premiums Paid and Net Losses Recovered Under Reinsurance Ceded Abroad by U.S. Insurers—1960, 1965, 1970, 1975, 1980 and 1982 (in millions of dollars)*

Area	Net Premiums Paid						Net Losses Recovered					
	1960	1965	1970	1975	1980	1982[1]	1960	1965	1970	1975	1980	1982[1]
All Areas	$267.1	$305.8	$447.7	$899.5	$1,896.5	$2,127.9	$185.3	$288.8	$287.8	$597.9	$1,031.8	$1,422.2
Western Europe (total)	252.6	285.8	392.5	652.4	1,054.2	1,082.0	177.0	273.1	253.8	436.4	617.7	890.0
Switzerland	25.1	16.3	22.4	33.5	75.7	101.5	20.0	13.2	14.5	30.1	34.1	108.3
United Kingdom	219.4	250.5	321.1	509.0	642.5	629.5	149.0	237.6	203.7	327.5	349.5	453.2
European Communities (6)	[2]	[2]	[2]	[2]	274.5	276.9	[2]	[2]	[2]	[2]	191.2	255.7
Other	8.1	19.0	49.0	109.9	46.7	58.9	8.0	22.3	35.6	78.8	30.5	59.8
Canada	3.4	3.7	12.3	34.2	56.3	81.7	3.4	5.8	12.5	34.2	37.8	44.5
Latin American Republics	[3]	[3]	[3]	[3]	40.7	47.1	[3]	[3]	[3]	[3]	29.9	30.6
Other Western Hemisphere	3.0	7.1	25.8	163.7	636.9	804.5	1.9	3.2	12.6	92.0	278.3	358.3
Japan	[4]	[4]	11.4	25.2	68.9	78.6	[4]	[4]	5.2	17.5	41.9	69.7
Other Countries	8.1	9.2	5.7	24.0	34.0	39.5	3.0	6.7	3.7	17.8	26.2	29.1

1. Preliminary estimate.
2. Included in Other Western European.
3. Included in Other Western Hemisphere.
4. Included in Other Countries.

*Compiled from U.S. Department of Commerce data.

Exhibit 7-12
Net Premiums Received and Net Losses Paid Under Reinsurance *Assumed from Abroad* by U.S. Insurers—1960, 1965, 1970, 1975, 1980 and 1982 (in millions of dollars)*

Area	Net Premiums Paid						Net Losses Recovered					
	1960	1965	1970	1975	1980	1982[1]	1960	1965	1970	1975	1980	1982[1]
All Areas	$56.8	$107.0	$251.4	$683.5	$896.3	$958.5	$44.7	$ 98.0	$174.2	$479.5	$660.7	$765.3
Western Europe (total)	33.6	67.9	165.2	395.2	516.4	471.1	28.5	70.2	121.4	293.4	379.8	404.2
Switzerland	[2]	1.4	10.4	32.2	66.0	36.5	[2]	1.5	6.6	19.7	50.1	36.7
United Kingdom	20.1	39.8	101.3	193.9	230.0	217.6	18.4	43.4	72.5	154.8	185.1	199.9
European Communities (6)	[2]	[2]	[2]	[2]	182.4	177.6	[2]	[2]	[2]	[2]	111.6	133.2
Other	13.5	26.7	53.5	169.1	30.4	28.3	10.1	25.3	42.3	118.9	28.0	23.3
Canada	7.9	16.9	32.2	135.3	165.5	203.7	3.4	10.8	20.0	86.5	138.3	184.2
Latin American Republics	[3]	[3]	[3]	[3]	72.4	95.3	[3]	[3]	[3]	[3]	49.7	60.6
Other Western Hemisphere	11.5	15.4	31.9	64.2	35.7	34.5	10.5	9.9	19.3	47.0	28.4	18.6
Japan	[4]	[4]	7.0	30.5	39.0	43.6	[4]	[4]	3.9	18.5	18.3	25.3
Other Countries	3.8	6.8	14.1	58.3	67.3	110.4	2.3	7.1	9.6	34.1	46.2	72.4

1. Preliminary estimate.
2. Included in Other Western European.
3. Included in Other Western Hemisphere.
4. Included in Other Countries.

*Compiled from U.S. Department of Commerce data.

Exhibit 7-13
Fifteen Largest Professional Reinsurers—1981*

Company or Company Group	Country of Domicile	1981 Premiums (millions of dollars)
Munich Re	Germany	$3,593.8
Swiss Re	Switzerland	3,059.8
General Re	United States	1,200.2
Gerling Group	Germany	766.5
Mercantile & General	United Kingdom	559.6
Cologne Re	Germany	514.9
SCOR[1]	France	468.2
Employers Re	United States	449.2
Frankona Re	Germany	434.7
American Re	United States	331.8
Prudential Re	United States	323.7
Bavarian Re	Germany	297.9
INA Re	United States	263.9
Toa Fire & Marine Re	Japan	259.7
Hannover Re	Germany	243.1

[1]Societe Commerciale de Reassurance.

*Reprinted with permission from *International Insurance Monitor*, April/May 1983, p. 5.

professional reinsurer (the word "professional" is used to denote a company whose principal business is reinsurance, as opposed to primary companies who may have a "professional" reinsurance department, but whose principal business is not reinsurance). An additional indication of the international nature of the reinsurance market is the fact that four of the top ten reinsurers in the U.S., as measured by premium volume, are alien reinsurers or controlled by alien reinsurers.

In addition to the geographic spread of the fifteen largest professional reinsurers, one other fact stands out in Exhibit 7-13. Many professional reinsurers are substantially smaller than the direct insurers to which they provide reinsurance protection. However, it should be remembered that any one professional reinsurer does not write or retain for its own account all of the exposures assumed under a treaty with a major ceding company. A major treaty may be shared by several reinsurers on a percentage basis, or if one reinsurer initially writes the entire treaty, it may cede much of it to other reinsurers under retrocession agreements.

Multiplicity of Reinsurers

In addition to its geographic spread, there is another reason that the boundaries of the reinsurance market are difficult to define. Any insurer can provide reinsurance unless it is subject to statutory or charter prohibitions. Few such prohibitions exist, and a great many insurers provide some reinsurance. Even relatively small insurers may engage in the reinsurance business by participating in various reinsurance pools and syndicates, their participation sometimes being a very small fraction of a percentage point of the pool business. Such small companies are not, of course, major factors in the reinsurance market, either individually or collectively.

As a practical matter, the reinsurance market for United States insurers is composed of (1) U.S. insurers or licensed alien insurers that specialize in reinsurance, frequently referred to as *professional reinsurers*; (2) U.S. insurers or licensed alien insurers whose primary business is direct insurance with the public but who have professional reinsurance departments; and (3) nonlicensed (nonadmitted) alien reinsurers. Exhibit 7-14 shows the relative positions of these three groups in the U.S. reinsurance market for the years 1960, 1965, 1970, 1975, 1980, and 1982. The insurance exchanges incorporated in New York, Illinois, and Florida may become important sources of reinsurance in the future, but they are only minor factors at the present time.

As shown by Exhibit 7-14, the professional reinsurers have increased their market share from 36 percent in 1960 to 54.4 percent in 1982. Their gain has been primarily at the expense of the nonadmitted alien reinsurers, and, to a lesser degree, at the expense of primary insurers with professional reinsurance departments. Part of the gain of the professional reinsurers has resulted from the fact that several large primary insurers that had professional reinsurance departments in 1960 have since incorporated professional reinsurance companies and transferred their reinsurance business to them. However, the exact magnitude of such changes is not known. Also, several alien reinsurers that were unlicensed in 1960 have since become licensed in the U.S.

Note that the market share of unlicensed alien reinsurers declined steadily from 1960 to 1975. To some extent, this decline resulted from some alien insurers obtaining licenses rather than losing premiums. The decline was reversed after 1975, and the market share of unlicensed alien reinsurers increased by 2.5 percentage points from 1975 to 1982. At least a part of this increase came from fronting operations of U.S. insurers on behalf of captive insurers in Bermuda and other places around the world.

Exhibit 7-14
Group Shares of United States Reinsurance Market — 1960, 1965, 1970, 1975, 1978, 1980 and 1982 (in millions of dollars)*

Year	Professional Reinsurers		Direct Insurers with Reinsurance Departments		Nonlicensed Alien Reinsurers	
	Net Premiums	Percent of Total	Net Premiums	Percent of Total	Net Premiums	Percent of Total
1960	$ 385	36.0%	$ 223	20.8%	$ 462	43.2%
1965	592	39.6	392	26.2	510	34.2
1970	1,007	43.4	598	25.8	714	30.8
1975	2,321	50.0	1,102	23.7	1,221	26.3
1980	4,841	50.3	1,803	18.8	2,961	30.9
1982	5,703	54.4	1,766	16.8	3,018	28.8

*Reprinted with permission from John R. Zech, "Re Premiums Up in '75, But So Are Losses," *National Underwriter* (Property and Casualty Edition), December 10, 1976, part 2, p. 37; John R. Zech, "U.S. Reinsurance Market: Deterioration Continues," *National Underwriter* (Property and Casualty Edition), December 11, 1981, Part 2, p. 31; and John R. Zech, "U.S. Re Premiums, Surplus Rise, Underwriting Results Deteriorate," *National Underwriter* (Property and Casualty Edition), August 26, 1983, Part 2, p.1.

Reciprocity

Another complicating factor in the measurement of the reinsurance market is the practice of reciprocal reinsurance among primary insurers. In reciprocal reinsurance, two (or possibly more) primary insurers enter into an agreement under which each cedes to the other an agreed percentage of its business. In an example mentioned earlier in this chapter, a United States automobile insurer and a Canadian automobile insurer entered into an agreement whereby the United States company ceded approximately 80 percent of its business to the Canadian company in exchange for 30 percent of the Canadian company's direct premiums. Because of the sizes of the two companies, the dollar amounts of ceded premiums were approximately equal. The transaction provided both companies with some protection against fluctuations in loss experience both by sharing losses and by providing each company with a better spread of exposures geographically and in numbers.

In this case, both insurers were writing substantially the same class of business—private passenger automobile insurance predominantly for blue collar workers. Similarity of business is a prime consideration in any reciprocal reinsurance arrangement. If the exchanged business is not substantially similar, one insurer is likely to profit at the expense of the other.

The two insurers in this case also possess another characteristic that is highly desirable for successful reciprocal reinsurance. They do not compete in the same market area. Since each partner in a reciprocal arrangement must furnish the other partner with a great deal of proprietary information, such arrangements generally are not satisfactory in a competitive situation. This fact, perhaps more than any other, contributed to the decline of reciprocity as a major force in the reinsurance market.

During the last century, when professional reinsurance was less available and few insurers operated nationally, reciprocity was an important reinsurance technique. Today, its use is relatively limited except for the special case of reciprocal reinsurance arrangements among several insurers under common ownership or common management or both. In that special case, reciprocity is still common.

Chapter Notes

1. For a discussion of these practices see Kenneth Thompson, *Reinsurance,* 4th ed. (Philadelphia: The Spectator, 1966), pp. 135-136; and Robert A. Bailey, "Phony Surplus Aid," *Best's Review,* Property/Casualty Insurance Edition, February 1972, p. 30.
2. Carol J. Loomis, "How Fireman's Fund Stoked its Profits," *Fortune,* 28 November 1983, p. 99; and Daniel Hertzberg, "Insurers' Move to Lift Profits is Questioned," *Wall Street Journal,* 7 September 1983, p. 33.
3. Julie Schlenger, "Insurers Turn More to Loss-Selling," *Journal of Commerce,* 21 July 1983, p. 1, 6A; and James E. Dwane, "Financially-Oriented Treaty Reinsurance," *Reinsurance,* August 1983, p. 208, 210, 212.
4. Jonathan F. Bank, "The Contract v. The Contact," *Reinsurance,* August 1983, p. 161.
5. Jonathan F. Bank, "Cut-Through Endorsements: Puerto Rico Ruling Tarnishes Their Attractiveness," *Business Insurance,* 10 October 1983, p. 51.
6. For a brief review of such cases, see the references cited in the two immediately preceding footnotes.
7. *Glossary of Reinsurance Terms,* Washington: Reinsurance Association of America, 1976, p. 5.
8. "Reinsurance Underwriting: Compiled by the Reinsurance Association of America," *International Insurance Monitor,* September 1983, pp. 4-5.
9. William J. Langler, *The Business of Reinsurance,* (Hartford: Northeastern Insurance Company of Hartford, 1954), pp. 181-182.
10. *Reinsurance and Reassurance* (New York: Munich Reinsurance Company, 1965), Vol. 5, p. 107.
11. William J. Langler, p. 241.
12. William J. Langler, p. 164.
13. Richard D. McClure, *A Review of Nuclear Energy Insurance,* a paper presented before the Casualty Actuarial Society at Washington, D.C., in November 1968.

CHAPTER 8

The Reinsurance Transaction

MAJOR CONSIDERATIONS

The reinsurance transaction may be conducted along a number of routes, depending on the nature of the ceding company and the reinsurer, the kind of reinsurance concerned, and other factors. This section will discuss in general terms some of the considerations in the negotiation of reinsurance agreements.

Of course, the first step in negotiation of any contract is for the parties to get together. In reinsurance transactions, the parties may be brought together in two ways. First, one party may approach the other directly, without the involvement of an intermediary. In most cases of this kind, an employee of the reinsurer makes the first approach to the primary insurer, though an approach from the opposite direction is not uncommon. The second method of bringing the parties together is through the efforts of a reinsurance broker, or as it frequently is called, a reinsurance intermediary.

Use of Reinsurance Brokers

The function of a reinsurance broker is essentially the same as that of any other broker: to act as an intermediary to bring together two potential contracting parties and to assist them in reaching agreement on the terms of the contract. The broker, in this case, is compensated for these efforts through a commission paid by the reinsurer. The percentage commission may be small in comparison with the commission rates paid to primary insurance brokers, frequently as low as 1 percent of the reinsurance premium. However, the premiums often are very large, so that the dollar amount of commission also may be quite large.

Unlike primary insurance brokers, reinsurance brokers are not required to be licensed in most states, nor are they required by law to demonstrate any special aptitude or skill in their chosen field. The principal purpose in licensing primary insurance brokers, at least in theory, is to protect the public against being victimized by dishonest or incompetent brokers. Since reinsurance brokers deal only with insurers, this protection has not been deemed necessary in their case. There has been some discussion of licensing reinsurance brokers as the result of the much publicized failure of a large brokerage firm during the mid-seventies. It should be noted that many reinsurance brokers are also excess and surplus lines brokers and must be licensed to write those lines.

New York requires licensing of reinsurance intermediaries, and makes them subject to examination by the superintendent of insurance. Regulation 98, adopted by the New York Superintendent of Insurance, establishes the regulatory pattern for that state. It provides that:

1. Reinsurance intermediaries act in a fiduciary capacity for all funds received in their professional capacity and must not mingle them with other funds without the consent of the insurers and reinsurers they represent;
2. Reinsurance intermediaries shall have written authorization from the insurers and reinsurers they represent, spelling out the extent and limitations of their authority;
3. The written authority above must be made available to ceding or assuming companies with which the intermediary deals;
4. No licensed intermediary shall procure reinsurance in an unlicensed reinsurer unless the reinsurer has appointed an agent for the service of process in New York;
5. The intermediary must make full written disclosure of
   (a) any control over the intermediary by a reinsurer,
   (b) any control of a reinsurer by the intermediary,
   (c) any retrocessions placed by the intermediary, and
   (d) commissions earned or to be earned on the business.
6. Records of all transactions must be retained for at least ten years after the expiration of all reinsurance contracts.

The foregoing requirements do not apply to managers of reinsurance pools, syndicates, or associations, or to managers of syndicates at the New York Insurance Exchange.

Should a primary insurer use a broker in the negotiation of its reinsurance program even though most large reinsurers are willing to deal directly? The question has been asked on many occasions, but there still is no one answer applicable to all cases. It depends on the needs and circumstances of the particular insurer.

If the primary insurer is well staffed with people who are

thoroughly familiar with reinsurance markets, capable of designing its reinsurance program, and negotiating its reinsurance contracts, it does not need a broker. Consequently, it may be able to negotiate a slightly lower reinsurance cost because of the absence of a brokerage commission.

However, many insurers, especially the small- and medium-sized ones, do not have the skilled personnel needed to manage their reinsurance affairs effectively. They must rely on some outside person for advice. That person could be a consultant or an employee of a reinsurer, but frequently it is a broker.

A broker handles the reinsurance needs of several, or perhaps many, insurers. This exposure to a variety of problems enables brokerage personnel to develop considerable expertise in handling reinsurance problems. This expertise, when coupled with a knowledge of available reinsurance markets and access to such markets, can make a reinsurance intermediary a very valuable ally for the negotiation of a reinsurance program.

Brokers may have one other advantage. Some reinsurers may not be staffed to deal directly with potential buyers of reinsurance. This is particularly likely with respect to small professional reinsurers and primary insurers with limited reinsurance operations. A broker may be the only practical means of access to such reinsurers, either through a pool managed by the brokerage firm or through individual negotiation.

Precise figures are not available to show the proportion of U.S. reinsurance handled by intermediaries. One estimate places the market share of all intermediaries combined at approximately 75 percent of U.S. reinsurance premiums.[1] Most of the reinsurance premiums controlled by intermediaries are for treaty reinsurance. Many intermediaries prefer not to handle facultative covers because of the large amount of effort and paperwork involved in that phase of the reinsurance business.

Historically, reinsurance intermediaries were small, independent business firms, controlled by one or a few individuals. Most recently, the trend has been to larger intermediaries controlled by even larger direct brokerage firms or insurance companies. Of the ten largest U.S. reinsurance intermediaries, five are controlled by large direct brokerage firms, and one is controlled by an insurance company group.[2]

It is not always clear whether the reinsurance intermediary is a representative of the ceding company or the reinsurer. The question is more than academic, since it may determine, among other things, whether or not a reinsurance contract is void because of misrepresentation or concealment.

For example, the ceding company may make full disclosure to the intermediary, but the intermediary may fail to transmit some material fact to the reinsurer. In this situation, if the intermediary is the agent of the ceding company, the treaty might be voidable at the option of the reinsurer for concealment. If the intermediary is the agent of the reinsurer, the treaty would not be voidable because the reinsurer would be charged with the knowledge of the intermediary. Consequently, there would not be any concealment.

In most cases, the courts have held that intermediaries are agents of the ceding company. However, the intermediary may become the agent of the reinsurer either by specific contractual agreement to that effect or by actions of the reinsurer that lead the ceding company to believe that the intermediary is the agent of the reinsurer.[3]

Reinsurance Commissions

Two kinds of commissions may be involved in reinsurance transactions: (1) ceding commissions paid by the reinsurer to the ceding company and (2) brokerage commissions paid by the reinsurer to the intermediary. Ceding commissions are intended to reimburse the ceding company for the expenses it incurred in selling and servicing the business ceded to the reinsurer. Such commissions are common under pro-rata treaties but not under excess treaties. The ceding commission is subject to negotiation between the parties, and usually depends upon (1) the actual expenses of the ceding company (including acquisition costs and extraordinary administrative, EDP, and accounting costs), (2) the reinsurer's estimate of the premium volume and loss experience expected under the treaty, and (3) the competitive state of the reinsurance market at the time the treaty is being negotiated. Treaties frequently provide for a retrospective adjustment of the ceding commission if the actual loss ratio under the treaty varies substantially from the expected loss ratio.

Brokerage commissions vary but a typical commission scale might be 1 percent to 2 percent on pro-rata treaties and 5 percent to 10 percent on excess treaties. The higher commission percentage on excess treaties reflects the fact that they produce lower premiums while requiring substantially the same amount of effort on the part of the broker. Thus a higher percentage commission is needed in order to provide the same dollar remuneration.

Information Needed

The information required in reinsurance negotiations varies with the kind of reinsurance arrangement under negotiation. In treaty negotiation, the reinsurer is interested primarily in information concerning the operations of the ceding company. Little or no attention is given to individual loss exposures insured other than product mix and geographical spread. In negotiations for facultative cessions, the reinsurer is interested primarily in the details of the individual loss exposure and only secondarily in the general operations of the ceding company. Of course, if the subject of negotiation is an obligatory facultative treaty, the information needed would be essentially the same as any other treaty. However, the reinsurer might underwrite the ceding company even more carefully because of the greater opportunity for adverse selection under an obligatory facultative treaty.

As noted, the reinsurer's principal considerations in underwriting a treaty are the management characteristics, underwriting policies, underwriting results, and financial conditions of the ceding company. The integrity of the ceding company's management is a primary consideration. There are numerous opportunities for fraud in the administration of a reinsurance treaty, and a substantial amount of fraud could be perpetrated by the ceding company with a limited chance of detection, as has been demonstrated by some actual cases.

However, the reinsurer is interested in more than just honesty. It is also interested in the demonstrated capability and stability management and the experience and capabilities of the underwriting staff. Reinsurance treaties are intended to be long-term arrangements. Consequently, the reinsurer is concerned with the possibility of a change in management personnel or a change in management objectives or both.

A reinsurer is also concerned with the financial strength of the ceding company. The insolvency of a ceding company normally does not increase the liability of the reinsurer, but it does complicate the administration of a treaty and it would often involve the loss of part of the reinsurer's premium corresponding to the liabilities accepted. The reinsurer's role may get especially complicated if many cut-through endorsements are outstanding, since the reinsurer may be required to adjust losses under such endorsements directly with the original insured. If local courts permit, the reinsurer will offset net premiums due against claims payable. Otherwise, the reinsurer is just another general creditor of the insolvent ceding company. Also as noted above, reinsurance treaties usually are considered to be long-term relationships, and the insolvency of the ceding company is hardly consistent with that concept.

The reinsurer would be especially interested in the solvency of the ceding company if the treaty provides for payment of premiums as earned rather than as written, or if the treaty permits the ceding company to hold funds of the reinsurer so the ceding company can take credit for the reinsurance in calculating its unearned premium or loss reserves. The latter provision is fairly common if the reinsurer is unlicensed in the ceding company's state of domicile. Of course, the ceding company is also quite interested in the financial strength of the reinsurer, for reasons that are obvious.

Perhaps the most important considerations are the underwriting policies and underwriting results of the ceding company. A number of factors would be considered in assessing underwriting policy:

1. What classes of business is the ceding company writing?
2. Is it writing primarily personal lines, small mercantile, industrial, or others?
3. What is its geographic area of operation?
4. Are the ceding company's underwriting guidelines (e.g., acceptable, prohibitive, and submit for approval lists) satisfactory?
5. Are its gross line limits and net line limits satisfactory?
6. Are the ceding company's loss control and loss adjustment practices adequate for the classes of business written?
7. Have the ceding company's underwriting results been satisfactory in the lines covered by the proposed reinsurance treaty?
8. Does the ceding company anticipate any substantial changes in its management, marketing, or underwriting practices?

The existence of other reinsurance and the terms of other reinsurance would also be important considerations. In property insurance, for example, the pro-rata reinsurers would be interested in the terms of any catastrophe treaty. Is it written only for the interest of the ceding company or does it apply to the interest of pro-rata reinsurers as well?

Of course, the reinsurer would also be interested in the ceding company's loss experience over the most recent several years. Loss ratio is especially important in connection with a pro-rata treaty because it is used for underwriting selection, rating, and setting commission terms. The reinsurer will be interested not only in the level of the loss ratio, but also in its stability, or lack thereof, over time.

For a per risk excess treaty, one additional bit of information will be needed. A distribution of losses by size will be needed for the establishment of the ceding company's retention and the reinsurance premium. A distribution of amounts of insurance by size may also be required.

The discussion up to this point has concentrated on the information the reinsurer is likely to require from the ceding company. However, reinsurance negotiations are two sided in most cases. That is, the ceding company is also interested in obtaining information about the reinsurer. However, the information needed by the ceding company is less detailed and is approximately the same as that needed by any consumer in purchasing insurance. Is the reinsurer financially sound and well managed? Are its claims practices satisfactory? Can it offer the services needed by the ceding company? Are its rates competitive? Is it licensed in the ceding company's state of domicile, or can it make other arrangements so that the ceding company can take credit for the reinsurance in calculating its unearned premium and loss reserves?

Role of the Ceding Company

After the reinsurance agreement has been negotiated and has become effective, the reinsurer is heavily dependent upon the capabilities, good faith, and good luck of the ceding company. The ceding company is obligated to conduct its underwriting and loss adjustment operations in the manner contemplated by both parties when the reinsurance was negotiated or to notify the reinsurer of any substantial changes.

Within the contemplated policies, the ceding company is free to exercise its best judgment in underwriting individual cases or adjusting individual claims, and the reinsurer is bound by the ceding company's actions in such matters. In the words common to reinsurance, the reinsurer "follows the fortunes" of the ceding company. Reinsurers generally even honor so-called *ex gratia* claim payments, those made by the ceding company in the absence of legal liability because of good will or other business considerations. However, the courts have held that reinsurers are not legally required to share in *ex gratia* payments unless the reinsurance contract specifically provides coverage for them.

The treaty may require the ceding company to notify the reinsurer promptly upon receiving notice of a large loss, and the reinsurer may reserve the right to associate itself in the investigation or defense of such claims. However, such right is exercised only in unusual circumstances which are becoming more frequent.

The ceding company is required to report premiums and losses, and perhaps other data, to the reinsurer by bordereaux or by such other means as may be specified in the treaty. It may also be required to make its books and records available to the reinsurer at reasonable times and places so the reinsurer can verify the reported data.

Traditionally, reinsurance treaties were considered "gentlemen's agreements" and contracts of utmost good faith. Disputes were to be settled by negotiation and arbitration, rather than by legal action. Unfortunately, these concepts have been somewhat weakened by the pressures and practices of recent years.

Role of the Reinsurer

As noted above, the reinsurer follows the fortunes of the ceding company. Under a smoothly functioning treaty relationship, the reinsurer's duties, other than collecting premiums and paying claims, are minimal. Many reinsurers prefer to write excess treaties with very high retentions, so that even the claim function is minimal.

Of course, this oversimplification understates the functions of the reinsurer to some degree. While it ordinarily does not become involved in the underwriting of individual insureds or the adjustment of individual losses, the reinsurer must track the underwriting and claims practices of the ceding company to be sure they are being conducted as anticipated. Large, individual losses may be examined partly as a verification that proper adjustment and reserving practices were followed and partly to extract whatever underwriting implications they may provide. The reinsurer may also be consulted by the ceding company on individual underwriting or claims problems, though this seems to be less common in property and liability insurance than in life insurance.

There has been a substantial amount of litigation concerning the obligation of the reinsurer to share in punitive damage judgments or judgments for bad faith against the ceding company arising out of the ceding company's handling of claims covered under the reinsurance contract. In most cases, the courts have held that the reinsurer is not liable for such judgments because they did not arise from the reinsured policy but from errors or unfair practices of the ceding company. However, bad faith judgments have been held to be covered in a few cases because of the wording of the specific reinsurance contract.[4]

Certificates of Reinsurance

A facultative reinsurance transaction is evidenced through the issuance of a certificate of reinsurance by the reinsurer. Under a pro-rata facultative cession, the reinsurance follows the form of the original insurance policy. As in any other pro-rata reinsurance transaction, the reinsurer accepts a fixed share of the coverage, gets the same share of the premium, and pays the same share of the losses.

After the reinsurance is agreed to, the ceding company must notify the facultative reinsurer of any change in the underlying policy. The reinsurance agreement itself can be canceled by either party, but cancellation usually requires five or ten days' advance notice.

Claim Settlement

The adjustment of claims under the ceding company's contracts with its policyholders is left to the judgment of the ceding company in the vast majority of cases. Reinsurance contracts usually permit the reinsurer to participate in the adjustment of direct claims which may result in reinsurance claims, but that right is exercised very infrequently.

Adjustment of claims by the ceding company against the reinsurer may vary from one agreement to another and by type of treaty. Under a pro-rata treaty, the ceding company may be required to file a monthly bordereau showing premiums due to the reinsurer and claims due from the reinsurer. If the premiums exceed the losses, the ceding company remits the difference. If the losses exceed the premiums, the reinsurer remits the difference. Exceptionally large individual losses might well be paid individually before the end of the reporting period as a convenience to the ceding company.

Losses under a working level per risk excess treaty probably would be handled in the same manner outlined above for pro-rata treaties. Catastrophe excess treaties would not come into play until the accumulated losses exceed the retention. At that point, the ceding company would begin presenting claims to the reinsurer as soon as they have been paid by the ceding company. The reinsurer usually is obligated to make payment to the ceding company as soon as reasonable proof of loss has been received. Proof of loss is often simply a statement of total claims paid, and as additional information, the reinsurer would want reserve estimates.

Stop loss treaties usually provide for an initial payment a short time, perhaps sixty days, after the end of the year. If the ceding company's loss ratio has not been determined finally at that time, a subsequent adjustment may be made. Although there usually is no contractual requirement for it, it is likely that most reinsurers would begin to make initial payments before the end of the year if it becomes clear that the ceding company's loss ratio will exceed the retention.

Loss Experience in Reinsurance

Under excess treaties and facultative reinsurance, there is no necessary relationship between the loss experience of primary insurers and reinsurers. In times of rapid inflation, excess reinsurers are likely to have poorer underwriting experience than the ceding companies. The poorer experience results from two factors. First, the excess reinsurer covers the top of the large losses, where inflation comes into play, while the primary insurer's payment is limited by the agreed retention.

Second, inflation pushes more of the smaller losses over the retention amount, resulting in payment by the reinsurer. Of course, fluctuations in the number and size of catastrophes also affect the loss experience of reinsurers.

Consequently, the loss experience of reinsurers, as a whole, may be better or worse than the experience of primary insurers in any given year. The annual reinsurance issue of *National Underwriter* shows the following combined ratios (loss ratio plus expense ratio) for U.S. professional reinsurers:

Year	Combined Ratio All Lines of Property and Liability Insurance	Combined Ratio U.S. Professional Reinsurers
1968	99.7	100.0
1969	100.6	99.0
1970	98.6	97.9
1971	94.9	95.9
1972	94.5	97.4
1973	97.5	99.5
1974	104.1	109.6
1975	106.7	109.9
1976	101.4	101.2
1977	96.2	99.7
1978	96.1	99.5
1979	99.1	103.0
1980	101.4	104.7
1981	104.2	105.6
1982	107.7	109.5

Of course, combined ratios of individual companies varied rather widely from the averages shown above. The averages seem to follow the primary insurer experience reasonably closely, though they are usually slightly higher. For the five years ending in 1982, the average combined ratio for the professional reinsurers was 104.5 as compared to a combined ratio of 101.7 for the entire industry.

A REINSURANCE PROGRAM FOR AN INSURER

It is evident from the preceding discussion that there are many kinds of reinsurance, each designed to serve a specific purpose. Each insurer must select that combination of contracts which best provides the protection and assistance it needs.

Systematic Plan

It may be possible for an insurer to meet all of its reinsurance needs with a single form of reinsurance contract, but it is far more common to have a combination of two or more forms. The combination is not likely to be exactly the same for any two insurers, since it depends on the coverages written, the territory, the financial resources of the ceding company, the attitude of management toward uncertainty, and perhaps other factors. Each insurer must shape its own reinsurance program in a systematic way after considering all relevant factors.

An insurer with limited financial resources may be interested primarily in the financial assistance it can obtain through pro-rata reinsurance, especially quota share. However, a quota share treaty may not provide the needed assurance of loss ratio stability, since the ceding company's dollar retention varies with the amount of insurance. Consequently, it may be desirable to supplement the quota share treaty with a per risk excess treaty applicable to the part of each loss retained under the quota share treaty. Of course, both the excess reinsurer and the pro-rata reinsurer would need to know of the existence of the other treaty. Also, if the ceding company is a property insurer, it most likely would need a catastrophe treaty to absorb the loss fluctuations resulting from hurricanes, tornadoes, earthquakes, and other catastrophes.

Of course, these various treaties cannot be purchased independently without consideration of the way they interact at the time of loss. For example, does the catastrophe treaty apply only to the primary insurer's retention under its other treaties, or does it apply to the direct loss, before the application of other treaties? Does the per risk excess apply before or after the quota share treaty? Treaties can be written to apply in almost any order acceptable to the ceding company and the reinsurers, but the method must be agreed upon in advance for two reasons. First, the order of payment will determine the rating of the treaties. Quite obviously, a per risk excess treaty that applies to the direct loss will cost more than one that applies to the net loss after quota share reinsurance, all other things being equal. Second, prior agreement is necessary so that the same order of payment can be specified in all of the treaties. Of course, this is less of a problem if all of the treaties are written by a single reinsurer, but this is not the usual case.

If the primary insurer is strongly financed and does not need the financial aid of pro-rata reinsurance, it probably should rely on excess treaties, possibly supplemented by facultative cessions, to provide the needed large lines capacity and loss stability. Excess treaties serve these purposes whle minimizing the amount of presumably profitable premium volume ceded to reinsurers.

At first glance, it would appear that a stop loss (or excess of loss ratio) treaty would be the only kind of treaty needed by a primary insurer that did not need the surplus relief provided by pro-rata reinsurance. However, this is seldom the case. In the first place, the stop loss treaty may cover only 90 percent of losses in excess of the retention, and the retention normally is set at a point above the ceding company's break-even point. These two conditions combined can result in a substantial underwriting loss for the ceding company.

Second, the stop loss reinsurer may insist, as a condition of providing the stop loss treaty, that the ceding company purchase a catastrophe treaty to protect both the ceding company and the stop loss reinsurer. In some cases, the stop loss reinsurer has also insisted upon the purchase of a per risk excess treaty. Of course, the rates for the stop loss treaty would reflect the existence or absence of other reinsurance written to benefit the stop loss reinsurer as well as the ceding company.

Finally, the ceding company may prefer to place most of its reliance on per risk excess because of the difference in the timing of reinsurance loss payments. Stop loss treaties usually provide for payment by the reinsurer at some time after the end of the contract year when all or nearly all losses have been reported. A per risk excess treaty, on the other hand, provides for payment as soon as the amount of the individual loss can be determined accurately. This difference is important to any ceding company, but it may be crucial to an insurer with limited financial resources.

Some large insurers may rely on a combination of a catastrophe treaty and a *spread loss treaty* for their property insurance portfolio. Of course, the catastrophe treaty would be unnecessary for most liability lines or for other lines without a catastrophe exposure. A per risk excess treaty, not on a spread loss basis, might be superimposed on the spread loss treaty to protect against large individual losses, and facultative cessions might be used for unusually large or hazardous loss exposures.

A *spread loss treaty* usually is a working level per risk excess treaty. That is, its retention usually is sufficiently low so that there is some frequency of losses. Frequency of losses, but not extreme severity, is desirable because of the rating method used. The premium for a spread loss treaty is determined by adding an expense loading to the average annual amount of losses that would have been paid under the treaty if it had been in effect for some specified number of years in the past, usually five years. Specified minimum and maximum premiums prevent extreme fluctuations in reinsurance costs. Rate stability requires that the retention under a spread loss treaty be low enough so that there is some frequency of loss and that the reinsurance limit be low enough so that the rates will not fluctuate too widely because of one or a small number of large individual losses.

As can be seen from the foregoing discussion, there is no single standard reinsurance program which will be satisfactory for all insurers or even for any substantial number of insurers. Each insurer must design its own reinsurance program, carefully balancing desired protection against reinsurance costs.

Cost of Reinsurance

The cost of reinsurance may not be easy to determine in advance. The cost is not, of course, simply the premium paid to the reinsurer. Several other factors must be considered. One of the major factors to be considered is the losses recovered or to be recovered under the reinsurance agreement. The losses are an especially important factor under a pro-rata treaty or a working level excess for which substantial loss recoveries are anticipated.

Of course, a ceding company is expected to pay its own losses and the reinsurer's expenses and profit under any treaty if the treaty is continued over a sufficiently long period of time. Consequently, the amount included in the premium for the reinsurer's expenses and profit becomes an important factor in assessing the cost of reinsurance.

Reinsurance transfers some loss reserves and unearned premium reserves from the ceding company to the reinsurer. Since the assets offsetting these reserves are invested, this transfer results in some loss of investment income to the ceding company. The loss of investment income is likely to be greater under a pro-rata treaty than under an excess treaty because the reinsurance premium for a pro-rata treaty usually is greater. However, some investment income is lost in either case, and the lost income is an additional cost of reinsurance.

The cost to the ceding company of administering the reinsurance program must also be considered. Facultative reinsurance is especially expensive to administer because each reinsurance transaction must be negotiated individually. Pro-rata treaties, especially surplus share, generally are more expensive to administer than excess treaties because of the more detailed record keeping and the greater frequency of reinsurance claims. In any case, the cost of administering the program must be considered in comparing reinsurance costs.

Finally, one additional factor must be considered in reciprocal reinsurance. The business accepted may be less profitable (or more unprofitable) than the business ceded. If so, the difference must be added to the cost of reinsurance. Of course, the relationship could be reversed, resulting in a reduction in the cost of reinsurance.

Setting Retentions

Although some actuaries have experimented with mathematical methods for establishing reinsurance retentions, those methods have not been generally accepted. The setting of retentions is still more of an art than an exact science. However, some general considerations can be mentioned.

It is apparent that the method of setting retentions will vary with the kind of treaty as well as other factors. The reasons for buying a pro-rata treaty differ from the reasons for buying an excess treaty, and so the factors considered in setting the retention also differ.

The principal reason for choosing a pro-rata treaty in preference to an excess treaty is to aid the policyholders' surplus. Consequently, the amount of policyholders' surplus aid needed must be an important factor in the selection of the retention. The amount of policyholders' surplus aid received will be a function of the percentage of premiums ceded and the percentage ceding commission received. Exhibits 7-1 and 7-2 illustrating the effect of pro-rata reinsurance on policyholders' surplus indicate the general method of making such calculations.

The principal purposes of excess treaties are to stabilize loss experience and to provide large line capacity. Providing large line capacity is a function of the treaty limit, rather than the retention. Therefore, the principal consideration in setting the retention of a per risk excess treaty is the size of loss which can be absorbed by the ceding company without undue effect on the policyholders' surplus or the loss ratio for the line or lines covered by the treaty. That amount is, in turn, a function of the premium volume and the policyholders' surplus of the ceding company.

There is a statutory provision in most states which puts an upper limit on an insurer's retention under its reinsurance treaties. That provision usually states that an insurer cannot retain net for its own account an amount on any one loss exposure in excess of 10 percent of the insurer's surplus to policyholders. Thus, if an insurer has surplus to policyholders of $10 million, its legal maximum net retention for any one loss exposure would be $1 million. However, it should be noted that very few, if any, insurers retain an amount near the legal maximum.

One of the principal purposes of excess reinsurance is to stabilize loss experience. It seems logical, therefore, that the ceding company should retain that part of its aggregate losses which is reasonably stable and predictable and should cede that part which is not reasonably stable and predictable. However, that simple statement raises two complex questions. First, what is meant by "reasonably stable and predictable"? Second, given criteria for "reasonably stable and predictable," how does one determine what portion of aggregate losses meets the criteria?

Managers of insurers will differ in their criteria for what is reasonably stable and predictable. However, some general rules can be given. Losses can be said to be reasonably stable and predictable if the maximum probable variation is not likely to affect the insurer's loss ratio or surplus to an extent unacceptable to management.

For example, the management of one insurer might conclude that they could accept a maximum variation of 3 percentage points in the loss ratio and 9 percent in surplus to policyholders due to chance variation in losses during the year. Another insurer with less surplus or less venturesome management might decide that it could risk only 2 percentage points of the loss ratio and 4 percent of surplus to policyholders. All other things being equal, it is apparent that the second insurer would elect a lower retention. Of course, the selection of a retention requires a balancing of the desirability of stability against the undesirability of high reinsurance costs. Lowering the retention tends to increase stability, but it also tends to increase reinsurance costs.

Based on the foregoing considerations, two methods have been used to select the retention level under an excess treaty. Both assume that the ceding company should retain losses within the size category in which there is sufficient frequency for reasonable predictability. Consequently, both methods require an analysis of a loss-size distribution, such as that shown in Exhibit 8-1, but the method of analysis differs somewhat. The losses in Exhibit 8-1 have been adjusted for inflation from the date of occurrence to the midpoint of the period for which the treaty will be effect.

The simpler of the two methods is to examine a table such as Exhibit 8-1 for the point at which there seems to be a sudden change in the frequency trend. For example, in Exhibit 8-1 the frequency of each size bracket is approximately one-half of the next lower bracket for losses up to $20,000. However, the frequency for the $20,001 to $25,000 bracket is only one-third of the next lower bracket. Consequently, a retention of $20,000 might be selected. A retention of $20,000 would include 97 percent of the number of claims and 94 percent of the dollar amount of losses (all of the losses up to $20,000 plus the first $20,000 of each loss in excess of $20,000).

Alternatively, management might prefer a retention of $15,000 at which a smaller break in the trend occurs. That retention would include 91 percent of the losses by number and 89.6 percent by amount.

The second method of setting the retention under an excess treaty

Exhibit 8-1

Distribution of Losses by Size for Last Ten Years—Adjusted for Inflation

| Loss Size | Losses | | Percentage of | |
	Number	Total Amount	Number	Amount
$ 1— 5,000	11,381	$ 23,774,909	48%	14.4%
5,001—10,000	6,639	48,033,165	28	29.2
10,001—15,000	3,557	43,804,455	15	26.6
15,001—20,000	1,423	24,664,859	6	15.0
20,001—25,000	474	10,564,986	2	6.4
over 25,000	237	13,845,777	1	8.4
	23,711	$164,688,151	100%	100.0%

involves a determination of the largest loss for which underwriting results are acceptably stable. The first step is to restructure the loss distribution from Exhibit 8-1 into a new distribution as shown in Exhibit 8-2. This table shows the losses by size for each of the last ten years, but instead of showing the number or dollar amount of losses, it shows them as loss ratios. That is, the dollar amount of losses in each bracket has been divided by the earned premium for the year. Of course, the premiums and losses must be adjusted to reflect rate changes and inflation, respectively, before the loss ratios are calculated.

The retention is set at the upper limit of the highest loss size class for which the variation in loss ratio is acceptable to management. In Exhibit 8-2, the statistics probably would indicate a retention of either $15,000 or $20,000, depending on the amount of variation management is willing to accept. In the $15,001 to $20,000 bracket, the difference between the worst year and the best year is 7.9 percentage points of loss ratio, or about 84 percent of the mean loss ratio for that bracket for the ten-year period. In the $20,001 to $25,000 bracket, the difference between the best year and the worst year is 8.7 percentage points of loss ratio, or approximately 229 percent of the mean loss ratio for that bracket for the ten-year period.

In this hypothetical illustration, both methods resulted in the same retention, depending on the choice between the two possible retentions in the second method. They would not necessarily be in such close agreement in actual practice.

The first step in setting the retention for a catastrophe treaty is the same as for a per risk excess treaty. That is, management must decide how much policyholders' surplus and how many points of loss ratio can

Exhibit 8-2
Loss Ratios by Loss Size for Last Ten Years—Adjusted for Rate Changes and Inflation

Loss Size	Loss Ratios by Year										
	1	2	3	4	5	6	7	8	9	10	Mean
$ 1– 5,000	8.6%	8.4%	8.8%	8.7%	8.9%	9.0%	8.8%	8.5%	8.5%	8.8%	8.7%
5,001–10,000	16.9	17.4	17.4	17.6	17.0	18.1	18.3	17.1	17.3	17.9	17.5
10,001–15,000	15.0	16.1	16.3	16.9	17.3	14.8	16.0	16.3	15.2	16.1	16.0
15,001–20,000	8.4	9.7	9.3	5.8	10.8	13.4	12.1	6.0	5.5	9.0	9.0
20,001–25,000	1.3	3.5	4.6	5.4	2.1	2.9	1.1	1.0	9.7	6.4	3.8
over 25,000	6.3	4.9	9.8	7.3	8.1	1.0	4.1	5.7	2.1	0.7	5.0
Totals	56.5%	60.0%	66.2%	61.7%	64.2%	59.2%	60.4%	54.6%	58.3%	58.9%	60.0%

be risked on one year's catastrophes. These must, of course, be translated into dollars.

The second step is to estimate the maximum number of catastrophes that might reasonably be expected to occur in one year. This number would depend, of course, on the line or lines of insurance concerned, the territory in which the company operates, and the concentration of insured properties within the territory. The retention per catastrophe would be found by dividing the number of dollars from the first step by the number of catastrophes from the second step.

Retention setting is easier under a stop loss treaty than under any other kind of reinsurance. Basically, the ceding company should select for its retention the lowest loss ratio (1) for which the reinsurance premium is affordable and (2) which is acceptable to the reinsurer. These two considerations almost inevitably result in a retention loss ratio somewhat higher than the ceding company's break-even loss ratio.

Most of this discussion of retention setting has ignored the cost of reinsurance and the role of the reinsurer in setting retentions. However, these factors cannot be overlooked in actual practice. Most ceding companies under excess treaties accept retentions higher than they would prefer, either to reduce reinsurance costs or because the reinsurer insists upon it.

Under surplus share treaties, the position of the reinsurer may be reversed. That is, the reinsurer may sometimes insist on a lower retention than the ceding company would prefer. Under a surplus share treaty, no reinsurance is ceded on properties for which the amount of insurance is less than the retention. Consequently, a very high retention would mean that the reinsurer would be excluded from participating in a large part of the ceding company's business. If the business below the retention is the most desirable part of the ceding company's portfolio, the reinsurer may insist on a lower retention to enable it to participate in that business.

If the ceding company carries several treaties which may cover the same loss, the retention under each of them should be set with due consideration for the relationships between them. For example, an insurer might have (1) a quota share treaty, (2) a per risk excess treaty, and (3) a catastrophe treaty. The retention under the catastrophe treaty should be higher if that treaty is written for the benefit of both the ceding company and quota share reinsurers than if written only for the benefit of the ceding company.

To illustrate the difference, assume that the retention under the quota share treaty is 25 percent and the retention under the catastrophe treaty is $1 million. Assume further that a catastrophe causes aggregate losses of $3 million under coverages reinsured under the treaty. If the catastrophe treaty is written for the benefit of the ceding company only, it will not pay any of the loss. The ceding company's portion of the losses would be 25 percent, or $750,000, which is less than the catastrophe retention.

If the catastrophe treaty is written for the benefit of the ceding company and quota share reinsurers, it would pay $2 million, assuming that the treaty limit is at least that high. The quota share reinsurer would then pay 75 percent of the remaining $1 million, leaving the ceding company with a net retention of only $250,000.

A similar analysis could be made for the per risk excess treaty and the quota share, or, for that matter, for all three of them. This is, of course, another indication that an insurer's reinsurance program should be a carefully integrated program and not merely a collection of treaties.

Setting Reinsurance Limits

Setting reinsurance limits is only slightly, if at all, less subjective than setting retentions. Pro-rata and per risk excess treaties, in whatever combination carried, should have sufficiently high limits to cover, in combination with the ceding company's retention, a substantial majority of the loss exposures insured by the ceding company. Exactly how large a majority will be covered will depend on cost considerations, since reinsurance costs can be expected to increase as the limit increases and the retention remains constant. This increased cost for a higher limit must be weighed against the premium, administrative expense, and inconvenience of facultative reinsurance for those exposures not fully covered by treaties.

Limit setting for a catastrophe treaty is even more subjective. The goal, of course, is to select a limit just adequate to cover the largest catastrophe that might reasonably be expected. The difficulty is in determining the potential amount of loss in the largest catastrophe likely to occur. The ceding company's past experience is not a statisfactory guide. Catastrophe losses are notoriously variable, and the largest catastrophe the company sustained in the past may not be the largest that is likely to occur in the future.

In addition, circumstances change. For example, the company may now be writing more business in a catastrophe-prone area than it wrote in the past.

Perhaps the best way to set the limit for a catastrophe treaty is through a careful analysis of the concentration of loss exposures. For example, a company that writes a large amount of extended coverage along the Gulf Coast might plot on a map the amounts of insurance written in various areas. It would then be possible to make a reasonable estimate of the resulting damage if a hurricane of maximum intensity should pass through the area of greatest concentration of business. Of course, the same could be done for floods, earthquakes, tornadoes, and similar disasters. The estimated maximum damage from any one catastrophe would be the desirable limit for the catastrophe treaty. However, cost considerations, or the unwillingness of reinsurers to provide that limit, might compel the acceptance of a lower limit.

The limit for a stop loss treaty should be set at an amount adequate to cover the highest loss ratio the ceding company might reasonably expect to sustain, provided the reinsurance premium for such a limit is affordable to the ceding company. Unfortunately, there is no reliable method of estimating accurately the highest loss ratio a company might expect to sustain. However, some general considerations can be given. First the variations in loss ratio is, in part, a function of the lines of insurance written. A property insurer can expect a greater variation in loss ratios than a liability insurer because of the catastrophe exposure in property insurance. Of course, the existence of a catastrophe treaty (in addition to the stop loss treaty) would lessen the variation from catastrophe.

The size of the insurer is another important determinant of loss ratio variability. All other things being equal, a smaller insurer (measured by premium volume) can expect more variation in loss ratio than a larger one. It would therefore need a higher treaty limit relative to its premium volume.

Perhaps the most important factor is geographical distribution of business. A company writing property classes in one-state territory is much more vulnerable to loss ratio fluctuation than one having a nationwide spread. Again, this is due to catastrophe possibilities.

In setting the limit for any kind of reinsurance, the interaction between all applicable treaties must be considered. For example, the limit for a stop loss treaty can be lower if adequate catastrophe reinsurance is carried than it would in the absence of such protection. Also, the limit of a catastrophe treaty can be lower if it applies only to the retention of the ceding company after recoveries from pro-rata reinsurance, rather than to the direct losses.

Reinsurance Pricing

As one might expect, pricing methods for reinsurance vary with the kind of reinsurance. Pricing methods also vary from one reinsurer to another, so it is not practical to discuss here all of the methods in use. Consequently, the discussion in this chapter will stress general principles rather than detailed calculations.

Pro-Rata Treaties For quota share and surplus share treaties, it is customary for the reinsurance rate to be the same as the rate used by the ceding company for the original policy. In other words, the pro-rata reinsurer usually charges a pro-rata part of the original premium, based on its pro-rata share of the amount of insurance. However, the ceding commission paid to the ceding company will vary according to the reinsurer's estimate of the loss ratio to be incurred and the premium ceded under the treaty.

For example, if the pro-rata reinsurer expects to incur a loss ratio of 60 percent under the treaty and is willing to accept 15 percent of the premium for expenses, profit, and contingencies, it would pay a ceding commission of 25 percent of reinsurance premiums. On the other hand, if it expected a loss ratio of only 50 percent with the same allowance for expenses, profit, and contingencies, it would allow a ceding commission of 35 percent.

Retrospective (or profit sharing or sliding scale) commission arrangements are quite common. Under such an arrangement, the ceding commission varies with the actual loss ratio incurred under the treaty. For example, in the first illustration given in the foregoing paragraph the treaty might provide for a provisional commission of 35 percent, to be adjusted after the end of the year according to the commission rates and loss ratios shown in Exhibit 8-3. Thus, if the actual loss ratio for the year is 50 percent, instead of the expected 60 percent, the ceding company would receive an additional 5 percent ceding commission. In effect, the retrospective commission scale in Exhibit 8-3 shares the unexpected profit approximately equally between the ceding company and the reinsurer.

The reinsurer's estimate of the loss ratio to be incurred usually is based primarily on the past experience of the ceding company. However, that experience may be adjusted for industry trends, changes in the ceding company's underwriting practices, and other factors the reinsurer considers relevant.

Per Risk Excess Treaties The rate-making procedure for per risk excess treaties is somewhat more complicated than that for pro-rata treaties. The first step is to estimate the losses which will be paid under the treaty. The past losses under an excess treaty are sometimes referred to as *burning cost*. The term burning cost originated in fire insurance, but it is used frequently with liability and other lines at the present time.

The beginning point for estimating burning cost is a distribution of losses by size such as that shown in Exhibit 8-1, which was used in the discussion of retentions. The data from Exhibit 8-1 must be restated as shown in Exhibit 8-4. Note that the losses in Exhibit 8-1 have been

Exhibit 8-3

Retrospective Ceding Commission (Sliding Commission) Scale— Pro Rata Reinsurance

Actual Loss Ratio	Commission Rate
60% or more	35%
59% but less than 60%	35.5
58% but less than 59%	36
57% but less than 58%	36.5
56% but less than 57%	37
55% but less than 56%	37.5
54% but less than 55%	38
53% but less than 54%	38.5
52% but less than 53%	39
51% but less than 52%	39.5
50% but less than 51%	40
less than 50%	41

adjusted for inflation to the midpoint of the treaty term and the premiums have been adjusted to anticipated rate levels for the same time.

The dollar amount of burning cost for any retention level is calculated as follows:

$$BC = T - A - N(R)$$

where BC = burning cost, T = total dollar losses, A = total dollar amount of all losses less than the retention, N = number of losses greater than the retention, and R = retention.

For example, the dollar amount burning cost for a retention of $5,000 is:

$$BC = \$164,688,151 - \$23,774,909 - 12,330(\$5,000)$$
$$= \$79,263,242$$

The *burning rate* in column (5) of Exhibit 8-4 is simply the burning cost divided by the premium volume for the period. Note that both the burning cost and the burning rate decline rapidly as the retention increases.

The rate, as a percentage of the ceding company's earned premium, would be calculated by (1) adding a loading for expenses and contingencies to the burning rate in Exhibit 8-4 and (2) making any

Exhibit 8-4
Burning Cost for Last Ten Years—Adjusted for Rate Changes and
Inflation

(1)	(2)	(3)	(4)	(5)
	Number of	Amount of Losses Less than		
	Losses Greater	or Equal to	Burning	Burning
Retention	Than Retention	Retention	Cost	Rate[1]
$ 0	23,711	$ 0	$164,688,151	60.0%
5,000	12,330	23,774,909	79,263,242	28.9
10,000	5,691	71,808,074	35,970,077	13.1
15,000	2,134	115,612,529	17,065,622	6.2
20,000	711	140,277,388	10,190,763	3.7
25,000	237	150,842,374	7,920,777	2.9
	Total Amount of Losses	$164,688,151		

[1]Based on a ten year premium volume of $274,480,252, after adjustment
to the anticipated rate level during the treaty period.

necessary adjustment to reflect the treaty limit. The burning rates shown in Exhibit 8-4 are for an unlimited treaty. However, burning rates for a treaty with both a retention and an upper limit can be determined from the table. For example, the burning rate for a treaty with a retention of $5,000 and a limit of $20,000 would be calculated by subtracting the burning rate for an unlimited treaty with a $25,000 retention from the burning rate for an unlimited treaty with a $5,000 retention. Thus, from Exhibit 8-4, the burning rate for such a treaty would be 26 percent, which is calculated by subtracting 2.9 percent from 28.9 percent.

The gross rate for the treaty in the foregoing paragraph would be calculated by adding a loading for expenses and contingencies. In reinsurance rating, the loading usually is added by multiplying the burning rate by a fraction, such as 100/80, in which the numerator is greater than the denominator. Using the burning rate of 26 percent from the preceding paragraph, the gross rate would then be 32.5 percent of the ceding company's earned premiums under the treaty.

Multiplying the burning cost by the fraction 100/80 is equivalent to dividing it by the expected loss ratio of 80 percent, the technique usually used in making rates for direct insurance. The reasons for and origin of the use of fractional loadings in reinsurance are lost in antiquity, but the practice is widespread if not universal.

Catastrophe Treaties In theory, the method of making rates for catastrophe treaties is the same as that for per risk excess treaties, except the loss distribution would show aggregate amounts per occurrence rather than for individual losses. In practice, reliable catastrophe data are not available on a company-by-company basis because of the large element of chance variation in catastrophic occurrences. Consequently, judgment plays a much larger role in the rating of catastrophe treaties than it does in per risk excess treaties. Of course, national, regional, and state catastrophe data are available and are used to the extent they are applicable. However, an individual insurer's catastrophe experience can be expected to differ from industry experience because of its geographic spread of business and the differing nature of insured exposures.

Stop Loss Treaties Theoretically, the premium for a stop loss treaty can be calculated from a probability distribution of loss ratios. In practice, that method is seldom, if ever, used because the nature of the probability distribution is not known. In any case, the mathematical manipulations involved in such a calculation are well beyond the scope of this text.

In practice, the premium for a stop loss treaty is likely to be based very largely on the judgment of the reinsurance underwriter. Of course, the underwriter will reinforce judgment with an analysis of the ceding company's loss ratios over the last several years, probably five or more. The class of business and territory of operation of the ceding company will be important factors, as will the magnitude of the retention and the treaty limit. Beyond these general statements, it is difficult to describe rate making for stop loss treaties in terms that are not both highly mathematical and highly theoretical.

Effect of Competition Reinsurance is a highly competitive business, both domestically and internationally. This competitiveness results, in part, from the ease of entry into the market. As noted earlier, reinsurers tend to be relatively small in comparison to direct insurers, so less capital is needed to start a reinsurer. This is especially true of reinsurers domiciled in some foreign areas, such as Bermuda.

Entry into the market is relatively easy for another reason. There are many reinsurance intermediaries and pools that are willing to accept a new reinsurer to write a small part of each reinsurance contract issued. Consequently, a new reinsurer does not need to invest large sums in building a marketing force.

In the United States, with one or two exceptions, a company's charter to write primary business also includes reinsurance for the same lines. Thus, little or no additional funds are required to start a reinsurer.

Finally, a new reinsurer needs only a minimal home office staff. Services to the insured are furnished by the direct insurer, and the reinsurer need not become involved in them except in very unusual circumstances. Even the reinsurer's claims department can be minimal, since the reinsurer must follow the fortunes of the ceding company in the vast majority of cases.

Because of this ease of entry, new reinsurers are formed frequently, and direct insurers move in and out of the reinsurance business as market conditions change. These changes in the market tend to unsettle reinsurance rates and cause fluctuations in the availability of reinsurance coverage.

When reinsurance is profitable, new reinsurers are formed and more direct insurers enter the market to sell reinsurance. These new reinsurers must offer some inducement to prospective ceding companies, and that inducement usually is price, either in the form of lower rates or higher ceding commissions, possibly coupled with higher commissions to intermediaries. Of course, the established reinsurers must meet the prices of their new competitors, and the result is lower profits, or possibly underwriting losses, and the resulting withdrawal of marginal reinsurers. The absence of rate regulation in reinsurance facilitates such cycles.

Effect of Inflation For pro-rata reinsurance, the effect of inflation is approximately the same as the effect on direct insurers. That effect is discussed in the chapters on rate making for direct insurance and need not be repeated here.

Excess reinsurers are affected by inflation to a substantially greater degree than pro-rata reinsurers. The effects are felt at both ends of the treaty: the retention and the reinsurance limit. The excess reinsurer covers the top part of the claims in excess of the retention, and, of course, as those claims increase from the inflation, the increase is at the top. If a fixed retention rather than a variable one is used, the inflationary increase in losses above the retention does not affect the ceding company's net loss.

If a fixed retention is used, the excess reinsurer also suffers at the lower end of the loss distribution. The inflationary increase in the smaller losses pushes more and more of them over the ceding company's retention, so the reinsurer must pay part of them.

Perhaps an illustration will help clarify these points. Assume that a ceding company, reinsured under an excess reinsurance treaty with a $100,000 retention, sustains two losses: one for $95,000 and one for $225,000. These losses would be divided as shown in Exhibit 8-5.

Now assume that two losses causing the same amount of actual physical damage as those above occurred two years later. Although the

Exhibit 8-5

Loss Allocation Between Ceding Company and Reinsurer

Loss	Amount	Amount Paid by Ceding Company	Amount Paid by Reinsurer
A	$ 95,000	$ 95,000	$ 0
B	225,000	100,000	125,000
	$320,000	$195,000	$125,000

Exhibit 8-6

Loss Allocation Between Ceding Company and Reinsurer
Showing the Effect of Inflation

Loss	Amount	Amount Paid by Ceding Company	Amount Paid by Reinsurer
C	$115,000	$100,000	$ 15,000
D	270,000	100,000	170,000
	$385,000	$200,000	$185,000

actual physical damage was the same, higher prices caused the cost of repairs to increase to $115,000 and $270,000 respectively. These two losses will be divided as shown in Exhibit 8-6.

The total loss has increased by $65,000 and the reinsurer's share has increased by $60,000, but the ceding company's share has increased by only $5,000. Of course, this simplified example overstates the relative effect somewhat, but it does illustrate the nature of the problem.

Reinsurers have attempted to combat this problem by adopting treaties, with *variable retentions*, sometimes called *indexed retentions*. Under such treaties, the amount of retention increases automatically with an increase in some price index, such as a construction cost index or a consumer price index. For example, in the illustration used above, prices seem to have increased approximately 20 percent, so the ceding company's retention would have increased from $100,000 to $120,000. The resulting division of losses would be as shown in Exhibit 8-7. Thus the inflationary increase has been spread more evenly between the ceding company and the reinsurers.

Inflation has a greater effect on loss reserves for reinsurance than

Exhibit 8-7
Loss Allocation Between Ceding Company and Reinsurer
Using Indexed Retentions

| | | Amount Paid by | |
Loss	Amount	Ceding Company	Reinsurer
C	$115,000	$115,000	$ 0
D	270,000	120,000	150,000
	$385,000	$235,000	$150,000

Exhibit 8-8
Comparison of Loss Development Rates for Direct Insurers and
Reinsurers—First and Fourth Years*

| | Reported Losses as a Percentage of Ultimate Incurred Losses | | | |
| | First Year | | Fourth Year | |
	Reinsurer	Direct	Reinsurer	Direct
Auto liability	35%	80%	80%	100%
General liability	10	45	40	85
Medical malpractice	5	40	25	80
Workers' compensation	20	70	50	95

*Reprinted with permission from *Loss Development Study: 1983 Edition* (Washington: Reinsurance Association of America, 1983), p. 15.

for direct insurance. The difference is especially large for excess reinsurance. This greater effect results from the slower payout of reinsurance losses. Exhibit 8-8 shows the percentage of ultimate incurred losses that have been paid or reserved by the end of the first and fourth year by direct insurers and reinsurers for specified lines of insurance.

There are two major reasons for the slower development of loss reserves for excess reinsurance. In many cases, the direct insurer may not report a loss to the reinsurer initially because its reserve is less than its retention under the reinsurance treaty. Later, when the reserve is increased above the retention, the loss is reported to the reinsurer. Also, the direct insurer's loss reserves are limited by its retention, so that a large increase in the reserve for an outstanding loss may have no effect or only a minor effect on the direct insurer's reserves (and incurred losses) while causing a substantial increase in the reinsurer's reserves. This increased effect of inflation greatly complicates the reinsurer's problems in the estimation of loss reserves, especially during periods of rapidly rising inflation.

IBNR also applies to reinsurers.

REGULATION OF REINSURANCE

Traditionally, reinsurance has been subject to very limited regulation. The principal purpose of insurance regulation is to protect insurance consumers from unfair practices of some insurers and from the insolvency of insurers. This protection was deemed necessary because of the unequal knowledge and bargaining power of insurers and insurance consumers. Since the reinsurance business is conducted between two insurance companies, the knowledge and bargaining power of the parties were deemed to be more equal, so that the protective shield of regulation was not considered necessary. There was also a fear that rigid regulation of U.S. reinsurers would limit their ability to compete with alien reinsurers, both here and abroad.

Another factor that reduced the need to regulate reinsurance was the nature of the market and the participants in the market. There were only a few reinsurers, and those were well financed firms with a long history of ethical and sound business dealings. The market situation has changed drastically in recent years. Many new firms, both reinsurers and intermediaries, have entered the market. It is quite evident that some of them were lacking in ethical standards, financial strength or both. The staid old world of reinsurance has been shaken by several scandals in the U.S., the United Kingdom, Panama, Bermuda, and other places. These scandals have brought about increased pressure for more detailed regulation of reinsurance. The New York regulation dealing with reinsurance intermediaries, mentioned earlier in this chapter, arose from one of these scandals—the insolvency of a reinsurance intermediary with large losses to both reinsurers and ceding companies.

The United Kingdom also tightened its regulation of reinsurance following several scandals there. A regulation adopted by the Department of Trade requires ceding companies to furnish a report to the Department each year showing:

1. the names and addresses of all reinsurers to which business has been ceded during the year;
2. any connection (other than the reported reinsurance) between the ceding company and any of its reinsurers;

3. the amount of premium payable to each reinsurer; and
4. any indebtedness of a reinsurer to the ceding company at the end of the year.[5]

With the exception of New York Regulation 98, there has been little change in the regulation of reinsurance in the United States. Many changes have been proposed, and some of the proposals are discussed later in this chapter. First, a brief review of the current regulatory pattern is in order.

Present Reinsurance Regulation

Reinsurers domiciled in the U.S. and alien reinsurers licensed in the U.S. are subject to the same solvency regulations as other insurers. They are required to file annual, and sometimes quarterly, financial statements with state regulatory authorities and adhere to state regulations regarding reserves, investments, and minimum capital and surplus requirements. They also must undergo periodic examination by the appropriate state authorities. However, these regulations cannot be applied to unlicensed alien reinsurers because they are not within the authority of state (or federal) regulatory bodies. There has been much concern in recent years about the possible insolvencies of unlicensed alien reinsurers, but there is little that our regulatory agencies can do to prevent such failures. Ceding insurers and intermediaries must rely on their own efforts to detect impending insolvencies of alien reinsurers. The solvency tests for reinsurers are the same as those applied to direct insurers. They are discussed at length in the CPCU 8 text (*Property-Liability Insurance Accounting and Finance*) and need not be repeated here.

Reinsurance rates are not regulated directly in this country. The regulation of direct insurer rates may have an indirect effect on reinsurance rates, however. The establishment of the ceding company's rates may place an effective ceiling on the amount it can pay for reinsurance.

Reinsurance contracts are regulated to only a slightly greater degree. Such contract regulation is aimed at the ceding company rather than the reinsurer, since many reinsurers are beyond the reach of our regulatory agencies.

Ceding insurers usually are anxious to be able to take credit against their unearned premium and loss reserves for premiums ceded to and losses recoverable from reinsurers. The availabililty of these credits reduces the drain on the ceding company's surplus from writing new business. Regulators motivate ceding companies to require some desirable provisions in their reinsurance contracts by withholding permission to take credit for the reinsurance unless it contains the specified clauses. Note that these provisons are not mandatory. A ceding company that is willing to forgo the reserve credits can enter into a reinsurance contract that does not include them.

The first clause to be required by this device was an insolvency clause. Before the insolvency clause was required, reinsurers sometimes escaped the payment of losses if the ceding company became insolvent. The required insolvency clause provides that the insolvency of the ceding company does not affect the liability of the reinsurer for losses under the receiver or liquidator of the insolvent ceding company reinsurance contract. The reinsurer makes payment to the for the benefit of the ceding company's creditors.

More recently, some states have required an intermediary clause in reinsurance contracts. This clause provides that the intermediary is the agent of the reinsurer for the collection of reinsurance premiums. Thus, the reinsurer assumes the risk of the intermediary being unable or unwilling to pay over to it all of the premiums collected under its reinsurance contracts. This clause is very beneficial to ceding companies because the courts have held in most cases that the intermediary is the agent of the ceding company. Consequently, in the absence of this clause, the risk of insolvency of the intermediary would fall most often upon the ceding company and not upon the reinsurer.

The regulatory authorities also use the leverage of reserve credits to limit the reinsurers with which a ceding company can deal. Some states permit the ceding company to take the reserve credits only if the reinsurer is licensed in the state. Others permit the credit if the reinsurer is licensed in any state of the United States. Finally, there are some states that permit the reserve credits even if the reinsurer is not licensed anywhere in the U.S., provided the ceding company obtains the permission of the state insurance department before entering into the contract.

Proposed Reinsurance Regulation

The present minimal regulation of reinsurance seems unlikely to continue. The National Association of Insurance Commissioners (NAIC) is developing a model reinsurance regulatory act which will be submitted to the various state legislatures for possible enactment.[6] The American Institute for Certified Public Accountants (AICPA) has promulgated guidelines for accountants to follow in auditing the reinsurance operations of either ceding companies or assuming reinsurers.[7] The Reinsurance Assocation of America (RAA) also has developed a model act. All three of these documents are intended to solve essentially the same problems and take essentially the same approach to the solutions.

The principal problems addressed by the proposed regulations are:

1. potential losses to ceding insurers and their policyholders resulting from the insolvency of alien reinsurers;
2. potential losses to ceding insurers and their policyholders resulting from the insolvency or fraudulent activities of reinsurance intermediaries;
3. the difficulties for U.S. ceding insurers in litigating disputed claims against alien reinsurers not licensed in the U.S., and
4. potential losses to stockholder and policyholders of ceding companies resulting from the fraudulent use of reinsurance by company management.

Since the RAA model act is representative of all of the new approaches to reinsurance regulation, it will be discussed in more detail here to illustrate the probable course of future regulation. Like current reinsurance regulations, the RAA model act uses the leverage of reinsurance reserve credits to motivate ceding insurers to require desirable provisions in their reinsurance contracts and to select reinsurers in sound financial condition.

The RAA model act provides that reserve credit will not be allowed for reinsurance unless the reinsurer meets one or more of the following conditions:

1. the reinsurer is licensed in the state concerned;
2. the reinsurer is licensed in another state of the United States and meets solvency tests similar to those required by the state concerned;
3. the reinsurer maintains a trust fund in the United States for the sole benefit of U.S. insureds, including ceding companies of at least $20 million for insurance companies and of $100 million for associations of individual insurers (such as Lloyd's); or
4. the ceding company holds assets of the reinsurer or an irrevocable letter of credit issued by a U.S. bank in an amount at least equal to the reserve credit.

In addition to the above, the reserve credits will not be allowed unless the reinsurance contract provides that:

1. the reinsurer will submit to the jurisdiction of U.S. courts and be bound by the decision of such courts in any dispute under the contract;
2. the state insurance commissioner is appointed the reinsurer's agent for the service of process; and

     3. the liability of the reinsurer for loss under the contract shall not be reduced by the insolvency of the ceding company.

The RAA model act also includes provisions to control the use of bulk reinsurance, in which an insurer cedes all or substantially all of its business to a reinsurer. Bulk reinsurance sometimes has been used to deprive the stockholders of a stock company or the policyholders of a mutual company of all or a part of their ownership rights in the company.

The model act provides that no bulk reinsurance contract can become effective without the prior written approval of the insurance commissioner. The commissioner can approve such a contract only if it is found (1) to be fair and equitable to the ceding company, and (2) not to reduce the protection provided to policyholders of the ceding company. In addition, no director, officer, agent or employee of either the ceding company or the reinsurer can receive any fee, commission, or other valuable consideration for aiding or promoting the bulk transfer. For mutual ceding companies, there are additional provisions regarding approval by policyholder vote and payment in cash to policyholders for their equity in the business ceded.

There are several other minor provisions in the RAA model act. However, they provide for minor revisions of code provisions that already exist in most states and need not be discussed here. It seems likely that the RAA model act is a close approximation of the reinsurance regulatory pattern that will eventually emerge. It should provide the state regulatory authorities with the necessary authority to deal with the growing problems of reinsurance. However, the effective administration of the act will require greater reinsurance expertise than most state insurance departments now possess.

Reinsurance and the Capacity Problem

One of the principal purposes of reinsurance, as discussed earlier in this chapter, is to provide capacity, both for large loss exposures and for premium volume, for ceding companies. Without reinsurance facilities, it would be very difficult for the primary insurers to meet the insurance needs of the public. However, the success of reinsurers in providing the needed capacity varies from time to time, depending on several factors.

A major factor in capacity availability is price adequacy. Both primary insurance and reinsurance are subject to pricing cycles in which rates vary from grossly inadequate to excessive. These cycles result from competition, inability to cope with inflation, and, in the case of primary insurers, from excessive zeal on the part of state regulatory authorities in the control of rates. Of course, a reinsurer is less than anxious to write business for which it has no reasonable expectation of profit.

Reinsurers may have poor loss experience for at least two reasons. One reason is inadequate rates. The other is that chance fluctuation in losses, especially from catastrophes, may cause poor loss experience in a single year even though rates are adequate for the long term. This is especially true, of course, of those reinsurers that write a substantial amount of catastrophe coverages. One or a few years of poor underwriting experience restrict reinsurance capacity in two ways. First, existing reinsurers become less interested in writing new business and may even terminate some existing business, either because of poor profit expectations or because of shrinkage of surplus. Second, poor investment experience, especially sharp declines in the stock market, may have much the same effect because of the resulting drop in policyholders' surplus.

There have been attempts to find a satisfactory solution to the recurring capacity shortages in insurance and reinsurance. During the years when rating bureaus were successful in keeping primary insurance rates adequate by controlling competition, capacity shortages were less common. However, a return to that kind of rate control in the near future seems very unlikely.

Any move by reinsurers to fix rates at a high level would be certain to run afoul of federal antitrust laws and probably would not succeed even in the absence of antitrust laws. Rates fixed at an unrealistically high level would merely attract new reinsurers willing to write business at lower rates. The ease of entry into the reinsurance business and the relatively low capital requirements of the business virtually preclude effective price fixing.

One can only conclude that reinsurance capacity shortages will continue to occur. Fortunately, they tend to be relatively brief and to cause less inconvenience than might be expected from a casual reading of the speeches and magazine articles that usually accompany them.

Chapter Notes

1. Len Strazewski, "Intermediaries' Historical Image Clashes with Modern Role," *Business Insurance*, 10 October 1983, p. 3.
2. Len Strazewski, p. 3.
3. For a more thorough treatment of this subject see Anthony M. Lanzone, "Analyzing Reinsurance Disputes," *National Underwriter*, Property & Casualty Edition, 19 August 1983, p. 19; and 26 August 1983, p. 15.
4. See Anthony M. Lanzone, "Analyzing Reinsurance Disputes," *National Underwriter*, Property & Casualty Edition, 9 September 1983, p. 27; and "Reinsurer Bound When Insurer Follows Policy," *Business Insurance*, 26 September 1983, p. 36.
5. "Supervision of U.K. Reinsurance Tightened Up," *International Insurance Monitor*, January/February 1983, p. 12.
6. Carol Cain, "NAIC Reinsurance Bill Being Reviewed," *Business Insurance*, 3 October 1983, p. 10.
7. Douglas McLeod, "New Guidelines to Spell Out Reinsurance Procedures," *Business Insurance*, 10 October 1983, p. 18 and William J. Kane, Reinsurance Accounting: Whose Responsibility?," *National Underwriter*, Property & Casualty Edition, 26 August 1983, part 2, p. 26.

Index

D

E

F

G

H

Hazard evaluation, *202*
Hazards, common, *226*
  moral, *202, 238*
  morale, *203, 238, 239*
  off-premises, *291*
  on-premises, *286*
  physical, *202*
  special, *226, 228*
Heating, *228*
High-rise buildings, *222*
Homeowners, profitability of, *95*
Homeowners and dwelling
    underwriting, *240*
Horizontal mergers, *143*
Housekeeping, *227, 286*
Human relations, *25*
Hurricanes, *240*
  paths of, *241*

I

ICC certificate/endorsement, *284*
ICC regulations on commercial
    automobiles, *284*
Ignition sources, *225*
IIR/ACORD, *111*
IIAA (Independent Insurance
    Agents of America), *68*
Implementing the decision, *207*
Independent agency firms, *55*
Independent agency system, *53, 54*
Independent contractor exposure,
    300
Independent contractors, *54*
Independently filed, *6*
Independently filed forms, *6*
Indexed retentions, *392*
Indirect or consequential losses, *251*
Industrial accidents, *288*
Industrial Risk Insurers (IRI), *354*
Inflation, effect of, on reinsurance,
    391
Information, external sources of,
    198
  internal sources of, *200*
  objective, *199*

subjective, *199*
Information gathering, *197*
Information needed, reinsurance,
    370
Inland marine, *264*
Insolvency clause, *396*
Inspection reports, *200*
Instrumentalities of transportation
    and communication, *265*
Insulation, *220*
Insurance activities,
    interdependency among, *32*
Insurance company loss control
    reports, *297*
Insurance departments, illustration
    of interdependency among, *38*
Insurance exchanges, *117*
  operating methods of, *118*
Insurance industry trends, *187*
Insurance operations, overview of,
    1
Insurance principles and coverages,
    46
Insurance sales compared to sales
    of other products, *49*
Insureds, selection of, *174*
Insurer networks, *110*
Insurers, admitted, *73*
  nonadmitted, *74*
  reinsurance program for, *376*
Interior finish, *218*
Intermediary clause, *396*
Internal sources of information, *200*
Investment, finance and, *28*
Investment strategy, *28*
IVANS, *112*

J

Joint underwriting associations, *355*
Joisted masonry construction, *216*

L

Large line capacity, *145, 324*

U

V

W

Y